Sports Cars

Classic
Sports
Cars

Cyril Posthumus and David Hodges

Artwork by Malcolm Ward

IVY LEAF

Contents

First published in Great Britain by
The Hamlyn Publishing Group Limited

This edition published in 1991 by
Ivy Leaf
Michelin House
81 Fulham Road
London SW3 6RB

ISBN 0 86363 023 5

Printed in Hong Kong

Acknowledgements
The publishers are grateful to the following for the photographs
reproduced in this book: *Autocar*, Foto Bachmann, Diana Burnett,
Geoffrey Goddard, David Hodges, Leigh Jones, LAT, *Motor*.

Introduction

High performance in one form or another, allied with a special quality of motoring above that of a basic mechanical conveyance, are major criteria for the choice of subjects in this book. Definitions are too easily blurred in this field of motoring, and the subjects are very numerous and widely varied; to justify *our* choice we would observe that sports cars are for sport – and that sport is amusement, diversion, fun, or simply something to enjoy, according to which dictionary one consults. Sport, of course, is also competition, and the competition content in this book is strong, running from cars suitable for club driving tests through those which have taken part in major rallies, to the exalted few with Le Mans-winning status.

We do not claim to include every 'sports car' ever built. Some omissions are deliberate: for instance, we stopped short of including competition versions of production saloons, even though the fiercest of these can frequently out-perform contemporary 'traditional' sports cars. Certain American GT models have nevertheless been included, both for their interest, and for their degree of departure from stock, which in our eyes – and certainly those of their native clientele – brings them within the catholic selection. One might add that such cars are as valid as some of the *poseurs'* machines which enjoyed the looks of full-blooded sports models.

Other omissions are by reason of their borderline importance, lack of space, or even lack of accurate data, but the overall contents aim to provide representative coverage of an intimidatingly broad field of 'performance' designs: a car may have a vee-twin or four-cylinder side-valve engine just about able to give 30bhp, or a voracious 1100bhp turbocharged flat-12, and yet both can rate as 'sports cars'. Ever-changing conditions and some very flexible competition regulations through the years have produced many such anomalies, and it is essential to look back to the origins to understand how such things came about.

In essence, although not in definition, the sports car has existed almost as long as motoring. The real pioneers had to be enthusiasts, in deadly earnest too, as they struggled to make the horseless carriage a realistic form of transport and a commercial proposition. By the early years of the 20th century, however, the concept of the automobile had advanced sufficiently for enthusiasts, sometimes too glibly termed playboys, to begin to appreciate superior performance qualities in their motor vehicles. Thus were various redundant racing cars rebodied in more habitable styles to convert them into unusually fast tourers; certainly 'sports cars' if not yet so termed.

The trend towards (and beyond) a fast touring category was accelerated by important German road events held in the Edwardian years, including the Herkomer Trophy Tours of 1905-1907 (and the Prince Henry Tours which succeeded them), the Kaiserpreis of 1907 – often recalled as a race for *racing* cars but in fact a race whose regulations called for sensible bodywork – and the pre-1914 Alpine Trials. The Prince Henry Tours in

A mixed bunch at the Nurburgring as mid-engined cars became the norm, including three Ford GT40s, a Ford Mustang, Porsche 906, Ferrari 250 LM and an Alfa Romeo TZ

Practical touring qualities demonstrated at Le Mans in 1926, as the field leave the start with hoods raised, led by an OM and a Bentley (above). *Below left: birth of a tradition – the 3-litre Bentley at the pits during the first Le Mans 24-hour Race, in 1923. Below right: American in Europe – a Stutz at Le Mans, totally in keeping with contemporary 1920s large-capacity European sports cars*

particular inspired both high performance engines and advanced bodywork, as well as some purpose-built sporting cars which started a style that lasted into the 1920s.

As engines grew lighter and more efficient generally, quite mundane manufacturers were tempted to produce 'speed models' of their normal cars. Meanwhile there was a vogue for two-seater sporting cars in the USA, where numerous speedsters, raceabouts or roadsters were listed. The earliest cars in this book are from those formative late-Edwardian years.

The birth of sports car racing

The sports car as such is a child of the years immediately following the First World War, the specific term 'sports car' first appearing in a motoring journal in 1919. As for modern sports car racing, this can be traced back to the Corsican Grand Prix run in 1921 – although who would deny the claims of those Targa Florio races run around the coast of Sicily between 1912 and 1914, or even the Kaiserpreis of 1907, at least in their spirit?

The regulations for the Corsican race marked it out, however, stipulating as they did four-seater cars of up to 3 litres, properly equipped with mudguards and windscreens. Regulations on similar lines were soon applied to other races, such as the first Belgian Grand Prix and in 1923 to what would become the pre-eminent sports car race: *Les Vingt Quatre Heures du Mans* or the *Grand Prix d'Endurance*, which was conceived as an endurance test for 'touring cars of the fast sporting type'. In its duration it was not a complete novelty, for there had been several 24-hour races run over rather primitive tracks in America, and the French *Bol d'Or* for light cars in 1922.

But Le Mans was different. Initially, each race was not even an end in itself, but a round in the 'Rudge Whitworth Triennial Award', the *Coupe Annuelle à la Distance* not being inaugurated until 1928. In those early races cars over 1100cc had to have four seats, while all had to carry ballast equivalent to passengers; from 1924 to 1927 part of the distance had to be covered with hoods erected. Slowly the regulations changed, until in 1937 all entries had merely to have 'two seats facing forward', and in 1949 prototypes were admitted.

The Le Mans 24 Hours Race became the single most important road race on the calendar, to the extent that its organisers, the Automobile Club de l'Ouest, could influence the formulation of international regulations, or – if these did not suit their race – could ignore them! In view of its stature, winners are given (page 17).

By the late 1920s, however, sports car racing was firmly established, even becoming an acceptable substitute for Grand Prix racing when costs of the latter soared beyond reason in harsh economic times. Sports cars thus proliferated at all levels, the French and British industries being particularly attracted to the type or at least having the most appreciative markets. Italy naturally produced some outstanding examples, the sports car seeming especially suited to the Latin temperament, and to the demanding races run in Italy, epitomised by the Mille Miglia, held annually for 30 years over a near-1000-mile course on public roads. Austria and Germany also contributed sports cars large and small, some of them truly outstanding; only in America did interest in sporting automobiles wane.

Success in major racing events was nationally important in prestige and economically important in sales terms, and the practice of marking success through model names spread, with a spate of types such as 'Brooklands', 'Montlhéry', 'Mille Miglia', 'Le Mans', and 'Nurburg', their names not always fully earned. This practice only began to lapse in the late 1960s, when the association of racing success with road cars became rather anti-social, or perhaps as sports-racing cars became ever further removed from the cars one could use on the road. By that time, however, such examples as 'Targa' and 'Carrera' had become so much part of the motoring vocabulary that their origins were almost forgotten (as, sadly, are the races from which they derived).

The 1930s, even more than the 1920s, saw the spread of mass-produced cheap 'sports cars', many of which were at best 'sporting' cars, however much they looked the part. In outward appearance the break with the Vintage years was obvious by the late 1930s (although the cycle-wing look lingered in odd corners for a surprisingly long time after the Second World War). There had been streamlined essays in the 1920s, mainly from French concerns such as Chenard-Walcker, Voisin and Tracta, but the next decade saw a positive swing towards efficient body shapes on cars by Bugatti, BMW, Adler and, of course, by leading Italian coachbuilders on chassis from Alfa Romeo.

Thus the closed coupe, anathema on Vintage sports cars, found acceptance and did not seem out of place on prominent cars in major races. The flowing lines were carried through quite logically on post-war models, gaining full expression on open and closed examples built by companies such as Jaguar, Mercedes-Benz and the great Italian coachbuilders.

By the 1950s the era of the 'sports-racer' had firmly arrived; there had been false dawns for years, with 'production-derived' but clearly rather special sports cars being admitted to races.

Changing shape of the sports car in the 1930s: a pair of Alfa Romeos, looking very "traditional", in the 1934 Mille Miglia (above); the Alfa Romeo team before the 1936 Mille Miglia (left); varied approaches at Le Mans in 1939 – a Talbot and a Lagonda are nearest the camera, while the fifth car in the line-up is a Talbot coupe (below, left); a trio of BMW 328s at the Nurburgring in 1938 (below)

An all-round sports car in a classic rally – an Austin-Healey 3000 in the last Liege-Rome-Liege (left) and two purpose-designed cars on the Monte Carlo Rally, a Renault Alpine in 1973 (above) and a Lancia Stratos in 1977 (below)

Enter the prototype

Recognition of a 'prototype' category encouraged this trend, incidentally leading to an ever-widening diversification of the concept of the sports car. Its role now encompassed machines ranging from straightforward roadgoing open two-seaters with no really outstanding performance qualities, to ludicrous buggies and out-and-out cars for very specialised and varied purposes, from trials freaks to rally cars such as the Lancia Stratos, and to the most-powerful road-racing cars ever built, the CanAm Porsche 917s.

The admission of prototypes to that first post-war 24-hour race at Le Mans had opened the way to sports-racing cars which would eventually bring about a decline in the status of sports car racing. Some manufacturers did honour the spirit of the prototype category, but for others it provided a convenient loophole for the use of pure racing-car design and equipment; it was a loophole which the rule makers

championship of less demanding events, and the rise of GT racing; it also inspired the construction of many outstanding cars. Its high noon came in the mid-1960s, with Ford's multi-million-dollar assault on Le Mans; its rosy afterglow came at the beginning of the next decade, with mighty 600bhp 5-litre cars (Le Mans in 1970 saw a quarter of the entry made up of such Porsches and Ferraris).

The decline of the championship

Racing became the poorer when such machines were followed by two-seater Grand Prix cars with detuned 3-litre engines; the decline showed in entry lists and in public interest, to the degree that the publicity value of a championship victory became questionable. The situation arose where one or two powerful manufacturers dominated the championship seasons almost by rota, and major efforts were confined to that French 24-hour race. Even Porsche, whose support had been as constant as Ferrari's, accepted that competing

Extreme sports-racing cars – the absurd twin-boom Nardi which was allowed to run as a prototype at Le Mans in 1955 (left), and the Chaparral 2J "sucker" car run in 1970 CanAm races

then seemed incapable of closing.

A review of the fluctuating international regulations would demand far too much space, yet these had their effect on sports car progress and led to some disheartening episodes. In terms of racing, inevitably focused on Le Mans, Ferrari was the one constant factor for more than two decades. Over-simplifying, the 30 years after the Second World War can be summarised as a series of challenges to Ferrari – by Mercedes-Benz, Jaguar, Aston Martin, Ford, Porsche, Matra and finally Alfa Romeo. In the mid-1970s, Ferrari abandoned sports car racing, accurately reflecting its decline.

The 'Ferrari era' saw superb seasons and a few that were mediocre; it encompassed the tragedy of Le Mans in 1955, the disappearance of classic races, the suppression of true endurance racing in favour of a

against its own customers was nonsensical.

Le Mans itself, however, continued to enjoy such prestige that some 'specials' were actually built simply to contest that one event, often at very considerable cost; some of these machines, such as the Gulf GR8 of 1977 and the Rondeau of 1980, actually won outright, but neither name was frequently encountered in any other sports car context.

The large sums of money required for such efforts were no longer easy to come by away from the glare of publicity enjoyed by Le Mans, however, and sports car racing in general became increasingly an expensive playground for independent entrants of production-related (if not derived) Porsches. Against such teams in 1980, only Lancia fielded works cars!

By then, the most extreme form of sports car racing,

A pair of Chevrolet Corvettes leading the Le Mans field into the first lap in 1960

the North American CanAm Championship, had followed another path towards oblivion, because its rules were too liberal, allowing the events to become dominated by extremely powerful, extremely costly machines; it was only revived in a curious form in the late 1970s as a series for single-seaters with enclosed wheels. The European 2-litre series, which had flourished in the first half of the 1970s, also faded away, its attractive little cars seeing out the decade in an Italian national series and as a class at Le Mans.

Here and there enclaves flourished: at a basic 'economy' level, the British-devised Sports 2000 category showed that sports racers could be attractive and popular; so did the much more expensive German Group 5 series. There were even signs of a resurgence in the World Endurance Championship with the 'FISA

Category C' or GTP class, which was foreshadowed to a degree by the IMSA (International Motor Sports Association) GT series in the USA, and paralleled by the IMSA GTP class.

GT racing as such was, in fact, well under way in 1962, when it seemed set to supplant sports car events in the Championship. But the Le Mans organisers effectively stopped that, taking the initiative with other race organisers to set up a championship for 'prototype and experimental cars', to regulations which broadly formed the basis for the World Manufacturers' Championship in 1963.

The separate GT Championship ran for only six seasons, before being absorbed into the Manufacturers' Championship, which then admitted Group 5 sports cars with a minimum production run of 25 examples.

Therein lay controversy, since those Group 5 cars were subject to a 5-litre capacity limit, while the Group 6 sports prototypes (with no production minimum) were restricted to 3 litres. No specialist manufacturer, it was reasoned, would build 25 out-and-out racing machines. But Porsche did, and Ferrari perforce followed. The spectacle was often superb, but it served the cause of sports car racing poorly …

The mid-engined trend

Meanwhile, as part of the road-going sports car world merrily carried on building and selling cars on 'traditional' lines, other manufacturers felt impelled to follow the mid-engined trend, perhaps spurred on by the first Le Mans victory for a mid-engined car, which fell to Ferrari in 1963. Few followed the Porsche rear-engined example. By the end of the 1960s there were some practicable mid-engined road cars on the market, although most had one or more shortcomings in such areas as visibility, luggage space, passenger space or wet-weather handling. At least racing could be said to have affected the breed, even though it did not necessarily improve it.

The appeal of two-seaters faithful to the old ideas always lived on, however. Morgans, MGs, Triumphs and others, even in the 1970s, closely reflected pre-war concepts; Panther actually set out to recapture their essence, and Lotus – of all companies – successfully did so with its Seven, although that car was far removed in many of its manners from the older cart-sprung generation. Datsun emulated the success of the 'traditional' British cars although it borrowed some of Italy's more advanced coachwork ideas.

Grass roots sports-car racing at Brands Hatch in 1962, Morgans and MGs leading a mixed bunch including Jaguar, Austin Healey 3000, Sunbeam Alpine, TVR and Lotus

GT line up for the 1960 Tourist Trophy at Goodwood

It was indeed an odd notion that a true all-round sports car should be noisy and uncomfortable, with sometimes indifferent roadholding and performance; it was even more irrational that this image should have lingered so long after the Second World War, when higher standards were being set in production saloons. Probably the biggest single jolt into a new age came with the Jaguar E-type in 1961: elegance, comfort and phenomenal performance were combined as never before in a sports car priced within reach of large numbers of enthusiast drivers. That car is universally rated as 'classic', although that over-worked distinction can by no means be applied to all the models in this book.

The modern era is perhaps epitomised by the Fiat X1/9, which successfully combines the virtues of mid-engined handling with the practicality of 'traditional' designs, something attempted with less success by the earlier VW-Porsche 914/916 series.

At the other end of the scale there were the *grand routiers*; Facel Vega perhaps built the last true cars in that genre, for GT cars with widely varying competition backgrounds merged into such vague categories as 'business-man's express' or the 'supercars' of more recent times. In truth the last two types had been around as long as the first, for there has always been a market, often of very small numbers, for cars combining high performance with high quality (and high cost). Oddly, this has often been achieved without the 'competition breeding' to which lip service is customarily paid.

Sports cars are studied more closely than mundane cars, for they are by no means regarded as mere transportation devices – by the buyer who wants the best fun for his money, by the designer who has to produce it, and by the majority who are simply interested and follow the state of the art. And art there unquestionably is in a good sports car, as there is in driving it and, moreover, in painting it. Malcolm Ward has completed a prodigious task in the detailed colour elevations and frontal aspects of so many sports or sporting cars spanning a period of over 70 years, which appear in this book. These are not drawn to a common scale; more importantly, however, Ward has achieved accuracy in dimensions and proportions, in some cases after painstaking research for references and accurate data.

Virtually every successful sports car has appeared in more than one form during its life, often with different bodywork to suit particular purposes; the illustrations in this book depict each car as it might have come 'out of the box' – thus modern sports racing cars, for example, appear without decals and numbers which were often peculiar to just one event.

In addition to the models shown, others are referred to in the text or their specifications are given. Even within the apparently close limits of dimensions, however, other variations sometimes existed – on modern sports racing cars, for example, a change to wider wheels can affect the track measurement. One detail is worth mentioning: where specifications mention dampers, these can generally be assumed to refer to friction dampers on cars before the mid-1930s and to hydraulic dampers on post-1940s models; for the intervening period of change, we have recorded the type, as we have any exceptions.

Cyril Posthumus
David Hodges

Sports-racing cars in contrasting races in 1970: a Porsche 908 lined up to pass a Carrera in the 1970 Targa Florio (above), and two Porsche 917s leading a Ferrari 512 off the banking at Daytona (left)

THE RACING CHAMPIONSHIPS

World Sports Cars Championship

1953	Ferrari
1954	Ferrari
1955	Mercedes-Benz
1956	Ferrari
1957	Ferrari
1958	Ferrari
1959	Aston Martin
1960	Ferrari
1961	Ferrari

GT Championship		Prototype Championship
1962	Ferrari	Ferrari
1963	Ferrari	Ferrari
1964	Porsche	Ferrari
1965	Ferrari	Shelby
1966	Porsche	Porsche
1967	Ferrari	Porsche

Manufacturers' Championship

1968	Ford
1969	Porsche
1970	Porsche
1971	Porsche
1972	Ferrari
1973	Matra
1974	Matra
1975	Alfa Romeo
1976	Porsche
1977	Porsche
1978	Porsche
1979	Porsche
1980	Lancia

Start of the 50th anniversary Le Mans race in 1973, with Ferraris and Matras leading the field away

16

WINNERS OF THE LE MANS 24-HOUR RACE

Year	Car	Driver/Driver	Distance	Speed
1923	Chenard-Walcker	Lagache / Léonard	2208km / 1372 miles	92·06kph / 57·20mph
1924	Bentley	Duff / Clement	2076km / 1290 miles	86·55kph / 53·78mph
1925	La Lorraine	De Courcelles / Rossignol	2234km / 1388 miles	93·08kph / 57·84mph
1926	La Lorraine	Bloch / Rossignol	2551km / 1585 miles	106.·35kph / 66·08mph
1927	Bentley	Benjafield / Davis	2369km / 1472 miles	98·74kph / 61·35mph
1928	Bentley	Barnato / Rubin	2668km / 1658 miles	112·02kph / 69·60mph
1929	Bentley	Barnato / Birkin	2844km / 1767 miles	118·49kph / 73·63mph
1930	Bentley	Barnato / Kidston	2931km / 1821 miles	122·11kph / 75·88mph
1931	Alfa-Romeo	Howe / Birkin	3017km / 1875 miles	125·73kph / 78·13mph
1932	Alfa-Romeo	Sommer / Chinetti	2953km / 1835 miles	123·08kph / 76·48mph
1933	Alfa-Romeo	Sommer / Nuvolari	3143km / 1953 miles	131·00kph / 81·40mph
1934	Alfa-Romeo	Chinetti / Etancelin	2885km / 1793 miles	120·29kph / 74·74mph
1935	Lagonda	Hindmarsh / Fontes	3006km / 1868 miles	125·28kph / 77·85mph
1937	Bugatti	Wimille / Benoist	3288km / 2043 miles	136·99kph / 85·12mph
1938	Delahaye	Chaboud / Tremoulet	3180km / 1976 miles	132·54kph / 82·35mph
1939	Bugatti	Wimille / Veyron	3354km / 2084 miles	139·78kph / 86·85mph
1949	Ferrari	Chinetti / Selsdon	3177km / 1974 miles	132·42kph / 82·28mph
1950	Talbot-Lago	Rosier / Rosier	3465km / 2153 miles	144·38kph / 89·71mph
1951	Jaguar	Walker / Whitehead	3610km / 2243 miles	150·46kph / 93·49mph
1952	Mercedes-Benz	Lang-Riess	3734km / 2320 miles	155·57kph / 96·67mph
1953	Jaguar	Rolt / Hamilton	4088km / 2540 miles	170·33kph / 105·84mph
1954	Ferrari	Gonzalez / Trintignant	4060km / 2523 miles	169·21kph / 105·14mph
1955	Jaguar	Hawthorn / Bueb	4134km / 2569 miles	172·31kph / 107·07mph
1956	Jaguar	Flockhart / Sanderson	4035km / 2507 miles	168·12kph / 104·46mph
1957	Jaguar	Flockhart / Bueb	4397km / 2732 miles	183·22kph / 113·84mph
1958	Ferrari	Hill / Gendebien	4101km / 2548 miles	170·91kph / 106·20mph
1959	Aston Martin	Shelby / Salvadori	4347km / 2701 miles	181·16kph / 112·60mph
1960	Ferrari	Frére / Gendebien	4216km / 2620 miles	175·73kph / 109·19mph
1961	Ferrari	Gendebien / P Hill	4476km / 2781 miles	186·53kph / 115·90mph
1962	Ferrari	Gendebien / P Hill	4450km / 2765 miles	185·47kph / 115·24mph
1963	Ferrari	Scarfiotti / Bandini	4561km / 2834 miles	190·07kph / 118·10mph
1964	Ferrari	Guichet / Vaccarella	4694km / 2917 miles	195·64kph / 121·56mph
1965	Ferrari	Rindt / Gregory	4677km / 2906 miles	194·88kph / 121·09mph
1966	Ford	Amon / McLaren	4842km / 3009 miles	201·79kph / 125·39mph
1967	Ford	Gurney / Foyt	5232km / 3251 miles	218·04kph / 135·48mph
1968	Ford	Rodriguez / Bianchi	4451km / 2766 miles	185·53kph / 115·29mph
1969	Ford	Ickx / Oliver	4997km / 3105 miles	208·25kph / 129·40mph
1970	Porsche	Herrmann / Attwood	4607km / 2863 miles	191·99kph / 119·30mph
1971	Porsche	Marko / van Lennep	5335km / 3315 miles	222·30kph / 138·13mph
1972	Matra-Simca	Pescarolo / G Hill	4691km / 2915 miles	195·47kph / 121·46mph
1973	Matra-Simca	Pescarolo / Larrousse	4854km / 3016 miles	202·25kph / 125·67mph
1974	Matra-Simca	Pescarolo / Larrousse	4606km / 2862 miles	191·89kph / 119·27mph
1975	Gulf	Ickx / Bell	4582km / 2847 miles	191·44kph / 118·98mph
1976	Porsche	Ickx / van Lennep	4768km / 2963 miles	198·75kph / 123·49mph
1977	Porsche	Ickx / Barth / Haywood	4672km / 2903 miles	194·65kph / 120·95mph
1978	Renault Alpine	Pironi / Jaussaud	5044km / 3134 miles	210·19kph / 130·60mph
1979	Porsche	Ludwig / Whittington	4173km / 2593 miles	173·91kph / 108·07mph
1980	Rondeau	Jaussaud / Rondeau	4508km / 2863 miles	192·00kph / 119·30mph

AC Ace and Aceca

For a decade after its introduction in October 1953, when it caused a stir as the first post-war British production sports car with all-round independent suspension, the Ace was among the most attractive of cars, as was the Aceca coupe which followed. That the well-balanced lines of the Ace recalled early Ferrari *barchettas* was no coincidence, for they came directly from a Tojeiro sports-racing car so bodied at the behest of Cliff Davis.

John Tojeiro collaborated in the design of the Ace, which followed his cars in having a ladder-type chassis with two large-diameter longitudinal members carrying welded-up supports for the wishbones and transverse leaf springs front and rear. This arrangement made for roadholding of a high standard, with first-class controllability and a good ride. The open body was practical as well as attractive, and in 1954 the Aceca coupe was added to the range, with curved screen and hinged rear window panel (in anticipation of a later wide-spread fashion). The 160kph (100mph) four-seat Greyhound followed in 1959, but was built in small numbers. It had a longer wheelbase, revised nose and separate boot lid, and coil and wishbone ifs and revised irs similar to that on the Ace which Bolton and Stoop placed eighth at Le Mans in 1958 (although this suspension was not used in any production version of the Ace).

The first Aces were powered by that famous AC 1991cc (65 × 100mm) ohv six designed by John Weller in 1919, in this use modified to give 85bhp at 4500rpm. This would be available as an option until the end of Ace production in 1963, when it was rated at 102bhp in competition tune. In 1956, however, AC responded to customer demand for more performance by offering the pushrod-ohv Bristol six, initially in 105bhp and 120bhp forms; these were listed until 1961, when a Ruddspeed-modified 2·6-litre Ford six became the alternative to AC's own venerable unit, in states of tune giving from 90bhp to 170bhp (and allowing the nose lines to be made a little finer).

The earliest cars had a 103mph top speed, while the standard Bristol-engined version could exceed 185kph (115mph).

An all-round sports car, the Ace had a good record as a production competitions model. A racing highlight was seventh place at Le Mans in 1959, following an eighth and a ninth in 1958.

The Ace did not date rapidly, and AC maintained an excellent quality control reputation with it, but production ceased almost suddenly as demand for Cobras became almost overwhelming . . .

1956 Aceca coupe

Specification (*Ace-Bristol*)
Engine: Bristol straight-six 66 × 96mm, 1971cc; pushrod ohv; three Solex carburettors; 125bhp at 6000rpm.
Gearbox: four-speed manual, with optional overdrive.
Chassis: tubular; independent suspension front and rear, by wishbones, leaf springs and dampers; disc front/drum rear brakes.
Dimensions: **wheelbase** 229cm/90in; **track** 127cm/50in.

AC Cobra

This was one of the last blatantly masculine cars, in some ways a throwback to the post-Vintage generation yet enormously successful in the sophisticated 1960s. It was an Anglo-American hybrid, but an unusual example as the initiative came from California and the funding from Detroit.

Carroll Shelby was the match maker, bringing together AC and a compact new short-stroke Ford V-8, together with related transmission components. AC readily adapted an Ace chassis to accept the V-8 – there was ample room in the engine bay – and conducted initial testing in the autumn of 1962 before shipping the first Cobra to the USA. The programme then got under way remarkably quickly, with AC sending complete chassis/body assemblies out for engines and transmissions to be fitted by Shelby American at Santa Fe, and later in the old Scarab shops in California. AC production for European markets started early in 1963.

The chassis was strengthened, as were the suspension and rear axle, and cooling arrangements were revised; at first only the new nose betrayed the changes under the bonnet, but later came louvres at the sides. The first 75 cars had the 4·2-litre (260cu in) 250bhp V-8, subsequent cars the 4·7-litre (289cu in) version giving 271bhp in standard form, or up to 370bhp in full Shelby race trim.

Late in 1964 wishbones and coil springs replaced the transverse leaf rear suspension. Tyres grew fatter and wheel arches were flared with the introduction in 1965 of the Shelby Cobra 427, using the 7-litre (427cu in) V-8 from the Ford Galaxie, giving up to 345bhp, and up to 260kph (160mph).

The standard 289 – AC in some markets, although Cobras were increasingly Shelby or Ford in the USA – was a fairly demanding, noisy and heavy car to drive, but was in turn a rewarding road car, with a 220kph (135mph) maximum speed. But a prime Ford consideration had been competitions use, and after a shaky start on the circuits and development by Ken Miles, the Cobras built up a splendid racing record. This extended from club to international level, where the purposeful Daytona coupe version very nearly won the world GT championship in 1964, and actually did so in 1965. In 1964 one car also finished fourth overall at Le Mans.

British and American paths had diverged considerably before Cobra production ended in 1968, when just over 1000 had been built. AC continued with its own 428 derivative, with a sleek Frua body on a chassis lengthened by 15cm, building 80 of these between 1967 and 1973. But it is for the aggressive, bellowing racing Cobras that the model is remembered . . .

1967 Shelby 427 roadster

Specification *(289)*
Engine: Ford 90-degree V-8, 101·6 × 72·9mm, 4727cc; pushrod ohv; one Ford carburettor; 271bhp at 6000rpm.
Gearbox: four-speed manual.
Chassis: tubular; independent suspension front and rear, by wishbones, coil springs and dampers; four-wheel disc brakes.
Dimensions: wheelbase 229cm/90in; **front track** 138cm/54½in; **rear track** 137cm/54in.

Alfa Romeo RLS and RLSS

The rough roads and hilly terrain in much of Italy have – in the past, at least – endowed many of her 'touring' cars with the liveliness and agility of sports models. When Italian manufacturers set out to build real sports cars, therefore, their performance seemed positively outstanding to connoisseurs in other countries. One of the most famous examples is Alfa Romeo's Type RL touring car. Designed by Giuseppe Merosi and introduced in 1922, this provided a firm basis for Alfa's future forays into the high performance market.

The RL had a 2994cc pushrod-ohv six-cylinder engine mustering 56 horsepower, in a conventional semi-elliptically-sprung chassis, and with a lusty performance which was quickly exploited. The first sports version, the 71bhp Type RLS (S for Sport), was given twin carburettors, a quick-lift camshaft, a shorter wheelbase, a handsome vee radiator, and Rudge Whitworth quick-release wire wheels. It was marketed in Britain – home of the 3-litre Bentley and the 30/98 Vauxhall – as a 22/90 in chassis form, with various open and closed British bodies available.

An even shorter edition of the RL, with a boosted power unit, was developed for racing. It proved extremely successful, winning the 1923 Targa Florio and several lesser Italian road races. Seven-bearing crankshafts were used in 1924, bringing further successes, although the competition RLs were superseded that same year by the famous straight-eight supercharged Grand Prix Alfa Romeos.

An updated version of the RL six, with more power, dry-sump lubrication, and less weight, was introduced in 1925. Termed the RLSS (Super Sport), it was a spirited sports machine with excellent roadholding and steering, and a claimed maximum of 137kph (85mph); superbly nimble on Italian roads, it was somewhat hampered in flatter countries by low intermediate gear ratios. These fine Alfa sixes were notably flexible, however, and could amble along in top gear at 13kph (8mph). They were bought by connoisseurs in Europe and South America, and by fortunate Italians, including *Il Duce* Benito Mussolini, who rated himself quite an expert on high performance machinery.

1925 RLS Spyder

Specification

Engine: *RLS* – straight-six; 76 × 110mm, 2994cc; pushrod ohv; twin carburettors; 71bhp at 3200rpm.

RLSS – as above, but 83bhp at 3600rpm.

Gearbox: four-speed manual.

Chassis: pressed steel side members; semi-elliptic springs front and rear; friction dampers; four-wheel drum brakes and transmission brake.

Dimensions: wheelbase 312cm/123in; **track** 146cm/57½in.

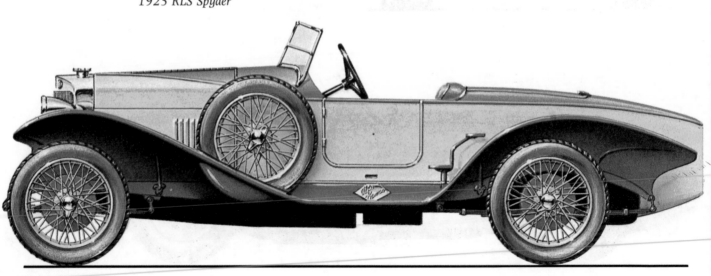

Alfa Romeo 6C types

By 1925, Alfa Romeo's pushrod ohv RL models and the smaller four-cylinder Type RM were beginning to date, and the famous Milan concern – in the glow of numerous Grand Prix victories with the superb P2 straight-eights – set out to produce a new range of road cars. Designer Vittorio Jano's aim was a smaller, more nimble car with a high-efficiency, fast-turning engine capable of extra development for high speed use.

The first fruit was a 1½-litre single-ohc six, the Tipo 6C Turismo which appeared at the 1926 Milan Show. With its fully counter-balanced five-bearing crankshaft rotating at 4200rpm, this commendably smooth fixed-head unit gave 44bhp and powered a refined new range of fast touring Alfa Romeos.

Jano then produced a faster version, the 6C 1500 Sport, with inclined valves and detachable twin-ohc head, giving 54bhp at 4500rpm; installed in a 290cm wheelbase chassis able to carry a wide variation in bodywork from roomy saloons to open two-seaters, this was good for speeds of up to 125kph (77mph). Brakes and roadholding were excellent, and Jano's inevitable next step was to combine these with higher engine performance, achieved by fitting a Roots-type supercharger.

The resultant 6C 1500SS (15/85) mustered 76bhp· and a 140kph (87mph) maximum, making it a 'must' for the sports car racing then staged extensively in Europe. Cavaliere Campari's victory in the 1928 Mille Miglia (1000 Miles) race was the first of many which made this car, and the 1929 1750cc-engined (17/95) edition, renowned all over Europe for their masterful balance of speed and agility.

Both supercharged and unsupercharged 1750s were available to customers, with 290cm and 274cm chassis, the latter adorned by a choice of beautiful open two-seater *spyder* bodies by Zagato and other Italian body craftsmen. These delightful Alfa sixes were built right up to 1933.

1929 4th series Zagato 6C 1750

Specification

Engine: *1500S* – straight six; 62 × 82mm, 1487cc; twin ohc; single carburettor; 54bhp at 4500rpm.

  1500SS – as above, but with Roots-type supercharger; 76bhp at 4800 rpm.

  1750S – as 1500S, but 65 × 88mm, 1752cc; 55bhp at 4400rpm.

  1750SS – as above, but with Roots-type supercharger; 85bhp at 4500rpm.

Gearbox: four-speed manual.

Chassis: pressed steel side members; semi-elliptic springs and friction dampers front and rear; four-wheel drum brakes.

Dimensions: wheelbase 289cm/114in or 274cm/108in; track 137cm/54in.

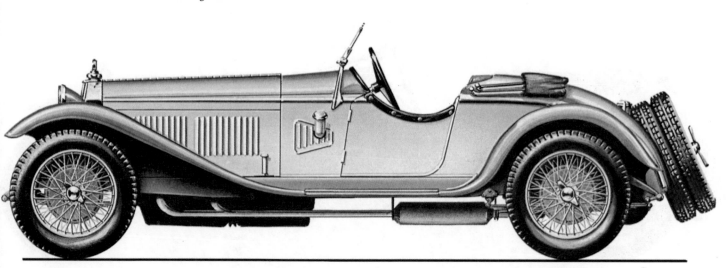

Alfa Romeo 8C types

Like Ettore Bugatti, Alfa Romeo's Vittorio Jano was an artist as well as a designer, requiring his cars and engines to look as well as they performed. His work at its peak was epitomised by the straight-eight supercharged Tipo 8C, in which he embodied several basic 6C engine features including the same 65 × 68mm bore and stroke as the 1750 six, with the addition of two more cylinders to give 2336cc and 142bhp.

The blocks were cast in two pairs, with a central gear train driving the twin ohc, a single Roots compressor and oil and water pumps. The paired cylinder heads were of light alloy with phosphor-bronze valve inserts, and the crankshaft, built in two halves, bolted centrally to the primary timing gear and ran in ten plain bearings at up to 5000rpm. It was an engine of classic beauty but considerable cost, and without the spur of Mussolini's government and the will to win races, Alfa Romeo could scarcely have afforded to produce it.

It was installed in chassis of three different lengths, having semi-elliptic springing all round and wheelbases of 264cm, 274cm or 310cm. The shortest was for Grand Prix racing, when the 8C became known as the Monza; the medium length was the two-seater sports car, wearing rakish *spyder* bodywork; the longest carried four-seater bodywork complying with contemporary AIACR race regulations.

Displacing Britain's big Bentleys from domination at Le Mans, Alfa's lithe, high-revving, blown straight-eights won the 24-hour classic four years in a row, from 1931 to 1934. Similar domination was enjoyed by the shorter wheelbase 8Cs in the Mille Miglia and other long-distance European races, indicating that the car was more substantial than its feline grace suggested.

As road cars they were dramatically fast, with a maximum of over 185kph (115mph). They required more careful maintenance than the older sixes and handled like the thoroughbreds they were, highly sensitive and very fast but stable in cornering. Aesthetically, few other cars could match the glorious sweeping lines achieved by Italy's best coachbuilders, such as Zagato, Touring and Castagna, and the cars' appearance was further enhanced by the large wire

Specifications
8C
Engine: straight-eight; 65 × 88mm, 2336cc; twin ohc; Roots-type supercharger; single carburettor; 142bhp at 5000rpm.
Gearbox: four-speed manual.
Chassis: pressed steel side members; semi-elliptic springs and friction dampers front and rear; four-wheel drum brakes.
Dimensions: wheelbase 274cm/108in or 310cm/122in; track 138cm/54½in.

1931 8C (factory Le Mans car)

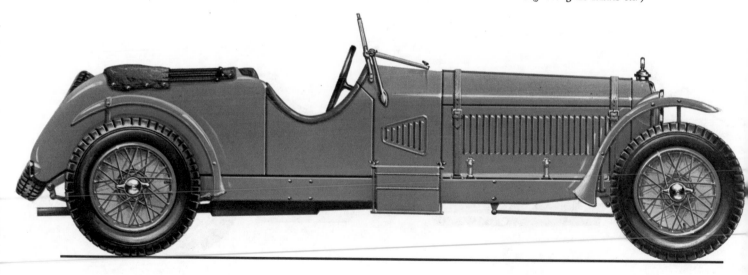

wheels with huge-diameter aluminium alloy drum brakes.

In the forcing house of motor racing, Alfa Romeo's 8C 2300 engines grew to 2·6, 2·9 and then to 3·2 litres, powering the famous P3 Monoposto Grand Prix single-seaters from 1932 to 1935 in twin-supercharged form. By then, however, they were outmoded by the much more powerful German cars, and new 12-cylinder units were developed. The old straight-eights nevertheless remained eminently suitable for use in sports cars and sports car racing.

A batch of 2·9-litre twin-supercharged units was prepared, detuned to give 180bhp at 5200rpm, and fitted to all-new chassis with welded box-section side members. Instead of the time-honoured rigid axles and semi-elliptic springs, they had all-independent suspension of the type used on the 1935-37 Grand Prix Alfas, comprising trailing links and coil springs in unit with hydraulic dampers at the front, and swing axles and a transverse leaf spring at the rear, with combined hydraulic and friction dampers.

A four-speed gearbox was mounted rigidly in unit with the final drive, connected with the front-mounted engine by a dry multi-plate clutch and a long propeller shaft with a centre bearing. Three prototypes of this advanced new sports car took the first three places in the 1936 Mille Miglia, and a production model, the Type 8C 2900B, was marketed in 1937 with the usual long (300cm) and short (274cm) wheelbase options.

Beautiful coachwork by such firms as Touring and Pinin Farina was available, outstanding examples being the works cars (with more powerful 220bhp engines) bodied by Carrozzeria Touring for the 1938 Mille Miglia. Based on the 274cm chassis, these had superbly formed two-seater *spyder* bodies built to the firm's *Superleggera* (super-light) system of construction, with light alloy tube framing supporting light alloy panelling; their weight was slightly over 1000kg and two of them finished first and second in the Mille Miglia.

Thirty examples of the 2900B, probably the world's fastest pre-war production sports car, were produced. They were the last Alfa Romeo sports cars to be designed under Jano's supervision.

1938 8C 2900 (1938 Mille Miglia car)

8C 2900

Engine: straight eight; 68 × 100mm, 2905cc; twin Roots-type superchargers; twin carburettors; 180bhp at 5200rpm (competition cars 225bhp at 5200rpm).
Gearbox: four-speed manual transaxle.
Chassis: box-section side members; front suspension independent by trailing links and coil spring/damper units; rear suspension independent by transverse leaf spring, swing axles and hydraulic/friction dampers; four-wheel hydraulic drum brakes.
Dimensions: wheelbase 279cm/110in or 300cm/118in; **track** 135cm/53in.

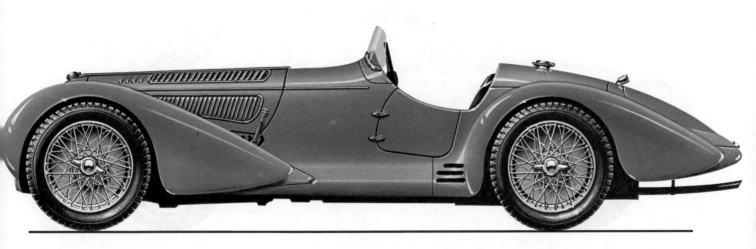

Alfa Romeo Giulietta variants

In the early 1950s, Alfa Romeo lacked the resources to develop a successor to the 158/159, which had ruled the Grand Prix world from 1946 until 1951, but the competitive urge remained strong and in the following year the Disco Volante (flying saucer) sports car appeared. It was featured in brochures, although not put into production, and sports-racing versions were developed. These were only modestly successful, despite the services of Fangio, and a win in the 1953 Supercortemaggiore GP and second place in the Mille Miglia were the high points.

Sights were therefore lowered again, to competition cars based on production models, the Giulietta and the bigger Giulia. These became much more than tuned saloons, however, and led – in a slightly circuitous (and typically Italian) way – via Bertone and Zagato conversions to the fierce SZ and TZ, to the establishment of Autodelta, to the TZ2 (which resembled a miniature Ferrari GTO) and finally to the Tipo 33 sports prototypes ...

The Giulietta Sprint coupe was introduced in 1954, with a wheelbase 15cm shorter than the saloons but with the same five-bearing twin-ohc 1290cc engine, smooth and flexible throughout its range. There was also an exemplary *spyder* variant by Farina; in looks, neither version dated in a decade of production. The coupe was widely used in racing and in rallies and eventually over 44 000 of these Giulietta sporting models were produced.

In 1957 Bertone introduced the Giulietta SS (Sprint Speciale), built on the Sprint undertray, with a sleeker body and high-compression 100bhp version of the engine, which gave it a speed in excess of 190kph (120mph). Next came a no-nonsense competition derivative, the Zagato SZ, with a spaceframe married to the undertray and with considerably less weight (giving better acceleration, although top speed was little higher). The first body was corpulent, but aerodynamic work led to a longer, leaner body with Kamm tail. The SS and SZ had adequate speed in standard form, and there was no lack of tuning expertise to improve on that. Handling was also good and both models were formidable class contenders on the Continent.

The SZ pointed the way to the Giulia TZ of the early 1960s. This Tubolare Zagato owed its basic engine to the 1·6 Giulia (catalogued at 112bhp, but so responsive to tuning that it could take an improvement of almost 50 per cent); transmission and running gear also came from the Giulia, but there was a new spaceframe and irs, while the body followed the lines of the later Giulietta SZ. It proved to be a class winner in events as diverse as the Sebring 12 hours, Tour de France, Le Mans 24 hours, Nurburgring 1000km and Targa Florio; rallying TZs won the 1964 Coupe des Alpes and Tour de Corse outright. Production of the TZ, from 1963, was entrusted to a new Alfa offshoot, Autodelta ...

1954 SS Coupe

Specification (SS)

Engine: straight-four; 74 × 75mm, 1290cc; twin ohc; Solex carburettor; 80bhp at 6300rpm.
Gearbox: five-speed manual.
Chassis: unitary; front suspension independent by wishbones, coil springs, dampers and anti-roll bar; rear suspension by live axle, radius arms, coil springs and dampers; four-wheel drum brakes.
Dimensions: wheelbase 225cm/88½in; front track 129cm/51in; rear track 127cm/50in.

Alfa Romeo Montreal

This was Alfa Romeo's top-of-the-range model through the first half of the 1970s, a modest-production car true to the company's old tradition in being a practical high-performance machine – a true GT car rather than a supercar 'extravaganza'. It used mass-production components and – again echoing its forbears – a detuned racing engine; against the trend of the period, this was front-mounted.

The Montreal had a gestation period almost as long as its production life, indirectly going back to a 1965 Bertone show car and directly to the Montreal first shown in that city during Expo '67. That car was little more than a design study, with a Giulia engine; three years were to pass before the definitive Montreal appeared, with a detuned version of Alfa's competitions V-8 from the T33 sports-racing programme, in 2·6-litre form. It was still a light alloy unit, with dry sump lubrication, electronic ignition and fuel injection hinting at its racing background, but in its Montreal form it proved to be smooth and flexible. It was rated at 200bhp, and as the car was no lightweight (1270kg unladen), the Montreal's top speed of 220kph (135mph) was commendable, modest though it may have seemed by contemporary supercar standards.

Oddly, Alfa Romeo chose to use a ZF gearbox, which had well-chosen ratios, and retained the Giulia suspension layout incorporating a live rear axle (with limited-slip differential). However, the company had ample experience in controlling live axle movement, and the arrangement proved more than adequate for the average driver, and it did give a comfortable ride.

The coupe body did not inhibit visibility, while the cockpit was reasonably laid out and comfortable. Allowance for luggage was almost a joke in a front-engined car that had so many other grand touring qualities, although more could be stowed on the rear seats, which were an even greater joke!

In most respects, the Montreal was sound rather than sensational. A few years earlier, it would have been regarded as a natural competition car – especially as there was a race-proved engine in effect available for it – but it had a little-noticed career until production ended in 1976, when 3925 Montreals had been built, fewer than half the originally planned 10 000.

Specification
Engine: 90-degree V-8; 80 × 64·5mm, 2593cc; twin ohc per bank; Spica fuel injection; 200bhp at 6500rpm.
Gearbox: five-speed manual.
Chassis: unitary; front suspension independent by wishbones, coil springs, dampers and anti-roll bar; rear suspension by live axle, radius arms, coil springs and dampers; four-wheel disc brakes.
Dimensions: wheelbase 235cm/92½in; **front track** 137cm/54in; **rear track** 131cm/51½in.

Alfa Romeo T33

Alfa Romeo's participation in racing was more or less limited to modified production cars once the Disco Volante programme had been axed in 1953, but in the early 1960s a new competition department, Autodelta, was gradually built up. Carlo Chiti was appointed to run this late in 1964, and under him the move back towards top-flight racing gathered momentum, first with the TZ *Tubolare*, and then with the first of the T33 sports-racers.

This was a mid-engined 2-litre prototype, with a chassis of large-diameter tubes and cast magnesium subframes front and rear, all-independent suspension, and a 90-degree oversquare 256bhp V-8 (78 × 52·2mm, 1995cc) designed by Satta and Busso, which drove through an Alfa six-speed gearbox (five speeds were soon found adequate). It had coupe and *spyder* glass fibre bodywork.

Despite a first-time win, in a minor Belgian hill climb in 1967, the T33 was not competitive in the 2-litre class, and chassis, suspension and body were extensively revised for 1968, when there was the encouragement of second, third, fifth and sixth places in the Targa Florio and fourth, fifth and sixth at Le Mans. A total of 27 competition T33s were built, and a road-equipped variant, the Stradale, was essayed.

During 1968 a 2·5-litre version of the engine had been used occasionally, and for 1969 a 3-litre V-8 appeared in the T33/3, which also had an aluminium monocoque chassis. Substantial modifications were needed during the year, before Andrea de Adamich gained a first victory for the model in Austria. In the face of intense competition, 1970 had to be a year of development (finding more power, losing weight), and the rewards did not come until 1971. That year Alfa won the Targa and their first world championship race, at Brands Hatch. Autodelta then reverted to a tubular frame in the 33/3TT, but enjoyed little success and turned to 12 cylinders for 1974.

An optimistic 500bhp was claimed for the flat-12, which was intalled in a modified 33/3TT tubular frame. In this form it was disappointing, however 'right' it may have seemed in specification and looks, for throughout 1974 only one race of any significance, at Monza, fell to the team. In 1975 the cars were fully developed, and their opposition was slight, and Alfas run by the Kauhsen team won seven of the eight championship races. Sports cars took second place to the Formula One engine programme in 1976, but with a new monocoque-chassis car Autodelta returned with its own team in 1977. Opposition was again negligible, and Chiti let his drivers race each other. The turbocharged version (which had made its debut late in 1976) was not really needed, and its extra weight and power led to tyre and brake problems. Overall, this final fling with sports cars ended on a high note for Alfa Romeo, with the 33SC/12s winning all eight championship races.

1967 33/2 'Telescopica' (2-litre)

Specification

Engine: *33/3* – 90-degree V-8; 86 × 64·4mm, 2998cc; twin ohc per bank; Lucas fuel injection; 440bhp at 9800rpm.
   33TT/12 – flat-12; 77 × 53·6mm, 2995cc; twin ohc per bank; Lucas fuel injection; 500bhp at 11 000rpm.
Gearbox: five-speed manual.
Chassis: monocoque (although early versions of both types had tubular frames); front suspension independent by wishbones, coil springs and dampers; rear suspension independent by swinging and radius arms, coil springs and dampers and anti-roll bar; four-wheel disc brakes (inboard rear on some cars).
Dimensions: *33/3* – wheelbase 224cm/88in;
front track 150cm/59in; **rear track** 138cm/54½in.
   33TT/12 – wheelbase 208cm/82in;
front track 143cm/56½in; **rear track** 150cm/59in.

T33/3 (1969 Sebring 12 hours)

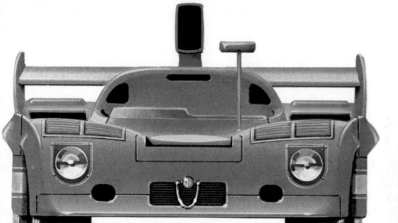

1975 33TT/12

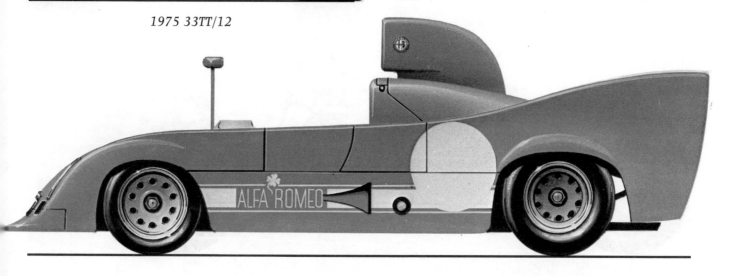

Allard J2

Sydney Allard was a pioneer constructor of Anglo-American hybrids, using big American engines with British chassis, body and running gear. He built his first special on these lines in the mid-1930s, started to make replicas late in the decade, then returned to his embryo company in 1945 to become a more serious manufacturer. The first post-war Allards used the British Ford 3622cc V-8, in models designated by body styles: L (four-seater) and K1 (two-seat roadster) which ran from 1946 until 1950, and the short-chassis two-seat J1 of 1946-47. The M and P1 were slightly later models in a bespoke line, and in mid-1949 the company introduced the archetypal J2.

This was a new design, with a rigid tubular-braced ladder frame, and a stark alloy body with cycle wings and small aero screens, or a full-width screen in 'road trim' – as with most Allards, there were many variations on the base specification. A de Dion arrangement was used at the rear, with coil spring ifs in place of Allard's previous split axle and transverse leaf scheme (further modification came with the J2X in 1951, which had radius arms ahead of the axle and engine set further forward in the chassis). 'Standard' engine was the side-valve Mercury V-8, bored and stroked to 4375cc, which gave

the J2 a 175kph (110mph) top speed, and the fierce acceleration which was an Allard speciality. Later, the Ardun ohv conversion became available for standard capacity units, giving approximately 140bhp and diminished reliability.

Most J2s, however, were supplied without engines to US customers, for the chassis would take almost any combination of V-8 and transmission. The Cad-Allards from among these held almost undisputed sway in US sports car racing for a brief period. The most powerful of the ohv Cadillac V-8s used gave over 300bhp, and married to Allard's peculiar brand of roadholding, that made for a very hairy sports-racing car. Thus cars with even modestly sophisticated handling, exemplified by the Jaguar XK120, saw off the J2s by the mid-1950s.

By that time Sydney Allard's great racing moment had been achieved by a 5·4-litre Cadillac-engined J2 at Le Mans in 1950, when with Tom Cole as co-driver he finished third, not far behind a pair of Talbots.

Fewer than 200 J2 Allards were built, and although Allard would win the 1952 Monte Carlo Rally in a P1 coupe, none of his later cars lived up to the awesome brute-force reputation of the J2 series.

1950 J2 (Cadillac engine)

Specification *(J2X)*
Engine: Mercury 90-degree V-8; 81 × 95·2mm, 3917cc; Ardun ohc; two Solex carburettors; 140bhp at 4000rpm.
Gearbox: three-speed manual.
Chassis: ladder frame; front suspension independent by split axles radius arms, coil springs and dampers; rear suspension by de Dion axle, coil springs and dampers; four-wheel drum brakes.
Dimensions: wheelbase 254cm/100in; **track** 142cm/56in.

Alpine A110

Automobiles Alpine had its beginnings in 1952, with a sports-bodied Renault 4CV; this was followed by a succession of Chappes-bodied Renault-based sports cars until Jean Redelé moved his company out of the special builder category with the A106 Mille Miles (after Michy's 1956 Mille Miglia class victory). In 1957 the A108 was introduced, with backbone chassis, glass fibre bodywork and Renault Dauphine running gear and engine tuned to give 60bhp. This led to the A110 in 1963. In 1965, Alpine's already strong Renault affiliations were cemented: Renault agreed to distribute the cars under the name Alpine-Renault, while Alpine agreed to use only Renault components.

The A110 followed the A108 in having a large-diameter steel tube backbone and platform floor, with subframes front and rear, Renault ifs and swing axle at the rear. The first engine – markedly rear-mounted – was the 998cc Renault four, giving 77bhp; the 1108cc R8 engine was soon introduced (with a five-speed gearbox), and then the 100bhp Gordini twin-cam version became available to Alpine.

Redelé turned his competitions attention towards sports-racers and single-seaters in the mid-1960s, when the principal role of the A110 was as a well-equipped and lively road car. At the end of the decade, however, Matra's circuit programme was given official preference, so Redelé looked to rallying, where the A110 already had a reasonable secondary-level record. At the highest level, it now proved tough, despite bodywork which seemed almost flimsy; distinctively noisy; well-mannered, despite its swinging half axle suspension; and very effective.

A 1300S version was followed in 1969 by the 1600S, which used the R16 engine, initially giving 138bhp but developed by Mignotet to give 155bhp in the main-line 1600S Berlinette of 1970. That was Alpine's breakthrough year, when the Acropolis and Tour de Corse fell to the team, and Jean-Claude Andruet took the European championship. 1971 opened with one-two-three in the Monte Carlo Rally (Ove Andersson, Jean-Luc Therier, Jean-Pierre Nicolas), and other victories gave Alpine the world championship. Both the Monte Carlo and championship successes were repeated in 1973, but in the following year the A110 was suddenly eclipsed.

While in no way related, the motor sport situation reflected the commercial fortunes of Alpine, which in that year was saved only by a complete Renault takeover.

1969 1600S factory rally car

Specification *(1600S)*
Engine: Renault straight-four; 77 × 84mm, 1565cc; pushrod ohv; one Weber carburettor; 138bhp at 6000rpm (see text).
Gearbox: five-speed manual.
Chassis: tubular backbone; front suspension independent by wishbones, coil springs and dampers and anti-roll bar; rear suspension by swinging axles, radius arms, coil springs and dampers and anti-roll bar; four-wheel disc brakes.
Dimensions: wheelbase 210cm/82½in; **front track** 130cm/51in; **rear track** 128cm/50½in.

Alvis 12/50

An impressive testimony to the longevity and hard-wearing qualities of the Alvis 12/50 is the number still performing lustily in Vintage events today. The first Alvis to have overhead valves, the 1½-litre 12/50, was evolved from the side-valve 10/30 model, appearing in mid-1923.

Its rugged but remarkably flexible 1496cc four-cylinder engine had a three-bearing crankshaft, detachable cylinder head with pushrod-and-rocker valve gear, and thermosyphon cooling. Dimensions were 68 × 103mm (a 69 × 110mm, 1650cc version appeared in 1926) and a healthy 50bhp at 4000rpm meant a 110kph (70mph) sporting car able also to potter pleasantly in town traffic and pull away in top gear from 20kph (12mph), or to tackle the toughest gradient, thanks to excellently chosen ratios in the four-speed gearbox. The frame and suspension were typically vintage, strongly built from the best materials, while the makers took great pains to ensure first class steering and handling.

Touring and sports versions of the 12/50 shared the same wheelbase and track, with a diversity of open and closed bodywork by Alvis and outside coachbuilders, one of the most popular styles being the handsome two-seater 'duck's back' Super Sports in polished aluminium. This had a bold outside exhaust system and a minimal 'dickey' seat in the turned-up tail, with spare wheel bolted below it. It was succeeded by an equally pleasant-looking 'beetle-back' in 1927.

The launch of the 12/50 was greatly assisted by Alvis' remarkable victory in the 1923 200 Miles Race at Brooklands with a racing version. This had a modified rear axle and brakes and special bodywork, but the engine and transmission were basically of production type. The car won at a remarkable speed of 150·14kph (93·29mph), and averaged an impressive 24mpg in an 'all out' race lasting over two hours.

The versatile 12/50 was driven to innumerable class successes in racing, speed trials, hillclimbs, driving tests and reliability trials, the bulk of them achieved by private owners. Apart from its performance and modest fuel consumption (30 or more mpg in road cars), the 12/50 above all embodied quality: no Alvis was ever cheap, but the purchase price was amply repaid by long life and seemingly inexhaustible vigour. The 12/50 was produced with periodic improvements from 1923 to 1929, was revived in late 1930 and survived in modified form until 1932 – a remarkable lifespan at a time when lesser marques brought out new models every 12 months.

Specification

Engine: straight-four; 68 × 103mm, 1496cc; pushrod ohv; single carburettor; 50bhp at 4000rpm. Optional engine (from 1926) as above, but 69 × 110mm, 1645cc.

Gearbox: separate four-speed manual.

Chassis: pressed steel side members; suspension by semi-elliptic springs and friction dampers front and rear; two-wheel drum brakes until 1925, four-wheel drum brakes thereafter.

Dimensions: wheelbase 286cm/112½in; **track** 127cm/50in.

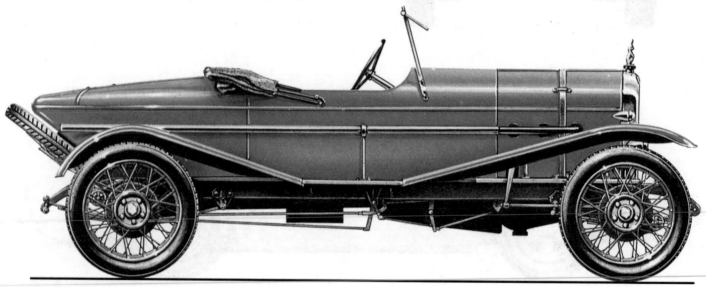

Alvis front-wheel drive models

That the Alvis concern was imaginative as well as practical was very evident from its front-wheel-drive cars. Virtually nothing was known of the technique of driving a car through the front (steering) wheels when the Alvis designers began experimenting in late 1924. Their target was more power, less weight and improved stability, so they supercharged one of their 12/50 engines and installed it back-to-front to drive the front wheels of a sprint special. A low, light duralumin chassis was made, and front suspension followed the old de Dion system, employing two parallel tubes as the 'axle' and two pairs of quarter-elliptic springs, with drive by two half-shafts carrying inboard brakes and pot-type universals.

Three years of experimentation culminated in a daring but abortive Grand Prix straight-eight and in 1928 Alvis surprised the motoring world by announcing a catalogue front-drive sports model. This had a 68 × 102mm, 1482cc four-cylinder engine with single ohc, driving forward through a four-speed gearbox; a Roots-type supercharger was optional, output thereby being raised from 50 to 75bhp.

Front springing was fully independent by eight quarter-elliptics, mounted transversely four per side. Heavy cost prohibited the use of constant-velocity joints of Gregoire or Rzeppa type, and pot joints were retained. Rear suspension was also independent by reversed quarter-elliptics and jointed half-shafts, making this Alvis sensationally advanced.

Inevitably such cars were raced. At Le Mans first time out in 1928, a front-drive Alvis won the 1½-litre class, while the Ulster TT saw one finish a close second to the winning Lea-Francis.

A total of 145 front-drive fours, carrying a variety of bodywork, was built during the next two years, but design complexities, exacting servicing, excessive noise from the straight-cut timing gears and final drive, mechanical temperament and harshness threatened to undermine Alvis' proud reputation for refinement and quality and this, together with the high price and sales resistance, forced an end to production in 1929.

Alvis was not quite finished with front drive, however. A batch of all-independent 1½-litre twin-cam straight-eight sports cars, based on the 1927 Grand Prix design, was built and raced in 1929-30. The three-car works team was foiled in the 1½-litre class by the more mature Alfa Romeos in the 1929 Ulster TT, but in the 1930 race they scored a fine one-two-three class win, being deprived of outright victory only by the Italian team cars. After that, Alvis regrettably abandoned further research into the front-wheel-drive principle which today features so strongly in the world's passenger cars.

Specification (*1928/29 production sports model*)
Engine: straight-four; 68 × 102mm, 1482cc; single ohc; 50bhp at 4500 rpm (75bhp at 5000rpm with optional Roots-type supercharger).
Gearbox: four-speed manual.
Chassis: pressed steel side members; front suspension independent by eight transverse quarter-elliptic springs (two upper/two lower on each side); rear suspension independent by reversed quarter-elliptic springs and longitudinal torque arms; friction dampers front and rear; four-wheel drum brakes, inboard at front.
Dimensions: wheelbase 259cm/102in or 305cm/120in; track 137cm/54in.

1928 supercharged TT

Amilcar CC and variants

Two outside factors helped bring this popular little French sports car into existence. One was a 1919 French fiscal measure which reduced annual tax by 75 per cent for 'cyclecars' weighing less than 350kg, having two seats and an under-1100cc engine. The other was the acquisition by André Citroen of the Le Zèbre marque's designer, leaving the latter's two engineers, Moyet and Morel, unhappy in an ailing concern.

Resolving to build a car to the new cyclecar class, Moyet and Morel secured financial backing from Messrs Lamy and Akar, left Le Zèbre and launched Amilcar, its name a somewhat abstruse anagram on the two financiers' names. While others toyed with four-wheel motorcycle ideas, Moyet plumped for a real car to small scale, prescribing a 904cc watercooled monobloc four with side valves and a splash-lubricated two-bearing crankshaft which proved an unintentional but effective rev limiter!

A simple rectangular chassis with quarter-elliptic springs projecting front and rear was employed, and final drive was via a unit gearbox with three well-chosen ratios and a differential-less rear axle. An open two-seater body with light wings and running boards completed a sound little car, the Model CC, weighing 430kg and capable of a maximum speed of 80kph (50mph).

Proof of the CC's speed and stamina came in 1922, when Morel won the first Bol d'Or 24-hours race outside Paris, after which Amilcar dropped the economy image in favour of sport and never looked back. The CC was soon followed by the rakish CS (Petit Sport) with 985cc engine and two-seater body wearing a vee-screen and shapely pointed tail; 1924 brought the improved CGS (Grand Sport) with pressure-lubricated 1078cc engine, semi-elliptic front springs and four-wheel brakes. Weight had risen to 580kg, but the engine's 28bhp meant a guaranteed 120kph (75mph).

Long, stylish wings and the pointed stern made this a very pretty car, many being imported into Britain and providing an *entrée* for young amateurs into club-type sporting events. Amilcars were also built under licence in Germany, Italy and Austria, and in 1926 the famous 145kph (90mph) *Surbaissé* or lowered version, the CGSS (Super Sport) was introduced. This had a 33bhp engine in a lowered chassis, while a four-speed gearbox further improved it in its last year of production. The Amilcar side-valve fours were built until 1929, over 15 000 of all models being produced, despite strong competition from the rival 1100cc ohv Salmsons.

Specification

Engine: *CC (1921-24)* – straight-four; 55 × 95mm, 904cc; side valves; single carburettor; 20bhp at 2500rpm.

CS (1922-24) – as CC but 57 × 95mm, 985cc; 23bhp at 3200rpm.

CGS :1924-29) – as CC, but 60 × 95mm, 1078cc; 28bhp at 3600rpm.

CGSS (1926-29) – as CGS, but 33bhp at 4500rpm (40bhp with supercharger).

Gearbox: three-speed manual (four-speed in CGSS).

Chassis: pressed steel side members; suspension by quarter-elliptic springs front and rear (CC and CS), but with semi-elliptic front springs on CGS and CGSS models; friction dampers; rear-wheel drum brakes on CC and CS, four-wheel drums on CGS and CGSS.

Dimensions: wheelbase 233cm/91½in; **track** 110cm/43½in.

1926 CGSS

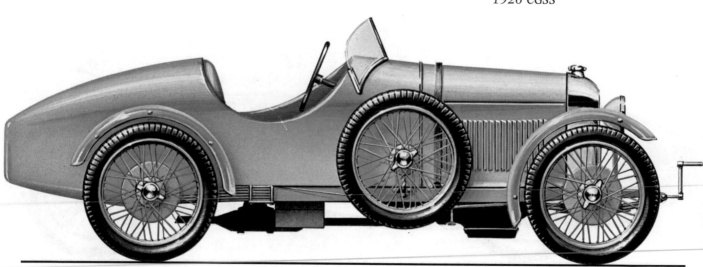

Aston Martin 1½-litre

Through dogged perseverance and sound, sturdy construction, the Aston Martin has proved one of the longest-living of British sports cars, enduring from 1920 to the present day despite many difficulties. After the first 'side-valve' phase the concern changed hands in 1926, with A C Bertelli taking over, his first Aston Martin design being a 1½-litre single-ohc four which was quietly introduced in 1927.

This promising if overweight car underwent considerable development to emerge in 1929 as the International with two- or four-seater bodywork. The chassis which had the customary semi-elliptic springs and friction dampers of Vintage days, was underslung at the rear, and although very rugged for a 1½-litre car, it endowed it with excellent roadholding and steering. Truly excellent large-diameter four-wheel brakes were fitted, and some serious racing at Le Mans, Brooklands, Ulster and elsewhere helped mature the design.

The 1495cc four-cylinder engine had a detachable head, single chain-driven ohc with Weller tensioner, two in-line valves per cylinder in Ricardo-type combustion chambers, twin carburettors, a sturdy three-bearing crankshaft and dural connecting rods. Dry sump lubrication was an innovation, the system being supplied from a shallow ribbed 11-litre oil tank housed between the front chassis dumbirons.

A separate sliding-pinion gearbox provided four usefully close ratios, and final drive was via torque tube and underslung-worm rear axle. The International had the shorter of two optional wheelbase lengths, being suitable in standard form for sports car racing anywhere in the world. The rear seats were very 'occasional' and the low body lines were enhanced by neat cycle-type mudguards.

With transmission and other improvements, the basic 1½-litre Aston Martin endured until 1936, scoring some highly significant racing successes at home and abroad, and establishing a great reputation for dependable high performance. The International was succeeded by the Le Mans in 1932 and then by the glorious Ulster competition model in 1934, while a long-wheelbase MkII four-seater was also produced. All were heavy (the Ulster at 940kg was one of the lightest), but in their weight lay their durability, while aesthetically the pre-war Bertelli Aston Martins were hard to equal, the Ulster in particular being one of the finest-looking British competition cars of any era.

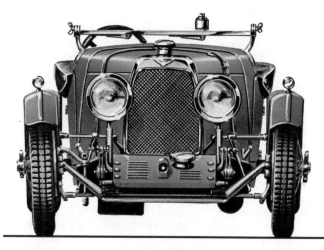

1930 International

Specification

Engine: straight-four; 69·3 × 99mm, 1495cc; single ohc; twin carburettors; power/rpm figures not quoted.

Gearbox: four-speed manual (separate on International)

Chassis: pressed steel side members, underslung at rear; semi-elliptic springs front and rear; friction dampers; four-wheel, cable-operated drum brakes.

Dimensions: wheelbase 259cm/102in (305cm/120in on MkII); track 132cm/52in.

Aston Martin DB2 and DB2/4

In the years immediately following the Second World War, Aston Martin still made modest-sized 2-litre sports cars, but that policy changed considerably during the next two decades. When David Brown took over the ailing Feltham concern in 1947, he inherited a 2-litre four-cylinder pushrod ohv engine and a prototype saloon called the Atom, an advanced design with a triangulated spaceframe of rectangular tubing and ifs by coil springs, trailing links and an anti-roll bar.

A light, open two-seater competition car was developed from this, surprising and delighting British race followers by winning the 1948 Belgian 24-hour race at Spa. The first David Brown production sports model, initially called the '2 litre Sports' and then the DB1, evolved directly from that Spa winner, and was itself the basis of the next model.

In 1947 Brown had also taken over the Lagonda company, and with it a fine 2·6-litre six-cylinder twin-ohc engine designed by W O Bentley. For the revived Le Mans 24-hour race of 1949 this six was fitted into an improved DB1 spaceframe with shorter wheelbase, and carrying superb aerodynamic two-seater coupe bodywork of stressed alloy skin construction. The DB1 live rear axle (located by twin trailing arms and a Watt linkage) remained, but with coil instead of leaf springing.

With triple SU carburettors, the Bentley-designed engine gave 120bhp and the car proved fast but unreliable at Le Mans, retiring early. At Spa, however, it placed third in the Belgian 24-hour race,

and Brown decided to put the car into production as a fast road coupe designated the DB2. With 105bhp and twin carburettors, even the poor fuel of the time allowed a maximum speed of 170-180kph (105-110mph); with excellent roadholding and controllability, the DB2 proved a fine, fast, durable car of undeniable beauty.

Numerous racing successes in Britain and Continental Europe spread its fame internationally, and although the production DB2 was almost hand-built and expensive in comparison with rivals such as the Jaguar XK120, demand strained Feltham's limited output.

Owners irked by the limited space in the shapely coupe were mollified by the introduction in 1953 of the DB2/4, with a longer body on the same wheelbase containing two extra 'occasional' seats and a luggage boot, and a higher-compression, 125bhp Vantage engine to propel it at a luxurious 185kph (115mph). Two years later, engine size was raised to 2922cc, further increasing performance.

A drophead coupe version was also available, and the DB2/4 was produced until late 1957, when the MkIII appeared. This 190kph (120mph) car embodied some restyling, having the wider, shallow radiator grille of the DB3S competition model, and the race-developed triple-Weber 162bhp engine. Girling disc front brakes and a new hydraulic clutch were fitted, and overdrive was optional, but this model was quickly superseded by the DB4 in 1959.

1953 DB2/4

Specification

Engine: *DB2* – straight-six; 78 × 90mm, 2580cc; twin ohc; twin SU carburettors; 107bhp at 5000rpm (but 125bhp at 5000rpm on Vantage models).

　　　DB2/4 – as above, but 83 × 90mm, 2922cc; 125bhp.

　　Mark III – as above, but triple Weber carburettors; 162bhp at 5500rpm.

Gearbox: four-speed manual.

Chassis: multi-tube spaceframe; front suspension independent by trailing links, coil springs, anti-roll bar and dampers; rear suspension by twin radius arms, Panhard rod, coil springs and dampers; four-wheel Girling drum brakes (but disc front brakes on Mark III).

Dimensions: wheelbase 251cm/99in; **track** 137cm/54in.

Aston Martin DB4, DB5 and DB6

Although sports car racing absorbed so much time and money at Aston Martin, the famous Feltham company did not neglect its road models and lessons learned on the circuit were passed on to the catalogue cars. Thus the big 3·5-litre all-alloy six-cylinder engine with seven-bearing crankshaft, developed for Le Mans 1957 and which won the 1958 British Empire Trophy race, was detuned and adapted for a new model, the DB4, introduced at the 1958 Earls Court Motor Show.

Replacing the DB2/4 MkIII, this had a very different chassis of platform type fabricated from sheet metal, carrying shapely aluminium 2 + 2 coupe bodywork styled by Carrozzeria Touring of Turin, over their *superleggera* system of tubular subframes.

This new Aston Martin had race-developed coil-spring-and-wishbone front suspension in place of trailing links, but at the rear the DB2-type live axle with coil springs was retained. Brakes were disc all round, an all-synchromesh four-speed gearbox was employed, and rack-and-pinion steering was new to a road Aston Martin. The DB4 weighed about 1320kg, which with 240bhp made it a 225kph (140mph) car of refinement and elegance. Wheelbase and track differed minimally from those of the old DB2, but the wide body and grille and deep side panels gave it a heavier look. It was, in truth, a car in the then-new Grand Touring class rather than a sports car in the old sense, although its reliability was somewhat marred by lubrication problems in the alloy engine.

A more sporting variant, the DB4 GT, was introduced in September 1959, having a wheelbase 13cm shorter, a triple-Weber engine for which 302bhp was claimed, a limited-slip differential and a speed potential of 240kph (150mph). It was raced in events such as the Goodwood TT, although was generally eclipsed by the GT Ferraris, while a Zagato-bodied DB4 GT of even lower profile was also produced in small numbers. This was lighter, more spartan within (a 136-litre fuel tank occupied the boot) and with a speed potential of 260kph (160mph) or more, according to gearing.

In 1964, the year in which Aston Martin moved from Feltham to Newport Pagnell, the DB4 was given a larger bore (96mm), 3995cc engine and a five-speed all-synchromesh gearbox, becoming the 230kph (145mph) DB5. This was a quieter, smoother, and more reliable car which sold well despite its high price.

Two years later it was succeeded by the DB6, a roomier two-door four-seater with 95mm longer wheelbase and extra GT refinements including electric winding windows, optional automatic transmission and power steering. The lengthened roofline of the DB6 ended in an abrupt tail embodying a spoiler, improving the car aerodynamically (if not aesthetically), but also affording extra seat and luggage space. This was a superb car of formidable performance, achieving 0 to 80kph (50mph) in only 4·9 sec, yet vying with Bentley or Rolls-Royce in finish, trim and equipment. An exotic and even more expensive variant was the Volante drophead, claimed to be the first European car with a power-operated soft-top as standard.

Engine: *DB4* – straight-six; 92 × 92mm, 3670cc; twin ohc; twin SU carburettors; 240bhp at 5500rpm (260bhp on Vantage models).

DB4GT – as above, but triple twin-choke Weber carburettors; 302bhp at 6000rpm.

DB5 and DB6 – as DB4, but 96 × 92mm, 3995cc; triple SU carburettors; 282bhp at 5500rpm (325bhp on Vantage models).

Gearbox: *DB4* – four-speed all-synchromesh manual or optional three-speed automatic.

DB5 and DB6 – five-speed manual or optional three-speed automatic.

Chassis: box section platform-type; front suspension independent by coil springs, wishbones and dampers; rear suspension by rigid axle, twin trailing links, Watt linkage, coil springs and dampers; four-wheel disc brakes with servo assistance.

Dimensions: *DB4* – **wheelbase** 249cm/98in; **track** 137cm/54in.

DB4GT – **wheelbase** 236cm/93in; **track** 137cm/54in.

DB5 – **wheelbase** 249cm/98in; **track** 137cm/54in.

DB6 – **wheelbase** 261cm/102½in; **track** 138cm/54½in.

1958 DB4

Aston Martin sports-racing cars

The 'R' in DBR1 meant 'Racing', and this model was the ultimate Aston Martin competition sports car, taking the marque to its peak achievement of victory in the Le Mans 24-hour race and the 1959 World Sports Car Championship.

Outright success at Le Mans had been a particular ambition of David Brown since he had taken over Aston Martin; he tried for ten years running, from 1949 to 1958, scoring numerous high placings and class wins but never outright victory. During that time, Aston Martin's works competition cars were constantly developed, from a DB2 coupe with boosted engine to open sports-racing cars of ever-increasing potency, climaxing in the DBR1.

The DB3 with tubular frame, de Dion rear axle and torsion bar suspension appeared late in 1951 and won the 1952 Goodwood Nine Hours race. It was succeeded in 1953 by the DB3S, a more handsome machine with better streamlining, tubular ladder chassis and a 180bhp triple-carburettor engine driving through four speeds and an improved de Dion back end. The DB3S won four major British victories that season, but failed at the all-important 24-hour race at Le Mans.

Disc brakes all round, an alloy cylinder head and twin ignition helped take second place at Le Mans both in 1955 and 1956, but Brown was not satisfied, and sanctioned the building of a redesigned car, the DBR1. Appearing quietly at Le Mans in 2½-litre form in 1956, this had an all-alloy six-cylinder engine with 12-plug head, valves at 95 degrees, triple Weber carburettors and dry sump lubrication, a rear-mounted five-speed transverse gearbox in unit with a ZF differential, de Dion back end and a tubular spaceframe with front springing by wishbones and longitudinal torsion bars.

The new car retired at Le Mans, but reappeared in 3-litre form as the DBR1/300 in 1957, winning its first two races – the Spa GP and the Nurburgring 1000km – in the latter defeating full Maserati, Ferrari and Jaguar teams. A second Belgian win in the Spa 3 Hours followed, and in 1958 the DBR1 again won the Nurburgring 1000km, plus the Goodwood TT and Empire Trophy races, the latter with a larger, 3·7-litre engine.

With the design nearing obsolescence, Brown decided on one more try for Le Mans in 1959, and his patience was richly rewarded: Aston Martin's 3-litre cars ran the Ferrari and Porsche opposition into the ground, taking first and second places, while a third car led the race and broke the lap record before retiring. That same exciting year the DBR1 won the Nurburgring 1000km for the third successive year and the Goodwood TT again, these three victories clinching the 1959 World Sports Car Championship for Aston Martin, the only British marque ever to have won this title.

Specification (*DBR1*)
Engine: straight-six; 83 × 90mm, 2992cc; twin ohc; three Weber twin-choke carburettors; 250bhp at 6300rpm.
Gearbox: five-speed manual, transversely-mounted in unit with the final drive.
Chassis: tubular spaceframe; front suspension independent by wishbones, longitudinal torsion bars and dampers; rear suspension by de Dion-type axle, transverse torsion bars and dampers; four-wheel Girling disc brakes.
Dimensions: wheelbase 483cm/190in; track 135cm/53in.

DBR1

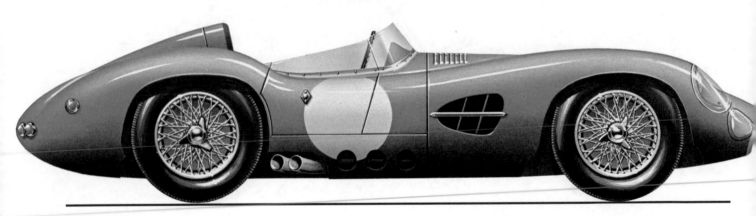

Aston Martin DBS

Early in 1966 Aston Martin's chief engineer, Polish-born Tadek Marek, began an arduous 12 months' task: designing and developing a replacement for the DB6. The main change was the power unit, which was to be an all-new four-cam V-8, the rest of the specification (including the platform chassis and ifs) being much as before, but for a de Dion rear axle with inboard disc brakes, and cast alloy wheels replacing the traditional wire type.

Superleggera bodywork designed by Carrozzeria Touring of Milan was planned, but the Italian firm had to withdraw owing to financial problems which ended its coachbuilding career; Aston Martin therefore passed the brief to resident stylist Bill Towns, who produced a distinctive new two-door four-seater coupe. Gone was the portliness of the DB6, even though the new body was 15cm wider, and Towns gave it sharp, incisive lines of striking purity, and – equally important – a structure complying with the stringent American safety regulations which came into force in 1968.

The one thing missing at the DBS' debut was the V-8 engine. A prototype unit tried at Le Mans in 1966 required drastic redevelopment, and the production 5·3-litre engine, built entirely at Newport Pagnell, was not ready until 1969. In the interim the tough old twin-cam alloy six served on in 3995cc form, and the DBS introduced in September 1967 was well received.

When the DBS V8 finally appeared two years later, it got an even better reception, 200 being ordered in the first week.

The all-alloy 90-degree V-8 engine was well 'over-square', with five main bearings and chain-driven twin-ohc to each block. Although Aston Martin, following Rolls-Royce's example, declined to divulge bhp or rpm figures, the output was estimated at well over 300bhp. Initially Bosch fuel injection was employed, but US emission regulations made the use of four twin-choke downdraught Weber carburettors more suitable from 1973. A maximum of 260kph (160mph) made the DBS V8 one of the world's fastest four-seater road cars.

The departure of Sir David Brown from the board in 1971 preceded the sale of the company, which emerged as Aston Martin Lagonda (1975) Ltd, the car thereafter shedding its 'DB' prefix and becoming known simply as the V8 – one of Britain's finest prestige GT cars, albeit one of the heaviest at 1760kg and one of the costliest.

Specification *(DBS V8)*
Engine: 90-degree V-8; 100 × 85mm, 5340cc; twin ohc per bank; fuel injection from 1969, four twin-choke Weber carburettors from 1972; estimated 300bhp (see text).
Gearbox: five-speed all-synchromesh manual; optional three-speed automatic.
Chassis: platform-type frame; front suspension independent by wishbones, coil springs and dampers; rear suspension by de Dion-type axle, parallel trailing arms, Watt linkage, coil springs and dampers; four-wheel disc brakes (inboard at rear) with servo assistance.
Dimensions: wheelbase 261cm/102½in; **track** 150cm/59in.

Atalanta

Born at the wrong time, in early 1937 when sabres were already rattling in Europe, the Atalanta had too short a life to influence British sports car design widely. Yet it was a car of bold concept, with novel all-round independent suspension. The first model was the 1½-litre with a four-cylinder, eight-plug, 12-valve single-ohc engine designed by Alfred Gough, an Atalanta director (racing drivers Peter Whitehead and Denis Poore were others) who had earlier produced a basically similar eight-valve engine for Frazer Nash.

The 1496cc Atalanta unit produced 78bhp with twin-SU carburettors, while a driver-engaged Centric or Arnott supercharger was an optional fitment. There were also two transmission options: a US-built four-speed Warner manual gearbox with overdrive, or the French Cotal clutchless magnetic unit. The ifs employed twin coil springs on each side, mounted vertically in conjunction with rigid twin trailing arms made in Hiduminium, and hydraulic dampers. The rear springs were installed horizontally, close to the chassis side members, with swinging half-shafts located by single trailing arms, a combination which, even with restricted deflection, produced curious handling but eliminated wheelspin and gave a

comfortable ride. Powerful hydraulic brakes with 16-inch electron drums were employed.

The short-chassis open sports two-seater was notably good looking with its low build, 'helmet' wings, elegant vee radiator and neat tail, and performance to match the looks – it could attain 145kph (90mph). Open four-seater and closed bodywork was also offered on a 274cm chassis.

Essentially hand-built, using many light alloys, and of high quality, the 1½-litre Atalanta was expensive in 1937 at £582 (when the contemporary 2½-litre SS100 Jaguar cost £395). There were, moreover, production problems with the four-cylinder Gough engine which persuaded the company to substitute the 4·4-litre 90degree V-12 Lincoln Zephyr side-valve unit. This added little to the maximum speed but increased the acceleration and brought comforting reliability and flexibility at modest cost. The Lincoln three-speed gearbox was also used.

About 20 Atalanta cars were built at the Staines, Middlesex, factory, and the marque was starting to making a name for itself in competition when the Second World War began in 1939, sadly killing off the enterprise.

1937 long wheelbase 1½-litre (supercharged)

Specification

Engine: *1½-litre* – straight-four; 69×100mm, 1496cc; single ohc; three valves per cylinder; twin SU carburettors; 78bhp at 4500rpm.

4·4-litre – Lincoln 90-degree V-12; $69·8 \times 95·2$mm, 4379cc; side valves; single carburettor; 112bhp at 3900rpm.

Gearbox: *1½-litre* – Warner four-speed manual with overdrive or Cotal electro-magnetic four-speed.

4·4-litre – three-speed manual with synchromesh.

Chassis: pressed steel side members with cruciform bracing; front suspension independent by double coil springs and twin trailing links; rear suspension independent by horizontal coil springs, swing axles and single trailing links; four-wheel hydraulic drum brakes.

Dimensions: wheelbase *1½-litre* – 244cm/96in or 274cm/108in; *4·4-litre* – 274cm/108in; **front track** 135cm/53in; **rear track** 137cm/54in.

Auburn Speedsters

American sports cars were extremely rare before the Second World War, one of the best known being the Auburn Speedster, produced erratically between 1929 and 1937. More 'sporting' than 'sports', the first model bearing the name had a 115bhp, 4·4-litre straight-eight Lycoming engine with side valves, three-speed gearbox, a heavy touring-type chassis and a characteristic high 'boat-tail' two-seater open body with vee windscreen. For all its ponderous size, this car could attain almost 145kph (90mph), and a strikingly attractive short-wheelbase two-seater coupe version called the Cabin Speedster was even faster, although few were built.

In 1932 the open two-seater was revived in more purposeful form, with cleaner lines, long sweeping wings, a tall vee radiator inherited from Auburn's associates, Cord and Duesenberg, and the fashionable white-wall tyres. Major interest lay under the bonnet, for in quest of more power Auburn now employed a 6·4-litre Lycoming V-12 engine – a 45-degree unit with horizontal valves, twin carburettors and a claimed 160bhp, taken through a three-speed gearbox and Columbia two-speed rear axle.

One such Speedster clocked 162·17kph (100·77mph) through the flying mile in 1932, and the new car was remarkably cheap.

Production of the V-12 engines ended in 1934, so a new straight-eight Speedster was introduced, its outstanding feature being the Schwitzer-Cummins centrifugal supercharger which boosted output of the 4596cc side-valve engine to 148bhp at 4000rpm. This comfortably upheld the Speedster's traditional 160kph (100mph) maximum, the two-speed rear axle with highest ratio of 3·47:1 playing an important part in the accomplishment.

The boat-tail two-seater body style was gracefully updated by the Cord stylist Buehrig, who prescribed helmet-type wings, four flexible outside exhaust pipes, and the chrome legend 'Super-Charged' on the bonnet sides to distinguish this final edition of the Speedster. One such car covered five miles (8km) at 104mph (167kph) at Bonneville, and every one bore a silver plaque signed by record-man Ab Jenkins, testifying that he had topped 100mph with it on test.

The dry weight of 1680kg contributed to the car's notable steadiness at all speeds, while the big engine took care of the acceleration. Handling was not so good, but this Auburn has endeared itself to many American preservationists as a classic. Auburn itself was ill-rewarded for its individuality by closure in 1937, with the collapse of the Auburn-Cord-Duesenberg Corporation.

1935 supercharged 851

Specification

Engine: *1929* – Lycoming straight-eight; 83 × 114mm, 4394cc; side valves; single carburettor; 115bhp at 3400rpm.

1932-34 – Lycoming 45-degree V-12; 79 × 108mm, 6417cc; horizontal valves; single carburettor; 160bhp at 3400rpm.

1935-37 – straight-eight; 78 × 121mm, 4596cc; side valves; single carburettor; Schwitzer-Cummins centrifugal supercharger; 148bhp at 4000rpm.

Gearbox: three-speed manual; Columbia two-speed rear axle optional 1932-34, standard from 1935.

Chassis: pressed steel side members; semi-elliptic springs front and rear; four-wheel drum brakes, mechanically operated from 1929, hydraulic from 1932.

Dimensions: *1929* – wheelbase 317cm/125in; track 147cm/58in.

1932-34 – **wheelbase** 323cm/127in or 338cm/133in; **track** 147cm/58in.

1935-37 – **wheelbase** 323cm/127in; **front track** 150cm/59in; **rear track** 157cm/62in.

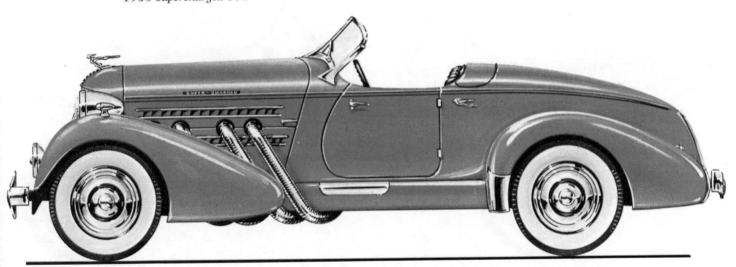

Audi Alpensieger

Cars built for climbing Alps are essentially sporting, and the 14/35 3·6-litre Audi was one of the true ancestors of the sports car. Although young in years, this German marque from Zwickau in Saxony gained a great reputation in the annual Austrian Alpine Trials, in those days Europe's premier road contest. It lasted over a week and involved contestants in well over 1600km of extremely rugged and gruelling mountain driving.

Dr August Horch was an old hand at such events, having driven cars bearing his own name with considerable success, but in 1909 he fell out with the original Horch company and promptly moved further up the same street in Zwickau to start another car factory. Forbidden by his former board to use his own name, he called his new marque Audi, at the suggestion of a fellow executive's son who was versed in Latin. *Horch* in German means hark or listen; in Latin the word is *Audi*.

In 1911, Audi laid down a new model, the Typ C 14/35, with four-cylinder bi-bloc engine having overhead inlet valves and side exhausts, four-speed gearbox and shaft drive. With a short chassis carrying well-formed open aluminium bodywork, this car was capable of 100kph (60mph) and could tackle almost any Alpine gradient, with the extra virtues of remarkable robustness and reliability.

It gave the first inkling of its potential in the 1912 Austrian Alpine Trials when one car finished without loss of marks, alongside a small 2·6-litre 10/28 Audi. In 1913 a team of 14/35s won the team prize, and they repeated this feat in 1914, when no less than five Audis finished with clean sheets, gaining the premier award. The title *Alpensieger* (Alpine victor) was thus fully earned.

The outbreak of the First World War unfortunately interrupted further development of the Typ C, but when Dr Horch resumed Audi production in 1920 a batch of the rakish Alpensiegers was put through. A new Model K was also based on the successful pre-war design, using the same bore and stroke, but gaining the overhead valves which Horch had intended to employ in 1915.

Specification *(Typ C 14/35)*
Engine: straight-four; 90 × 140mm, 3564cc; overhead inlet valves, side exhaust valves; single carburettor; 35bhp at 1800rpm.
Gearbox: separate four-speed manual.
Chassis: pressed steel side members; semi-elliptic springs front and rear; rear-wheel drum brakes and transmission brake.
Dimensions: wheelbase 304cm/119½in (competition model 290cm/114in); track 130cm/51in.

1914 Typ C14/35

Austin Seven Ulster

That so utilitarian a vehicle as the Austin Seven could become a lively sports car and go racing successfully was inconceivable when it first appeared in 1922. Puny and underpowered, the original Chummy tourer had a 190cm wheelbase, a 10bhp engine and a weight of 356kg. Yet its tiny side-valve engine, with two-bearing crankshaft only 28·6mm in diameter, proved tough enough to win long distance races at Monza, Brooklands, Ulster and elsewhere, and to withstand supercharging.

A sporting Seven appeared as early as 1924, but the Ulster or Super Sports, as it was first called, was Austin's most serious effort in the sports car market. It retained the touring Seven's 'basics' – the A-form frame, transverse leaf front and quarter-elliptic rear springing and tiny four-wheel brakes. The 747cc side-valve engine, however, was fitted with a gear-driven Cozette supercharger, special cylinder head, valve gear and camshaft, and pump cooling, while the two-bearing crank, required to turn at over 5000rpm, was pressure-lubricated and balanced.

The three-speed gearbox had closer ratios, while a dropped front axle and flatter springs lowered the car. Wings, hood, windscreen and lights were quickly removable for competition work, and the weight with a doorless open two-seater body and spidery outside exhaust system was around 435kg. With 33bhp available, the little car could exceed 120kph (75mph) reliably: an unblown 24bhp version could touch 100kph (60mph), but the blown car, raced by the factory in 1929, scored four class wins in major British races, besides finishing third and fourth in the Ulster TT.

That earned it the name Ulster and in 1930 the little orange cars took three more British class wins and won the 500 Miles Race at Brooklands outright at 134·25kph (83·42mph), but the advent of the ohc MG Midget intruded on further Austin successes in the 750cc racing class.

Production of the blown Ulster was very small, but more plebeian sporting Sevens provided enthusiasts with a wide variety of 'fun' motoring at minimal cost for many years.

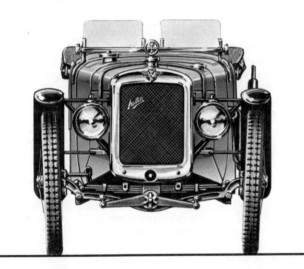

Specification
Engine: straight-four; 56 × 76mm, 747cc; side valves; single carburettor; 24bhp at 4500rpm, or 33bhp at 5000rpm when fitted with Cozette supercharger.
Gearbox: three-speed manual
Chassis: pressed steel side members; single transverse leaf front suspension; quarter-elliptic rear suspension; four-wheel drum brakes.
Dimensions: wheelbase 191cm/75in; track 102cm/40in.

Austin Healey 100 and 3000

The 'big Healey' evolved from a design framed around a manufacturer's existing components, as have several notable sports cars; but in this case there was the odd distinction that to all intents and purposes these were left-overs from the abruptly-terminated run of a less-than-successful model with sporting pretensions, and yet the eventual outcome was a car worthy of that overworked appellation 'classic'.

The failure was the Austin A90 Sports, whose pushrod-ohv 2660cc engine and gearbox fitted in with Donald and Geoffrey Healey's ideas for a sports car to take the place of the Nash-Healey, at least for some markets. That coincided with Sir Leonard Lord's thoughts about a stock-based sports car, which he instantly recognized in the metal of the Healey 100 shown at the 1952 London Motor Show. Agreement was quickly reached, giving Austin the right to use the Healey name on a royalty basis, and to build the cars at Longbridge (the first 20 were built by Healeys at Warwick). Little changed outwardly, with wire wheels substituted for the A90 wheels of that first batch, the 100 was put into real production in

the spring of 1953. It was a smoothly styled car, solid on its box-section side-member chassis, wishbone and coil spring ifs and rigid rear axle on leaf springs; mechanically unexciting but sound, as low as the engine would permit and low to the ground as well, with a top speed to justify the '100' – 102mph (164kph) in production versions, 117mph (188kph) achieved by a pre-production 100 at Jabbeke. Handling could be rude but the cornering power could strain the spokes of its traditional wire wheels.

Immediate demand was high, especially from the USA, for the car slotted into a market gap between MG or Triumph and Jaguar. They soon appeared on the circuits (12th at Le Mans in 1953) and modified versions started to appear. The S and the M had aluminium

Specifications

100

Engine: straight-four; 87·3 × 111·1mm, 2660cc; pushrod ohv; twin SU carburettors; 90bhp at 4000rpm (132bhp on the 100S).
Gearbox: three-speed manual with overdrive (four-speed on 100S).
Chassis: ladder-type; front suspension independent by wishbones, coil springs and dampers; rear suspension by live axle, semi-elliptic springs and dampers; four-wheel drum brakes.
Dimensions: wheelbase 234cm/92in; **track** 126cm/49½in (129cm/51in on 100S, 100M).

3000

Engine: *MkI* – straight-six; 83·36 × 88·9mm, 2912cc; pushrod ohv; twin SU carburettors; 124bhp at 4600rpm.
　　　　MkII – as above, but 130bhp at 4750rpm.
　　　　MkIII – as above, but 150bhp at 5250rpm.
Gearbox: four-speed manual.
Chassis: ladder-type; front suspension independent by wishbones, coil springs and dampers; rear suspension by live axle, semi-elliptic springs, radius arms and dampers; disc front/drum rear brakes.
Dimensions: wheelbase 234cm/92in; **front track** 123cm/48½in (124cm/49in on MkIII); **rear track** 127cm/50in (126cm/49½in on MkIII).

1953 100

and steel bodies respectively (the 'S' being owed to Sebring, where a disc-braked forerunner had finished third in the 1954 12 hours), a 50 per cent power increase to 132bhp, four-speed-plus-overdrive gearboxes, improved suspension and disc brakes.

The 100-Six came in 1956, with the BMC C-series 2639cc six, rated at 102bhp, a restyled and longer 2+2 body, heavier and smoother. That became the 3000 in 1959, with the engine in 2912cc, 124bhp form, beefed-up chassis and disc front brakes, and a 195kph (120mph) top speed. Development then progressed naturally, with a 132bhp engine in the MkII of 1962 (190kph/116mph top speed) and 150bhp in the MkIII of 1964 (198kph/123mph), gaining in torque as well as power. Wind-up windows and an optional one-piece top came as part of a 'civilizing' process, and the noise was subdued, but the car always retained its 'character', its firm ride and its marginal ground clearance. A 4-litre MkIV project reached an advanced stage, but in the face of US safety regulations the 3000 was discontinued in 1968, when some 43 000 had been made.

The big Healey became one of the legendary cars of rallying, especially the red works cars prepared at Abingdon and managed by the first guru of the sport, Stuart Turner, when for five years the 3000 was the mainstay of the BMC team in its golden days. The works cars had light-alloy bodies, engines giving up to 210bhp, and that restricted ground clearance, which should have ruled them out of contention on rough events, but which never did. They were hard work to drive, but the results came: from a Coupe des Alpes in 1958 through to the mid-1960s their strength paid dividends in overall terms and in the GT categories. The outstanding victory was perhaps that scored by Pat Moss and Ann Wisdom in the 1960 Liege-Rome-Liege (it hardly matters that by then the event did not go near Rome, but used the rough roads of the Balkans); Rauno Aaltonen and Tony Ambrose also won the last-ever Liege, in 1964.

They were raced, without the same degree of outright success, but at least with the consistent reliability that came from toughness; but it is for its 40 class victories in major international rallies that the 'big Healey' is recalled with affection . . .

1964 3000 MkIII

Austin Healey Sprite

This little fun car was launched in 1958 to complement the A-H 3000. A cheap and economical two-seater, it was designed to use BMC stock components – A-series engine, four-speed gearbox, wishbone front suspension and live rear axle with quarter-elliptic springs. A platform chassis supported the body, its protruding headlights helping to give it a 'character' only appreciated after many of the early 'frog-eyed' Sprites had been thoughtlessly modified ...

It was light (648kg), so its 42bhp gave it a very reasonable performance, maximum speed topping 130kph (80mph), and it was responsive. The tuning specialists of the day, such as Speedwell, soon got at it and engine modifications giving up to 70bhp led to top speeds of up to 160kph (100mph). The Sprite became a popular club racing model, and production was climbing towards 50 000 when the MkII appeared in the spring of 1961. This had a completely new body (with a real boot) which was smart but undistinguished, and 46·5bhp available from its 948cc to give 140kph (85mph). That hardly matched up to sporting pretensions, so a 1098cc version of the A-series engine (55bhp, 145kph/90mph) came late in 1962, together with disc front brakes (and a badge-engineered MG Midget variant). A slightly better-equipped and marginally more powerful

MkIII came in 1964; in this semi-elliptics replaced the rear quarter elliptics. It was quieter and more comfortable, and had a maximum speed of just over 145kph (90mph).

Nevertheless, performance had no more than kept pace with advancing saloon standards, so the MkIV, which came late in 1966, had a version of the Cooper S 1275cc engine, initially rated at 65bhp, but with fractionally less power and improved torque after 1968. This was a 150kph (95mph) car.

Sprites were extensively raced, a works team run by the Healeys rather than from Abingdon contesting the classic endurance races in search of class honours through the mid-1960s. The works cars were normally coupes, with variations of fastback shape according to the nature of circuits, and were substantially lighter than standard cars owing to the use of aluminium bodies on tubular structures. In amateur categories, such as SCCA championships, the standard cars were frequently seen.

In road form, the Midget naturally had precisely the same qualities as the Sprite – economical, lively and well-balanced – and it lasted to the end of the 1970s. The Sprite, however, was phased out in 1971, and the name Austin-Healey disappeared.

1963 MkII

Specification

Engine: *MkI* – straight-four; 62·9 × 76·2mm, 948cc; pushrod ohv, twin SU carburettors; 42bhp at 5200rpm.

MkII (from 1962) – as above, but 64·58 × 83·72mm, 1098cc; 55bhp at 5500rpm.

MkIV – as above, but 70·64 × 81·33mm, 1275cc; 65bhp at 6000rpm.

Gearbox: four-speed manual.

Chassis: steel monocoque; front suspension independent by wishbones, coil springs and dampers; rear suspension by live axle, quarter-elliptic springs (semi-elliptics on MkIV) and dampers; four-wheel brakes – all drum on MkI, disc front/drum rear from MkII.

Dimensions: wheelbase 203cm/80in; **front track** 117cm/46in on MkI, 120cm/47in from MkII; **rear track** 112cm/44in on MkI, 114cm/45in on MkII, 117cm/46in on Mk. IV.

Austro-Daimler ADM

Although extinct since the Second World War, Austro-Daimler was once a central European marque with a great sporting pedigree. Launched at Wiener Neustadt in 1899 as the Austrian branch of the pioneer German Daimler company, it became independent in 1906 and its cars quickly developed sporting characteristics under Dr Ferdinand Porsche, its designer until 1923.

Porsche produced the advanced ohc cars which took the first three places in the 1910 Prince Henry Trials, and in 1921 he designed a very clean six-cylinder single-ohc 4·4-litre Austro-Daimler engine of up-to-date specification. It had an alloy cylinder block with press-in nitralloy liners, full-pressure lubrication, a unit four-speed gearbox, and a radiator and steering column rigidly attached to the engine. Intended for a touring car, the 348cm chassis had semi-elliptic front springing and long cantilever-type springs at the rear.

The subsequent ADM range of higher performance, four-wheel-braked models were direct descendants. The first ADM, appearing in 1923, had a 2·6-litre single-carburettor engine giving 50bhp, with a new and attractive flat radiator in place of the more usual vee-type. The twin-carburettor 60bhp ADM 2 was announced in 1925, and in 1926 came the ADM 3 with an engine enlarged to 2994cc.

Fitted with twin Zenith carburettors, the ADM 3 engine put out an impressive 100bhp at 4000rpm, and in a special lightened 274cm Sport chassis could exceed 160kph (100mph), with better handling than the long-chassis models. Known in Britain as the 19/100, the ADM 3 Sport generally wore light and rakish open two-seater bodywork. It was the basis of Hans Stuck's famous hillclimb Austro-Daimler with which he won literally scores of European events and gained the first European Mountain Championship in 1930. A team of more standard ADM 3s, with four-seater bodies, ran in the 1928 Ulster TT, finishing third, fourth and tenth, winning their class and taking the Team Prize.

The main characteristics of Porsche's ohc engine were repeated in the larger sixes he subsequently developed for Mercedes-Benz; apart from its somewhat dated cantilever rear springing, the ADM3 might thus be regarded as a smaller, nimbler edition of the famous 38/250 Mercedes and its variants.

Specification *(ADM 3)*
Engine: straight-six; 76 × 110mm, 2994cc; single ohc; twin Zenith carburettors; 100bhp at 4000rpm.
Gearbox: four-speed manual.
Chassis: pressed steel side members, underslung at rear; front suspension by semi-elliptic springs; rear suspension by cantilever leaf springs and radius arms; friction dampers; four-wheel drum brakes.
Dimensions: wheelbase 345cm/136in (275cm/108½in on Sport model); **track** 135cm/53in.

1926 ADM 3

Ballot 2LS and variants

Ballot was a curiously unlucky French marque which plunged into the deep (and expensive) end of motor racing just after the First World War, building a team of advanced double-ohc straight-eight Grand Prix cars. Although undeniably fast, success attended them rarely, thanks to diverse ill fortunes, and after 1922 Ballot concentrated on producing sports and touring cars. Inheriting racing practice, these were fine performers, although high price inhibited sales of the most exciting, the 2LS sports model.

One of the earliest production road cars to have a twin-ohc engine, the 2LS was a direct descendant of the 2-litre four-cylinder racing Ballot which finished third in the 1921 French GP and second in the 1922 Targa Florio. Its engine was of almost pure racing type, having twin-ohc, four valves per cylinder, and a ball-bearing crankshaft which topped 4000rpm, when some 80bhp was produced. In road trim, bearing open two- or four-seater bodywork, the 2LS could comfortably exceed 145kph (90mph), while road-holding was excellent by 1922 standards, backed by high-efficiency Isotta-Fraschini-type brakes. The last of Ballot's disappointingly few race victories was scored by a privately owned 2LS in the 1925 San Sebastian 12-hours. With its need for frequent maintenance, the 2LS was a poor seller, however, and less than 100 had been built when production ended in 1924.

Meanwhile, Ballot evolved a cheaper and more rational 2-litre four, the 2LT, with a longer wheelbase able to carry roomy closed bodywork. The engine had a single skew-driven ohc operating two valves per cylinder, the four-speed gearbox now in unit with the engine, and vacuum servo brakes. Purchase price was barely half that of the 2LS, but it had more touring than sporting character, and in 1925 the higher performance 2LTS with larger, inclined valves and a 116kph (72mph) maximum appeared. These were strong, comfortable, well-braked cars which proved popular in Britain, particularly in Weymann fabric saloon form, thanks in part to the then-favourable rate of exchange for the French franc. These Ballot fours continued in production until 1928.

1924 2LT

Specification *(2LS)*
Engine: straight-four; 69·9 × 130mm, 1986cc; double ohc; four valves per cylinder; single carburettor; 80bhp at 4000rpm.
Gearbox: separate four-speed manual.
Chassis: pressed steel side members; semi-elliptic springs front and rear; friction dampers; four-wheel drum brakes.
Dimensions: wheelbase 279cm/110in; **track** 130cm/51in.

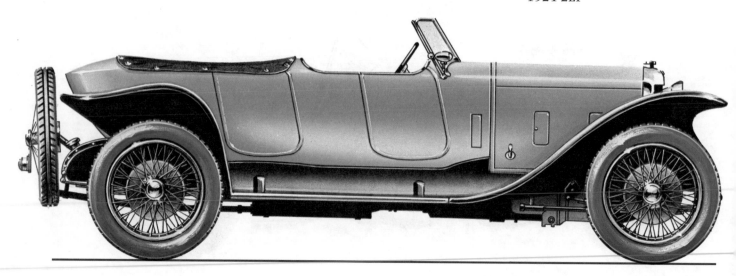

Bentley 3-litre

Although the entire Bentley story occupied a mere 13 years from formation to liquidation, no marque more nobly epitomised the classic British vintage sports car, its reputation surviving to the present day, when many dozens are still in use, fondly cherished by their proud owners.

The first Bentley of all was the 3-litre, a rugged ohc long-stroke four broadly following 1914 racing pattern. Designed by W O Bentley, who was responsible for the successful Bentley rotary engine used in First World War fighter aircraft, the prototype 3-litre appeared in 1919, while the first production model, built at Hendon, North London, and delivered in September 1921, departed little from his original conception.

The engine measured 80 × 149mm (2996cc), there were four narrow-angled valves operated by a single shaft-driven ohc, and two plugs per cylinder were sparked by twin magnetos. A five-bearing crankshaft and aluminium pistons featured, and the initial output was 65bhp at 3500rpm. A separate four-speed gearbox took the drive to a spiral-bevel rear axle, and the pressed steel chassis

with friction-damped semi-elliptic springing was notably sturdy, helping to account for the Bentley's renowned longevity. Powerful rear brakes sufficed until mid-1923, after which a Perrot-type front-wheel system was added.

It was not the means whereby the 3-litre Bentley performed, but the manner in which it did it, that endeared the car to sportsmen who took a pride in their driving. The engine was remarkably flexible, strong and reliable, the gear ratios admirably chosen, the handling excellent and the quality unremittingly high. So, also, was the price, but an ever-growing reputation, augmented by striking racing victories – including the Le Mans 24 hours of 1924 and 1927 – ensured its success.

In the quest for durability, the design erred on the massive side and the weight of the various models ranged between 1300kg and 1700kg. Three chassis lengths were available, and altogether 1920 3-litre Bentleys were produced between 1921 and 1929, the most handsome and popular model being the Vanden Plas open four-seater.

Specification

Engine: straight-four; 80 × 149mm, 2996cc; single ohc; four valves per cylinder; single or twin carburettors; 65bhp at 3500rpm on introduction, rising to 85bhp from 1925.
Gearbox: separate four-speed manual.
Chassis: pressed steel side members; semi-elliptic springs front and rear; friction dampers; two-wheel drum brakes until mid-1923, four-wheel drums thereafter.
Dimensions: wheelbase 'Red Label' – 298cm/117½in, 'Blue Label' – 298cm/117½in or 331cm/130½in, 'Green Label' – 274cm/108in; track 142cm/56in.

1925 'Red Label' (Vanden Plas four-seat sports bodywork)

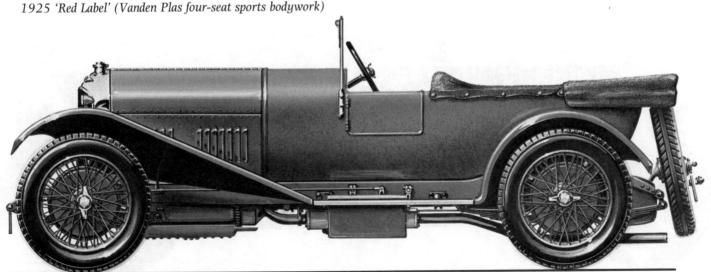

Bentley 4½-litre

In his quest 'to make a fast car, a good car, the best in its class', in 1919 W O Bentley settled on the basic specification of the famous 3-litre model. Inevitably, a marque endowed with the Bentley philosophy was drawn into racing, and although the 3-litre won twice at Le Mans, it also suffered defeat twice, at the hands of the French 3½-litre Lorraine-Dietrich.

The answer was to improve on the 3-litre's performance, and the simplest way was to enlarge its engine. This coincided with the need for a road model to replace the obsolescent 3-litre, and the four-cylinder 4½-litre was the impressive result. The new engine was not, however, a mere 'pumped-up' 3-litre, but rather a four-cylinder version of the 6½-litre straight-six Bentley which had been introduced in 1925. By using the same 100×140mm bore and stroke, a capacity of 4398cc was achieved. The connecting rods and pistons were of 6½-litre type, but some 3-litre components were still used, and the fixed single-ohc 16-valve cylinder head design was little changed. The shorter stroke and larger valve area meant greater potential for the larger engine, demonstrated in the years since the Second World War by some highly-developed '4½s' which

have put up remarkable performances in Vintage racing.

The first 4½-litre car, built for Le Mans in 1927, used a 3-litre chassis, axles and transmission; the production road model, which made its debut at Olympia that year had, however, a more robust gearbox and a longer wheelbase of 331cm able to carry more capacious open or closed bodywork. The '4½' was naturally even more flexible than the smaller-engined car, while full use of the separate four-speed gearbox would achieve 0-to-60mph (96kph) in 15 secs and a maximum of 148kph (92mph).

Although heavy, the car handled superbly, the steering being lower-geared than that of the 3-litre and having predictable under-steer, while braking was first rate. The '4½' was the most popular Bentley with the team racing drivers; with few modifications apart from raised compression, modified carburation and competition gear ratios, the model won the 1927 24 hour GP de Paris, the 1928 Le Mans 24 hours and the 1929 Brooklands 500 Miles, all long, gruelling races which emphasised the remarkable stamina and sustained high performance of which Bentley's biggest four-cylinder model was capable.

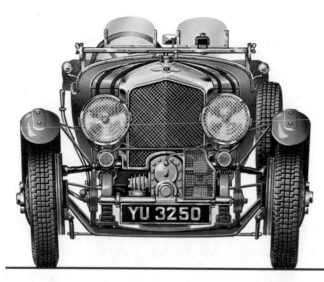

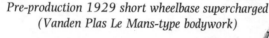

Pre-production 1929 short wheelbase supercharged (Vanden Plas Le Mans-type bodywork)

Specification

Engine: straight-four; 100×140mm, 4398cc; single ohc; four valves per cylinder; twin carburettors; 110bhp at 3500rpm.
Gearbox: separate four-speed manual.
Chassis: pressed steel side members; semi-elliptic springs front and rear; friction dampers; four-wheel drum brakes.
Dimensions: wheelbase 298cm/117½in (standard) or 331cm/130½in (short); **track** 142cm/56in.

Bentley Speed Six

Once Bentley Motors Ltd of Hendon was well established, its clientele widened to include those seeking cars of high performance with luxury standards of comfort, space and silence – the category now known as 'grand touring'. For such customers W O Bentley turned to six cylinders, producing a superb 100 × 140mm 6597cc unit with an eight-bearing crankshaft and an output of 147bhp at 3500rpm.

To minimise mechanical noise the single ohc was driven, not by the shaft and bevels of the four-cylinder Bentleys, but by a system of three-throw coupling rods and eccentrics driven off the crankshaft. The usual separate four-speed gearbox and massive semi-elliptically-sprung chassis featured, with three wheelbase options to accommodate all kinds of luxury coachwork. With a road weight of well over 2000kg and a speed potential of 140kph (85mph), large-diameter vacuum-servo-assisted four-wheel brakes were employed.

Three years after the first 6½-litre Bentley was seen at the 1925 Olympia Show, a more sporting version, the Speed Six, was introduced with two optional wheelbases. Twin SU carburettors were fitted, the engine giving 160bhp with astonishing flexibility. Such was the torque that the four-speed gearbox was scarcely needed, and with a wide variety of special coachwork this splendid car provided grand touring of the highest calibre for those with money to spend.

The Speed Six was the natural basis for a Le Mans car when the 4½-litre four-cylinder Bentley became outmoded, and for 1929 a special short (335cm) wheelbase version with an engine modified to give 200bhp was built. This awesome sports car, so large yet so beautifully proportioned, a truly classic wearer of British racing green, proved unassailable in the great 24-hour race, winning both in 1929 and 1930, and raising Bentley's Le Mans victory score to five. It also won two long-distance races at Brooklands in 1929 and 1930, and the 500 Miles Race there in 1931 – the latter a bittersweet victory achieved after the Bentley company had gone into liquidation, victims of the world economic slump.

Specification

Engine: straight-six; 100 × 140mm, 6597cc; single ohc; four valves per cylinder; twin carburettors; 160bhp at 3500rpm (200bhp on Le Mans cars).
Gearbox: separate four-speed manual.
Chassis: pressed steel side members; semi-elliptic springs front and rear; friction dampers; four-wheel drum brakes, servo-assisted.
Dimensions: wheelbase 357cm/140½in or 387cm/152½in; track 142cm/56in.

1930 Le Mans car

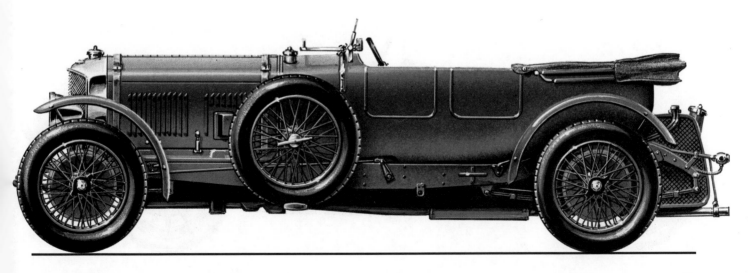

Benz 'Prinz Henry'

These imposing German machines owe their name, and their fame, to those prestigious early rally-type events, the Prince Henry Tours, inaugurated by Prince Heinrich (Henry) of Prussia, brother of Kaiser Wilhelm II of First World War notoriety. Heinrich's interests were more pacific, including automobiles, for which he even invented and patented a windscreen wiper. The 'Tour' bearing his name consisted, in fact, of several long and gruelling road sections across Germany, punctuated by strenuous timed hillclimbs and speed tests, all ostensibly for touring cars.

The first event took place in 1908, and the Benz factory of Mannheim made the best of the rules by producing a 'special'. This owed much to racing practice, having a big 50bhp 115 × 180mm four-cylinder ohv engine, chain final drive, minimal bodywork and a 120kph (75mph) maximum. With factory star Fritz Erle driving, the Benz won the Tour from a Mercedes, an Adler and another Benz. In reaction, the formula for the 1909 event did not favour big-bore engines, thwarting Benz's chances, but for the 1910 Prince Henry they produced a significant new car.

Eschewing the Grand-Prix-style chain drive and draughty racing body, the 1910 Prince Henry Benz carried low-built four-seater coachwork of striking shape and advanced streamline concept, with a peaked radiator, faired headlamps, a sweeping scuttle line, 'tulip'
body sides, and a short, pointed 'torpedo' tail. The engine was a 7·3-litre four with two inlet and two exhaust valves to each cylinder, operated by pushrods and rockers. It put out some 115bhp at just over 2000rpm, although it was fully capable of close on 3000rpm.

Transmission was through a close-ratio four-speed gearbox and propeller shaft, and standard wood-spoked wheels were fitted, some of the Tour cars wearing wheel discs. Ten of these 'Prince Henry' Benz were built for the contest, four having 115 × 175mm (7270cc) engines, and six 105 × 165mm (5715cc), thus widening their chances in two classes. None of them won, however, thanks to an adverse handicap, but seven Benz finished in the first twenty, the highest placed being fifth and attaining a record 138kph (85·8mph) in one 5·6km (3·5mile) sprint test.

Subsequently, a so-called Prince Henry Benz went into limited production with chain or shaft final drive to choice, some being exported to the USA and to Britain. Their engine performance was well below that of the actual Tour cars, however, one of which performed with distinction at Brooklands, winning several races and creating numerous speed records, including a flying kilometre at 165·75kph (102·99mph), which gave some indication of the machine's potential.

Specification
Engine: straight-four; 115 × 175mm, 7271cc; pushrod ohv; four valves per cylinder; 115bhp at 2100rpm.
Gearbox: separate four-speed manual.
Chassis: pressed steel side members; semi-elliptic springs front and rear; friction dampers; rear-wheel drum brakes and transmission brake.
Dimensions: wheelbase 300cm/118in; track 123cm/49in.

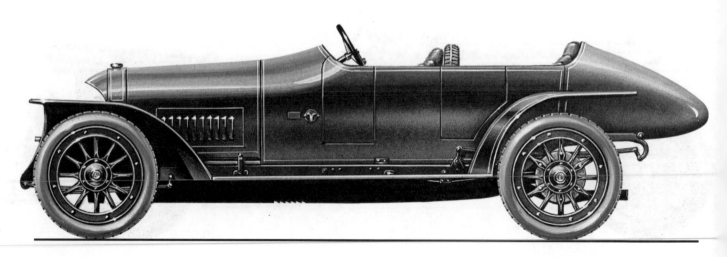

Benz Tropfenwagen

Although Porsche set the fashion for rear-engined sports cars with the VW-based Type 356/2 of 1949, the layout was anticipated over a quarter-century earlier by a German marque of equally high repute – Benz of Mannheim. Notably conservative, Benz amazed the automobile world in 1923 by fielding a team of revolutionary mid-engined Grand Prix racers, nicknamed *Tropfenwagen* (teardrop cars) owing to their streamlined shape.

These cars employed principles patented earlier by the Bohemian inventor Dr Edmund Rumpler, a pioneer aircraft manufacturer who in 1921 had produced a radical mid-engined streamlined saloon car with irs. The racing Benz embodied the Rumpler-type chassis and cantilever springing, with swing axles at the rear and a rigid I-beam at the front. The engine was a Benz design, an advanced twin-ohc in-line six with 24 valves, electron pistons, twin Zenith carburettors, a built-up roller-bearing crankshaft, and roller big ends, which gave some 90bhp at 4500rpm.

This engine was located between the cockpit (containing the driver and riding mechanic), and the rear axle, which it drove through a three-speed gearbox mounted in unit. Inboard rear brakes were employed, a separate crescent-shaped radiator was mounted above the engine cover, and the car had excellent stream-lining with a clean, rounded nose and tapering tail. Two of these revolutionary cars finished fourth and fifth in their only Grand Prix, the 1923 Italian, when they were well eclipsed in power and speed by the rival supercharged Fiats.

Faced with a costly development programme at a time of dire inflation in Germany, Benz opted instead to convert two *Tropfenwagen* into sports cars, entailing a slight lengthening of the wheelbase and the fitting of some very slick mudguards and headlights. In this form they weighed around 820kg and could achieve 150kph (95mph), winning several German hillclimbs in both 1924 and 1925.

Regrettably the design was not developed further when Benz and Mercedes combined in 1926, and these fantastic cars, unappreciated portents of the future, were abandoned. Their influence showed significantly, however, in the mid-engined Auto Union GP cars which appeared in 1934 and which won many Grands Prix between then and 1939.

Specification
Engine: straight-six; 65 × 100mm, 1997cc; twin ohc; four valves per cylinder; twin Zenith carburettors; 90bhp at 4500rpm.
Gearbox: three-speed manual.
Chassis: pressed steel side members; front suspension by non-independent beam axle and cantilever leaf springs; rear suspension by swing axles and cantilever leaf springs; friction dampers; four-wheel drum brakes (inboard at rear).
Dimensions: wheelbase 283cm/111½in; **front track** 140cm/55in; **rear track** 130cm/51in.

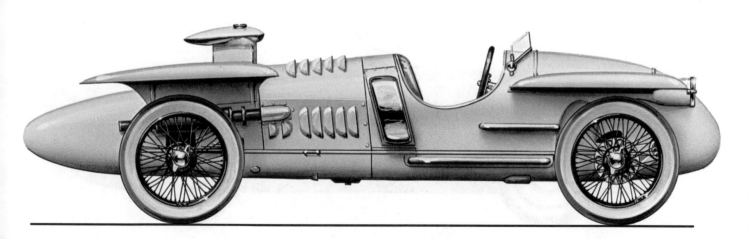

Berkeley

The little Berkeleys were far from conventional, however much they may have looked like scaled-down normal sports cars, but in some respects were very effective in providing low-cost sporting motoring. The ingenious front-wheel drive design by Laurie Bond had strong motor cycle associations, and the cars were built by an established caravan manufacturer who made good use of experience with plastics construction.

Introduced in the autumn of 1956, the car comprised three main glass-reinforced polyester resin mouldings (nose, pontoon undersection and tail), bolted together and reinforced with alloy members; there was no chassis as such, merely a steel subframe linking engine, transmission and bulkheads. Suspension was independent at the front, using motor cycle type coil springs and dampers, with swing axles at the rear. Outwardly the body changed little in its life of under five years; wider doors came after a year, as did flamboyant wheel trims, while the oval grille gave way to a large square aperture; a hard top was added to the range in 1957, and a few four-seaters were made in 1958-59.

The first 163 cars had an air-cooled 322cc British Anzani two-stroke twin, but its 15bhp was hardly adequate, even for this car's 280kg unladen weight, nor was a similar 328cc Excelsior. In 1957, therefore, a three-cylinder air-cooled Excelsior of 492cc and 30bhp took its place, mounted transversely ahead of the centre-line of the front wheels, and this propelled the car to 130kph (80mph). Finally, in the B105, a tuned 692cc Royal Enfield four-stroke was fitted, to give a daunting 145kph (90mph) maximum speed. Drive was carried to the gearbox and differential by chains.

The assemblage was a little temperamental, and drivers had to learn its quirks as well as endure vibration and noise, but there was normally-safe handling and flat cornering, while acceleration matched top speed. The little Berkeleys offered economy and exhilaration, but they were too far outside the motoring mainstream to enjoy any lasting success and the company faded away at the end of 1960.

Specification (1958)

Engine: Excelsior two-stroke straight-three; 58 × 62mm, 492cc; three Amal carburettors; 30bhp at 5000rpm.
Gearbox: four-speed manual (three-speed on some early cars).
Chassis: metal-braced plastics unitary; front suspension independent by driveshafts, wishbones and coil spring/damper units; rear suspension independent by swing axles and coil spring/damper units; four-wheel drum brakes.
Dimensions: wheelbase 174cm/68½in; **front track** 108cm/42½in; **rear track** 107cm/42in.

BMW 328

The Type 328 was one of those rare designs which set new standards for production sports cars, although in some respects it was no more than a logical BMW progression. All late-1930s BMWs were endowed with good looks, and the appearance of the 328 would not date for years after production ceased, as well as inspiring post-war designers; its engine, too, enjoyed a long second life as a Bristol unit.

Chief designer Dr Fritz Fiedler achieved reliability and competitive power in a series of sixes built from the mid-1930s. The 328 unit was similar to that used in the 326, save for its aluminium cylinder head which had inclined inlet valves directly operated by pushrods and corresponding exhaust valves operated by rockers and secondary pushrods. Quoted power output on introduction in 1936 was 80bhp; 20 years later Bristol rated the same basic unit at 105bhp in their 405, and tuned versions produced considerably more. It was mounted in a tubular chassis, which had a high degree of rigidity to complement the transverse leaf ifs.

Outwardly, the 328 had integrated lines, aerodynamically effective and aesthetically pleasing even with the hood erected. As a whole, it demonstrated that a sports car did not have to be a crude, stark device, and its performance underlined this. In Britain, the home of the 'traditional' sports car, it was marketed by AFN, with their own marque badge Frazer Nash hyphenated to BMW.

The 328 proved an outstanding competition car, even without the 'performance' parts available: in standard form it was shown to be a 100mph (160kph) car in official and private one-hour runs at Brooklands. 328s gained many 2-litre class victories in major races, and a high point came in 1940 when a works coupe version won the truncated Mille Miglia at 166·6kph (103·5mph). Only 462 had been built when production ceased in that year, although a handful was later assembled from parts. A number were raced independently for years after the Second World War.

Specification

Engine: straight-six; 66 × 96mm, 1971cc; pushrod ohv (see text); three Solex carburettors; 80bhp at 4500rpm.
Gearbox: four-speed manual.
Chassis: tubular ladder-type; front suspension independent by transverse leaf spring, lower wishbones and hydraulic dampers; rear suspension live axle, semi-elliptic springs and hydraulic dampers; four-wheel drum brakes, hydraulically operated.
Dimensions: wheelbase 244cm/96in; **front track** 132cm/52in; **rear track** 140cm/55in.

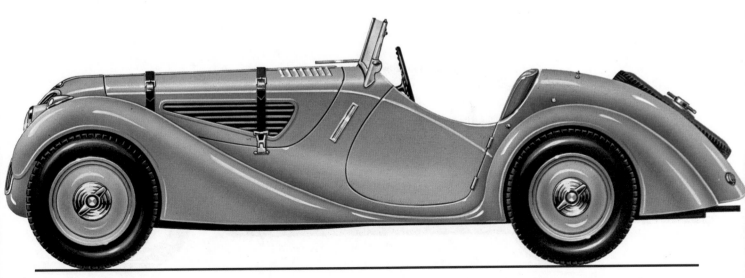

53

BMW 507

The famous Bayerische Motoren Werken was slower to recover from the Second World War than other German makers. The Eisenach plant was in the Russian Zone, while the potential of BMW's Munich factory, which survived to the war's end despite bombing, was effectively destroyed by the US occupation forces, who commandeered all the machine tools and other equipment, leaving BMW to start again from scratch.

The company managed to resume motorcycle production by 1948, and by 1952 had built its first post-war car, the Type 501 with pre-war pattern 2-litre six-cylinder engine. The next development was an all-new 2·6-litre five-bearing V-8 engine, used in the Type 502 announced in 1954. This advanced unit had its eight cylinders angled at 90 degrees in a single aluminium casting with wet liners. A single camshaft in the centre of the vee operated parallel overhead valves by pushrods and rockers, with the plugs on the outside of each bank and a twin-choke carburettor between. This engine was the world's first production all-alloy V-8.

A 3·2-litre version, specially tuned to give 140bhp against the standard 95bhp, was developed for the Type 503 saloon, and it did not take the firm long to put the tuned V-8 into a special short chassis carrying light coupe bodywork. The resulting Type 507 was

hailed as 'the pearl' of the 1955 Frankfurt Show. The chassis and suspension were of 502/503 type, but the wheelbase was 36cm shorter, while the body styling, with low 'angled-back' radiator grille and masterful blending of body curves, was thought by many to be of Italian design. In fact it was the work of Albrecht Goertz, outdoing the contemporary Mercedes-Benz 300SL in its graceful looks, and at the same time offering very high standards of comfort and finish.

The aluminium coupe top was quickly detachable, overall weight was 1120kg, and a maximum speed of 220kph (136mph) was claimed. Quick-release wheels, aeroscreen, undershield and limited-slip differential were optional extras, and the BMW 507 was acclaimed a worthy post-war successor to the famous Type 328. In European hillclimbs the Austrian ace Hans Stuck scored many class victories with a works-prepared 507 (which is now owned by ex-GP driver John Surtees).

Unfortunately BMW's fine sporting V-8 was marketed at the wrong time and at the wrong price for a nation still recovering from a devastating war. Exported, its 140bhp could not compare with the 210bhp of the contemporary Jaguar XK150 costing half the price, and only 253 were produced.

Specification
Engine: 90-degree V-8; 82 × 75mm, 3168cc; pushrod ohv; two twin-choke carburettors; 140bhp at 4800rpm.
Gearbox: five-speed manual.
Chassis: oval-tube side members with steel plate reinforcement; front suspension independent by wishbones, longitudinal torsion bars and dampers; rear suspension by rigid axle, central A-bracket, longitudinal torsion bars and dampers; four-wheel drum brakes.
Dimensions: wheelbase 248cm/98in; track 145cm/57in.

BMW M1

BMW's sporting reputation through the 1970s rested on their high-performance saloons, but towards the end of the decade the Bavarian company introduced its mid-engined M1 'supercar', to maintain its racing image as saloon categories declined, and to be sold in standard form as a practical road-going car.

That the sleek two-seater was reminiscent of similar models from Italian low-volume manufacturers was no coincidence, for it was styled by Italdesign and the original (1977) intention was that Lamborghini would be responsible for M1 production. That arrangement fell through as Lamborghini's business problems grew, so Marchesi took over production of the tubular and sheet steel chassis, Italdesign undertook the interiors, and Baur of Munich became responsible for fitting engine, transmission, running gear, and final trim.

The multi-national nature of the programme became more complex as teams such as Ron Dennis' in England became responsible for building competition versions for a series of 'Procar' races, run in 1979 as supporting events at European Grands Prix, and in 1980 as an independent series. Meanwhile, March built the first out-and-out sports-racing M1 in 1979: this departed considerably from the production original, for example in having a new monocoque chassis.

The engine for all versions was based on the 635 unit, with a light-alloy twin-ohc head and pressurized dry-sump lubrication. It produced 277bhp in the road version, around 470bhp in the Procar cars, and with up to 850bhp envisaged in a turbocharged version for world championship races. Transmission was through a five-speed ZF transaxle, and ATE ventilated disc brakes were used.

The rigid chassis was designed to cope with potential power, and the main differences between road and Procar versions were in suspension detail, while outwardly the racing version was obviously distinguished by a large rear aerofoil.

Orders for the road cars built up rapidly, although production was not fast enough to achieve Group 4 homologation as soon as BMW would have liked; the 400 required were finally completed in 1980, and production then ceased, as the M1 was not a realistic commercial proposition. Meanwhile, the Procar series provided an unusual (if expensive) and successful type of one-model racing, while Jim Busby gained some good IMSA placings and at the end of 1979 Procar M1s finished first and second in an endurance race at Kyalami. Initial outings for the March car were unsuccessful, however, and in 1980 the M1 made little impression even on the few sports-car events which could warrant the term 'important'. Then developed versions in 1981 were more competitive.

Specification (*road car*)
Engine: straight-six; 93·4 × 84mm, 3453cc; twin ohc; Kugelfischer-Bosch fuel injection; 277bhp at 6500rpm.
Gearbox: five-speed manual.
Chassis: tubular; independent suspension front and rear by double wishbones, coil springs, dampers and anti-roll bars; four-wheel disc brakes.
Dimensions: wheelbase 256cm/101in; **front track** 155cm/61in; **rear track** 157cm/62in.

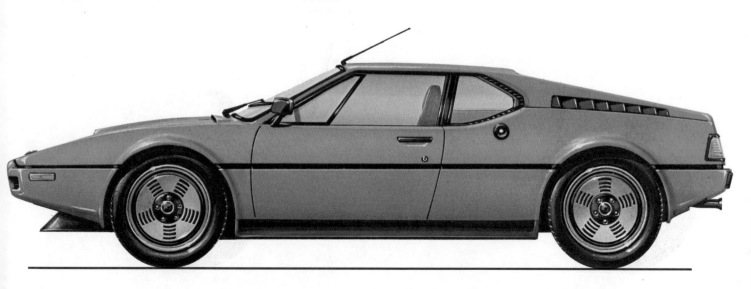

BNC Monza and Montlhéry

This pretty little sports car vied with Salmson, Amilcar, Derby, Rally and other French marques of the 1920s for the popular 1100cc sporting market. The makers were Bollack, Netter et Cie, and the first car to bear their initials appeared in 1923, using the four-cylinder 900cc SCAP side-valve proprietary engine. This served equally well in BNC vans and economy cars, but when more sporting models appeared, these employed the livelier Ruby 972cc side-valve and ohv units made locally.

The early BNC chassis was quite high-built, with vertical radiator, semi-elliptic front springs and quarter-elliptics at the rear, a three-speed gearbox and torque-tube transmission. Almost inevitably in France, the BNC was soon being raced, and in 1927 new and rakishly good-looking sports-racing models were introduced, with very low chassis, steeply inclined radiators, and pointed tails of the type known as 'Bordino', after the style of that great driver's Grand Prix Fiat.

These new BNCs were marketed in two forms: the Monza with

unsupercharged 35bhp ohv Ruby engine and three-speed gearbox, and the Montlhéry, with Cozette-supercharged SCAP four-cylinder ohv unit having an output of 60bhp and a four-speed gearbox. Excellent Perrot-type four-wheel brakes were fitted, and in stripped form the Montlhéry could exceed 145kph (90mph). In full road trim, one car in the hands of French woman driver Violette Morriss won the Bol d'Or 24-hour race at Fontainebleau in 1927; another car – in unsupercharged form – won the 1100cc class of the Paris 24-hour GP at Montlhéry, indicating that the little cars had stamina as well as good looks.

The BNC factory at Levallois also assembled the 1100cc four-cylinder twin-ohc Lombard sports car in small numbers for André Lombard, one winning the Bol d'Or in 1929. The BNC factory closed down in 1932, but the foresight of one Andre Siréjols in acquiring all the stock and spares kept the marque alive until 1940, and thanks to this and their attractive appearance, over 30 examples of the breed are still cherished today in France alone.

Specification

Engine: *Monza* – Ruby straight-four; 60 × 97mm, 1097cc; pushrod ohv; single carburettor; 35bhp at 3500rpm.
Montlhéry – SCAP straight-four; 61 × 94mm, 1099cc; pushrod ohv; single carburettor; Cozette vane-type supercharger; 60bhp at 4000rpm.
Gearbox: *Monza* – three-speed manual; *Montlhéry* – four-speed manual.
Chassis: pressed steel side members; semi-elliptic front springs, quarter-elliptic rears; friction dampers; four-wheel drum brakes, with Perrot actuation.
Dimensions: wheelbase 235cm/92½in; front track 115cm/45½in; rear track 108cm/42½in.

1928 Montlhéry

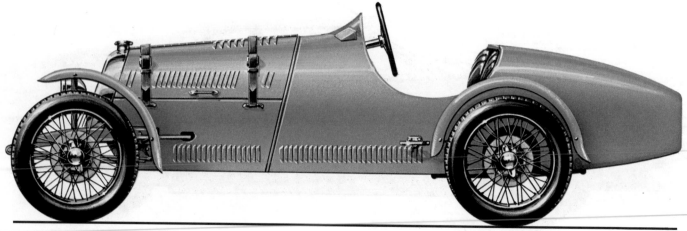

Bristol Type 450

Coming from the makers of an expensive and finely-engineered grand touring car, the Type 450 Bristol was a distinct surprise. It was a competition sports car with racing origins in the 1952 Formula Two G-type ERA designed by David Hodkin; that car's links with the Bristol Aeroplane Company included the 2-litre six-cylinder, three-carburettor engine and the four-speed gearbox, both of BMW origin but Bristol manufacture.

After an unsuccessful Grand Prix season, ERA Ltd sold the G-type – conveniently an offset single-seater readily convertible to a two-seater – to Bristol as a basis for the latter's new competition sports car. The broad specification was retained, but the 15·2cm deep oval magnesium tubing used as side members by ERA was replaced by 11·4cm diameter steel tubes. Construction in general was sturdier, but the rather long-stroke, four-bearing 1971cc Bristol engine was in highly tuned F2 form, with dry sump lubrication, and gave 142bhp at 6000rpm.

The gearbox was built in unit with the final drive, and inboard rear drum brakes were employed. Front suspension was by wishbones and single coil springs, with a coil-sprung de Dion rear end, and unusual alloy detachable-rim wheels were fitted. Bizarre closed streamlined bodywork, embodying a steeply inclined screen, twin stabilising fins on the tail, and curved plastic side windows, was somewhat hastily developed in the Bristol wind tunnel in time for the 1953 Le Mans race, where two 450s made their debut.

They proved fast but brittle, both breaking connecting rods. Quickly recovering, the team reappeared a fortnight later in the Reims 12-hour race, where one car took first place in the 2-litre class at 149·14kph (92·67mph).

The Bristol aerodynamicists then had time to refine the shape of the 450, which was much improved about the nose, before the team appeared at Montlhéry for some record breaking. Six new 2-litre class records were set, from 200 miles (322km) to six hours, at speeds of up to 202·57kph (125·87mph).

Le Mans in 1954 saw the Bristols further cleaned up, their engines now with new 12-port cylinder heads contributing to the 155bhp, which took them to a triumphant one-two-three class victory. For the 1955 24-hour race the closed body was scrapped in favour of an open roadster, somewhat resembling a D-type Jaguar with prominent head-fairing-cum-tail fin. In this form the 450s proved even faster, a trio repeating their 1954 one-two-three class win. On that high note, the sports car racing career of the Bristol marque was concluded.

1954 Le Mans car

Specification

Engine: straight-six; 66 × 96mm, 1971cc; pushrod ohv; three Solex twin-choke carburettors; 142bhp at 6000rpm, rising to 155bhp.

Gearbox: four-speed manual transaxle.

Chassis: tubular side members; front suspension independent by wishbones, coil springs and dampers; rear suspension by de Dion axle, coil springs and dampers; four-wheel drum brakes (inboard at rear).

Dimensions: wheelbase 248cm/97½in; front track 130cm/51in; rear track 134cm/52in.

BSA Scout

Like today's Morgan cars, the BSA Scout of 1936-39 was the descendant of a three-wheeler. The parallel ends there, however, for whereas Morgan four-wheelers are as lively and exhilarating to drive today as when first introduced over 40 years ago, the Scout was a disappointing performer. Although a pretty little car with its smart vee-radiator, folding windscreen and customary 'Le Mans' uniform as popularised by MG – two seater open body with cutaway sides and slab rear tank supporting a spare wheel – the Scout's engine was a side-valve four of touring type with two-bearing crankshaft, the main design novelty being the fact that it drove the front instead of the rear wheels.

Weight was only 580kg unladen, but the engine's 26bhp could manage little more than 100kph (60mph) flat out, although a twin Solex carburettor version managed 108kph (67mph) with screen folded flat, and the 1939 Series 6 had a 32bhp three-bearing engine capable of 115kph (70mph). The BSA's front-wheel drive, descended from the BSA three-wheeler of 1930-34, was a clever solution for its time, the short four-cylinder engine driving forward through a three-speed gearbox. Final drive was through an underslung worm gear with differential and open half-shafts, each with two fabric universals and all, unfortunately, proving fine media for wear.

The front track was 102mm wider than the rear, giving a pronounced 'crab track'. Front suspension was independent by four quarter-elliptic leaf springs to each side (as on the earlier front-drive Alvis). Ride was firm but roadholding was excellent, the driven front wheels permitting fast cornering while steering remained light and positive – so long, that is, as the front and rear wheels retained the correct track.

The gearchange was unusual, being of dash-mounted 'pistol-grip' type, working with the 'push, pull and twist' horizontal action later used on the famous Citroen 2CV. A four-seater tourer and a coupe were also available on the same basic BSA chassis with slight wheelbase variations. While the Scout was more sporting in appearance than performance, it was economical, safe and modestly priced.

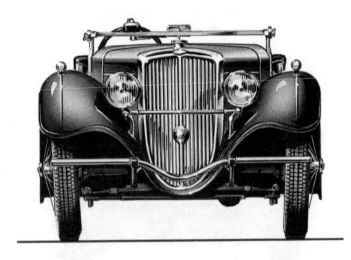

Specification

Engine: straight-four; 63·5 × 95mm, 1203cc; side valves; single carburettor; 26bhp at 4000rpm (32bhp at 4200rpm from 1939).
Gearbox: three-speed manual.
Chassis: pressed steel side members; front suspension independent by transverse quarter-elliptic springs (four per side); rear suspension by semi-elliptic springs; friction dampers; four-wheel drum brakes.
Dimensions: wheelbase 229cm/90in; **front track** 122cm/48in; **rear track** 112cm/44in.

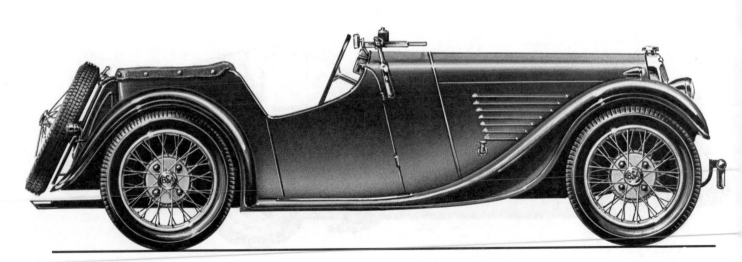

Bugatti T13 to T23

Bugatti is a much revered name in the sports car world, and although the Brescia was not the first product from the famous Molsheim factory, it widened its reputation internationally and provided unique super-sports motoring for many private owners. Its origins went back to before the First World War, when the little town of Molsheim was in German Alsace, and Bugatti was technically a German marque. After the war the territory reverted to France, and the Bugatti swiftly became one of that nation's principle contenders in motor racing.

The Brescia, so-called after its sweeping one-two-three-four victory in the feebly contested 1921 Italian Voiturette GP at Brescia, descended from the first Type 13 Bugatti which, with a 65×100mm, 1327cc ohc four cylinder engine, had been introduced in 1910. Ettore Bugatti himself was among the successful drivers of these cars, while Ernest Friedrich ran a remarkable second to a 9·6-litre Fiat in the 1911 GP de France at Le Mans. The first Type 13 had eight valves and distinctive curved 'banana' tappets which dispensed with rockers. In 1914, a 1368cc 16-valve edition was produced for racing but the outbreak of war deferred its debut until 1920, when it won the Coupe des Voiturettes race at Le Mans.

Next came a full 1½-litre version with the crankshaft running in two ball races and one plain bearing, roller-bearing big ends, and a bore and stroke of 68×100mm (1453cc). Twin Zenith carburettors and twin magnetos featured, the 'mags' protruding behind the engine into the cockpit. The standard Type 13 short wheelbase of 200cm was retained, and this was the racing 'Brescia-to-be' which won that prestigious victory in Italy.

A catalogued sports model soon followed – a short, cobby two-seater characterised by the pear-shaped radiator and reversed quarter-elliptic rear springs and (frequently) the bolster tank of the racers. Two longer chassis variants were the Types 22 and 23, these also being termed Brescia Modifié from 1923, when the bore was increased to 69mm to produce 1496cc; in 1925 four-wheel brakes were adopted.

Brescia production ended in 1926, by which time nearly 2000 examples had been sold, all endearing for their superb steering and roadholding, responsive engine, striking acceleration, fine gearbox, and the easily attained (and guaranteed) 80mph (130kph) maximum. Raced extensively by Raymond Mays, B S Marshall, Leon Cushman and others, the Brescia was undoubtedly one of the finest little sports cars of its time. Moreover, despite its delicate appearance, it was remarkably strong and reliable, many still being used in the 1930s.

Specification *(road cars)*

Engine: straight-four; 69×100mm, 1496cc; single ohc; four valves per cylinder; single carburettor; 33bhp (approx) at 3500rpm.
Gearbox: separate four-speed manual.
Chassis: pressed steel side members; semi-elliptic front springs, reversed quarter-elliptic rears; friction dampers; rear-wheel drum brakes, but four-wheel drums from 1925.
Dimensions: wheelbase *Type 13* – 202cm/79½in, *Type 22* – 242cm/95in, *Type 23* – 257cm/101in; **track** 115cm/45in.

1923 Type 23

Bugatti T35 and T43

Although the Type 35 is best known as a Grand Prix car, its adaptability was such that it could be equipped with wings, lights, screen, starter etc, and serve as a highly exciting if spartan road machine, and also compete successfully in sports car races. Indeed, its straight-eight engine with single ohc operating three vertical valves (two inlet and one exhaust) was descended from a road car prototype, the 3-litre Type 28 Bugatti, but motor racing developed the design to full maturity.

After his experience in building the 2-litre, eight-cylinder Grand Prix cars of 1922 and 1923, Ettore Bugatti gave his artistry full rein to produce the 1924 GP car, designated Type 35 and of a mechanical beauty seldom equalled. From its exquisite horseshoe radiator, swelling out to the scuttle and cockpit, and tapering into a shapely tail covering the renowned reversed quarter-elliptic rear springs, its proportions and grace were exquisite.

There were many pleasing features: the ingeniously-tapered tubular front axle; the chassis following the contours of the body and varying in chord along its length, and the unique alloy eight-spoked wheels with integral brake drums. But the Type 35 differed in one other important aspect from its Grand Prix rivals – it was to be produced for sale to private buyers. During the following seven years over 350 were built, some in racing form, others as sports cars, with engine sizes ranging from $1\frac{1}{2}$ litres (just five cars) to 2·3 litres, and with or without superchargers from 1926.

Real Type 35 engines contained built-up five-bearing crankshafts (three ball and two roller races) and roller bearing big ends, and although power output was less than that of their sternest rivals, these Bugattis contrived by superior chassis design and superb steering, handling and roadholding to turn competitive lap times. In racing guise, of course, their victories became legion, but sports versions of the supercharged Type 35 also did well, winning the French and Spanish GPs of 1928 and the German GP of 1929.

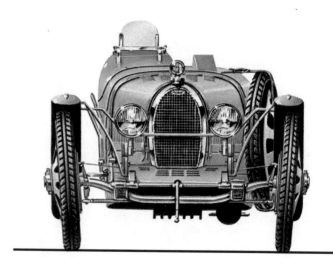

Type 35

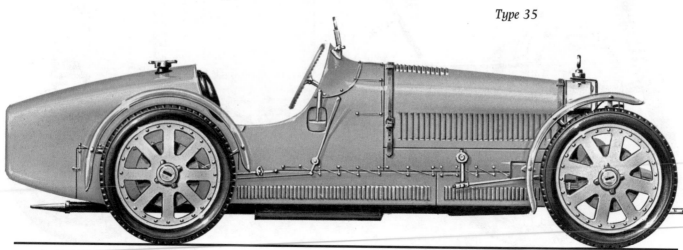

60

Such jewels were naturally expensive, but the realist in Ettore Bugatti saw another market for a 'lesser' Type 35 with all the grace but minus some of the design sophistication. Thus came the unsupercharged Type 35A or *Técla*, implying 'imitation', with three ball-bearing crankshaft, plain big ends, Delco coil ignition, wire wheels and a 145kph (90mph) maximum – against the 190kph (120mph) of the real Type 35s. Costing just over half the price of the latter, however, and with much of its aesthetic beauty, it sold well.

As it matured, the Type 35 became so tractable and reliable, even when supercharged, and its production at Molsheim was proceeding so smoothly, that a proper passenger-carrying sports version became a practical proposition. It meant a longer wheelbase – 297cm against 240cm – to enable full four-seater bodywork to be mounted on the chassis. Road weight was raised to about 1000kg, but with the Roots-supercharged 2·3-litre power unit, performance was well up to Bugatti standards, with a maximum approaching 180kph (110mph), a 0-to-60mph (96kph) figure of under 12 sec, and characteristic flexibility.

A separate dynamo and heavier starting unit were fitted, plus other road-going equipment, and the new model, introduced in 1927, was given the Type number 43. A particularly attractive body option was the 'Grand Sport' with fixed cycle wings, single door on the nearside and an open 3/4-seater body ending in a deeper version of the typical Bugatti vee-tail. The reversed quarter-elliptic springs were not housed within this, as on the 35, but were mounted further out, parallel to the frame and exposed.

Descended as it was from a Grand Prix car, the Type 43 – although highly desirable – was not cheap, and only 151 were produced between 1927 and 1932, yet it was succeeded by the even more sophisticated (and expensive) Type 55, based on the more complex twin-camshaft Type 51 racing car.

Type 43

Specification

Engine: *Type 35* – straight-eight; 60 × 88mm, 1991cc; single ohc; three valves per cylinder; twin Zenith carburettors; 95bhp at 5000rpm.

   Type 35A – as Type 35 (but with three-bearing crankshaft); 70bhp at 5000rpm.

   Type 35B – as Type 35, but 60 × 100mm, 2262cc; supercharged; 130bhp at 5500rpm.

   Type 35C – as Type 35, but supercharged; 120bhp at 5500rpm.

   Type 35T – as Type 35B, but supercharged.

   Type 43 – as Type 35B, but 120bhp at 5000rpm.

Gearbox: separate four-speed manual.

Chassis: pressed steel side members; semi-elliptic front springs, reversed quarter-elliptic rears; friction dampers; four-wheel drum brakes integral with alloy wheels.

Dimensions: *Type 35 (all models)* – **wheelbase** 240cm/94½in; **front track** 125cm/49in; **rear track** 119cm/47in.

   Type 43 – **wheelbase** 297cm/117in; **track** 125cm/49in.

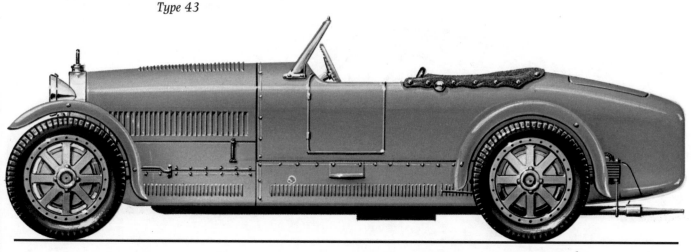

Bugatti T57

Ettore Bugatti's eldest son Jean brought a new and practical approach to Molsheim's products, reflected in the Type 57 range over which he had considerable influence. He realised that a cramped and noisy 'racing car with mudguards' no longer attracted customers in the pampered 1930s. Delage, Delahaye and Talbot were offering fast but civilised motoring at competitive prices, and he felt that Bugatti, with its wider experience, could compete for the same clientele.

Although the Type 57, introduced in 1934, retained the classic Bugatti suspension, axles and straight-eight engine, it was refined in many respects. The 72 × 100mm, 3·3-litre power unit had twin-ohc driven by a gear train at the rear, and two valves per cylinder angled at 90 degrees. Articulated rockers were interposed between the cams and the valve stems, the one-piece crankshaft ran in six plain bearings, and dual-coil ignition and a single carburettor were employed. A refined and supple 135bhp at 5000rpm was the result.

A new four-speed gearbox was in unit with the engine, a single-plate clutch replaced Molsheim's traditional multi-plate type, and wire wheels served instead of Ettore's unique eight-spoked alloy type. The standard Type 57 was, indeed, more a grand tourer than a sports car, with the speed and power of a Bugatti while at the same time managing to be smooth and quiet.

Inevitably, customers demanded a sports edition, and thus the 57S appeared late in 1935, with a shorter, lower chassis through which the rear axle actually passed, and having expensive and rather complex de Ram dampers. The engine, set lower, was given dry-sump lubrication, and had raised compression, Scintilla magneto ignition, and 35 more horsepower. The production 57S was also distinguished by a strikingly beautiful vee-radiator retaining the classic horseshoe form.

Two years later a Roots-type supercharger was fitted, the resultant 200bhp Type 57SC being capable of 200kph (125mph) with prodigious acceleration. Sports-racing Bugattis of Type 57S origin won several European events between 1936 and 1939, including the French, Marne, Comminges and Pau GPs and two Le Mans 24-hour races.

Some very striking bodywork was fitted to 57S and SC chassis, often designed by Jean Bugatti himself, a bizarre example being the Atlantic coupe (illustrated) with its unique central spine running from the vee-windscreen to the tail. Hydraulically-operated brakes were adopted in 1938 but production of the 57S and SC ended that same year and it was doubly sad that the brilliant Jean should have died in a road crash in 1939, which fateful year also brought an end to markets for such exotica as Bugattis.

Specification *(Type 57S)*
Engine: straight-eight; 72 × 100mm, 3257cc; twin ohc; single carburettor; 170bhp at 5500rpm.
Gearbox: four-speed manual.
Chassis: pressed steel side members; semi-elliptic front springs, reversed quarter-elliptic rears; de Ram hydraulic dampers; four-wheel drum brakes, mechanically-operated from 1934, hydraulically from 1938.
Dimensions: wheelbase 298cm/117½in; **track** 135cm/53in.

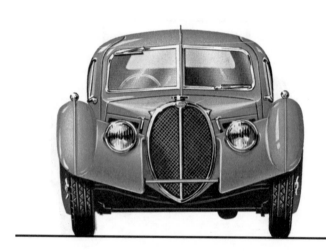

1937 Type 57SC Atlantic coupe

Chenard-Walcker

Among the earliest makers to apply streamlining successfully to a competition sports car was Chenard-Walcker of Gennevilliers-sur-Seine. Facing strong opposition from French rivals in 1924, they called on aerodynamics to augment limited horsepower, and surprised all Europe with their success.

The curious beetle-like blue machines, which won first time out in the 1924 Boillot Cup race at Boulogne, had coachwork echoing features of both the 'tank' Bugatti and the Voisin Aerodynamique which had enlivened the 1923 French Grand Prix. Helmet-type wings merged into full-width bodywork enclosing the rear wheels, and tapered into a curved tail. Frontal treatment was uglier, the body shrouding the dumbirons but leaving a blunt, recessed radiator intake; wheel discs were sometimes worn, and the overall reduction in drag clearly paid off.

Beneath the unusual exterior was an unusual engine, a Touté-designed all-alloy long-stroke four with pushrod-operated ohv, augmented by extra rotary-type exhaust ports in the cylinders at the base of the stroke, thus ensuring maximum extraction of burnt gases despite remarkably small exhaust valves, which in turn permitted the use of large inlet valves. A dropped chassis kept the overall height under 92cm, with two-part radiator header tanks,

one in front of the engine, the other in the scuttle.

The bodywork was formed in duralumin sheet over angle-iron framing with flexible mountings, and the driver sat on the left. The braking arrangements were also unorthodox, with very large-diameter drums at the front, but no rear-wheel brakes; instead, a single large-diameter external contracting brake worked on the transmission shaft. No differential was used, helping to keep the road weight down to 700kg. With some 44bhp from the engine this meant a 151kph (94mph) '1100', which dominated its class.

The Boillot Cup win was repeated in 1925 and 1926, both Rudge-Whitworth Cups (for the Index of Performance) were won at Le Mans in 1925, and in 1926 the 'Tank' Chenards won the 1100cc class of the Belgian 24-hours and took the Spanish 12-hours outright. Revived eleven years later, two of them finished first and second in the Bol d'Or 24-hour race – a remarkable testimony to their stamina. Cozette superchargers were fitted for some races, raising output to over 60bhp and speed to 164kph (102mph). A fully equipped 1½-litre road version of the 'Tank', the Y8 with much improved nose treatment and cleaner lines, was shown at the Paris Salon in 1927 in open and coupe forms, and although few were produced one survives today.

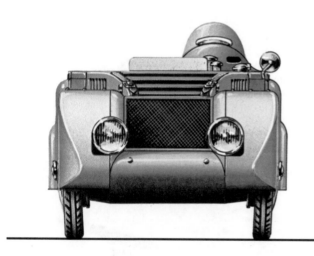

Specification
Engine: straight-four; 66 × 80mm, 1094cc; pushrod ohv with auxiliary exhaust valves (see text); single carburettor; 44bhp at 4200rpm (60bhp when fitted with Cozette supercharger).
Gearbox: four-speed manual.
Chassis: pressed steel side members; semi-elliptic springs front and rear; friction dampers; front-wheel drum brakes (servo assisted) and transmission brake.
Dimensions: wheelbase 224cm/88½in; track 104cm/41½in.

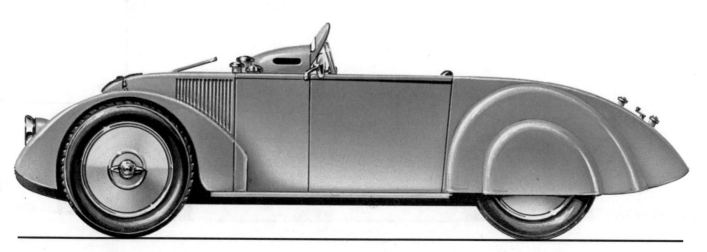

Chaparral

The sports car world has not generally been a hot-bed of innovation, least of all in the USA. However, the outstanding exception had its base and roots in Texas, and the snake-killing road runner bird of that region was adopted as its emblem and name, Chaparral. Jim Hall, a mechanical engineer, was a club racer in the mid-1950s and a GP aspirant in the early 1960s before turning to sports cars, and teaming with Hap Sharp to build them.

Their first Chaparral was an updated Scarab, which served only to confirm that the day of the front-engined sports-racer was past. So the Chaparral 2 was mid-engined, with a highly original glass fibre semi-monocoque hull which was light, strong and easily repaired. It became the basis for Hall's aerodynamic work, as he progressed from simply countering negative lift to using downforce positively and on into the then-strange world of balancing a car fore-and-aft with nose and tail spoilers. The hull was to be re-used on later Chaparrals.

The 2C was the first Chaparral with a driver-controlled rear aerofoil, and it was followed by the 2D coupe of 1966. This car had an all-aluminium stock-based 5360cc Chevrolet V-8 and a GM fluid torque converter automatic transmission which the team delighted in surrounding with mystery (neither item was truly stock, as Chaparral always enjoyed a close and fruitful liaison with GM tech-

nicians). The 2D made its European debut in the Nurburgring 1000km, when Phil Hill and Jo Bonnier drove it to victory.

The CamAm 2E was the first Chaparral to have a high-mounted 'wing', and this was carried through to the 2F coupe of 1967. This hub-mounted aerofoil was driver-actuated, and complemented by a nose flap which opened at high speeds to maintain fore-and-aft balance. The proven glass fibre chassis was used, with a body made of 60mm-thick PVC foam sandwiched by thin plastics skins. Engine was the staggered-valve ('porcupine') 7-litre V-8 producing 575bhp, which often proved too much for the automatic transmission. 2Fs started nine times in a 1967 eight-race programme (two cars were run at Le Mans) but finished only once. That was in the last championship race, the BOAC 500 at Brands Hatch, when Phil Hill and Mike Spence beat a strong field.

The 3-litre capacity limit effectively ruled Chaparral out of international championship racing after that, and in 1970 high wings were outlawed too. But Chaparral had one more sports car surprise before Hall turned to Lolas and racing single-seaters, the 2J 'sucker car'. This pioneer ground effects machine used fans to draw air from beneath it and skirts to seal it to the track – in 1970! Inevitably, it was banned, and with it the extraordinarily innovative line of Chaparral sports cars ended.

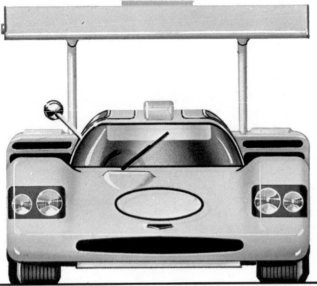

1967 2F

Specification *(2F)*
Engine: Chevrolet 90-degree V-8; 108 × 95·3mm, 6995cc; pushrod ohv; four Weber carburettors; 575bhp at 7500rpm.
Gearbox: three-speed automatic.
Chassis: reinforced glass fibre semi-monocoque; front suspension independent by double wishbones and coil springs; rear suspension independent by wishbones, transverse link, radius arms and coil springs; hydraulic dampers; four-wheel disc brakes.
Dimensions: wheelbase 231cm/91in; **front track** 139cm/55in; **rear track** 147cm/58in.

Chevrolet Camaro

Like most other GM products, the Camaro wore coats of many colours. It was a sporty car to most of the public, a sport coupe to its manufacturers; it was highly successful with Roger Penske's team in TransAm racing and as a Group 1 saloon in Europe; in its earlier Z-28 forms it was a real high-performance device, and once equipped with option packages the outwardly more standard models of the late 1960s and early 1970s were very sound GT cars within the American interpretation of the term.

The Camaro was Chevrolet's tardy response to the success of the Mustang, coming more than two years after the Ford had made such an impact on the market, and with a 400 000 production target for its first model year, 1967. It was a straightforward unitary construction car, deriving in part from the Chevy II, very cleanly styled with echoes of the Corvair and Corvette, but its fittings and equipment carefully avoided its becoming a market competitor for the latter. The first restyling by Bill Mitchell's studio, in 1970, gave it more restrained and distinctly 'European' lines – Pininfarina was reckoned to be the inspiration – and marked a high point in GM aesthetic achievement.

The mechanical permutations were numerous, but the 5·7-litre (350cu in) V-8 was the main line engine offered, rated in 1970 at 300bhp in the normal models, or up to 370bhp in the Z-28.

Towards the end of the 1970s, when the Z-28 was still among the faster American cars, the same basic 5·7-litre V-8 had been so emasculated by emission controls that it was rated at only 185bhp. Transmission was through the three-speed Turbo Hydramatic or a four-speed manual gearbox, with the option of close ratios on the Z-28.

The suspension followed conventional practice, with ifs and a live rear axle where the leaf springs located it as well as providing the springing, but one of the options included rear as well as front anti-roll bar to give acceptable 'GT' handling. The early-1970s standard 5·7-litre model was a 185kph (115mph) car.

Roger Penske was largely responsible for the Camaro's competitions reputation, running cars developed by Mark Donohue in the once-important TransAm series – dominating the 1968-69 championships – and later providing very substantially modified Camaros for the one-model IROC series. Camaros were also extensively raced in SCCA events, were dominant in British Group 1 saloon racing until outlawed by an engine capacity limit, and lingered through the 1970s in other European countries. Ironically, the Pontiac Firebird, which was badge-engineered Camaro hardware, remained true to the Pony Car concept for much longer than GM's first essay in this category.

1972 Z28

Specification

Engine (representative): *1968* – 90-degree V-8; 101·6 × 82·5mm, 5358cc; pushrod ohv; Rochester carburettors; 210bhp at 4600rpm.

1970 – as above, but 101·6 × 88·4mm, 5735cc; 300bhp at 4800rpm.

1978 – as above, but 185bhp at 4000rpm.

Gearbox: four-speed manual or three-speed automatic.

Chassis: unitary; front suspension independent by wishbones and coil springs; rear suspension by live axle, semi-elliptic springs and optional anti-roll bar; hydraulic dampers; disc front/drum rear brakes (front drums optional on early models).

Dimensions: wheelbase 274cm/108in; **front track** 150cm/59in, but 155cm/61in from 1970; **rear track** 150cm/59in, but 152cm/60in from 1970.

Chevrolet Corvette

The sobriquet 'America's Only Sports Car' may be disputed, but there is no denying the success of the Corvette down the years, or that it was a remarkable car to come out of General Motors in the 1950s ... Harley J. Earl was responsible for GM styling for three decades, and in the early 1950s he designed the 'dream cars' that tended to be featured in GM Motoramas. For the 1953 Motorama Earl decided to show a sports car; the GM brass approved, and more to the point agreed that plans for production could be put into effect if the public reaction to Motorama showings was favourable. It was.

Legend has it that designer Bob McLean started at the rear axle, placing seats and engine as far back in the chassis as possible, achieving a 53/47 weight distribution, and coincidentally ending up with the same wheelbase as the Jaguar XK120. A glass fibre body became part of the concept, and this daring novelty for a major manufacturer was mounted on a box-section chassis, X-braced and swept up over the rear axle. Expediency meant that stock parts had to be used, however, and this almost damned the Corvette. Handling was mediocre, the two-speed Powerglide automatic transmission was standard – which did not go down well with the growing number of sport-car buffs – while the only available engine was the rather aged and mundane 3·8-litre (235cu in) straight-six, which even in its Blue Flame appellation failed to provide more than 150bhp. Things could only be stopped, or made better. Ford's Thunderbird made the first option unpalatable; the second was realized when Zora Arkus-Duntov took charge of the programme. With a background in European sports cars, he was able to tackle it with a sure hand. A V-8 was obviously essential, and became 'optional' in 1955 (the six was soon dropped), then came an optional three-speed manual gearbox. Preparations for a serious racing effort with the space-framed 300bhp Corvette SS were set in train, but almost immediately killed by the AMA no-racing agreement.

The homely lines of the production car became sleeker in 1956, and for 1957 the 4·3-litre (265cu in) engine gave way to a 4·6-litre (283cu in) V-8 (for publicity purposes rated at 283bhp in works-tuned form). An initially troublesome and costly fuel injection system was offered to give this output, a four-speed gearbox was introduced, a limited-slip diff was available, as were suspension options. These made a 200kph (130mph) maximum speed production sports car of the Corvette – to make the point, there was a ninth place at Sebring for a rather special 5·2-litre (317cu in) car in 1956; 12th and 15th were achieved in 1957, and the model became a formidable SCCA championship contender.

The second basic shape lasted until 1962. While irs was tried and rejected, rear-end handling and traction problems were lessened with an anti-roll bar (the first on an American production car) and radius rods. Two of these 4·6-litre (283cu in) Corvettes placed eighth and tenth at Le Mans in 1960, during which year production exceeded 10 000 for the first time.

A complete revision came in 1963, with the Sting Ray line, still firmly a two-seater. On a slightly shorter wheelbase and marginally narrower track, the body was more purposeful and stronger with more steel in its centre section. The fast-back coupe was the most distinctive body, clean in its overall lines, fussy in its details. It sat on a new ladder-type frame, and transverse leaf irs was introduced. Basic engines were the 5359cc (327cu in) V-8, giving up to 395bhp and a 240kph (150mph) maximum in 'injection' form; and in 1966-67 the 7-litre (427cu in) V-8 rated at up to 435bhp, which made for a 225kph (140mph) Corvette.

A new body style based on the Mako Shark show car of 1965 came in 1968; apart from changes such as deformable bumpers, this was to last for more than a decade – the Corvette line continued to sell well, but never in the volume to justify frequent facelifts, let alone the mid-engined Corvette so often rumoured but never produced in more than show form. Adding to length increased the impression of sleekness in the glass fibre body.

Briefly top of the line was the lightweight ZL-1, with over 400bhp and searing acceleration, but the 1970s emission and safety regulations forced an inevitable reversion to lower performance. In the mid-1970s the LT-1 – the high-performance model – was still a 200kph (125mph) car, but for real hair-on-the-chest Corvettes one had to look to the circuits. Through much of the 1960s, Corvettes were out-run by Cobras, but the 1970s IMSA 'silhouette' Corvettes were formidable racing machines with 7-litres and 650bhp.

As the 1980s opened, the earlier multiplicity of engine options had gone, and only the L-81 5·7-litre (350cu in) V-8 was catalogued. The past was recalled in a Custom Industries roadster based on the 1980 coupe, devised with the blessing of Arkus-Duntov and dubbed Duntov Turbo ...

Total Corvette production was modest by US standards, the magic 500 000 only being reached in March 1977.

1958 model

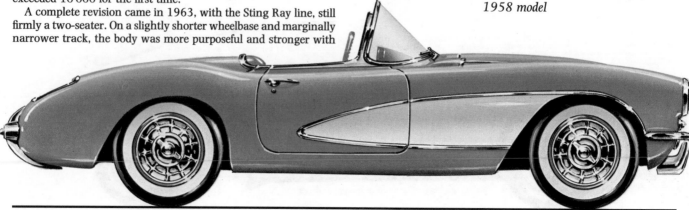

Specification

Engine: *1954* – straight-six; 90·4 × 100mm, 3851cc; pushrod ohv; Rochester carburettor; 150bhp at 4200rpm.

1957 – 90-degree V-8; 98·4 × 76·2mm, 4637cc; pushrod ohv; various carburettors (usually Rochester), but optional fuel injection until 1965; 283bhp at 6200rpm.

1963 – as above, but 102 × 82·6mm, 5359cc; 360bhp at 6000rpm.

1968 – as above, but 108 × 95·2mm, 6999cc; 435bhp at 5800rpm.

1973 – as above, but 101.6 × 88.4mm, 5734cc; 250bhp at 5200rpm.

1977 – as above, but 210bhp at 5200rpm.

Gearbox: *from 1954* – two-speed torque-converter automatic.

from 1956 – three-speed manual.

from 1958 – four-speed manual, with optional two- or three-speed automatic.

1963 Sting Ray

1968 model

Chassis: cross-braced box-section until 1963, ladder-type frame thereafter; front suspension independent by wishbones, coil springs, anti-roll bar and telescopic dampers; rear suspension by live axle and semi-elliptic springs until 1973, thereafter independent by lower wishbones, transverse leaf spring, jointed drive shafts, radius arm and telescopic dampers; four-wheel drum brakes until 1965, thereafter optional disc front/drum rear or four-wheel discs.

Dimensions: *from 1954* – wheelbase 259cm/102in; **front track** 145cm/57in; **rear track** 150cm/59in.

from 1963 – wheelbase 249cm/98in; **front track** 143cm/56in; **rear track** 145cm/57in.

from 1968 – wheelbase 249cm/98in; **front track** 148cm/58½in; **rear track** 151cm/59½in.

Chevron sports-racing cars

Derek Bennett's forte was the small sports-racing car, elegant and effective coupes and spyders which he designed, helped to build, and tested as the first of each was completed at his inadequate Victorian mill building in Bolton. The first of his sports cars to gain wide recognition was the BMW-engined B8, of which 55 were built in 1968-69 and which was homologated as a Group 4 GT car. It was succeeded in 1969 by the B16, a most attractive racing coupe.

In the B16, Bennett abandoned the pure spaceframe in favour of a semi-monocoque with tubular frames front and rear to carry suspension and engine/gearbox assemblies. The whole car was thus lighter than the B8, compact and very low. Suspension followed conventional racing lines, and while first tests were carried out with a BMW engine, the 'standard' B16 specification assumed use of the Cosworth FVC, a 1·8-litre (bored and stroked) version of the FVA Formula Two engine, initially rated at 230bhp at 8500rpm. The following year full 2-litre BDA-based engines were to become available, and in any case it was anticipated that customers would fit a variety of power units. This car was homologated into Group 5 in 1971.

The previous year had seen the introduction of a European championship for sports cars up to 2 litres, and the B16 was favoured to win this after Brian Redman's convincing victory in the car's debut race, the 1969 Nurburgring 500. However, the series saw a stern struggle, as the *spyder* Lola T210 was some 100kg lighter than the Chevron. Bennett's answer was a one-off B16S *spyder*, 50kg lighter than the coupe at 500kg, and with which Redman clinched the series by one point in the last race.

This car was the basis of the 1971 production model, the B19, in which Niki Lauda, Toine Hezemans and John Hine won championship races, although Lola took the overall title. The B19 led in turn to the B21, seen in the 1972 2-litre championship with three different engines (BMW, Cosworth FVCs of 1·9 litres and the troublesome Chevrolet Vega-based Cosworth EA); Chevron, with two race victories, were overall runners-up to Osella-Abarth, but their little cars also placed well in world championship races, notably when Hine and Bridges were third and fourth overall in 1000km races at Spa and the Nurburgring.

The B23 was the last of the direct derivatives of the B16S (these succeeding cars could all be updated to the new season's specification fairly easily). The B23 was again successful outside Europe, was again runner-up in the 2-litre championship (to Lola) and once again claimed third place in a 1000km race for Chevron (Burton and Bridges at the Nurburgring). Then a totally new 2-litre sports Chevron, the B26, superseded the B16-derived series; 148 of these had been built, forming the backbone of an attractive but short-lived class of sports car racing.

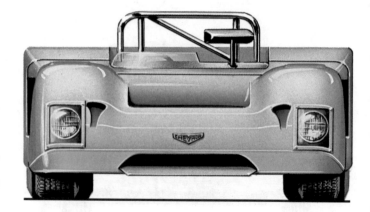

1972 B21

Specification *(B16)*
Engine: Ford-Cosworth FVC straight-four; 85·6 × 77·6mm, 1790cc; double ohc; Lucas fuel injection; 240bhp at 9000rpm.
Gearbox: five-speed Hewland manual transaxle.
Chassis: multi-tubular, with stressed-panel centre section; independent suspension front and rear by lower wishbones, top links and radius arms, coil springs and hydraulic dampers, anti-roll bars; four-wheel disc brakes.
Dimensions: wheelbase 236cm/93in; **front track** 133cm/52½in; **rear track** 135cm/53in.

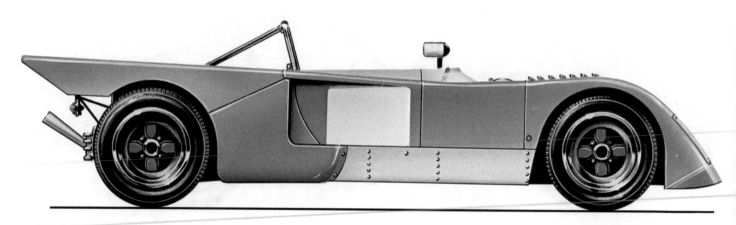

Cisitalia

Piero Dusio became involved with racing in the 1930s, and inched towards becoming a constructor during the Second World War, when he commissioned Dante Giacosa to design a voiturette single-seater and a sports car, both to use a modified version of the Fiat 1100 engine. The racing cars were effective enough in the 1100cc category, but in the immediate post-war years the racing world was not ready for the one-model series tried with the Cisitalias. The chassis conception was brilliantly original and also applied to the sports cars. These gained an excellent racing record and moreover, some of the bodies designed for them were to revitalize Italian coachbuilding, becoming the key to its later pre-eminence.

Before Fiat duties again demanded his full attention in 1945, Giacosa laid out a spaceframe design – significant in itself, facilitated by the happy chance that the Dusio consortium included a bicycle factory – modified the Fiat engine to the extent that only the block remained original, and designed transmission and suspension, also using some Fiat components. Giovanni Savonuzzi took over and, once the D46 single-seater programme was under way, turned his attention to the sports car project.

This followed the D46 in its ifs/live rear axle layout and its engine (which was to appear in 50, 60 and 65bhp forms) but with a four-speed gearbox. The welded steel tube chassis was extended to full width, hooped at front and back of the cockpit area.

The first car was a Savonuzzi-designed coupe; the second was a *spyder* with modest fins; the third made a feature of fins (and bonnet-side 'portholes') and brought the name of its designer, Vignale, to the fore. In 1946 Pinin Farina unveiled the definitive coupe (illustrated), which more than any other post-war car set an aesthetic standard. He followed this with a *spyder*, and the two bodies were put into production, by Stabilimenti Farina as well as Pinin Farina; a works coupe and a *spyder*, both dubbed Mille Miglia, had brief lives.

The sports Cisitalia had already made an indelible mark on the Mille Miglia, when a sick Nuvolari drove an open car into second place in 1947 – and but for an error by his mechanic would surely have won – while two other team cars were third and fourth. That was the high point, although Cisitalia racing director and test driver Piero Taruffi was second in the 1948 Giro di Sicilia, and numerous class successes fell to the car.

The intention was to build 500 Farina-bodied cars, but it is unlikely that production reached 200. Dusio wildly over-extended his resources in an ambitious Grand Prix exercise; his son tried to revive the company in the 1950s, but Cisitalia was really finished by 1949, when the promise of a brilliant sports car line was ended.

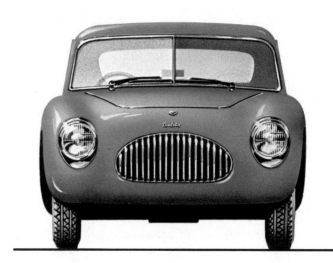

Specification *(1948 202)*
Engine: straight-four; 68 × 75mm, 1089cc; pushrod ohv; single Zenith carburettor; 65bhp at 5800rpm.
Gearbox: four-speed manual.
Chassis: tubular; front suspension independent by wishbones, transverse leaf springs and dampers; rear suspension by live axle, semi-elliptic springs and dampers; four-wheel drum brakes.
Dimensions: wheelbase 240cm/94$\frac{1}{2}$in; track 126cm/49$\frac{1}{2}$in.

1948 202

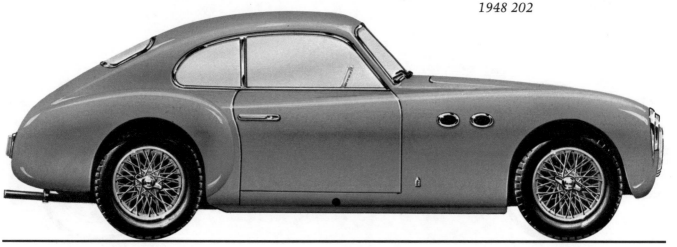

Cord 810 and 812

The Auburn-Cord-Duesenberg company was sliding towards extinction in the mid-1930s when the striking Cord 812 was announced; it did nothing to reverse that process. It appeared to be a sports car, and was certainly the closest approximation produced in America during the second half of that decade; it was an open car, and it was capable of 160kph (100mph) in its 812 form, but its other qualities were never put to the test of racing. If it had to be put into any category it should perhaps be rated a *grand routier* in the tradition of contemporary French models.

Whatever competition potential there might have been in the design was never developed, apart from some record runs for publicity, as there existed no racing in the USA for such a car. The 810/812 is therefore dismissed as a *poseur*, perhaps just a little too glibly ...

Beyond dispute is the fact that Gordon Buehrig's styling was effective, especially on the open versions. Overall it was unified, although the prominent 'coffin' nose belied the low build (overall height was 147cm). Detailing was careful, with retractable headlights in the wings, a soft top which folded away under a panel, an absence of external door hinges, running boards and so forth. The external chromed flexible exhausts of the supercharged models were at least functional and not intended purely to impress.

Mechanically it followed preceding Cords in having front-wheel drive, and a weak point was the transmission, a complex Bendix electro-vacuum gearchange mechanism with preselection, which was troublesome and sluggish. The engine was a three-bearing Lycoming V-8, which produced 125bhp in its standard 810 form. With Schwitzer-Cummins supercharger in the 812 it was rated at 170bhp, up to 195bhp with higher boost and over 200bhp in tuned forms. Suspension was fairly stiff by American standards; allied with front-wheel drive this made for stability and was dispassionately reported to give good handling qualities.

The car was conceived in 1933 to carry the Duesenberg name, but was eventually announced late in 1935 as the Cord 810 in saloon and convertible forms, a few of the open cars having a rumble seat. The FC supercharged engine appeared for 1937 with the 812, but by the late summer of that year production had ceased. The model's teething troubles had been widely publicized, and it was expensive, factors which weighed heavily against the success of this very distinctive sporting car, which proved to be the last serious attempt by a US manufacturer to market such a model for almost two decades.

Specification
Engine: *810* – Lycoming 90-degree V-8; 88·9 × 92·25mm, 4729cc; roller-operated horizontal valves; Duplex carburettor; 125bhp at 3500rpm.
   812 – as above, but with Schwitzer-Cummins supercharger; 195bhp at 4200rpm.
Gearbox: four-speed manual.
Chassis: unitary; front suspension independent by trailing arms, transverse leaf spring and dampers; rear suspension by dead beam axle, semi-elliptic leaf springs and dampers; four-wheel drum brakes.
Dimensions: wheelbase 317cm/125in; front track 142cm/56in; rear track 155cm/61in.

812

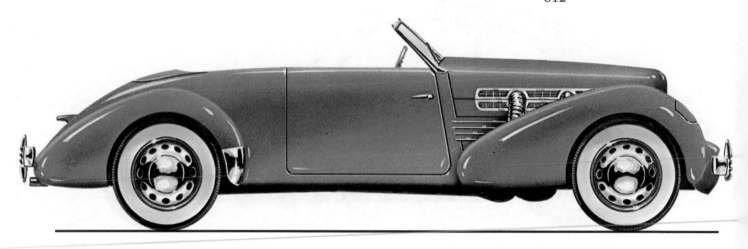

Cunningham

Briggs Cunningham was a sportsman in an old-fashioned manner, but with none of the dilettante attitudes which that sometimes implies – he played hard, and professionally, in his yachting and in his motor racing. In the latter, his aim was an American victory at Le Mans; to that end he created a sports car line, and came within sight of the cherished victory.

A Cunningham team made a trial sortie to Le Mans in 1950 with a pair of Cadillacs, a near-stock saloon and an oddly-bodied open car. These finished 10th and 11th. The fact that the saloon was less than 200 miles behind the winning Talbot 'GP car with wings and lights' was less than palatable to some purists, but the novelty value endeared Cunningham to the ACO, despite their requirement that in future prototypes could be entered only by established manufacturers.

Frick and Walters, who had prepared the 1950 cars, therefore moved to an establishment set up to build Cunningham cars at West Palm Beach. The C-1 prototype led to the 1951 C-2. This was built around the 5·4-litre Chrysler Firepower V-8, bulky and heavy but in production form giving 180bhp, with abundant torque, and reworked by Cunningham to produce 220bhp for Le Mans. It drove through a Cadillac gearbox, tough enough for the job but with only three speeds and thus not very useful in helping the brakes slow more than 1800kg of car. Most suspension components were stock items from Cadillac, Chrysler and Ford, with a Cunningham de Dion

rear axle. Chassis was tubular, the body substantial but well-proportioned.

At Le Mans two of the C-2s crashed, but the third climbed as high as second, before dropping back as poor fuel ruined the valves. It reached 245kph (152mph) on the Mulsanne straight. Back in the USA, engine development produced 270bhp by the end of the year, and there were victories at Elkhart Lake and Watkins Glen. Meanwhile, a small run of road-going C-3s, including some elegant Vignale coupes, were built to honour the 'production' requirement.

The open C-4R of 1952 was smaller and lighter, while the C-4RK was a Kamm-designed coupe; the V-8 gave 325bhp, there was a Chrysler live axle at the rear, and the wheels were designed to force air over the big Alfin drums. Two cars retired at Le Mans, but Cunningham – who drove for almost 20 hours – and Spear finished fourth in the third. The team gained more successes in the USA, while in 1953 a C-4R placed seventh at Le Mans and the C-4RK was tenth.

Into third place that year ran the C-5R, which had rigid axles front and rear, 17-inch brakes and a Siata four-speed gearbox. It crashed in the Rheims 12 hours, but the C-4Rs were run with success in several secondary events and in 1954 took third and fifth places at Le Mans. An Offenhauser-engined C-6R was not a success, and although Cunningham thereafter ran cars of other marques, his attempt to win Le Mans 'for America' petered out.

Specification

Engine: *C-2 to C-5* – Chrysler 90-degree V-8; 96·8 × 92·1mm, 5424cc; pushrod ohv; four Zenith carburettors; from 220bhp to 325bhp at 5200rpm (see text).

C-6R – Offenhauser straight-four; 100 × 92mm, 2891cc; twin ohc; two twin-choke carburettors ; 260bhp at 6000rpm.
Gearbox: Cadillac three-speed manual on C-1 to C-3, ZF five-speed manual on C-4R, four-speed manual on C-5R and C-6R.
Chassis: tubular; front suspension independent by wishbones, coil springs and dampers (except C-5R, which had a rigid axle with leading arms); rear suspension by de Dion axle, trailing links, coil springs and dampers, or by rigid axle, radius arms, coil springs and dampers; four-wheel drum brakes.
Dimensions: *C-2R* – **wheelbase** 267cm/105in; **track** 147cm/58in.

C-4R – **wheelbase** 254cm/100in; **track** 137cm/54in.

1952 C-4R

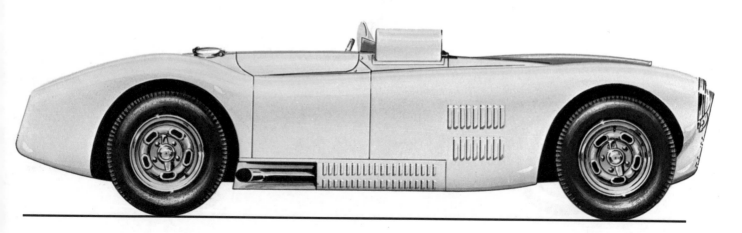

Daimler SP250

This was a late-1950s surprise from a company known through most of the 20th Century for its generally sedate saloons and stately limousines. It was first seen at the 1959 New York Motor Show, where it was named Dart but, soon after production got under way later that year, prior use of that name meant that it was redesignated SP250 (to which 'Sports' was often attached).

At the heart of the car was a 140bhp 2½-litre V-8, which was beyond criticism. The chassis was short, cross-braced and wholly orthodox, and on the early cars it flexed to an alarming degree (reports of doors flying open in corners were not uncommon). On it was mounted a resin-bonded glass fibre body in which both sleek and bulbous lines were combined in a distinct lack of harmony. An easily-detachable hardtop added rigidity, especially around the scuttle, which was undercut by the large doors. Efforts were soon made to strengthen the chassis, and in 1961 the flexing problem was finally solved when the bodywork was made to a higher specification.

Some of the shortcomings of the rigid rear axle set up were also overcome during the life of the SP250, although they remained apparent in hard driving on winding or bumpy roads. The cockpit was well laid out, and comfortable for two (the rear bench seat was very much in the 'occasional' category) and the unusually good luggage space helped to make this a genuine all-round sporting tourer. The SP250 did appear in secondary competitions, and a few were even used by the police.

The over-square engine was smooth and quiet throughout its wide effective rev range, and it was economical. It gave real sports performance to the light (960kg dry) SP250, which had excellent acceleration through well-chosen gear ratios, and a maximum speed of over 190kph (120mph). It promised well as the first of a possible line of sports cars, but the engine next appeared in a badge-engineered Jaguar Mk2 body shell, for in 1960 Daimler had been absorbed by Sir William Lyons' company. Popular though it was, the SP250 lasted only until the late summer of 1964.

Specification

Engine: 90-degree V-8; 76·2 × 69·85mm, 2548cc; pushrod ohv; twin SU carburettors; 140bhp at 5800rpm.
Gearbox: four-speed manual, or optional three-speed automatic.
Chassis: ladder-frame; front suspension independent by wishbones and coil springs; rear suspension by rigid axle and semi-elliptic springs; hydraulic dampers; four-wheel disc brakes.
Dimensions: wheelbase 239cm/94in; **front track** 128cm/50½in; **rear track** 122cm/48in.

Datsun 240Z

The Nissan Motor Company dabbled with sports cars through the 1960s, obviously looked closely at the European models which dominated this sector of the market, looked equally closely at the US legislation which frightened Europeans, and decided to start from scratch rather than use ready-to-hand components. They came up with a winner: the Datsun 240Z proved to be just the car the US market (and others less important) wanted, while it also proved to have real competition potential at international level.

It was introduced in 1969, as a fastback two-seater coupe (the 2 + 2 derivative came much later), with restrained lines which had been drafted by Goertz. The sohc straight-six derived from a 1·6-litre four; it delivered 151bhp, enough to give the 240Z a 200kph (125mph) top speed. It sat squarely on the front wheel centreline, with no attempt to achieve a 'mid-engined' effect, and this served to demonstrate that balanced handling is perfectly feasible with such a layout. The three-door unitary body was wholly orthodox, and while independent suspension all round was not novel in a car in this class, in the Z it did point up deficiencies in some of its contemporaries.

240Z sales had reached 153 000 when the 260Z appeared in 1974, with engine capacity increased from 2393cc to 2565cc, again to give 151bhp in cars sold outside the USA (US specification 240Z engines had been emission-emasculated to 129bhp in 1973). Other changes were slight, but their added weight told against acceleration, although top speed was marginally improved. A re-skinned version, the 280Z, with 2573cc fuel-injected engine, followed. While this retained much of the lusty 'man's car' appearance, some of the mystique which had attached to the 240Z was lost . . .

This outward impression was not contradicted by actual performance, for the 240Z gained a good rally reputation. The record is perhaps not as strong as one's recollections of these sturdy cars, which seemed so 'right' in a rally environment, but a 240Z was the first sports car to win the Safari Rally, the works team taking first and second places in 1971, while there was a third in the Monte Carlo Rally and success on lesser events such as the Welsh Rally. It was raced most commonly in the USA, notably in SCCA production events: this was appropriate, for it was a sports car aimed at the US market, and success there made it the world's best-selling sports car during the early 1970s.

1971 factory rally car

Specification (*road car*)
Engine: straight-six; 83 × 73·7mm, 2393cc; single ohc; twin Hitachi (SU) carburettors; 157bhp at 5600rpm.
Gearbox: five-speed manual.
Chassis: unitary; front and rear suspension independent by lower wishbones and MacPherson struts; disc front/drum rear brakes.
Dimensions: wheelbase 230cm/90½in; **front track** 136cm/53½in; **rear track** 135cm/53in.

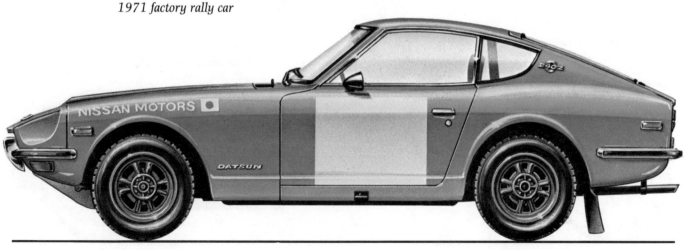

Delage DI and DM

Louis Delage was a remarkable character, whose love for racing and for 'cutting a dash' eventually caused his ruin. In 1923 he embarked on a costly Grand Prix racing programme which kept his personnel busy right up to 1927. Anguished accountants urged him to reduce expenditure, but Delage was determined to build France's champion racing car and nothing would stop him.

The staple products of his Courbevoie factory were some very fine touring and sports cars, which had to earn the profits to offset the racing costs. One very popular model, introduced in 1923, was the 2·1-litre Delage DI (known in Britain as the 14/40), a well-built 75 × 120mm, 2121cc pushrod-ohv four with excellent four-wheel brakes working on the Perrot system. The well-braced chassis and springing were conventional but the engine's potential was exploited in the more sporting DIS which followed in 1925. Larger valves, higher compression, alloy pistons and a higher rear axle ratio combined to raise the maximum speed potential to about 120kph (75mph).

In 1926 the DISS (Sport Surbaissé) was introduced, with a shorter, lowered chassis, a more sporting camshaft, single-plate clutch, closer gear ratios, and a tachometer. It was also distinguished by a Ducellier dynamometer (starter-cum-generator) mounted on the front of the crankshaft.

All these Delage DI variants were substantial but handsome vehicles, often carrying 'torpedo sport' open bodywork which was well set off by the elegant nickel-silver radiator (which followed Hispano-Suiza style) and by the large-diameter Rudge wire wheels. Steering was light and roadholding excellent, and while acceleration was impaired by the weight and the 'long' gear ratios (less so on the DISS) a remarkably high cruising speed could be maintained.

A six-cylinder edition of the 75 × 120mm power unit first appeared in 1926, in the touring Delage DM, followed in 1927 by the DMS (Sport). Capacity in both was 3181cc, and the valve gear followed DI pattern. The crankshaft ran in seven plain bearings, and the engine was beautifully smooth and flexible. Like that of the DI, the chassis was of sturdy and rather heavy construction with cruciform bracing, and the large diameter brakes had Dewandre vacuum-servo assistance. In 1928, a Grand Sport version was introduced, carrying some striking coachwork by various coachbuilders. These Delages were strong, reliable cars, comfortably able to exceed 130kph (80mph).

Specification

Engine: *DIS (1925-27)* – straight-four; 75 × 120mm, 2121cc; pushrod ohv; single carburettor; approx. 40bhp at 3200rpm.
   DISS (1926) – as above, but 48bhp at 3200rpm.
   DMS – straight-six; 75 × 120mm, 3181cc; pushrod ohv; single carburettor; 55bhp at 3300rpm.
Gearbox: four-speed manual.
Chassis: pressed steel side members with cruciform bracing; semi-elliptic springs and friction dampers front and rear; four-wheel drum brakes (with vacuum servo-assistance on DMS).
Dimensions: *DIS* – **wheelbase** 318cm/125in; **track** 132cm/52in.
   DISS – **wheelbase** 299cm/118in;
track 131cm/51½in.
   DMS – **wheelbase** 338cm/133in;
track 142cm/56in.
   DMS Grand Sport – **wheelbase** 323cm/127in;
track 142cm/56in.

1922 DI torpedo

Delage D8

Belonging more to the 'Grand Touring' class than that of outright sports models, the big Delage straight-eights which came in with the 1930s were nonetheless high performance cars. Too large and luxurious to perform on the race circuits, they figured rather more prominently in *Concours d'Elegance* at fashionable French seaside resorts, and are thus less well known than they deserve to be.

Although Delage's highly successful straight-eight Grand Prix cars had twin-ohc and superchargers, the road-going eights were less sophisticated mechanically, having pushrod-ohv of straightforward design, apart from the eccentricity of valve springs mounted on the rocker arms, which made adjustment a tricky matter. The first model, the D8, made its debut at the Paris Salon in autumn 1929, having a bore and stroke of 77 × 109mm (4050cc).

The chassis, suspension and brakes were similar to those of the six-cylinder DMS, but the radiator was even more elegant, with vertical slats and a stone-guard.

The long, low chassis attracted the French coachbuilders, who excelled themselves in creating exotic two-door coupes and convertibles with very long bonnets and shallow 'letter-box' windscreens.

The Delage's cruciform-braced frame with 363cm wheelbase was very heavy, but the powerful 4-litre engine could carry the car along at well over 145kph (90mph), although the DMS-type brakes were not quite up to stopping such a moving mass. Higher-tuned D8S and D8SS editions were also turned out in small numbers, with a 330cm wheelbase. The D8SS-100 was an even more special development, with 120bhp at 4000rpm under its bonnet and 160kph (100mph).

A track version of the D8SS-100 broke several speed records up to 12 hours at Montlhéry, the fastest being at 189·63kph (117·83mph). After Delahaye took over Delage in 1935, the D8 was enlarged to 80 × 107mm (4300cc), becoming the D8-120 and inheriting Delahaye-type ifs and a Cotal electro-magnetic gearbox. In 1938 the straight-eight engine was further enlarged to 84 × 107mm (4750cc), but the car lost much of its sporting character despite a quartet of flexible outside exhaust pipes in Mercedes-Benz Type 500 style.

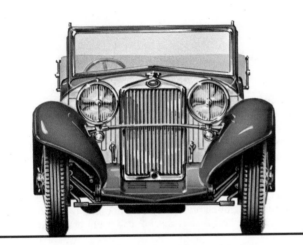

1933 D8SS drophead coupe

Specification

Engine: *D8S* – straight-eight; 77 × 109mm, 4060cc; pushrod ohv; single carburettor; 110bhp at 3500rpm.

D8-120 – as above, but 80 × 107mm, 4300cc; 115bhp at 4000rpm.

From 1938 – as above, but 84 × 107mm, 4570cc; 120bhp at 4000rpm.

Gearbox: four-speed manual; optional Cotal electro-magnetic from 1937.

Chassis: *D8* – pressed steel side members with cruciform bracing; semi-elliptic springs and friction dampers front and rear; four-wheel drum brakes.

D8S and later models – as above, but front suspension independent by transverse leaf spring and wishbones; hydraulic dampers; servo-assisted brakes.

Dimensions: *D8S* – wheelbase 310cm/122in or 330cm/130in; track 150cm/59in.

D8-120 – wheelbase 338cm/133in; track 150cm/59in.

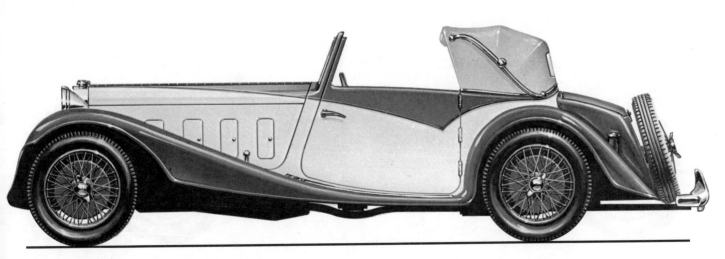

Delahaye Type 135

One of the best of the larger French sports cars before taxation killed off the class in the 1950s was the Delahaye. Succeeding a range of dull, heavy and uninspired touring cars, the 3½-litre six-cylinder Type 135 came as a pleasant surprise in the middle 1930s. It was descended from the 82bhp 3·2-litre Super-Luxe of 1933, a model which had the virtues of a robust six-cylinder ohv engine, and ifs by transverse leaf spring and radius arms.

One of these cars finished third in the 1934 Monte Carlo Rally, and that summer a lower, shorter, livelier edition with a 112bhp triple-carburettor engine won a coveted Coupe des Alpes in the prestigious Alpine Trial. By 1935 (the year in which Delahaye took over Delage) the 'Coupe des Alpes', as this new Delahaye was inevitably called, was winning sports car races in Algeria and France.

A year later an even lower, lighter and more agile 3558cc model appeared as the Type 135 Compétition, with bigger valves, higher compression, etc., producing 150bhp. Only 14 of these were built for sports car racing, for factory and private owners, but between 1936 and 1939 they scored over half a dozen race wins, including Le Mans itself in 1938. After the Second World War several were converted into Grand Prix racers, where their rugged durability and frugal fuel consumption offset their size, weight and modest specification to earn some honourable placings.

Meanwhile the Type 135 road models had been announced in late 1935 wearing a wide choice of French bodywork, some of it very beautiful, and some ludicrously overdone in the Gallic manner. Beneath their bodywork, the chassis and running gear was basically similar to that of the fiercer 135 Compétition models, although a single-carburettor version was available, and the engines had coil ignition, air cleaners and other refinements, giving a flexible, refined and reliable 120bhp; synchromesh or Cotal electromagnetic four-speed gearboxes replaced the 'crash' box of the racers. Strong, fast and agile, these 'Grand Tourers' won two Monte Carlo Rallies in 1937 and 1939 (sharing the latter with Hotchkiss).

After the Second World War the basic 135 was continued, with more modern, if less appealing, full-width bodywork made by Delahaye themselves, who augmented the range with the Type 175, in which the classic six-cylinder engine was enlarged to 4½ litres. Delahaye manufacture continued for a dwindling market until 1954, when the concern was taken over by the Hotchkiss-Brandt combine.

Specification

Engine: straight-six; 84 × 107mm, 3558cc; pushrod ohv; single or triple carburettors; 130bhp at 3850rpm.
Gearbox: four-speed manual (non-synchromesh on Compétition, other models with synchromesh); optional Cotal four-speed electro-magnetic.
Chassis: box section side members; front suspension independent by transverse leaf spring, swinging links and radius arms; rear suspension by semi-elliptic springs; friction and hydraulic dampers; four-wheel Bendix mechanical drum brakes, with servo assistance.
Dimensions: wheelbase 295cm/116in; **front track** 140cm/55in; **rear track** 147cm/58in.

1936 135 Compétition

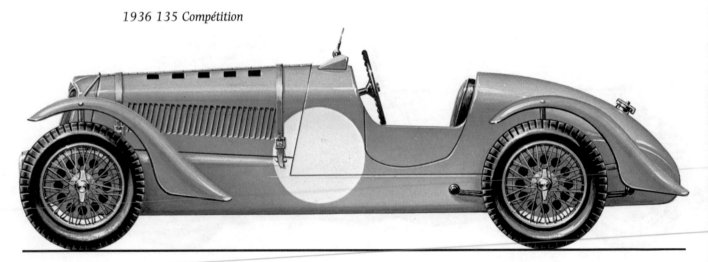

De Tomaso Pantera

Alejandro de Tomaso, an Italian-domiciled Argentinian, is one of the motoring entrepreneurs, a sometime racing driver, a constructor of usually abortive racing cars and, more successfully, a manufacturer of high-performance road cars, with the Vallelunga and Pampero leading to the elegant but less than perfect Mangusta. That was powered by a Ford V-8, and Ford distributed it in the USA for a period. A much firmer alliance with Ford centred on the Pantera – in the late 1960s, Ford had not discarded its 'performance image' and wanted a fitting car which could be produced in reasonable quantities (that alone ruled out the Mangusta). First ideas were to call the new model Cobra or Puma, but eventually Pantera (Panther) was agreed.

It was introduced for 1970, appearing to be a typical Italian 'supercar' in most respects. It had a monocoque chassis/body, with a subframe supporting engine and rear suspension, wishbone and coil spring independent suspension all round, and sleek lines by Ghia (inevitably, as it was an associated company). However, the Pantera was unlike others of the breed in that its engine was a 'no substitute for cubic inches' 5·8-litre (351cu in) V-8 supplied by Ford – making it more marketable in the USA, and at a substantially lower price than outwardly competitive models.

The base version of the engine in what was to become the L produced 330bhp, while the GTS had a 350bhp V-8; roughly ten per cent of that power was to be lost as noise and emission restrictions were introduced later in the decade. Respectively, they gave theoretical top speeds of 212kph (162mph) and 274kph (170mph), although in practice Panteras apparently fell a little short of those speeds. Acceleration was in the supercar class, however, roadholding and handling were excellent, the ride was good, and accomodation for two people and their luggage was reasonable.

In 1971 an ambitious racing programme was announced, but like several de Tomaso track enterprises this one – although encouraged by Ford – hardly took off. Competition engines were prepared by the redoubtable Bud Moore, to give around 400bhp, but apart from details like extended wheel arches the cars appeared to be almost standard, although purposeful in black and red. The works team appeared only three times, one car at least leading the Monza 1000km before finishing fifth, while the Le Mans effort was almost a *debacle*, only one car surviving to finish 17th. Thereafter, racing was left to independent teams, which achieved little with a car that was so heavy (unladen weight was over 1400kg).

It was as a road car that the Pantera survived into the 1980s, despite the ending of Ford's involvement in 1974 and the later cessation of production of the Cleveland-built 5·8-litre V-8 engine. De Tomaso then turned to Ford of Australia for his motive power, which further reduced the performance of the cars: the 1980 GTS could boast only 300bhp at 5000rpm and production was down to 25 cars per year.

Specification
Engine: *L* – Ford 90-degree V-8; 101·6 × 89mm, 5763cc; pushrod ohv; Autolite carburettor; 330bhp at 5400rpm.
   GTS – as above, but 350bhp at 6000rpm (see text).
Gearbox: ZF five-speed manual.
Chassis: unitary; front and rear suspension independent by wishbones, coil springs and dampers, with anti-roll bars; four-wheel disc brakes.
Dimensions: wheelbase 251cm/99in; front track 146cm/57½in; rear track 145cm/57in.

1972 L model

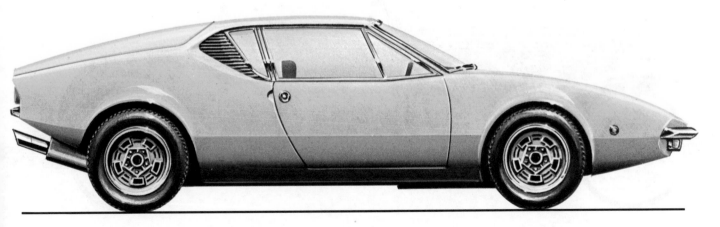

Duesenberg Models J and SJ

Whether the famous eight-cylinder Duesenbergs were strictly sports cars or simply fast road cars is open to question. What is certain is that with 6·8 litres of twin-cam, 32-valve, straight-eight engine, their performance was emphatically sporting, with maximum speed figures in defiance of their road weight of almost 2500kg – 185kph (115mph) for the unsupercharged J in open four-seater form, and approaching 210kph (130mph) for the SJ with the almost surplus assistance of centrifugal supercharging.

Even for American cars, Duesenbergs were vast, with optional wheelbases of 362cm or 390cm, enabling them to accommodate the most spacious of coachwork and yet retain superb proportions and perfect symmetry. Such was their horsepower – even if the factory claims of 265bhp and 320bhp seem over-generous – that three speeds sufficed admirably (the J could reach 145kph/90mph in second gear), although in contrast the formidable dead weight did require the very best of braking. The makers, pioneers of hydraulic brakes, employed their own system of large drums with vacuum servo assistance.

The engines, built by the associated Lycoming concern, clearly benefited from Duesenberg's racing experience, with twin overhead camshafts, four valves per cylinder, hemispherical heads, aluminium connecting rods and pistons and a massive, fully-balanced five-bearing chrome-nickel crankshaft, able to rotate at 5000rpm despite the long 121mm stroke.

Everything about the cars was massive; the frame side members were 216mm deep, with six large tubular cross members, and the chassis alone scaled over 2000kg, even before the world's master coachbuilders added the weight of their finest bodywork, superbly appointed for the millionaires who could afford Duesenbergs.

In Europe, the Model J cost almost £500 more in chassis form than the contemporary Rolls-Royce Phantom II; all bodies were made by outside coachbuilders, although the tall, striking Duesenberg vee-radiator with its elegant vertical slats was a standard hallmark of quality and grace. Considering its cost and limited clientele, the Duesenberg did well to live through the world depression of the early 1930s. Indeed, the ultra-expensive SJ – which could accelerate from 0-to-160kph (100mph) in 17sec – was introduced in the blackest year, 1932, yet this hyper-luxury marque survived to 1937, when car production ended and the plant was sold off. About 500 Duesenbergs were built between 1929 and 1937, and the marque remains a legendary American production, vastly revered today.

1932 Model J roadster

Specification

Engine: *Model J* – Lycoming straight-eight; 95 × 121mm, 6882cc; twin ohc; four inclined valves per cylinder; single twin-choke carburettor; 250bhp at 4250rpm.

Model SJ – as above, but with centrifugal supercharger; 320bhp at 4750rpm.

Gearbox: three-speed manual.

Chassis: pressed steel side members; semi-elliptic springs and hydraulic dampers front and rear; four-wheel drum brakes with hydraulic servo assistance, plus transmission brake.

Dimensions: wheelbase 362cm/142½in or (J only) 390cm/153½in; **track** 142cm/56in.

Facel Vega

Facel Vega were the harbingers of a post-war European re-discovery of the simple fact that one way to achieve high performance without high engine development costs was to buy-in the power of big American engines. The imposing luxury sporting saloons built by Facel SA (Forges et Ateliers de Construction d'Eure et de Loire) were hardly sports cars – certainly they eschewed competition – but echoed the *grands routiers* and were unquestionably grand touring cars. As such they had a real place in the European motoring scene, and might have survived alongside other Euro-US hybrids, had the company not chosen to branch out with smaller models (Facellias), with their own unreliable 1·6-litre engine, or with Austin Healey and Volvo power units, for the failure of these models contributed to their downfall.

Power was the essence of the HK500, lazily pushed out by Chrysler V-8s, 180bhp by the 4½-litre unit in the earliest (1954) Facel Vega, 360bhp by the 6·3-litre version in 1960, and as much as 390bhp by the same unit in the Facel II of 1962. Maximum speeds correspondingly rose, from 185kph (115mph) to 225kph (140mph). Although an automatic transmission was a natural complement – and, indeed, the Chrysler three-speed automatic was a Facel option – the four-speed manual box was more often specified.

In the rest of its make up, the HK500 was thoroughly orthodox, with a sturdy tubular chassis and a 2+2 coupe body which, although large, was so well proportioned that it appeared ponderous only from ahead. Over-ornamentation was avoided, although Facel was one of the few European companies to ape the wrap-round windshield fad, and HK500s were lavishly furnished and well finished (Facel built car bodies before they built cars, and obviously knew their business). Suspension was soft, almost 'American', but the big car was quiet and responsive in a manner which belied its size, and had very good ride and roadholding qualities by the standards of its day. Facel's day was over by 1964, however, leaving the French industry once again without a big high-performance car.

Specification (1960)

Engine: Chrysler 90-degree V-8; 107·95 × 85·85mm, 6286cc; pushrod ohv; twin Carter carburettors; 360bhp at 5200rpm.
Gearbox: four-speed manual; optional three-speed automatic.
Chassis: tubular frame; front suspension independent by coil springs, wishbones and dampers; rear suspension by rigid axle, semi-elliptic springs and dampers; four-wheel disc brakes.
Dimensions: wheelbase 267cm/105in; **front track** 141cm/55½in; **rear track** 146cm/57½in.

Ferrari 125 to 250

It was entirely appropriate that the marque Ferrari should start life with a V-12 engine, a classic Colombo 60-degree 1·5-litre unit that ran on a test bed in the autumn of 1946 and produced a modest 72bhp. This was used in the first Ferrari, the 125S which made its race debut in 1947. Only seven were built, and the three works cars were soon converted to 159s, with a 1·9-litre version of the engine. For 1948, Colombo's successor, Lampredi, further increased bore and stroke, to a 2-litre capacity, and around this the early Ferrari essays took definitive form as the 166.

Initially it was built as the Spyder Corsa with a narrow body and cycle wings, which made for easy conversion to formula guise, but for 1949 a Touring full-width body was introduced – the famous *barchetta* (little boat) which was to inspire other sports car designers. Various coachbuilders were also to offer coupe versions on the (original) long wheelbase chassis.

There was nothing extraordinary in chassis or running gear, a cross-braced frame of main oval tube members being carried on ifs and a live rear axle, a combination which had some uncertain qualities, for example in the transmission and drum brakes.

While Inter road cars were offered with a mild single-carburettor 105bhp V-12, the 166 will always be associated primarily with its up-to-150bhp competition versions. Its most notable early victory was scored by Biondetti in the 1948 Mille Miglia (in a coupe, although it was the *barchetta*-bodied 166 which gained the MM designation) and he won again in 1949. However, the outstanding achievement in that year was victory in the revived Le Mans 24-hour race, gained by Chinetti and Lord Selsdon.

For years Ferrari models tended to blend, at least in part, into succeeding models. While an improved 166 was listed through to 1953, it had been joined in 1950 by the 195, closely similar, but with a longer wheelbase (which lent itself to some shapely Vignale coupes) and a 2341cc version of the V-12, giving 180bhp in competition form.

The 212 which followed became more widely known. The engine was enlarged again, to 2562cc, to give 130bhp in its mildest form (the Inter) or 150bhp in the Sport (also called the Export), rising to 170bhp in the late 212s built in 1953. A *barchetta* Sport won the first Tour de France, while coupes were second and third, but the outstanding competition achievement of the 212 came in the second Carrera Panamericana eight-stage road race across Mexico in 1951. The cars – with beefed-up chassis and rear suspension, portly Vignale coupe bodies and Inter engines because of the low-octane fuels – took the first two places.

The engine size rose again, to 2715cc in the 225, which led to the 3-litre V-12 250 Sport and 250MM. That 'Mille Miglia' appellation came after Giovanni Bracco's famous 1952 victory in the 250 Sport prototype, when despite rain and tyre problems (but reputedly with the aid of quantities of brandy and cigarettes!) he defeated the mighty Mercedes team of lightweight 300SLs.

In its definitive form, the 250MM was shown in the autumn of 1952 with the 2953cc V-12 having the 73 × 58·8 bore and stroke that were to recur in many later 3-litre Ferraris. It was rated at 240bhp. Pininfarina provided coupe bodies with notably unfussed lines, while the open *spyders* were built by Vignale. The 250MM seemed more prone to rear-axle failures that its predecessors, but nevertheless had a good racing record in Europe and the USA.

1949 166 MM

Specification

Engine: *166* – 60-degree V-12; 60 × 58·8mm, 1995cc; single ohc per bank; three Weber carburettors; 140bhp at 6600rpm rising to 145bhp at 7000rpm by 1950.

250MM – as above, but 73 × 58·8mm, 2953cc; 240bhp at 7200rpm.

Gearbox: five-speed manual.

Chassis: tubular frame; front suspension independent by upper and lower wishbones, lower transverse spring and dampers; rear suspension by live axle, semi-elliptic springs and dampers; four-wheel drum brakes.

Dimensions: *166 Inter (road car)* – **wheelbase** 242cm/95½in; **front track** 125cm/49in; **rear track** 120cm/47in.

166MM – **wheelbase** 220cm/86½in; **front track** 127cm/50in; **rear track** 125cm/49in.

250MM – **wheelbase** 240mm/94½in; **front track** 130cm/51in; **rear track** 132cm/52in.

Ferrari 340 and 375

Ferrari's decision to attack the Grand Prix superiority of the 1·5-litre supercharged Alfa Romeo with unsupercharged 4·5–litre cars led directly to Maranello's 'big engine' sports car period, initially to counter the successful Anglo-American hybrids in US racing, and eventually to bring Ferrari success again in the premier sports car race, the Le Mans 24 hours.

A new Lampredi-designed V-12 first took shape in 3·3-litre form in 1950, but during the autumn of that year the Type 342 America was announced at the Paris Motor Show with a 4·1-litre version of the engine. This was initially rated at 220bhp, but was soon cut back to a more modest 200bhp as part of a general 'softening' to make this essentially roadgoing model more acceptable to US drivers. However, out of it came the 280bhp, competitions-orientated Type 340 Mexico (ironically the best placing achieved with this car in the 1952 Carrera Panamericana was third), and the 1953 Type 340MM, with power output up to 300bhp. *Spyder* and *berlinetta* versions were raced, but on sinuous circuits the unsophisticated suspension made life difficult for drivers, making Giannino Marzotto's record-breaking victory at 142·374kph (88·47mph) –

in the 1953 Mille Miglia all the more outstanding.

The 4·5-litre 375 which appeared later that year inevitably gained a 'Mille Miglia' appendage to its designation. A longer wheelbase contributed to better handling and the V-12's 340bhp output gave the 375MM the outright speed to match the Jaguars at Le Mans, where one of the coupes battled for the lead through the first half; however, the Ferrari's big (14-inch) drum brakes were no match for Jaguar's discs. The 375MM went on to win the Spa 24-hour and the Pescara 12-hour race.

Engine size was raised again in the 1954 375 Plus, to 4954cc. Normally rated at a modest 344bhp, the V-12 proved absolutely reliable in this form. A de Dion rear end took the place of the rigid axle of the earlier cars. In *spyder* form, the 375 Plus driven by Gonzalez and Trintignant gained a dramatic 'revenge' victory for Ferrari at Le Mans in 1954, and Maglioli also drove one to win the last Carrera Panamericana.

The 375 Plus was followed by the short-lived 4·9-litre 410 Sport, before Ferrari turned away from V-12s for a brief period, ending this series of belligerent sports-racing cars.

1953 4·5-litre 375MM

Specification

Engine: *340MM* – 60-degree V-12; 80 × 68mm, 4101cc; single ohc; Weber carburettors; 300bhp at 6600rpm.

375 Plus – as above, but 84 × 74·5mm, 4954cc; 344bhp at 6500rpm.

Gearbox: four-speed manual.

Chassis: *340MM* – tubular; front suspension independent by wishbones, transverse leaf spring and dampers; rear suspension by rigid axle, radius rods, semi-elliptic leaf springs and dampers; four-wheel drum brakes.

375 Plus – as above, but rear suspension by de Dion axle, wishbones, transverse leaf springs and dampers.

Dimensions: *340MM* – **wheelbase** 250cm/97½in; **track** 132cm/51½in;

375 Plus – **wheelbase** 250cm/97½in; **front track** 132cm/51½in; **rear track** 128cm/50½in.

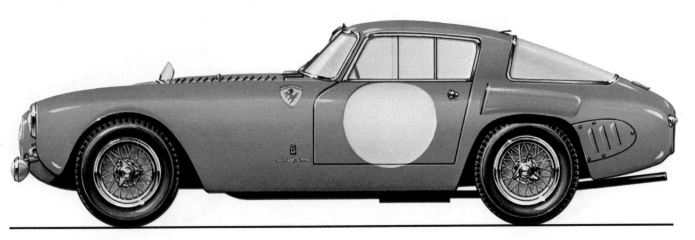

Ferrari Mondial and Monza

During the 1950s, Ferrari technicians were extraordinarily flexible; until trade unionism penetrated the gates of Maranello in the following decade, model followed model in over-lapping profusion. Formula racing threw up a requirement for a four-cylinder engine, and during the winter of 1950-51 Aurelio Lampredi was set to designing one. Although it departed from many Ferrari tenets, Lampredi's design moved swiftly from drawing board to test house; it produced both the outright power and the torque expected of it, and was the basis of the T500 which dominated the 1952-53 F2 world championship seasons.

Sports car use inevitably followed, and in 1953 the 3-litre T735 appeared, and showed considerable promise in its first races at Senigallia and Monza. It led to the 2-litre T500 Mondial and the T750 Monza. The capacity of the first engine corresponded with the F2 unit, modified to run on pump fuel and developing 260bhp; the second used a similar but distinct four derived from the T735, developing 260bhp. Although these were large-cylinder engines compared with the Ferrari V-12s, they had only two valves per cylinder, and a valve system of some complexity – features which restricted the rpm limit and hence the potential power output (competitive though the cars were at the start of their lives). The early cars had four-speed gearboxes, later versions five speeds, the boxes being in transaxles.

The definitive chassis consisted of two oval-tube longitudinal members, with numerous small tubes linking them and carrying the bodywork – an arrangement part-way towards a spaceframe. Rear suspension was de Dion, while at the front a transverse leaf arrangement soon gave way to coil-spring ifs.

The first bodies were very dumpy, but a smoother, sleeker Scaglietti body following lines devised by Dino Ferrari became standard; other bodies were also produced, notably the Pinin Farina *spyder*, and less notably the *berlinettas*.

These fours gained a reputation for speed and for handling which bordered on the perilous. Nevertheless, leading drivers got the measure of them, and victories came in events as diverse as the Supercortemaggiore race at Monza and the 1954 TT at Dundrod, and the cars became popular with US competitiors.

As the Mondial became less competitive, it was replaced by the T500TRC/Testa Rossa as a customer car for 1956, while to meet the 2·5-litre capacity limit at Le Mans that year the 2498cc, 225bhp T625 was contrived for the works team (one finished third). The last four-cylinder Ferrari was an uprated Monza with a 3431cc 280bhp engine, the T860. In 860M form this gained second places in the Mille Miglia, at Caracas, the Nurburgring and in the Swedish GP. But during that 1956 season, Ferrari was firmly steering away from four-cylinder engines ...

Specification

Engine: *Mondial* – straight-four; 90 × 78mm, 1985cc; double ohc; twin Weber carburettors; 160bhp at 7000rpm.
    Monza – as above, but 103 × 90mm, 2999cc; 260bhp at 6000rpm.
Gearbox: four/five-speed manual transaxle.
Chassis: tubular main members (see text); front suspension independent by wishbones, coil springs, dampers and anti-roll bar (see text); rear suspension by de Dion tube, radius rods, transverse leaf springs and dampers; four-wheel drum brakes.
Dimensions: wheelbase 225cm/88½in; **track** 128cm/50½in.

1954 Mondial 500 (Scaglietti body)

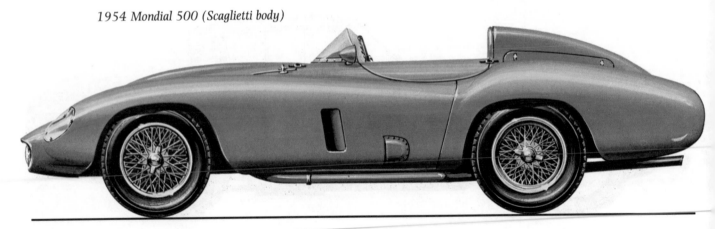

Ferrari Testa Rossa

Testa Rossa is an evocative name in the Ferrari story, recalling the lithe V-12 cars of the period before Maranello turned to mid-engined sports-racers. It was also applied to an earlier four-cylinder car which succeeded the Mondial, for the name derived from the simple fact that the cylinder heads were painted red ...

The first TR was built in two versions, the sleeker 500TRC coming in 1957, and was intended from the outset to be an uncomplicated car for private entrants, whom it served well as a 2-litre class contender. It was dropped when the 250TR was introduced for 1958; this proved to be a reliable and competitive customer car, while for the works team it succeeded the big V-12s and six-cylinder cars, just as the sports car championship capacity limit was set at 3-litres from 1958.

The concept was logical, with a chassis following the 2-litre TR, a de Dion rear axle after the prototype had run in 1957 with a live rear axle, and an engine based on the 250GT unit and producing an unstrained 300bhp. Early bodies had extravagant cutouts inside the front wings to scoop air to the drum brakes, but the nose lines became smooth when Dunlop disc brakes were adopted for 1959. The bodies were built by Fantuzzi, and a characteristic shared with contemporary six-cylinder Ferraris was a prominent bonnet-top airscoop, which was usually transparent.

The new cars won the first three championship races of 1958, although they were beaten at the Nurburgring, and the outstanding sports-car partnership of Phil Hill and Olivier Gendebien clinched the championship for Ferrari with a Le Mans victory. By contrast, 1959 was not a good year for the team, for after a victory at Sebring, Ferrari did not win another championship race.

The championship was regained in 1960, when the cars (TR60) had slightly shorter wheelbase, sometimes an experimental irs, and of course the high windscreen required by the regulations. Ferrari won the opening race at Buenos Aires, and the last race at Le Mans; good placings in the other two scoring races secured the title.

The TR61 had an aerodynamically-refined body, with the windscreen integrated into the overall lines and complemented by a high tail (which at Sebring incorporated the first rear spoiler to be seen in a race) while a split nose signalled the arrival of Carlo Chiti at Maranello. This was a year of transition to mid-engined cars, but the team still ran the TRs, works cars taking the first two places at Sebring, private TR60s the next two, while TR61s were first and second at Le Mans and an independent TR61 won the Pescara championship race. The last major victory for a Testa Rossa came at Sebring in 1962, while a TR-based 4-litre Prototype won at Le Mans, the last major race to fall to a front-engined Ferrari sports car.

1958 250 TR

Specification

Engine: 60-degree V-12; 73 × 58·8mm, 2953cc; single ohc per bank; Weber carburettors; 300bhp at 7200rpm.
Gearbox: four-speed manual.
Chassis: multi-tubular with large-section side members; front suspension independent by wishbones, coil springs, dampers and anti-roll bar; rear suspension by de Dion axle, coil springs and dampers (but wishbones and coil spring/damper irs from 1960); four-wheel drum brakes (discs from 1959).
Dimensions: wheelbase 235cm/93in (but 229cm/90in from 1960); **front track** 131cm/52½in; **rear track** 130cm/52in.

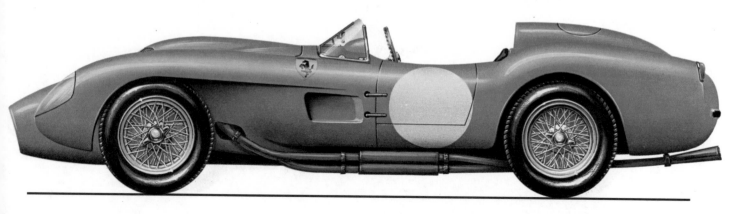

Ferrari 250 GTO and variants

The Grand Touring category became increasingly important through the second half of the 1950s, inspiring a succession of Ferrari *gran turismo berlinettas*, culminating in the 250GTOs of the 1960s, the last front-engined competition Ferraris.

The 250GT was announced at Ferrari's early-1962 press conference, but 250GTs had been competing in GT classes since the mid-1950s. These were built around the Colombo-designed, Lampredi-developed single-ohc 60-degree V-12, which gave around 240bhp in such forerunners as the Tipo 250MM of 1954. Out of this 112 engine the closely similar 128 was developed for 1956, when Ferrari began to take GT racing seriously; initially rated at 240bhp, by 1959 output had been increased to 260bhp.

These 1950s cars followed orthodox Ferrari practice in other respects, with well-braced main chassis tubes and outriggers to carry bodywork; unequal length wishbones and coil spring front suspension, and a leaf-spring-mounted live rear axle with radius arms to control longitudinal movement. Pininfarina's first bodies followed 375 Mille Miglia lines, which were gradually evolved in the Scaglietti-built bodies, while aesthetically less successful light-weight versions came from Zagato. An attractive open version was developed for road use at the behest of US distributors; it was named 250GT Spyder California and built by Scaglietti in 1958-59.

By that time the *berlinettas* had established almost complete domination of the GT categories, effectively starting in 1956 with class victories in the Tour of Sicily (fourth overall), the Mille Miglia (fifth overall) and the first of nine outright victories in the Tour de France. Many many more were to follow as the 250GTs became widely used, long wheelbase cars becoming known as TdFs (to mark the Tour de France victories).

Matters became more serious as GT races in 1959 – above all the Le Mans GT category – presaged the FIA GT championship that was to be introduced in 1960. The main-line Ferrari TRs retired at Le Mans in 1959, but there was consolation as the Beurlys-Eldé 250GT was third overall (at 166·74kph/103·61mph, which would have been a race-winning speed up to 1953), while cars with a new body shape were fourth and sixth.

The new body was carried through to the short wheelbase version announced in the autumn, which with minor revisions was produced in Competition and Lusso forms; the former title is self-explanatory, and with little more than a plug change it was a tractable road car, while the Lusso had a properly-trimmed cockpit and a heavier body using steel in place of light alloy. The revised

Specification

Engine: 60-degree V-12; 73 × 58·8mm, 2953cc; single ohc per bank; Weber carburettors; 260-300bhp at 7000-7200rpm (see text).

Gearbox: four-speed manual; five-speed manual on GTO.

Chassis: multi-tubular with large-section side members; front suspension independent by wishbones, coil springs, dampers and anti-roll bar; rear suspension by live axle, radius rods, half-elliptic leaf springs and dampers; four-wheel drum brakes (discs from 1960).

Dimensions: wheelbase 260cm/102½in (240cm/94½in on swb GT and GTO); **track** 135cm/53in.

1962 California

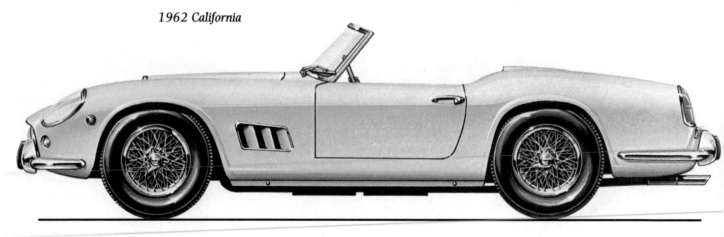

engine followed the Testa Rossa in its cylinder head (primarily with outside plugs) and produced 270bhp in the Competition version (280bhp in 1961). The chassis was developed towards a space-frame, while Dunlop disc brakes were standardized.

This 'new' 250GT was not homologated as a GT car until mid-1960, when it continued to uphold Ferrari's record in GT racing. The first success for the homologated car was at Le Mans, with fourth, fifth and sixth overall and the Group 3 GT victory. Among other events, two consecutive Tourist Trophy victories followed, while in 1961 these short wheelbase *berlinettas* conclusively won the GT championship for Ferrari.

Meanwhile, Ferrari had been working towards the 250GTO through these short wheelbase cars, one preoccupation being to achieve stability at high speeds, where the 250GT was suspect (broadly, a dry-sump engine facilitated a lower nose line, while rear spoilers were added, later becoming integral with the body). Engine output was raised to 300bhp.

'O' stood for *omologato*, Ferrari claiming that the 250GTO was a restyled 250GT, and that production therefore exceeded the required 100 cars; the claim was accepted and 39 production cars have been recorded, although some 250GTs were also independent-ly converted to GTO appearance and specification.

During its first season in 1962 the GTO continued to build up Ferrari's GT record, successes including second and third places at Le Mans. This near-invincibility continued in 1963, and Ferrari then had to rely on the 250GTO through 1964 as the FIA refused to homolgate the mid-engined 250LM as a GT car. The GTO design was modified in detail, with shorter body and wider track in the cars sometimes known simply as 'GTO 64'. That year, Ferrari gained a third GT championship, but by a very narrow margin, and the cars were defeated in the most important race, Le Mans.

These cars continued in competition with private teams, while a 275GTB derivative was occasionally run by or for Ferrari, finishing third overall and first in the GT category at Le Mans in 1965. By that time, the Ferrari team had turned away from GT racing, and the true successors to the 250 series were in a Lusso vein: the 250GT 2+2, with wheelbase extended by 30cm and a particularly elegant Pininfarina body, and the roadgoing 275GTB and GTS (coupe and convertible) which had independent rear suspension, rear-mounted gearboxes, and 3·3-litre 280bhp engines. These models pointed towards the more sophisticated generation of Ferrari road cars; in the history of racing, the 250GTO stands as an all-time classic.

1962 GTO

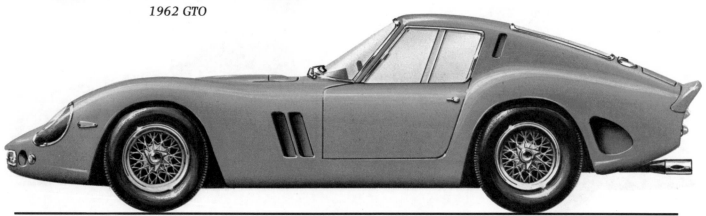

Ferrari mid-engined Prototypes

The Ferrari Prototypes of the 1960s followed a logical progression, as the team felt its way uncertainly into the new era of mid-engined two-seaters, gained confidence with success, and in the 330s produced some outstandingly efficient and handsome cars; although the rear spoiler was first seen on the forerunner of these cars, the 330s came when the age of aerodynamics was still in its infancy and the tendency was towards low frontal areas and slippery shapes rather than a plethora of wings and fins.

That forerunner was the 246SP of 1961, which closely followed the F1 car, with a wider tubular chassis to carry full-width bodywork and a version of the 2417cc V-6 engine used in the last years of the 2½-litre GP formula. At the front this car even reflected the 'nostril nose' of 1961's GP Ferraris, while the famous rear spoiler came into being when Richie Ginther encountered handling problems in fast corners during a Monza test session.

The 246SP retired from its debut race, at Sebring, but won the 1961 Targa Florio; in slightly modified form it won again in Sicily in 1962, and also won the Nurburgring 1000km. That year Chiti's 248SP appeared, briefly and unsuccessfully; this car is worthy of note only because it had a V-8, a real rarity in the Ferrari story.

By 1963 Ferrari had sufficient confidence in the mid-engined layout to put a V-12 into the neat 250P. This engine was a 3-litre Testa Rossa, rated at 310bhp. The car was slightly larger than the 246SP, similar in appearance but with a lower engine deck and full-width aerofoil-section roll-over bar behind the cockpit, while the nostril nose had been abandoned. It proved very successful, winning at Sebring, Nurburgring and Le Mans, and it led to the 3·3-litre 275P and the 4-litre 330P. The latter car needed more development, and the 275P carried the racing burden in 1964, winning the

same three championship events again, while the 330P won three late-season secondary races.

Meanwhile, there was a furore around the 250LM and Ferrari's efforts to get it homologated as a Cobra-beating GT car. It was not quite a 250P with a roof, as the frame was modified, and by the time it was 'in production' it had the 275P engine. Homologation did not come, however, despite typically wily Ferrari endeavours to obtain it by fair means or foul, but the 250LM did become a successful private entrants' Prototype (now there is a contradiction!) a high point being the 1965 Le Mans victory for a NART 250LM (and that same car was eighth at Le Mans in 1969).

As an answer to the growing Ford challenge, Ferrari introduced Forghieri's P2 in 1965, best-known in its 4-litre 330P2 form but also built as the 3·3-litre 275P2 and the 4·4-litre 365P2 customer car (with a single-ohc V-12, whereas the works cars had double-ohc engines). The P2s had tubular chassis, and followed contemporary Ferrari F1 practice in having some of the aluminium body panels welded to the tubes to add to the structure's rigidity. Suspension also followed the F1 cars. Coupe or open bodies were used, the latter having a refined version of the transverse aerofoil behind the cockpit and from some angles appearing to be a closed car. These cars won the Targa Florio and the Nurburgring 1000km in 1965, but the entire works team retired at Le Mans.

The 1966 330P3 appeared little different, but the car was lower and there was some glass fibre in the bodywork. Lucas fuel injection replaced Webers on the V-12, which was rated at 420bhp, while a

Specifications

246SP (1961)

Engine: 60-degree V-12; 85 × 71mm, 2417cc; double ohc per bank; Weber carburettors; 270bhp at 8000rpm.
Gearbox: five-speed manual.
Chassis: tubular; front and rear suspension independent by wishbones, coil springs, dampers and anti-roll bars; four-wheel disc brakes.
Dimensions: wheelbase 232cm/91½in; track 120cm/47in.

250P

Engine: 60-degree V-12; 73 × 58·8mm, 2953cc; single ohc per bank; Weber carburettors; 310bhp at 7500rpm.
Gearbox: five-speed manual.
Chassis: tubular; front and rear suspension independent by wishbones, coil springs, dampers and anti-roll bars; four-wheel disc brakes.
Dimensions: wheelbase 240cm/94½in; front track 135cm/53in; rear track 134cm/52½in.

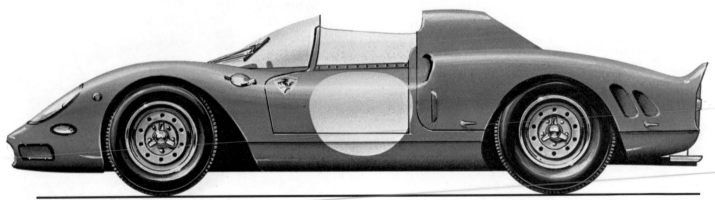

1965 275 P2

250P (1963 Le Mans)

ZF five-speed gearbox was used instead of a Ferrari unit, as industrial problems were rife at Modena. These also affected the team's season, when the P3s won only two 1000km races, at Monza and Spa.

A greater effort was made with the 1967 330P4, a complete redesign with a monocoque centre section, slightly wider and shorter, and with 450bhp from a revised V-12 (a three-valve version, with two inlet and one exhaust valve per cylinder), and a Ferrari gearbox. The theory that 4 litres of thoroughbred engine could combat the 7-litre pushrod engines used by Ford seemed well proven by a Ferrari one-two in the Daytona 24 hours, but the sole works Ford to run the 24 hours at Le Mans finished ahead of two P4s. However, a win in the Monza 1000km and good placings in other events ensured the championship for Ferrari, for the sixth time in the seven seasons that these mid-engined Prototypes had been run.

1967 330 P4

330P4

Engine: 60-degree V-12; 77 × 71mm, 3967cc; twin ohc per bank; Lucas fuel injection; 450bhp at 8000rpm.
Gearbox: five-speed manual.
Chassis: tubular with semi-monocoque centre section; front suspension independent by wishbones, coil springs, dampers and anti-roll bar; rear suspension independent by radius arms, wishbones, coil springs, dampers and anti-roll bar; four-wheel disc brakes.
Dimensions: wheelbase 240cm/94½in; **front track** 149cm/58½in; **rear track** 145cm/57in.

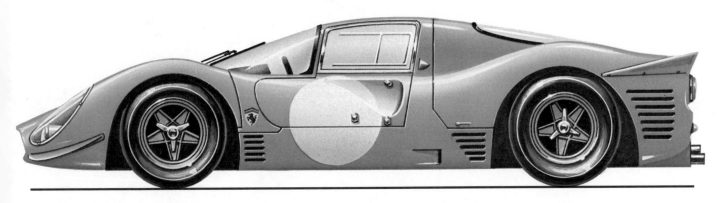

Ferrari Daytona

This was the ultimate front-engined Ferrari. Not the last, for the 400 lived on into the 1980s, but the last of the classic two-seater Ferrari Gran Turismo Berlinetta series which had its origins in the 275GTB of 1964. The Daytona was one of the fastest road cars ever marketed, although Ferrari's claimed 290kph (180mph) seemed beyond actual achievement.

The Daytona was announced in 1968, and in basic layout followed the 275GTB/4, with engine positioned well forward and rear-mounted gearbox combined with differential. That engine was a 4·4-litre twin-cam V-12 rated at 352bhp, with massive torque (318 1b/ft at 5500rpm), docile, flexible and unmistakably 'Ferrari'.

Pininfarina was responsible for the lines of the body, Scaglietti for building production bodies. The Daytona was more smoothly styled than the 275, with less aggressive lines, and was sensible from its headlight treatment to the adequate boot. Although from some angles the glass area appeared niggardly, visibility from the cockpit was good. The seats were thin and supported well – a detail example of the overall feel of refinement where it would have been so easy to mislead with an impression of 'luxury'. A large traditional steering wheel seemed odd, but was in keeping with the effort required to turn the fat front tyres at low to medium speeds.

This was a grand touring car in all respects, and it was therefore appropriate that independent teams, with scant factory recognition for their efforts, should achieve excellent results at Le Mans. These included fifth place in 1971, fifth, sixth, seventh, eighth and ninth places in 1972 (as well as the GT category victory), and sixth and ninth in 1973. Other good results came in the USA, notably second in the Daytona 24 hours in both 1973 and 1979, the latter gained by a NART Daytona when the model had been out of production for more than three years!

Specification
Engine: 60-degree V-12; 81 × 71mm, 4390cc; twin ohc per bank; six Weber twin-choke carburettors; 352bhp at 7500rpm.
Gearbox: five-speed manual transaxle.
Chassis: tubular; front and rear suspension independent by wishbones, coil springs, dampers and anti-roll bars; four-wheel ventilated disc brakes.
Dimensions: wheelbase 241cm/95in; **front track** 143cm/56½in; **rear track** 145cm/57in.

1969 GTB/4

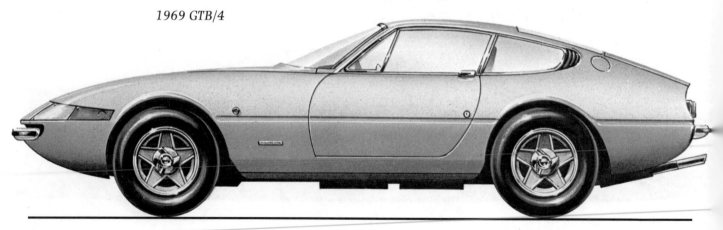

Ferrari Dino 246

Formula racing played a substantial role in the evolution of this exemplary little Ferrari, which was at once the cheapest Ferrari ever marketed and was absolutely 'right' in its mechanical make up, its lines and its performance.

Ferrari had used the Dino V-6 racing engine in various forms, and it remained attractive for the new Formula Two which came into effect in 1967. The regulations stipulated production-based engines, and a solution to this problem was found in a collaboration with Fiat – a detuned version of the engine was evolved, and used in the series-production Fiat Dino 206, introduced in *spyder* and coupe forms late in 1966.

Two years later, Ferrari launched their own up-market Dino, and in 1969 replaced this with the Dino 246GT. Like all save the prototypes of the earlier cars, this had its V-6 mounted transversely, and for this use it was enlarged to 2·4 litres (virtually its 1957 F1 capacity, although less 'square' in this Fiat-cast iron-block form). It was rated at 195bhp at 7600rpm in European specification, while engines destined for the USA had two Webers instead of three and

were consequently rated at 175bhp for this market.

This superb engine was mounted in a steel tubular-and-sheet chassis frame, with an aluminium body gracefully styled by Pininfarina. It was most commonly seen as a coupe, although almost a third of the 3900 production run was devoted to the GTS version, which had a removable roof panel, with the rear lines of the cockpit retained in a roll-over structure.

In its detuned form the V-6 proved to be truly 'road-civilized', pulling smoothly through a wide effective rev range without undue noise (that word has a nuisance connotation, which only an unsympathetic ear would associate with the sounds of Ferrari camshaft drive chains and valve gear!). Nevertheless, the car was heavy at 1090kg, and in all-out terms was no faster than its class rivals, the maximum speed being 238kph (148mph). In all-round terms – in traction, cornering and handling, low drag, braking, cockpit comfort, control layout and visibility – it excelled. However, it was never developed as a competition car as its Dino 206 forerunner was, and in 1973 it was discontinued in favour of the 308GT.

Ferrari Dino 246

Specification
Engine: 65-degree V-6; 92·5 × 60mm, 2418cc; twin ohc per bank; three Weber carburettors; 195bhp at 7600rpm.
Gearbox: five-speed manual.
Chassis: steel tubular and sheet; front and rear suspension independent by wishbones, coil springs, dampers and anti-roll bars; four-wheel ventilated disc brakes.
Dimensions: wheelbase 234cm/92in; **front track** 142cm/56in; **rear track** 140cm/55in.

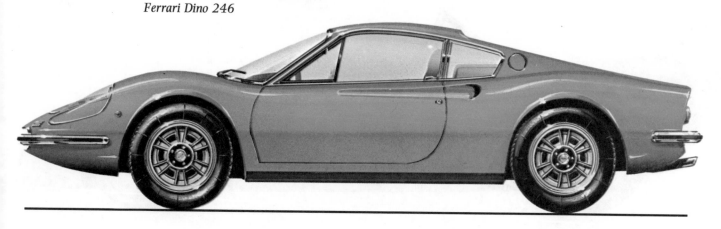

Ferrari 312P

Seldom was the ephithet 'Grand Prix car with wings and lights' more justified than when applied to the Ferrari which totally dominated the 1972 World Championship of Makes, when the red 312Ps won ten of the ten races the team entered. It was one of those seasons when everything clicked for the Scuderia: the team had a generous budget, a strong manager in Peter Schetty, driving strength in depth, mechanical components proven in Grand Prix cars, and (after the preceding years) there were no opponents exploiting loopholes in the regulations.

The first 312P was raced six times in 1969, finishing second at its Sebring debut, gaining another second and a fourth place. It was a Formula 1 car with sports bodywork, powered by the then-current V-12 rated at 420bhp – not enough to combat the 5-litre Group 5 Porsches, which Ferrari then tried to beat in 1970 with their own 5-litre 512S.

In 1971, however, a new 312P appeared, for a year of solid development in anticipation of a genuine 3-litre limit returning. This car used a spaceframe with aluminium sheet to produce a semi-monocoque in the Ferrari F1 mode, with a clean and attractive two-piece glass fibre body. The flat-12 F1 engine, slightly detuned for this use to give 440bhp, drove through a five-speed gearbox; suspension followed F1 lines, although experience led to detail modifications. Little improvement was called for in 1972, as the 1971 cars were almost at 1972's 650kg minimum weight; an outward distinction was the change from modest inboard tail fins to sleeker fins aligned with the car's flanks.

The team was able to rotate 'sets' of cars, one being overhauled while the other was raced; regular drivers were Jacky Ickx, Mario Andretti, Clay Regazzoni, Ronnie Peterson, Brian Redman and Tim Schenken, with Arturo Merzario and Sandro Munari as reserves. Ferrari withdrew the Le Mans entry at the last moment, as the durability of the boxer engine was suspect, but won everything else – taking ten wins from ten events, including eight one-two results – so that they had actually clinched the championship before the French 24-hour race was run.

The 312P was modestly revised for 1973 (a substantially different car was run only in tests late in the year). The 1973 312P had a longer wheelbase, bodywork revisions which included reprofiled noses, a full-width rear aerofoil and a long tail for fast circuits, and in some races the engine air intakes were raised above the rear deck. The engine was normally rated at 460bhp, although some in full F1 trim were used in a few sprint races. However, the team effort was reduced, and the opposition (primarily Matra) was stronger than anticipated. Wins came only at Monza and Nurburgring, and Ferrari were championship runners-up in their last sports-racing season.

Specification
Engine: flat-12; 78·5 × 52·5mm, 2991cc; double ohc per bank; Lucas fuel injection; 400bhp at 10 800rpm in 1971, rising to 460bhp at 11 000rpm in 1973.
Gearbox: five-speed manual.
Chassis: tubular and sheet monocoque; front suspension independent by wishbones, coil springs, dampers and anti-roll bar; rear suspension independent by radius arms, wishbones, coil springs, dampers and anti-roll bar; four-wheel disc brakes.
Dimensions: wheelbase 222cm/87½in; **front track** 142cm/56in; **rear track** 140cm/55in.

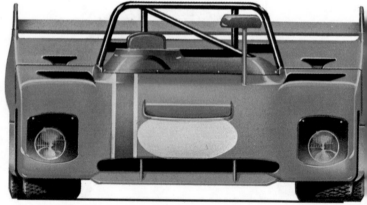

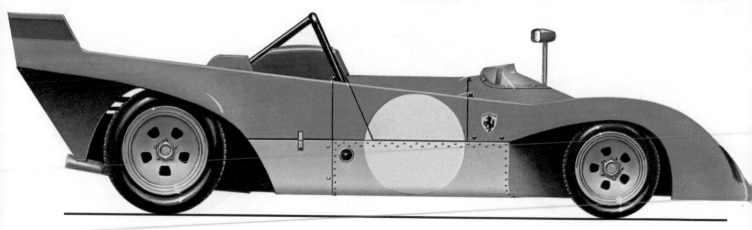

Ferrari Berlinetta Boxers

This was perhaps **the** supercar of the 1970s, the first large mid-engined Ferrari for road use, encapsulating all the Ferrari mystique, with a 12-cylinder engine and purposefully elegant Pininfarina styling. In conception it could be directly traced back to a Pininfarina show car of 1968, the year in which the classic front-engined Daytona was introduced, but two years after the first of the mid-engined supercars had appeared – the Lamborghini Miura, which must have been a spur to Ferrari. However, their reaction was not to panic something into production, and it was not until the 1971 Turin Show that the Berlinetta Boxer was exhibited.

Ferrari had used 'boxer' (horizontally-opposed) 12-cylinder engines in racing since 1964, and a 4390cc unit on these lines was chosen for the new road car rather than a traditional V-12. It was rated at 360bhp, and had abundant torque which made for shattering acceleration even if the claimed 290kph (180mph) maximum speed seemed around 20kph optimistic in the hands of independent testers. The drive was taken via a rear-mounted clutch through 180 degrees to a five-speed gearbox and transaxle below the engine. The chassis was conventional, with a square-tube frame and central sheet monocoque, steel-panelled save for glass fibre nose and tail sections.

The BB was a two-seater, with a functional cockpit, and good visibility ahead and to the sides, but with the rear-view restrictions common to this type of car; luggage space in the nose was also very limited . . .

Production of the 365 ceased in the summer of 1976, when almost 400 had been made, and at the Paris Show that year the 512BB, with a 5-litre version of the engine, was introduced. In this engine bore and stroke were increased and dry sump lubrication replaced the wet sump. The initial specification gave a power output of 360bhp, but this was later amended to 340bhp, which suggests that claims for the faster-revving 4·4-litre unit were based on traditional slightly puny Italian horses! The body was extended by 6½cm, while wider wheels were fitted and the arches extended correspondingly; a nose spoiler was also added.

Inevitably, a Ferrari with such an exciting specification was seen to have competition potential, although factory interest was limited to setting up a 'customer assistance' department to aid the efforts of independent teams, such as NART (North American Racing Team). These ventures enjoyed little real success, however, highlights being 12th at Le Mans in 1979 and 10th the following year, and the cars used tended to be marred by the addition of unsightly aerofoils at nose and tail.

None of this detracted from the real purpose of the Boxers, however, which were the most handsome and potent road cars of their time.

Specification

Engine: *365GT4BB* – flat-12; 81 × 71mm, 4390cc; twin ohc per bank; four Weber triple-choke carburettors; 360bhp at 7500rpm
   512BB – as above, but 82 × 78mm, 4924cc; 340bhp at 6800rpm.
Gearbox: five-speed manual transaxle.
Chassis: tubular, with monocoque centre section; front and rear suspension independent by wishbones, coil springs, dampers and anti-roll bars; four-wheel ventilated disc brakes.
Dimensions: wheelbase 250cm/98½in; **front track** 150cm/59in; **rear track** 151cm/59½in.

1976 512BB

Fiat Tipo 508 Balilla

With the double spur of the grim economic climate of 1931 and dictator Mussolini's commands to increase exports, Fiat of Italy set out to produce 'a car for Europe'. Light, lively and cheap, the resultant Tipo 508 Balilla of 1932 was built not only in Turin, but in France, Germany, Czechoslovakia and Poland. It had a short-stroke 995cc four-cylinder side-valve engine, three-speed gearbox, advanced hydraulic brakes, a choice of open or closed two-door bodywork, and a modest weight of 675kg.

As the economic situation slowly improved, thoughts inevitably turned to a sports version, exploiting the high cruising speed, good roadholding and general agility of the design. A captivating open two-seater *spyder* body with sweeping wings, neat tail with central spine, and wire wheels looked too fast for the first version, with its tuned side-valve engine giving 30bhp, but in March 1934 the design crystallised as the 508S, with 36bhp ohv engine and a four-speed close-ratio gearbox. Weighing only 610kg, the sports Balilla was good for 116kph (72mph), with a 109kph (68mph) cruising speed and modest fuel consumption of around 32mpg. Reasonably

priced, it sold briskly in Europe and Britain, where it intruded on established MG and Singer territory. Besides the *spyder*, a lighter Coppa d'Oro competition model with fixed cycle wings, and a beautifully formed Berlinetta aerodynamic coupe were also offered.

The 508S was plunged into competition work, proving highly versatile and scoring innumerable successes in racing, rallying, hillclimbing and record-breaking. Le Mans, the TT, the Bol d'Or, the Nurburgring, the Mille Miglia, and the Monte Carlo Rally all saw the pretty little Fiats in action. One was driven round and round the short Brooklands Mountain circuit until 1000 miles (1600km) had been covered at an average (in poor November conditions) of 88·7kph (55·11mph), while in France, where Simca was founded to build Fiats under licence, Amédée Gordini began his illustrious racing career with successful self-prepared Simca-Fiat Balillas.

The model was built until 1937. Had circumstances been different and Fiat been able to continue production, they could well have equalled the success enjoyed by the British MG Midgets in the sports car world.

Specification *(508S)*
Engine: straight-four; 65 × 75mm, 995cc; pushrod ohv; single Zenith carburettor; 36bhp at 4400rpm.
Gearbox: four-speed manual with synchromesh.
Chassis: pressed steel side members with cruciform bracing; semi-elliptic springs and friction dampers front and rear; four-wheel hydraulic drum brakes.
Dimensions: wheelbase 233cm/91½in; **front track** 119cm/47in; **rear track** 121cm/47½in.

1935 508S

Fiat 8V

This was Fiat's first post-war sports car, a surprising car to come from the Italian company in the early 1950s when their pre-occupation was with bread-and-butter vehicles. It was an experiment which slipped into limited production, a design with potential which was never really exploited. At most, 114 8Vs were built between 1952 and 1954 and efforts to market it were localized, although foreign-language brochures were produced for each of the two principal versions.

The 8V, Tipo 106, was one of the sensations of the 1952 Geneva Motor Show. It had come into being largely because its engine – a narrow-angle V-8 intended for a stillborn saloon – showed such promise that the technical men were able to persuade the business men not to abandon it. It was a short-stroke unit, oddly with a three-main-bearing crankshaft, exhaust manifolds on the outside of the cylinder head and a single overhead camshaft in the vee operating valves via pushrods and rocker arms. In both first and second series cars it was rated at 110bhp; competition versions produced up to 127bhp.

A straightforward cross-braced chassis was welded to a two-shell steel body, making for a car which was rigid and surprisingly light (dry weight was 930kg), with a cockpit so narrow that the two seats were staggered. The large steering wheel and instrument binnacle were typical of the period, and the apparently generous space within the fastback was in fact restricted by the horizontally-stowed spare wheel. Suspension was independent all round, by coil springs and wishbones. The claimed maximum speed of the standard cars was about 180kph (112mph), and if anything this was conservative.

In the second series version (illustrated) the lines were cleaned up, especially around the nose, while most of the leading Italian coachbuilders produced bodies for the 8V, with varying results: Farina were responsible for one of the best and one of the worst, Vignale had middling aesthetic success, and Zagato concentrated on light competition coupes.

Outside Italy, the 8Vs were rarities, and a 1953 Le Mans entry with experimental five-speed gearbox raced for only an hour. In Italy, they were used in races, rallies and hill climbs, with class successes in all three activities.

Final experiments included a glass fibre body which was outwardly standard, and the 8V was used as the basis for Fiat's 1954 gas turbine car. That was the year that half-hearted production of this under-exploited and inexpensive sports car ceased, probably because Fiat were just not ready for it.

Specification

Engine: 70-degree V-8; 72 × 61·3mm, 1996cc; single ohc per bank; twin Weber carburettors; 110bhp at 6000rpm.
Gearbox: four-speed manual.
Chassis: tubular, with integral steel bodywork; front and rear suspension independent by wishbones, coil springs, dampers and anti-roll bars; four-wheel drum brakes, with transmission handbrake.
Dimensions: wheelbase 240cm/94½in; track 129cm/51in.

Fiat 124

The elegant 124 *spyder* derived from the saloon introduced in 1966, and outlived it in the Fiat range. It became prominent in its Abarth competition form in the early 1970s, and – remarkably – continued in production into the 1980s as a by-then rare sporting open two-seater for the US market.

The 124 Sport started life with the toothed-belt-driven twin-ohc engine of the saloon in 1·5-litre form, producing 90bhp; the power unit was increased in size to 1·6 litres in 1970 and to 1·8 litres three years later, but with US emission equipment it had a lower output late in the decade, although capacity was up to 2 litres. Running gear was straightforward, with live rear axle, and disc brakes were fitted front and rear. By no means the least appealing feature was the simple, elegant and almost ageless body by Pininfarina, slightly improved around the nose in 1971 and then spoiled by the mandatory US bumpers. It was also built in two-door coupe form, with four usable seats. Open or closed, it was a 160kph (100mph) car, albeit only just.

Rally successes with the 1600 *spyder* led to the Fiat Abarth 124 Rally in 1972. This was a hard-top version of the open car, with additional air intakes below the grille, wheel arch extensions and modest rubber bumpers, with its interior revised for practical competitions use (including, for example, built-in roll cage elements), and independent rear suspension. Abarth work on the engine was not extensive, but resulted in a power output increase to 128bhp (20bhp up on the normal 1600 unit, 10bhp better than the 1800) in 'catalogue' form. Up to 30bhp more was extracted from works rally engines. In normal tune, the car had a claimed maximum speed of 190kph (118mph).

The 124 might have enjoyed as long a rally life as the Ford Escort, but it was available only until 1975 and Fiat policies meant that Lancia became their rally arm. Before that, the Italian marques indulged internecine strife; with the 124, Fiat were championship runners-up in three consecutive seasons (1972-74). The 124 was campaigned in world championship events by drivers such as Rauno Aaltonen and Markku Alen, but was most active in secondary Continental events, rallied by various Italian drivers.

1974 factory rally car

Specification

Engine: *Abarth 124 Rally* – straight-four; 84 × 79·2mm, 1756cc; twin ohc; two Weber twin-choke carburettors; 128bhp at 6200rpm.
   1800 roadster – as above, but single Weber carburettor; 118bhp at 6000rpm.
Gearbox: *Rally* – five-speed manual; *roadster* – four-speed manual.
Chassis: unitary; front suspension independent by wishbones, coil spring/damper units and anti-roll bar; rear suspension independent by lower swinging arms, coil spring/damper units and anti-roll bar; four-wheel disc brakes.
Dimensions: wheelbase 228cm/90in; **front track** 141cm/55½in; **rear track** 140cm/55in.

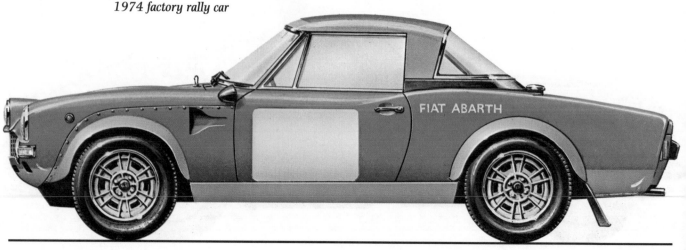

Fiat X1/9

The mid-engined gospel had been widely preached, and applied to road cars by specialist manufacturers, before Fiat introduced this small and relatively inexpensive sports car in 1972. Moreover, in a car which was to sell more than 140 000 units by the end of the decade, some of the shortcomings of the basic layout which dogged models from more exotic companies were avoided; for example, good rearward visibility was achieved by simply working along 'three box' lines.

Most X1/9 mechanical components were taken from the 128 (an early intention was to call it 128 Sport Spyder). The basis was a floorpan, with rigidity increased by a stressed control tunnel and boxed sills, and substantial front and rear bulkheads, which made for a strong structure and meant that a Targa-type detachable roof panel could be featured. Bertone was responsible for styling, successful in almost all respects, although the cockpit was cramped if either occupant was of above-average stature. Outward lines were well-balanced, with a subtle wedge profile, flared arches and retractable headlights; in 1978 American-specification bumpers and raised engine cover did absolutely

nothing to improve the car's over-all appearance.

The engine/transmission pack of the fwd 128 was used, in slightly modified form and turned through 180 degrees, with a four-speed gearbox until the 1500 was introduced late in 1978. With the original 1290cc engine, the X1/9 was just a 160kph (100mph) car; in 1978 the stroke of the engine was increased to give 1498cc capacity, and a five-speed gearbox was introduced. Top speed of this model was 177kph (110mph).

The X1/9 was relatively heavy (at 912kg) for its size, but this contributed to its good ride and excellent road holding, with a nicely balanced 47/53 front/rear weight distribution contributing to generally neutral handling.

To those for whom competition success is the acid test of a sports car, the X1/9 might be adjudged a failure, in that its competitions use was limited to amateurs and was largely insignificant, albeit sufficient to demonstrate potential (an X1/9 was placed fourth in the 1980 Giro d'Italia). The factory did produce a 2-litre prototype with considerable bodywork modifications, including a substantial rear aerofoil and a prominent air intake.

Specification (*road cars*)
Engine: *1300* – straight-four; 80·2 × 63·9mm, 1290cc; single ohc; single Weber carburettor; 73bhp at 6000rpm.
   1500 – as above, but 86·4 × 63·9mm, 1498cc; 85bhp at 6000rpm.
Gearbox: *1300* – four-speed manual; *1500* – five-speed manual.
Chassis: platform; front suspension independent by MacPherson struts and lower wishbones; rear suspension by MacPherson struts, wishbones and single links; four-wheel disc brakes.
Dimensions: wheelbase 220cm/86½in; **track** 135cm/53in.

Ford Thunderbird

To American enthusiasts, the early T-Bird was a sports car of promise, a counter to the Corvette and another sign that a new age of enlightenment was dawning in Detroit. Ford thought of it as a sports car, too, at least through most of its design period, which was accelerated as the Corvette was shown, and which led to a launch in 1954 before any cars had reached dealers. By that time, the decision had been taken to introduce it as a 'personal' car, in the hope that this would give it a wider market appeal than the GM model. While the early Corvettes may have been prestige loss leaders, the Thunderbird made money for Ford, initially at a break-even level perhaps, but making real profits as a Thunderbird Division was set up in the late 1950s. Ironically, that was when the car started to grow, away from the sporty image; although the name was still in catalogues in the 1970s, by then it applied to a run-of-the-mill gas guzzler far removed from divisional manager Lewis Crusoe's concept of the early 1950s.

In its earliest forms, the Thunderbird was a good-looking two-seater, low, functional and restrained, especially after its first face lift for 1956 when the spare wheel was mounted almost horizontally at the rear under a shaped metal cover (a sensible gimmick as boot space was limited in the first version). A folding hood or detachable port-holed hard top was available. A year later the car was to grow tail fins, albeit modest ones in that era of extravagant 'rocket' styling. In 1958 the main-line Thunderbird was a four-seater, with a short-lived Roadster two-seater option . . .

Under the skin was inevitably an assemblage of stock parts, with a substantially braced box-section side-member frame and a pressed-steel body which made no contribution to rigidity. The engine was set well back in the chassis, giving an initial 49/51 weight distribution, but any promise of good handling which might be read into that was offset by the sedan suspension, giving boulevard rather than sports characteristics. Ford did play with spring rates, but only to combat tail-heaviness from 1956.

All T-birds had V-8s, the first a Mercury 4785cc (292cu in) unit giving 198bhp; a 5112cc (312cu in) 225bhp engine came in 1956; the next year there were four V-8 options, the largest with 5768cc (352cu in) and over 300bhp. In the late 1950s some of Ford's NASCAR-aimed performance components were available for the T-Bird, and – as a response to the fuel-injected Corvette of 1957 – Ford built 100 cars with 5112cc in engines and Paxton-McCulloch superchargers, which produced outputs conservatively rated at 325bhp.

Once the name had been applied to mundane touring cars, the pre-1958 T-Birds achieved 'status'. More might have been achieved if the corporate minds had stayed closer to the original concept – in the early 1960s, Ford even toyed with the idea of resurrecting the original body and mounting it on a modified Fairlane floorpan, before deciding to go for the Mustang.

Specification (1956)
Engine: 90-degree V-8; 96·5 × 87·4mm, 5112cc; pushrod ohv; Ford carburettor; 225bhp at 4600rpm.
Gearbox: three-speed automatic (optional three-speed manual).
Chassis: pressed steel main members; front suspension independent by wishbones, coil springs and dampers; rear suspension by live axle, semi-elliptic springs and dampers; four-wheel drum brakes.
Dimensions: wheelbase 259cm/102in; **track** 142cm/56in.

1957 model

Ford Mustang

Ford cultivated a 'performance image' in the 1960s, but since the Thunderbird had been allowed to grow fat and soft, they started the decade without a sporting car in their range. When the Mustang arrived in the spring of 1964 it fitted the image and was the car many Americans wanted – sales of a million in two years put that beyond dispute – but purists criticized it as a special-bodied Falcon, and indeed the wide variety of engine and transmission options were borrowed freely from the Falcon, Fairlane and Galaxie lines. As a saloon, homologated as a four seater, it enjoyed a worthy competitions career; at the same time, Carroll Shelby was to make a fierce two-seater of it.

The variety of engines was intended to spread its initial appeal across the 'personal car' market. Initially a 2·8-litre 101bhp six, a 4·2-litre 164bhp V-8 and a 4·7-litre 210bhp V-8 were listed (but up to 7 litres and 335bhp would be on offer by 1968), with three- and four-speed manual gearboxes or Ford Cruise-O-Matic three-speed automatic transmission. A platform chassis with body panels welded to it resulted in effect in a unitary structure, and was novel for a US manufacturer. The option range was wide, and disregarding such frills as 'rally pac' instruments it included 'special handling' suspension and, soon after introduction, Kelsey-Hayes disc brakes in place of the inadequate Fairlane drums. More to the point, all the Cobra tuning expertise could now be applied to the V-8 Mustangs.

Shelby transformed the car, taking as a basis the fastback body which came late in 1964. In its best-known GT-350 (5·7-litre) form it had just two seats, revised suspension and steering, wide wheels, Warner gearbox, limited-slip differential and the 350bhp-plus Cobra engine. Then came the Thunderbird 428-engined – and nose-heavy – 210kph (130mph) GT-500, before the 'Shelby Mustang' was sold to Ford. The lighter, further-modified, competition GT-350s were good SCCA competitions cars, while as saloons the Mustangs were very competitive in Europe (following the Alan Mann-prepared cars which won the 1964 Tour de France).

Inevitably, the Mustang grew, was then 'downsized' until the cycle started again with the Pinto-based Mustang II which, with 2·3- and 2·8-litre V-6s (and a 5-litre V-8 from late 1974), did not compare well with its European counterpart, the Capri. The small Mustang that came in 1978, had notchback or fastback bodies, coil-spring suspension all round, and the same three basic engines with the option of a Garrett AiResearch turbocharger on the smallest unit.

Long before that, the Boss Mustang had been the dominant Trans Am car of 1970, notably the Bud Moore-prepared cars with competition 302 engines offering around 460bhp, refined suspension, reworked brakes and aerofoils. Together with the Shelby cars, that sort of machine created the Mustang image that lingered into the 1980s ...

1965 4·7-litre '289'

Specification (road cars)

Engine: *1964* – straight-six; 88·9 × 74·7mm, 2781cc; pushrod ohv; Ford carburettor; 101bhp at 4400rpm.

1964 – 90-degree V-8; 101·6 × 73mm, 4727cc; pushrod ohv; Ford carburettor; 271bhp at 6000rpm.

GT500 – as above, but 115 × 101mm, 7014cc; two Holley carburettors; 335bhp at 5400rpm.

1978 – straight-four; 96·04 × 79·4mm, 2301cc; single ohc; single Holley carburettor and Garrett AiResearch turbocharger; 118bhp at 5200rpm.

Gearbox: three/four-speed manual or three-speed automatic.

Chassis: platform (see text); front suspension independent by wishbones, coil springs, dampers and anti-roll bar; rear suspension by live axle, half-elliptic leaf springs and dampers; four-wheel brakes, drums on early models, then disc front/drum rear.

Dimensions: wheelbase 259cm/102in; **track** 142cm/56in (147cm/58in on GT500).

Ford GT40

In the mid-1960s Ford of America, like other manufacturers before and since, decided that if their motor sport programme was to have international impact it had to include victory in the Le Mans 24-hour race. Fundamental to this was European expertise, and once negotiations with Ferrari had fallen through, Ford set up a Ford Advanced Vehicles operation in Britain and established a liaison with Eric Broadley, to build a car owing much to his Lola racing coupe of 1963, the first European out-and-out sports-racing car to be designed around a US V-8.

The GT40 which appeared in the spring of 1964 was a striking mid-engined coupe. It had a sheet steel semi-monocoque centre section, with fuel carried in the two box side sills, and subframes fore and aft. Bodywork was in glass fibre, and noticeably clean, with radiator air flow from an under-nose pressure area; a rear spoiler was added after tests with the prototype had shown up high-speed handling shortcomings.

The proposed engine was a twin-ohc developed for USAC racing, but that programme fell behind schedule and a 4195cc (289cu in) 350bhp pushrod-ohv V-8 was substituted. Initially it drove through a Colotti gearbox in unit with the rear axle, but later a ZF unit was used. The GT40 made its race debut at the Nurburgring, but the 1964 season was one of frustration and learning. At Le Mans one of the team cars led the race, one set a new lap record, and a timed top speed of 317·8kph (197·5mph) was achieved, but all three cars retired.

The race cars were taken over by Carroll Shelby in 1965 and Broadley returned to his Lola activities, while the main FAV role became GT40 production – the car was increasingly favoured by private entrants (there were to be ten at Sebring in 1966) and its Le Mans career was to blossom astonishingly after Ford had turned their corporate back on this race. Reliability was the first aim in 1965, and a victory in the early-season Daytona 2000km must have seemed promising, but there were no further wins until the end of the year and all four GT40s retired at Le Mans.

Two of the works cars at Le Mans had been Mk2s – referred to just as that, not as 'GT40 Mk2' – which were prepared by Kar Kraft in the USA. The body was little changed, but a modified version of the 7-litre (427cu in) Galaxie V-8 was used. This produced up to 485bhp, less than in NASCAR tune in the interests of reliability. Galaxie components were also used in the transmission; failure of the T-444 gearboxes put the works cars out of the 1965 Le Mans race (where one was timed at 320kph/199mph).

The car was mildly revised for 1966, and its potential was fulfilled. The season started with first, second, third and fifth in the Daytona 24 hours, and second behind the open X-1 derivative at Sebring. Le Mans saw a strong entry of Fords – eight Mk2s and five

GT40s – and Mk2s dominated the 24-hour race, taking the first three places.

In 1967 the formidable Mk4 appeared. This outstanding sports-racing car used a unitary honeycomb body shell, lighter and stiffer than the Mk2. Engine was the 7-litre unit, rated at 500bhp, and reliable. Dan Gurney and A J Foyt shared one to gain Ford's second Le Mans victory, at 218kph (135·48mph), and then Ford withdrew from racing.

Meanwhile, 107 GT40s had been built by FAV at Slough, 31 of which were intended for road use (others were later converted). Seven Mk3s were also produced: this was announced as the definitive road version, with a detuned (306bhp) engine and improved interior trim, although there never seems to have been any serious intention of marketing it in quantity in the face of a general trend against high-performance cars. This concept was revived on a small scale in 1981, when Safir Engineering built a few roadgoing GT40s with a simplified specification including a 300bhp Boss Mustang V-8 engine.

Specification

Engine: *GT40 (representative 'production' model – see text)* – 90-degree V-8; 101·6 × 72·9mm, 4736cc; pushrod ohv; four twin-choke Weber carburettors; 390bhp at 7000rpm.

    Mk 2 – as above, but 107·5 × 96·1mm, 6997cc; single Holley carburettor; 485bhp at 6200rpm.

    Mk 4 – as above, but twin Holley carburettors; 500bhp at 5000rpm.

Gearbox: four-speed manual (five-speed manual on GT40 from 1965).

Chassis: *GT40 and Mk 2* – sheet steel semi-monocoque centre section with square-tube reinforcement and subframes front and rear; front suspension independent by double wishbones, coil springs and hydraulic coaxial dampers; rear suspension independent by single transverse top link, lower wishbones, twin trailing arms and hydraulic coaxial dampers; four-wheel disc brakes.

    Mk 4 – as above, but with unitary aluminium honeycomb monocoque.

Dimensions: *GT40* – wheelbase 241cm/95in; track 137cm/54in.

    GT40 (1969) – wheelbase 241cm/95in; front track 146cm/57½in; rear track 149cm/58½in.

    Mk 2 – wheelbase 241cm/95cm; front track 145cm/57in; rear track 142cm/56in.

    Mk 4 – wheelbase 241cm/95cm; track 140cm/55in.

1966 Mk 2

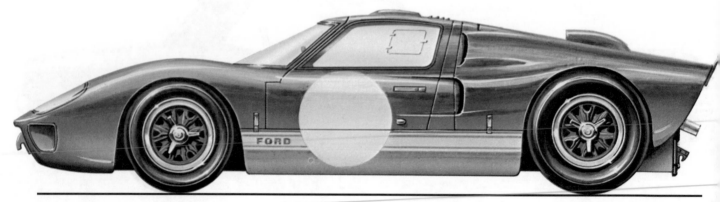

JW Automotive/Gulf GT40 (1968 Nurburgring 1000Kms)

1967 Mk 4

For the JWA-Gulf team, Len Bailey devised the 'Mirage' version, lighter and with a smoother body, using 4·7-, 5·0- and 5·7-litre engines, with a ZF gearbox. First victory for a Mirage came in the 1967 Spa 1000km. Changed regulations meant that JWA resorted to GT40s again in 1968-69, logically developed with a little less weight, uprated brakes and engines stroked to 4992cc. In 1968 they won the championship races at Brands Hatch, Monza, Spa and Watkins Glen; and one of their cars became the first GT40 to last through the 24 hours at Le Mans – it led for the last 18 hours, and won at 184·96kph (114·93mph). In 1969 the GT40 was theoretically outclassed, but once again a JWA car won at Le Mans, by around 100 metres after an extraordinary late-race duel between Jacky Ickx and Porsche driver Hans Herrmann. It was a fitting climax to the main-line career of the GT40.

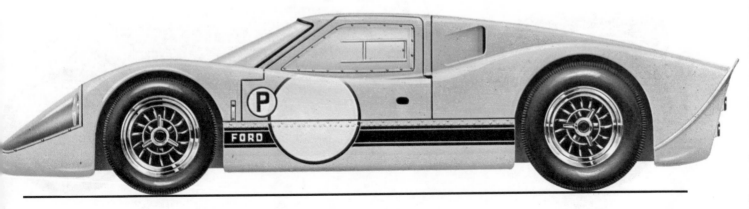

Frazer Nash chain-drive models

When the market for that very basic vehicle, the GN cyclecar, showed marked diminution in 1922, the partners Godfrey and Nash left the company, the latter establishing himself in Kingston, Surrey, to build a new sports car, the Frazer Nash. This employed the old GN-type transmission, unique for its solid rear axle and separate drive chains, with sprockets and dog clutches for each of three forward speeds and reverse – a light, quick-changing system conveniently accessible for changes of ratios in competition work.

Eschewing the old air-cooled vee-twin, Nash chose conventional power units, his first established model, the Boulogne in 1925, using the well-known 69 × 100mm Anzani side-valve engine. Installed in a light, simple frame of GN 'bedstead' type with quarter-elliptics at each end, the power-to-weight ratio, and hence acceleration, was highly stimulating, and the maximum speed was in excess of 110kph (70mph), coupled with direct and responsive handling.

When the Aldingtons took over the business from Nash in 1927 they developed a four-speed gearbox for the Boulogne and replaced the ageing Anzani engine with a 1½-litre ohv Meadows. By 1931,

this car had been developed into the TT Replica, one of the most popular of all 'Nashes and epitomising the breed with its stark lines, well set-back radiator, minimal open two-seater body, slab rear fuel tank and 'crab' track. As well as being aesthetically pleasing, however, the cars enjoyed the good handling qualities inherent in the solid rear axle and the high-geared rack-and-pinion steering, permitting extremely fast 'power-on' cornering and controlled four-wheel drifting. The TT Replica could exceed 130kph (80mph), but every example of the marque (of which there was a confusing variety of models such as Interceptor, Colmore, Nurburg, Exeter, etc.) was remarkably versatile, being able successfully to contest trials, driving tests, races, hillclimbs, sprints and long-distance rallies.

From 1933 a smoother Blackburne six-cylinder twin-cam engine in 1·5- and 1·65-litre forms became available as an alternative to the Meadows, and Frazer Nash's own Gough-designed single-ohc four, based on the Meadows, was also offered. Exponents of these unique chain-driven sports cars were dubbed 'the Chain Gang' for obvious reasons. The last car was assembled as late as 1939.

Specification

Engine: *From 1927* – Meadows straight-four; 69 × 100mm, 1496cc; pushrod ohv; twin carburettors; 62bhp at 4500rpm.
    From 1933 – Blackburne straight-six; 57 × 98mm, 1498cc or 60 × 98mm, 1667cc; twin ohc; two/three carburettors; 70/74bhp at 5000rpm.
    From 1934 – Gough straight-four; 69 × 100mm; 1496cc; single ohc; twin carburettors; 60bhp at 4500rpm.
Transmission: four-speed manual by multiple chain-and-sprocket drive (see text).
Chassis: pressed steel side members; reversed quarter-elliptic front springs; quarter-elliptic rear springs; friction dampers; four-wheel drum brakes.
Dimensions: wheelbase 259cm/102in, but from 1933, optional 274cm/108in; **front track** 122cm/48in; **rear track** 107cm/42in.

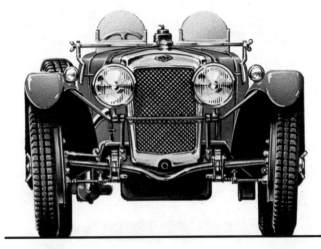

1934 TT Replica (Blackburne engine)

Frazer Nash 2-litre Le Mans replica

When the Aldington brothers of AFN Ltd sought another car design to augment their own highly specialised chain-drive Frazer Nash, they chose the advanced German BMW with its six-cylinder ohv engine, independent front suspension and tubular frame. The sports Type 328 Frazer Nash-BMW became a serious contender in British competitions between 1937 and 1939, only the Second World War bringing to a close a striking run of successes.

In 1946, with BMW of Munich out of action, AFN arranged with the Bristol Aeroplane Company for the latter to manufacture the 328 engine, with detail improvements, for installation in their own range of Bristol cars, and in a new, super-sports Frazer Nash model, the High Speed, which appeared in 1948. Beneath a very stark and purposeful exterior this had a welded tubular chassis and transverse-leaf ifs, much as they had been on the pre-war 328, although the live rear axle was now suspended on BMW Type 326 longitudinal torsion bars and located by a central A-arm.

BMW-type rack-and-pinion steering featured, and with up to 120bhp from the three-carburettor engine in a 690kg car, this exciting vehicle amply lived up to its name 'High Speed'. A private owner took his to Le Mans in 1949 and finished a brilliant third,

whereupon the model name was changed to 'Le Mans Replica'. Despite a high price the car sold briskly to drivers wishing to combine fast road use with competition work in sports-car racing and rallying.

The favourable power-to-weight ratio meant remarkable acceleration and a maximum speed of 185kph (115mph), with impressive reliability. Handling was light, precise and outstandingly controllable, and major race victories were scored in the 1951 Targa Florio and British Empire Trophy, and the 1952 Sebring 12 hours, while lesser wins at home and abroad were legion. Being made in small numbers, post-war Frazer Nashes were virtually hand-built, enabling buyers to specify their own degree of engine tune, body fitments, colour, etc.

In 1952 a lightened, slimmer Le Mans Replica Mark II appeared, finishing second in the Jersey Road Race, and in 1953, further improved with a de Dion-type rear axle, a Mark II won its heat and placed second overall in the British Empire Trophy race on the Isle of Man. Three years later AFN installed the 3168cc BMW V-8 engine in the de Dion-axled competition chassis, thereby producing an outstanding Grand Tourer which they called the Continental.

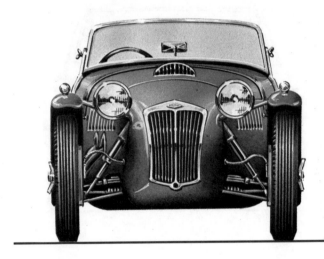

Specification *(Mk 1)*
Engine: Bristol-BMW straight-six; 66 × 96mm, 1971cc; cross-pushrod ohv; triple carburettors; 110-120bhp (according to tune) at 5500rpm.
Gearbox: four-speed manual.
Chassis: welded tubular side members; front suspension independent by transverse leaf spring and wishbones; rear suspension by longitudinal torsion bars and A-bracket; hydraulic dampers; four-wheel hydraulic drum brakes.
Dimensions: wheelbase 244cm/96in; **track** 122cm/48in.

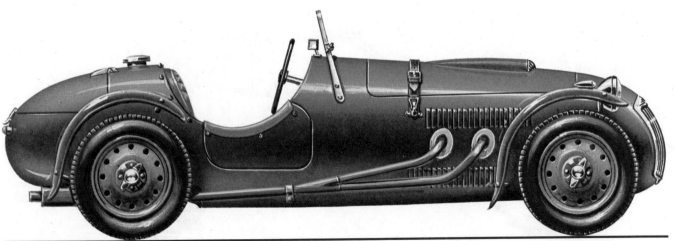

Ginetta G15

The well-proportioned little G15 sports coupe was the most successful of a long line of Ginetta models, with production surpassing the 500 G4s and eventually reaching 800. These figures lift the Walklett brothers' company well above the general run of British specialist constructors, although its origins were similar to many of the others – G1 was very much a one-off special, G2 turned out to be such a sound sports special that it created a demand for replicas, and so another minor marque was born, as a side-line to a general engineering firm.

The G15 was a tiny coupe, sometimes likened to the Lotus Elan (G14 could have been even closer, had it got into production). It was launched in the autumn of 1967, perhaps prematurely as considerable modification was needed before it actually became available in the summer of 1968. Like others of the type, it was offered in kit or assembled form, and bought-in components were used where feasible. Apart from its Triumph Spitfire front suspension, the Hillman

Imp was a major source: from it came the engine (in its twin-carburettor Sport form), transmission and semi-trailing arm rear suspension. The compact glass fibre body was bonded to a tubular chassis, and its unladen weight of only 570kg meant that even with a mere 875cc to propel it, the G15 was a brisk performer, with a maximum speed not far short of 160kph (100mph). It combined well-balanced road holding with a harsh ride, hinting at Ginetta's competition background and perhaps a lack of development resources in this sometimes difficult area. The two-seater cockpit was cramped, well equipped if not very well laid out, and luggage accomodation was surprisingly generous for such a small car.

The G15 was popular and successful in club racing, especially in its G15S version, which used a 998cc Imp engine developed by the Chrysler (née Rootes) competitions department. Production ended in the spring of 1974, leaving the larger and sleeker front-engined G21 as the sole Ginetta model.

Specification
Engine: Rootes straight-four; 68 × 60·37mm, 875cc; single ohc; twin Stromberg carburettors; 51bhp at 6100rpm.
Gearbox: Rootes four-speed manual.
Chassis: square-section tubular; front suspension independent by wishbones, coil springs and dampers; rear suspension independent by semi-trailing arms, coil springs and dampers; disc front/drum rear brakes.
Dimensions: wheelbase 208cm/82in; **front track** 124cm/49in; **rear track** 123cm/48½in.

GN Cyclecar

The GN was the most successful British example of that cross between the motorcycle and the car, the cyclecar. This spartan class of vehicle was born before the First World War as a more stable and less exposed option to the motorcycle-and-sidecar units then widely used by family men of modest means. Low cost was vital, and while many cyclecars were crude, the GN in maturity possessed engaging sporting characteristics, thanks to a high power-to-weight ratio combined with relative reliability.

Produced from 1911 to 1922 by H R Godfrey and A F (Frazer) Nash, the early catalogue models had a GN-designed 90-degree air-cooled vee-twin engine with inlet-over-exhaust valves, installed in line in a simple frame with wooden side members and quarter-elliptic springs front and rear. Transmission was through a chain-driven countershaft carrying two sprockets of different size, one or other being engaged by a dog clutch and driving the rear wheels by side belts.

The design was steadily improved, most tangibly by repositioning the engine across the frame to improve cooling and permit the use of a flywheel clutch, transmitting through a propellor shaft to a bevel cross shaft. This time the two sets of chains and sprockets served as the final drive to a solid axle, again with dog clutches actuated by bell cranks. After the First World War the number of chain sets was increased to four, providing three forward speeds and reverse, while the wooden frame was replaced by one of pressed steel.

The weight of the standard post-war GN two-seater was little over 400kg with road equipment, and this spidery machine could exceed 80kph (50mph). A somewhat brash sporting edition was the Légère with alloy pistons, polished aluminium body, wheel discs and plated parts, while still more special was the Vitesse, with its engine converted to ohv with vertical pushrods, extra-sparse bodywork and staggered bucket seats.

In 1922, the Vitesse gained a much improved engine with single chain-driven ohc operating inclined valves, and ball-and-roller engine bearings. This unit, evolved through racing, gave some 25bhp, and the Vitesse could attain a noisy, vibratory, exciting 108kph (67mph). The departure of both Godfrey and Nash from the company, and the advent of the Austin Seven in 1922 broke the spell. The new proprietors' efforts to turn the cyclecar into a respectable automobile failed, although the multi-chain and dog clutch transmission lived on in Nash's own Frazer Nash cars well into the mid-1930s.

1922 Vitesse

Specification

Engine: *standard model (1919-21)* – air-cooled 90-degree V-twin; 84 × 94mm, 1087cc; inlet-over-exhaust valves; single carburettor; 17bhp (approx.) at 2400rpm.

    Vitesse (1919-20) – as above, but pushrod ohv.

    Vitesse (1922) – as standard, but single ohc; 25bhp at 2600rpm.

Transmission: three speeds plus reverse, manually operated by quadruple chains and dogs.

Chassis: channel steel side members; reversed quarter-elliptic front springs with longitudinal radius arms; quarter-elliptic rear springs; rear-wheel drum brakes.

Dimensions: wheelbase 259cm/102in; **track** 107cm/42in.

Healey Silverstone

When Donald Healey introduced his first Healey in 1946, he already had a considerable reputation as past chief designer of Triumph and a leading rally driver. It followed that performance was a prime quality in his cars, and his alloy-bodied Elliot saloon was the fastest closed car produced in Britain at the time, even if its curvaceous lines were a little odd. A roadster, virtually identical below the waist line, was made in parallel at the modest Warwick works; the bulky and heavy Sportsmobile followed in 1948.

The faults of that car were corrected in the Silverstone, unveiled in the summer of 1949. The no-nonsense chassis of two sturdy 15cm side members, cross-braced, was inherited from the earlier Healeys with only slight modification, together with the suspension. The engine and transmission were also carried over, being the Riley 2½-litre unit (of pre-war origin) and four-speed gearbox.

The stressed-skin alloy body had contradictory lines, clean and functional, even sleek, but with cycle wings. Oddities were twin headlights within the deep, sloped grille at the front, a horizontally-stowed spare wheel projecting from the neatly-rounded tail so that it acted as a bumper, and a windscreen that retracted into the scuttle, save for the top which remained proud to act as a wind deflector. The car was light (940kg unladen) and the 104bhp engine gave it a top speed of just over 160kph (100mph).

The first version (D) was superseded by the E series in the late spring of 1950, with slightly wider body and thus roomier cockpit and improved luggage space; it was most easily distinguished by its front bumper and bonnet-top air intake. Demand for the Nash-Healey meant that the Silverstone was discontinued a year later, however, when production had reached the modest total of 105.

It achieved a stature out of all proportion to that modest figure through its sporting record. Appropriately, its sporting debut was in a rally, when Healey and Appleyard drove one to a class win in the 1949 Alpine. That success was repeated (by Wadsworth and Corbishley) in 1951, when there was also a class win in the Liege-Rome-Liege. But the Silverstone's reputation rested more on its record as a club-racing car through the 1950s, for it was relatively easy to drive and it had few vices.

Specification

Engine: straight-four; 80·5 × 120mm, 2443cc; pushrod ohv; two SU carburettors; 104bhp at 4500rpm, rising to 106bhp at 4800rpm in 1951.

Gearbox: four-speed manual.

Chassis: cross-braced frame; front suspension independent by trailing links, coil springs, dampers and anti-roll bar; rear suspension by rigid axle, Panhard rod, coil springs and dampers; four-wheel drum brakes.

Dimensions: wheelbase 259cm/102in; **front track** 137cm/54in; **rear track** 140cm/55in.

Hispano-Suiza Type 15T 'Alfonso'

The 'Alfonso' Hispano was a pioneer of the 'big flexible four' sports car formula, as emulated by Vauxhall and Bentley over the following 15 years. It was strange that such a car came from Spain, a country inexperienced in automobile production and marketing, but its creator, the Swisss engineer Marc Birkigt, knew European road conditions well and seized the opportunity of adapting a successful racing design for use on the roads.

Birkigt had produced a 2·6-litre long-stroke four which won important road races at Boulogne and Ostend in 1910, and he made this the basis of the Hispano-Suiza Type 15T, a direct forerunner of the sports car. The racing engine measured 65 × 200mm (2655cc) and had side valves in a T-head layout in which the inlet and exhaust valves were on opposite sides of the cylinders, operated by twin camshafts in the crankcase. However, it allowed for large inlet valves, and the engine produced over 60bhp in racing tune.

To achieve similar power with more tractability on the 15T road car, Birkigt increased the bore to 80mm and reduced the stroke to 180mm, giving 3620cc. The crankshaft ran in four plain bearings, and output claims varied between 57bhp and 64bhp at 2300rpm. The three-speed gearbox was in unit with the engine (advanced practice in those days), final drive was by propeller shaft at a time when chains were still extant, and springing was by semi-elliptics all round. Here, then, was the vintage sports car formula, eight years before what we now call the Vintage era had even opened.

That most enthusiastic motoring monarch, King Alfonso XIII, was one of the first to sample the 15T and appreciate its high top-gear performance, general flexibility and precise, high-geared steering, and the car soon came to be known as the 'Alfonso'. In 1911 main Hispano-Suiza production was moved from Barcelona to a new factory in Paris, where Alfonsos were turned out until 1914.

A four-speed gearbox, two chassis lengths and several body styles became available, one of the most popular among motoring sportsmen of the day being a short, open two-seater of rakish aspect, with long, lean wings and large-diameter wire wheels.

Specification

Engine: straight-four; 80 × 180mm, 3620cc; side valves in T-head; single carburettor; 60bhp (approx.) at 2300rpm (see text).

Gearbox: three-speed manual; optional four-speed manual from 1912.

Chassis: pressed steel side members; semi-elliptic springs front and rear, but three-quarter-elliptic rears from 1912; rear-wheel brakes and transmission brake.

Dimensions: *short-chassis model* – **wheelbase** 264cm/104in; **front track** 122cm/48in; **rear track** 122cm/48in.
    Long-chassis model – **wheelbase** 300cm/118in; **front track** 122cm/48in; **rear track** 130cm/51in.

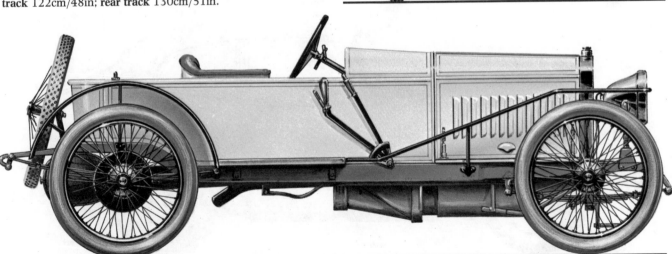

Honda S800

Inevitably, Honda's early cars echoed motor cycle practices, and none more so that the little sports cars which spread the name of this then-new car manufacturer widely during the mid-1960s. High-revving engines, with needle roller cranks and con-rod bearings and very close tolerances, were the norm for the little Hondas and most sports Hondas had chain final drive, none of these features being commonly favoured among the majority of the world's automotive manufacturers.

The first cars had a 360cc engine (33bhp at 9000rpm) or a 492cc 40bhp unit, a five-speed gearbox and chain drive from the differential via outboard sprockets – housed in 'chain cases' which ensured correct alignment and acted as trailing link suspension members – to each of the rear wheels. The first Honda car exported to Europe was the S500, which had a 531cc 44bhp engine. The neat aluminium chain-driven ohc engine was then taken out to 606cc, to give 57bhp at 8500rpm in the S600 of 1964. This model had a 145kph (90mph) top speed.

In the S800 engine size was further increased, to 791cc: this gave 70bhp at 8000rpm, with a wider torque band than the smaller unit and hence less need for constant gear-changing (four gears were standard, a five-speed gearbox being optional in this model). A conventional hypoid bevel transmission was fitted. The suspension, ifs and live rear axle, gave good handling but the ride varied considerably according to load. The cockpit was inevitably a little more cramped than that of the S800's rivals, such as the Midget, but it was better equipped. In performance terms it matched those market sector rivals, which had larger engines, with a maximum speed of 155kph (95mph).

Always more popular in export markets than in its native Japan through its 1967-70 life, the S800 became familiar in open and coupe forms. It was also raced at both club and international level, enjoying some success, particularly in class awards. After 1970, however, Honda's attentions turned to larger models (based on the Civic range) and the S800 seemed to fade away rapidly while outwardly similar British models with considerably less advanced engines continued to find buyers.

Specification

Engine: straight-four; 60×70mm, 791cc; twin ohc; four Keihin carburettors; 70bhp at 8000rpm.
Gearbox: four-speed manual.
Chassis: ladder frame, with separate body; front suspension independent by wishbones, longitudinal torsion bars, dampers and anti-roll bar; rear suspension by live axle, trailing arms, Panhard rod, coil springs and dampers; disc front/drum rear brakes.
Dimensions: wheelbase 200cm/78½in; **front track** 116cm/45½in; **rear track** 118cm/46½in.

Hotchkiss Grand Sport

Although the elegant and refined six-cylinder Hotchkiss Grand Sport may seem to epitomise Grand Touring, its performance in arduous competitions was of distinctly sporting calibre. Built at St Denis, a Paris suburb, this ancient marque had much of the character of a limited-production British quality car, partly perhaps because the company was run by an Englishman, H M Ainsworth. The basic design was conservative, with a six-cylinder pushrod ohv engine and semi-elliptic springing at a time when many European manufacturers were rapidly standardising ifs.

Like Delahaye and Talbot, Hotchkiss came suddenly to the forefront by pitching their designs into competition. They chose rallying in preference to sports-car racing, and succeeded brilliantly by winning no fewer than six Monte Carlo Rallies between 1932 and 1950. After achieving the hat-trick in 1932, 1933 and 1934, and also winning the 1934 Paris-Nice Trial, Hotchkiss introduced a new open sporting variant of their sturdy 3½-litre six, calling it the Paris-Nice Speed Model.

The 86 × 100mm, 3485cc engine had a statically- and dynamically-balanced seven-bearing crankshaft, twin Solex carburettors and high compression, mustering 115bhp at a mere 3500rpm, which made for a 150kph (95mph) roadster with every comfort. In 1935 Bertarione, the talented Sunbeam-Talbot-Darracq designer, joined Hotchkiss, and in 1936 a shorter-wheelbase 125bhp close-coupled saloon was introduced, capable of over 175kph (nearly 110mph) and called the Grand Sport.

In performance, stability and reliability, this model proved outstanding; it achieved 0–80kph (50mph) in 10sec and possessed excellent brakes and light steering. Although after the Second World War Hotchkiss adopted coil-spring ifs and offered Cotal electric transmission as an option, the pre-war Grand Sport accounted for three more Monte Carlo Rally victories in 1939, 1949 and 1950.

Harsh fiscal taxation in their native France killed off the splendid big-six Hotchkisses (as it did the rival Delahayes, Delages and Talbots) and after 1954 the St Denis plant was put to producing Jeeps, vans and lorries.

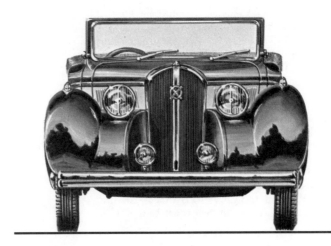

Specification
Engine: straight-six; 86 × 100mm, 3485cc; pushrod ohv; twin Solex or Stromberg carburettors; 120bhp at 3800rpm.
Gearbox: four-speed manual.
Chassis: pressed steel side members with cruciform bracing; semi-elliptic springs and hydraulic dampers front and rear; four-wheel Bendix mechanical drum brakes (but Lockheed hydraulic brakes in 1936 only).
Dimensions: wheelbase 279cm/110in, but 283cm/111½in from 1938; **track** 142cm/56in.

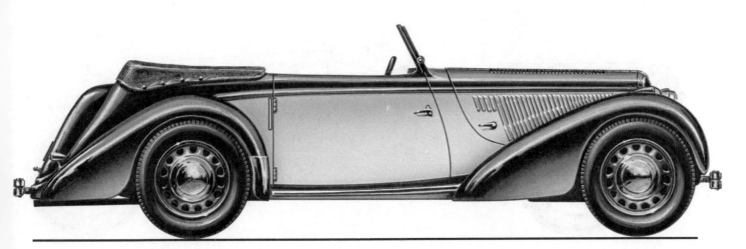

HRG

Sharing with Morgan the rarity of a Vintage specification in post-Vintage times, the HRG won many friends among discerning competition motorists. The three founders whose initials made up its name, E A Halford, G H Robins and H R Godfrey, all had strong links with the Vintage decade, Halford and Godfrey with GN and Robins with Trojan.

The 1½-litre sports two-seater they produced at Tolworth, Surrey, was totally purposeful and utterly devoid of 'styling', although it nevertheless contrived to be attractive in appearance. The simple, shapely radiator was set well back in classic style, exposing the tubular front axle, reversed quarter-elliptic springs and big brakes; rear suspension was by semi-elliptic leaves sliding in trunnions.

The engine was the classic four-cylinder 69 × 100mm Meadows 4ED, putting out about 58bhp on twin SU carburettors and a Scintilla magneto. It could propel the 710kg open two-seater at 145kph (90mph), although maximum speed was not as important a factor on the HRG as its acceleration, decceleration and phenomenal manoeuvrability.

The car was remarkably versatile, being equally at home in town, fast touring, speed hillclimbing, tackling the muddiest of trials, the trickiest of rally sections or an MCC High Speed Trial at Brooklands.

The first two-seater was delivered in 1936; for 1939 a switch was made from the ageing Meadows engine to the 68 × 103mm three-bearing Singer ohc unit and a synchromesh gearbox, while the smaller 60 × 95mm Singer engine went into the same chassis as the much cheaper '1100'.

In 1938 a 1½-litre Meadows HRG went to Le Mans, becoming the second 1½-litre car home, while in 1939 it won the class. After the Second World War, HRGs went 'new look' with the Aerodynamic, scientifically if not aesthetically superior, although the old hard-sprung chassis shook the 'tank' bodywork severely. The classic two-seaters were still produced, however, and after 30 Aerodynamics had been made their production ended. In 1949 three private Aerodynamics were rebuilt with lightweight open bodywork, winning the 1½-litre class both at Le Mans and Spa.

Meanwhile the 'vintage'-style 1500s and 1100s accumulated innumerable successes in races, hillclimbs and international rallies and in 1953 the newer Singer SM 1500 ohc engine replaced the old long-stroke unit. The last HRGs were completed in 1956, taking total production to 241. A revised Twin Cam with all-independent springing, tubular chassis, disc brakes and other modern features was projected but sadly did not get beyond the prototype stage.

Specification

Engine: *1½-litre* – Meadows straight-four; 69 × 100mm, 1497cc; pushrod ohv; twin SU carburettors; 58bhp at 4500rpm.

   1500 (from 1939) – Singer straight-four; 68 × 103mm, 1496cc; single ohc; twin SU carburettors; 61bhp at 4800rpm.

   1500 (from 1953) – as above, but 73 × 89·4mm, 1496cc.

   1100 (from 1939) – as above, but 60 × 95mm, 1074cc; 44bhp at 5200rpm.

Gearbox: four-speed manual, Moss non-synchromesh from 1936, Singer with synchromesh from 1938.

Chassis: pressed steel side members; quarter-elliptic front springs; semi-elliptic rear springs; friction/hydraulic dampers; four-wheel drum brakes.

Dimensions: wheelbase *(1½-litre)* 262cm/103in, *(1500)* 263cm/103½in, *(1100)* 255cm/100½in; **front track** 122cm/48in; **rear track** 114cm/45in.

1948 1500 model

Invicta S-type

Although widely known as the '100mph' or 'low-chassis' Invicta, the exciting 4½-litre sports model which first appeared at the 1930 Olympia Show was more correctly the S-type. The inspiration behind this marque was Noel Macklin, a prolific car producer who was earlier involved with the Eric Campbell and the Silver Hawk, and subsequently with Railton, displaying in all of them a predilection for incisive, straight-edge radiators and bonnets, and a profusion of rivets.

On looks alone, the S-type Invicta promised to be a winner, and undoubtedly in more propitious times and circumstances it would have survived longer than it did. Despite its distinctive low build (11½cm ground clearance) the S enjoyed several striking successes in European rallying, a field of competition which above all demanded ample ground clearance. An Invicta S-type driven by Donald Healey – who played a major part in its development – won the 1931 Monte Carlo Rally outright, while similar cars won Glacier Cups for losing no marks in the 1931 and 1932 International Alpine Trials, and were also placed second in the 1932 Monte Carlo Rally. Such success tended to discount a widely circulated claim that it was too low, and would spin out so suddenly as to be uncontrollable. Several fine performances on the twisty Shelsley Walsh hill further demolished this contention.

The engine of the Invicta S was the 4467cc pushrod-ohv six-cylinder Meadows proprietary unit, fitted with twin SU carburettors and dual ignition. A major charm of this rugged long-stroke engine – as 4½-litre Lagonda exponents could confirm – was its remarkable low-speed torque and flexibility, enabling the lazy driver to pull away in top gear from below 16kph (10mph), remaining there until the 150kph-plus (over 95mph) maximum was reached.

The chassis, substantially built and embodying numerous phosphor-bronze and gunmetal castings, was underslung at the rear and carried semi-elliptic springs all round, with hydraulic dampers. The compact open body seated four (just) and wore the popular slab rear fuel tank and Rudge wire wheels; two external flexible exhaust pipes graced the nearside bonnet. A small, handsome, squarish radiator with stone guard was set well back in bronze trunnions embodying shock-absorbing rubber balls.

This fine looking British sports car deserved a better fate than the Depression allowed it; less than 100 had been built when production ended in 1934.

Specification

Engine: Meadows straight-six; 88·5 × 120·6mm, 4467cc; pushrod ohv; twin carburettors; 115bhp at 3200rpm.
Gearbox: four-speed manual.
Chassis: pressed steel side members, underslung at rear; semi-elliptic springs and hydraulic dampers front and rear; four-wheel drum brakes.
Dimensions: wheelbase 300cm/118in; **track** 142cm/56in.

Jaguar SS100

Bill (later Sir William) Lyons was not only a clever designer and a shrewd businessman; he was a first-rate psychologist, who knew what his customers wanted – looks to please and impress, good performance, and value for money – and set out to provide them. When he founded the SS concern in 1931 he produced a striking if flamboyant two-door coupe which swiftly evolved into more elegant and practical form. It had a six-cylinder Standard side-valve engine, but Lyons' next aim was for SS to have its own ohv units, in the development of which W M Heynes and Harry Weslake played important roles.

In September 1935 details of the new SS Jaguar pushrod-ohv range were released; two handsome four-door saloons and a breathtaking 2½-litre short-wheelbase two-seat sports model, the SS100. This took the customary 'Le Mans' format: stoneguarded radiator, big headlights, long low bonnet, flared wings, big wire wheels and 77-litre slab rear tank, but the lines were masterfully incisive, and the price was sensational.

Although the '100' in the car's title referred to the bhp from the seven-bearing ohv engine (actually 104bhp at 4500rpm), many saw in it the promise of 100mph (160kph), although this was some 8mph (13kph) beyond its capabilities. At the autumn 1936 Brooklands meeting, however, a specially tuned and stripped SS100 lapped at 168kph (104·41mph) to finish second in a four-lap race. Twelve months later Jaguar sprang another surprise with an 82 × 110mm, 3½-litre version of the SS100, which in normal production form could attain the magic 'century', albeit with the windscreen folded flat to help.

One of these bigger-engined models, again specially prepared, bettered the 1936 Brooklands act, this time lapping at 189·9kph (118·02mph) and winning its race at 180kph (111·85mph), while the same car also set a new class record on Shelsley Walsh hill. Such successes apart, however, the SS Jaguar 100 was more a rally car than a racer: its short wheelbase, firm semi-elliptic springing and forward-biased weight distribution made it tricky on the twistier circuits.

Its four-speed gearbox with synchromesh on second, third and fourth had well chosen ratios, while the Girling brake system was powerful and effective. Good seating gave an ideal driving position, while engine flexibility further endeared this handsome car to its owners. Privately owned examples did well in major rallies, while the striking lines guaranteed innumerable *concours* successes. Production ended with the coming of war in 1939, but the SS100, superseded in 1948 by the even more sensational XK120, fired an effective parting shot by winning the 1948 Alpine Rally outright.

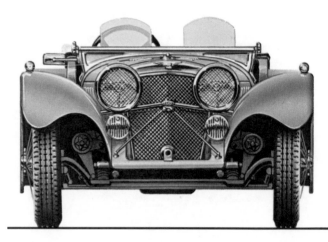

1936 2½-litre model

Specification

Engine: 2½-litre – straight-six; 73 × 106mm, 2664cc; pushrod ohv; twin carburettors; 104bhp at 4500rpm.
        3½-litre – as above, but 82 × 100mm, 3486cc; 125bhp at 4250rpm.
Gearbox: four-speed manual.
Chassis: pressed steel box-section side members, underslung at rear; semi-elliptic springs and friction/hydraulic dampers front and rear; four-wheel Girling drum brakes.
Dimensions: wheelbase 264cm/104in; **track** 137cm/54in.

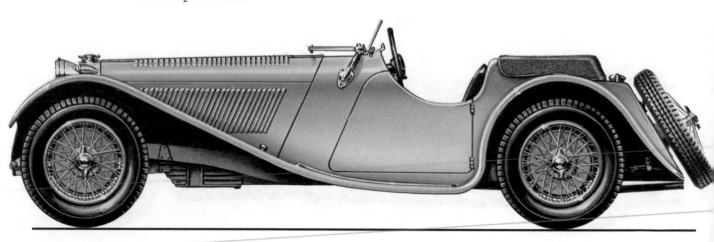

Jaguar C-type

Outwardly standard XK120s had performed well at Le Mans in 1950, one climbing to third before retiring, and this persuaded William Lyons that outright victory in the most prestigious of road races could be a very real possibility. So in the autumn of that year work started on a competitions version, designated XK120C, but which through usage became known simply as the C-type. The project was kept secret as late as possible, and that heightened the effect when the dramatically handsome cars appeared at Le Mans ...

The C-type was more closely related to the XK120 than many 'competition versions' of production cars, the engine having conventional improvements (catalogued or soon to be catalogued) to produce just over 200bhp at 5800rpm, even on low-grade fuel, while the standard gearbox and rear axle were used. The rear suspension was modified to a simple layout with a transverse torsion bar, centrally mounted so that in effect it acted as twin torsion bars, with trailing links to carry the axle. Weight was saved in the frame and body, the former a spaceframe of varying diameter tubes, advanced for its day, the latter a low drag shell of deceptively simple appearance, effective and elegant, practical in having a single front-hinged nose section for accessibility, and with an adequate cockpit giving a low seating position at a time when many sports car constructors took it for granted that a driver's upper torso should be exposed to the elements. Lower weight meant that the standard

drum brakes coped a little better than on the XK120.

Jaguar kept the car 'under wraps' until Le Mans in 1951, where it was sensational and successful: although one of the three cars retired early, Moss set a lap record in another before also retiring, and Whitehead and Walker won the race. Later came a one-two-four in the TT.

In 1952 the C-type gained disc brakes, first raced in a Mille Miglia entry. Despite this, Moss in that car was reputedly passed on a straight by a Mercedes 300SL, an episode which led to a panic revision to the nose; lower drag did presumably result, but so did severe overheating, which at Le Mans led to the retirement of all three team cars within two hours of the start.

Meanwhile, privately-owned C-types were appearing, one notable result being gained at Rheims, where Moss won in a car fitted with discs. Production eventually exceeded 50, and C-types were successful all over the world. Production models were slightly heavier than works cars and had drums as standard, but many were converted to discs.

The 1953 works cars had lighter chassis and bodies, modified rear suspension, disc brakes, and up to 220bhp. Although Jaguar ran Ferrari close in the sports car championship, Le Mans was again the main objective, handsomely achieved when the team cars were first, second and fourth.

1953 Le Mans car

Specification

Engine: straight-six; 83 × 106mm, 3442cc; twin ohc; twin SU carburettors (but three Weber carburettors on 1953 works cars); 210bhp at 5800rpm (see text).
Gearbox: four-speed manual.
Chassis: spaceframe; front suspension independent by wishbones, torsion bars and dampers; rear suspension by rigid axle, radius arms, transverse torsion bar and dampers; four-wheel drum brakes (but discs on 1953 works cars).
Dimensions: wheelbase 244cm/96in; track 129cm/51in.

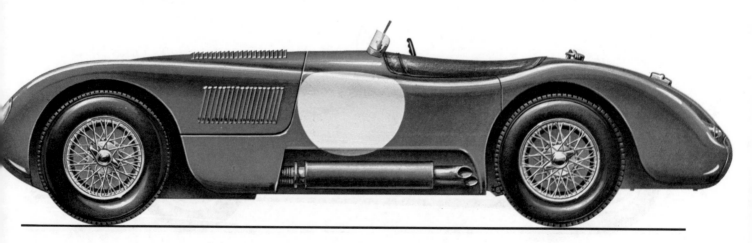

Jaguar XK models

Few cars remain as instantly recognisable throughout the motoring world decades after production has ended as the XK Jaguars; and few designs so influenced the changing shape of the sports car in the 1950s. There were other progenitors, but none of them was mass-produced, none remained so long in production, none had associated models with such illustrious competitions records. For all their faults – and undeniably there were faults, many stemming from the simple fact that they were built down to a price – the XKs achieved almost instant 'classic' status, and have retained it.

Yet this series of cars with which the name Jaguar will always be associated came into being almost incidentally, to publicize a new engine intended for saloons. Work had been started during the Second World War, progressing through XF and XG experimental units, to the XJ four- and six-cylinder units of 2·0 litres and 3·2 litres and the straight-six XK of 3442cc. This had twin overhead cam-shafts – the first mass-produced twin-cam unit – it was highly efficient, with excellent breathing (one of the basic criteria), it developed its target power from the start, and through over-engineering it had considerable development potential. It even looked purposeful. It was ready for production in 1948, when the MkVIII saloon for which it was intended was two years off.

Early in 1948, therefore, it was decided to introduce the engine in a limited run of sports cars, with the possibility that the four-cylinder unit might be offered as an alternative. The substantial chassis of the car owed something to the MkV saloon, and in part the body lines might have owed something to slightly earlier Continental cars, but the overall effect of the XK120 shown at the 1948 London Motor Show was stunning. It was styled as a whole, its lines flowing smoothly from neat grille to slender tail.

The suspension, torsion bars at the front and live rear axle with semi-elliptics, gave a ride which seemed more 'boulevard' than sporting but with a degree of softness not incompatible with good handling; the four-speed gearbox was heavy, but could cope with the power; the drum brakes were a weak point, until discs were introduced later. It was a two-seater, with a none-too-spacious cockpit and the oddity of a bench seat.

In retrospect, it seemed naive of Jaguar to plan a production run of 200, and build those in traditional manner with alloy panels over an ash frame. Most of them were sold in advance of early-1950 completion, and time was then lost while Pressed Steel prepared dies for steel bodywork production. Eventual sales exceeded 12 000, in three types – open, drophead coupe and hard top.

XK120s soon appeared in competition, and in 1950 won events as diverse as the Tourist Trophy and the Alpine Rally (one of Appleyard's three successive penalty-free Alpines, which gained him a Gold Cup), while Claes gained an outstanding victory in the 1951 Liege-Rome-Liege. By that time, however, racing interest in Jaguars had focused on the C-type sports-racer.

The successor to the XK120 was the XK140, introduced in autumn 1954. The straight-six was uprated to give 190bhp, it had revised suspension and weight distribution (within fractions of 50/50) and an increase in weight, the result of a wider body which allowed the cockpit to be opened up. With the optional 210bhp engine, maximum speed was up to 207kph (129mph), compared

1949 XK 120 Roadster

Specification

Engine: *XK120* – straight-six; 83 × 106mm, 3442cc; twin ohc; twin SU carburettors; 160bhp at 5000rpm.

    XK140 – as above, but 210bhp at 5750rpm (see text).

    XK150 – as above, but 210bhp at 5500rpm; also with 87 × 106mm, 3781cc; up to 265bhp (see text).

Gearbox: four-speed manual; optional automatic on XK140 and XK150.

Chassis: box-frame; front suspension independent by wishbones, torsion bars and dampers; rear suspension by live axle, semi-elliptic springs and dampers; four-wheel drum brakes (but discs on XK150).

Dimensions: wheelbase 259cm/102in; **front track** 129cm/51in; **rear track** 127cm/50in.

with the 190kph (120mph-plus) of the XK120.

The XK140 lasted until 1957, when the XK150 appeared. This was heavier again, even looking a little portly after the fine lines of the XK120, with more creature comforts built in (including the two child-size rear seats that had been introduced on the XK140). The 210bhp Blue Top engine was to all intents and purposes standardized (although the 190bhp unit was still listed), but top speed was down to 200kph (125mph). In 1958, however, a 250bhp 'S' version was offered, and for 1959 a 3·8-litre engine giving up to 265bhp was available, so that speed was not sacrificed for room and comfort, even if handling was marginal in some respects – indeed, the 3·8S was a 240kph (150mph) car. Most importantly, it had Dunlop disc brakes front and rear.

Borg Warner automatic transmission became an option on late XK140s and was continued on the XK150, underlining the transformation from sports car to GT car, or roadster. The basic format remained unchanged, however, and was therefore a little dated in several respects when XK150 production ceased in 1961 (after 9400 had been made) to make way for a replacement as headline-catching as the XK120 had been 13 years earlier.

XK 120 (Silverstone, 1951)

1958 XK 150S Coupe

Jaguar D-type

In 1953 Jaguar laid down the successor to the C-type, producing a car that was to become even more famous and which remains one of the best-remembered and most evocative sports cars. Although some production-based components were used – above all, the famous six-cylinder engine – the D did not derive from its predecessor, being smaller, lighter and more up-to-date in conception.

Central to this was a strong magnesium-alloy monocoque, with the engine and front suspension held in a tubular frame whose main members were carried through to the back of the monocoque (production versions differed in that they had an unstressed light-alloy central structure, while the tubular frame was in steel instead of magnesium alloy). Nose and rear body sections were unstressed. The front suspension came from production models, as in the C, but the rear axle was carried by four flat trailing arms (its unsprung weight was always a handicap to handling on twisting or bumpy circuits). Wire wheels gave way to alloy disc wheels, and disc brakes were naturally standard. A new Jaguar four-speed gearbox was used.

A dry sump version of the engine and separate radiator header tank enabled aerodynamicist Malcolm Sayer to achieve a low bonnet height, a worthwhile contribution to the superb overall shape, elliptical in basic cross section and with svelte longitudinal lines set off by the distinctive vertical stabilizing fin. Initially there was a screen round the driver's side of the cockpit (the other seat could be covered) but full-width screens appeared in 1955, as did lengthened noses.

In its 3442cc form the engine was first rated at 245bhp; some units were enlarged to 3781cc, while a change of rules led to a short-stroke 2986cc version, which proved oddly unsuccessful; a 2482cc version was also built for TT 'handicap specials'. The first fuel-injected units were raced in 1956; these were rated at 272bhp, compared with the 277bhp delivered by 1956 carburettor engines.

Two of the team cars retired at the 1954 Le Mans debut, the third being narrowly defeated, more by dirty fuel than by the winning 4·9-litre Ferrari. The first victory came within weeks, however, in the Rheims 12-hour race. In long-nose form, a works car won the sombre 1955 Le Mans 24-hour race, and the same event in 1956 saw the Jaguar team's last appearance with full-blooded sports cars. Only one of its cars finished sixth, but an Ecurie Ecosse D-type won, and this team won again in 1957. D-types won countless other races into the 1960s, even taking fourth, fifth and sixth places in a USAC-style race at Monza in 1957. D-types were actually manufactured on a production line basis – not inappropriate, as the car was quite tractable for road use – and out of this production 16 fully-road-equipped two-seaters designated XKSS were built.

Specification

Engine: straight-six; 83 × 106mm, 3442cc; twin ohc; three Weber twin-choke carburettors; 245bhp at 5500rpm, rising to 277bhp at 6000rpm in 1956.

    also (see text) – as above, but 87 × 106mm, 3781cc; Lucas fuel injection; 306bhp at 5500rpm.

Gearbox: four-speed manual.

Chassis: monocoque centre section with tubular frames front and rear (see text); front suspension independent by wishbones, torsion bars, dampers and anti-roll bar; rear suspension by rigid axle, trailing arms, transverse torsion bar and dampers; four-wheel Dunlop disc brakes.

Dimensions: wheelbase 230cm/90½in; **front track** 127cm/50in; **rear track** 122cm/48in.

1956 3·4-litre (Ecurie Ecosse team)

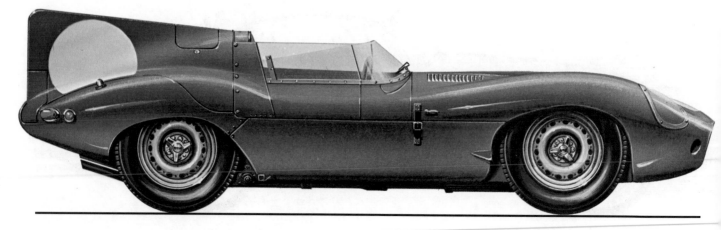

Jaguar E-type

The balanced and flowing lines of the E-type were justifiably rated 'sensational' when the car was announced in 1961, although they clothed detail shortcomings early in its life and would appear a little dated towards its end, in 1975. It followed the D-type in such respects as its fully-stressed steel monocoque with front and rear subframes, but its direct forerunner was a lightweight car which ran at Le Mans in 1960, with a fuel-injection engine and coil spring irs. The E-type was first offered with fastback and open bodies, both two-seaters.

In 1964 a 4·2-litre straight-six succeeded the first 3·8-litre unit, and drove through an improved, but still heavy, all-synchro gearbox. In 1966 the wheelbase was 'stretched' by 23cm, something of the elegant proportions being sacrificed to make a 2+2 coupe (a year later, detail changes to meet US safety regulations further detracted from the car's lines). There was early disappointment that the E had not turned out to be a full-blooded sports car, but the point that this was not the intention was later underlined when power steering and automatic transmission were offered.

The Series 3 came in 1971, with the long-awaited V-12 and the longer wheelbase standardized. The new engine was rated at 272bhp, well below its paper potential and improving only modestly on the six – and the extra weight of the V-12 resulted in slight loss of maximum speed, from the near-240kph (150mph) of the early cars to 233kph (145mph). But the V-12 delivered its power very smoothly, and the S3 inherited the excellent ride and handling qualities of the earlier versions, so that the new model remained an outstanding GT car.

As mentioned, the E-type's competitions career began with the prototype, run by Cunningham at Le Mans in 1960; it failed to finish, but later that year it enjoyed some success in the USA. True E-types were raced in 1961, in secondary events, and were placed fourth and fifth at Le Mans in 1962. A small batch of lightweight competition cars followed for 1963; these had alloy-block engines with D-type heads, Lucas fuel injection and power outputs of up to 344bhp, modified suspension and in some cases ZF five-speed gearboxes – no two were identical. Outright success was confined to secondary races, however, and aerodynamic appearances were shown to be deceptive as maximum speeds did not match those achieved by D-types a decade earlier (even with 'low-drag' bodies). The V-12 made an impression only in SCCA events, where the Group 44 team cars were very successful.

Total E-type production was 75 584, of which 15 292 were V-12s. The model marked the end of a line which brought enormous success and prestige to Jaguar, which bore the Lyons stamp and reflected his policy of giving extraordinary value for money. They were – and still are – striking motor cars.

1961 Series 1

Specification

Engine: *Series 1* – straight-six; 87 × 106mm, 3781cc; twin ohc; three SU carburettors; 265bhp at 5500rpm.

Series 3 – 60-degree V-12; 90 × 70mm, 5343cc; single ohc per bank; four Stromberg carburettors; 272bhp at 5850rpm.
Gearbox: four-speed manual; optional Borg-Warner automatic.
Chassis: monocoque; front suspension independent by wishbones, torsion bars, dampers and anti-roll bar; rear suspension independent by wishbones, radius arms, coil springs and dampers; four-wheel disc brakes.
Dimensions: *Series 1* – wheelbase 244cm/96in; track 127cm/50in.

Series 3 – wheelbase 267cm/105in; front track 138cm/54½in; rear track 135cm/53in.

Jensen-Healey

The earliest Jensens had some sporting qualities, but while the company built bodies for other companies' sports cars, their own range was limited to high-performance executive cars, businessmen's expresses. However, as outside contract work dried up in the second half of the 1960s, and the company was taken over, expansion became essential to survival. The group which took control in 1970 was headed by Kjell Qvale, a major US West Coast sports car distributor, and among appointments to the Jensen board were Donald and Geoffrey Healey. The much-loved Austin Healey 3000 had been axed in 1967, and now enthusiasts looked for a British replacement – after all, the "last of the Big Healeys", as the Datsun 240Z was cynically dubbed, was hardly the real thing . . .

Nor, by that yardstick, was the Jensen-Healey unveiled at the 1972 Geneva Motor Show. It was an open two-seater, with an integral steel body which had sensible rather than inspired lines (first and foremost in Jensen minds was the need to meet US regulations in all respects). Conception-to-production was quick, as Healey already had an AH3000 successor in mind, and bought-in components were used. Suspension, ifs and live axle came from the

Vauxhall Viva, the gearbox from the Sunbeam Rapier, and after several possibilities had been explored the Lotus twin-cam engine (with cam covers inscribed 'Jensen-Healey') was adopted – it was well-suited to the purpose, Lotus' surplus production capacity assured supplies, and it propelled the Jensen-Healey to a 190kph (120mph) maximum speed.

Cockpit was comfortable and well laid-out, while the luggage space was adequate for a car which really had a roadster role. Inevitably, a GT version followed, in 1976, but despite the designation the interpretation was interesting in that it resulted in a semi-estate car appearance which, if anything, enhanced the lines of the open model to which it was grafted. It was nominally a 2+2, but was in reality a two-seater with generous load space.

Both the Jensen-Healey and the Jensen GT were well-received, especially in America, and there was no lack of orders despite murmurings from early owners. However, as the GT appeared the company was running into problems with working capital; the Receiver tried hard to keep the company going, but the physical assets of Jensen had to be disposed of piecemeal in the summer of 1976.

Specification

Engine: Lotus straight-four; $95 \cdot 2 \times 69 \cdot 3$mm, 1975cc; twin ohc; twin Dellorto carburettors; 140bhp at 6500rpm.
Gearbox: four-speed manual, but five-speed on GT.
Chassis: integral; front suspension independent by wishbones, coil springs and dampers; rear suspension by live axle, upper and lower arms, coil springs and dampers; disc front/drum rear brakes.
Dimensions: wheelbase 234cm/92in; **front track** 135cm/53in; **rear track** 133cm/52½in.

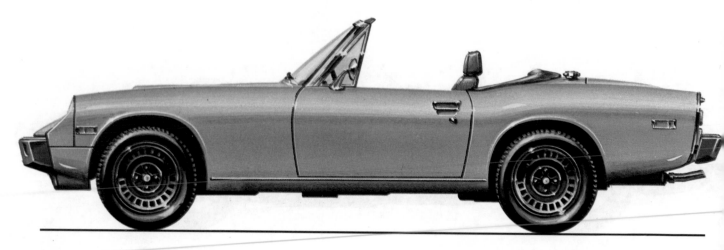

Jowett Jupiter

One of the bigger surprises of the post-Second World War British motor industry was that Jowett, after making sturdy, utilitarian flat-twin cars for over 25 years, should re-launch in 1947 with a sophisticated 1½-litre flat-four-engined saloon, designed by Gerald Palmer and featuring torsion-bar springing, unitary chassis/body construction, and good aerodynamic form. Called the Javelin, its potential encouraged the production of a sports version, using as many Javelin parts as possible.

Initial development was undertaken in 1949 by ERA, and the prototype was called the ERA-Javelin, with Prof Ing Eberan Eberhorst (joint designer of the 1938-39 Grand Prix Auto Union), contributing the chassis. The integral structure of the Javelin could not be adapted for use in an open two-seater, so an early tubular space-type frame was built, incorporating Jowett's torsion bar springing and with the flat-four engine 'hung' at the forward end of a sturdy bridge which also supported the front suspension.

A remote-control gear lever and rack-and-pinion steering were employed, the overall build was markedly lower than the Javelin, and with a weight of 940kg the new sports Jowett could approach 145kph (90mph), coupled with excellent acceleration and road-holding. The company put it into production in 1950 as the Jupiter, simultaneously embarking on a competition programme which produced success almost first time out, when one won the 1½-litre class at Le Mans.

The lessons of racing were applied both to the standard Javelin and the Jupiter, which appeared in 70bhp competition form in 1951 as the R1, less comely with cycle-type wings and narrow lower-drag body, but both lighter and faster. It enjoyed a splendid season, scoring class wins in the Sebring 12-hour, Le Mans 24-hour, Dundrod TT and Watkins Glen races, while standard Jupiters scored a one-two class victory in the Monte Carlo Rally.

In 1952 the R1 scored Jowett's third successive 1½-litre class victory at Le Mans. Unfortunately, the situation at Jowett deteriorated in 1953, and although at Earls Court the company showed a new fibreglass-bodied sports prototype – the Jupiter R4 – with electric fan-cooled engine, box-section frame and semi-elliptic rear springing, this car never went into production. In the following year, almost unbelievably, the courageous Bradford company had to close down after almost 50 enterprising years in the motor industry.

Specification

Engine: flat-four; 72·5 × 90mm, 1486cc; pushrod ohv; twin Zenith carburettors; 62·5bhp at 4500rpm.
R1 competition – as above, but 70bhp.
Gearbox: four-speed all-synchromesh manual.
Chassis: tubular frame; front suspension independent by wishbones, longitudinal torsion bars, dampers and anti-roll bar; rear suspension by rigid axle, transverse torsion bars, trailing arms, dampers and anti-roll bar; four-wheel Girling drum brakes.
Dimensions: wheelbase 236cm/93in; **front track** 130cm/51in; **rear track** 124cm/49in.

Kissel Speedster

Founded by a family of German immigrants, the Kissel concern graduated from making farm implements to gas engines, and then to automobiles by 1906. The factory was in Hartford, Wisconsin, the first cars being called Badger, changing to Kissel Kar a year later, and to plain Kissel just after the First World War.

The staple product was an 84 × 139mm, 4·6-litre six called the 6/45; the engine had side valves, alloy pistons and cylinder head, and gave 61bhp at 2300rpm. It powered a rakish open two-seater called the Speedster, with a double-dropped frame to lower the build, an attractive arched radiator, sliding seats (long before these became normal wear) and a moveable steering wheel to ease entry and exit. The body featured a 'rumble' seat for two passengers and two further 'reserve' seats which pulled out of each side like drawers.

The car was finished as standard in bright yellow, so they nick-named it the 'Gold Bug', although other colours were available – if you paid extra! Maximum speed was around the 110kph (70mph) mark – quite enough then with rear brakes only – and the Speedster became a serious rival to the Mercer Raceabout in the exclusive American sports-car field, offering top quality throughout, with enterprisingly-styled coachwork. The strong, precision-built chassis had automatic lubrication, but early models betrayed the age of their design with scroll-type three-quarter-elliptic rear springs, until these gave way to semi-elliptics in 1922.

Also in 1922, the Speedster's lines became sleeker, the combined wings and running boards being replaced by heavy, fixed cycle-type wings and individual cast-aluminium steps, while a golf bag carrier on the nearside and a rear luggage trunk emphasised the leisured status of the average Kissel customer. In 1923, the old 6/45 engine was phased out and an improved 6/55 side-valve unit, with stroke reduced to 130mm giving 4·3 litres, took its place.

From 1924, 4·7-litre straight-eight Lycoming engines in lengthened chassis became optional, and Lockheed hydraulic external contracting four-wheel brakes were adopted. By 1928, with the Depression looming large, the Wisconsin factory was encountering sales resistance; despite a 'new-look' range in 1929, the last Kissel appeared in 1931, only 16 cars being made that year by a company which had once produced over 2500 annually.

1923 model

Specification

Engine: *from 1920* – straight-six; 84 × 139mm, 4622cc; side valves; single carburettor; 61bhp at 2300rpm.
    from 1923 – as above, but 84 × 130mm, 4343cc.
Gearbox: separate three-speed manual.
Chassis: pressed steel side members; semi-elliptic front springs; rear springs three-quarter-elliptic, but semi-elliptic from 1922; friction dampers; rear-wheel drum brakes, but four-wheel Lockheed hydraulic drums from 1925.
Dimensions: wheelbase 307cm/121in; **track** 143cm/56½in.

Lagonda Rapide

At a time when the great Bentley sports car legend was fading, and world economic straits were leading to the production of numerous small, cheap and dull passenger vehicles, the exciting 4½-litre six-cylinder Lagonda M45 Rapide open four-seater sports car came as a distinct tonic to British motoring connoisseurs when announced in 1934. Built in a factory at Staines, Middlesex, Lagonda was founded by an American named Wilbur Gunn, and owed its name to a small creek near his birth-place in Ohio.

The Lagonda Rapide had a sturdy long-stroke Meadows engine with vertical overhead valves operated by pushrods. This big, flexible unit had earlier been used in the Invicta '100mph' sports car, and later served as a marine engine during the Second World War. As fitted to the Rapide, it had twin SU carburettors, raised compression and other modifications, and drove through a Lagonda-built four-speed gearbox, all mounted in a heavy chassis with semi-elliptic springing front and rear, and extremely powerful servo-assisted brakes with large finned drums.

With its sweeping lines, handsome vertically-slatted radiator and long, elegant wings, the Rapide lived up to its name, and achieved 173kph (108mph) in speed tests at Brooklands. Such was the manufacturer's confidence in its longevity that it was sold with a nine-year guarantee.

The Rapide's all-round potential was exploited by the famous Fox & Nicholl racing stable, which prepared a team of special M45Rs for international sports-car racing, with engines tuned to give around 150bhp. On their first appearance, these cars finished fourth, fifth and eighth in the 1934 Ulster TT, and in 1935 they scored a magnificent victory at Le Mans, breaking Alfa Romeo's four-year hold on the classic 24-hour race. By 1936 the design was growing old, but still managed class wins in the French GP and Belgian 24-hour events, while a year later one averaged 104·44 miles in one hour (168·01kph) at Brooklands with full road equipment.

The production 4½-litre had by then been given a cross-flow head and other modifications by W O Bentley, becoming the LG45, while the Rapide was restyled with revised wings and distinctive outside exhaust pipes. Production of this model was small, however, for it was soon superseded by newer W O Bentley-designed models.

Specification

Engine: *M45* – Meadows straight-six; 88·5 × 120·6mm, 4453cc; pushrod ohv; twin carburettors; 120bhp at 3200rpm.

LG45 – as above, but 130bhp at 4000rpm.

Gearbox: separate four-speed manual.

Chassis: pressed steel side members; semi-elliptic springs and hydraulic dampers front and rear; four-wheel Girling drum brakes.

Dimensions: wheelbase 312cm/123in; **track** 147cm/58in.

1937 LG45

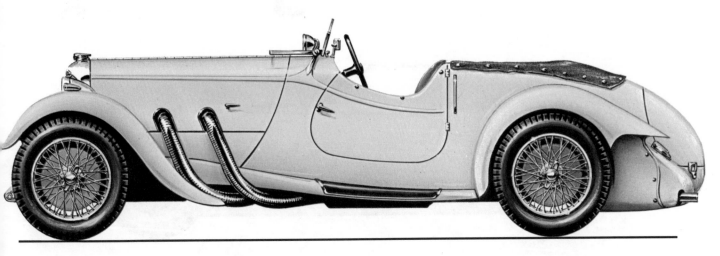

Lamborghini Miura

Ferruccio Lamborghini's entry into the motor industry in the early 1960s was seen as a challenge to Ferrari, even as a reaction to a supposed personal slight by Ferrari, but whatever the specific reason it was a timely entry, in a boom period for high-class, high-performance cars. A contemporary extrapolation of the 'Ferrari' story was that Lamborghini would extend his challenge to the circuits. That never happened, yet most of his cars had the characteristics traditionally ascribed to 'race-breeding' ...

The first were front-engined – the 3½-litre 350GT of 1963 and the 4-litre 400GT of 1966 – with V-12 engines based on a racing design by Bizzarini. Then at Turin in 1965, this engine was shown in a new chassis, transversely mounted between the cockpit and the centre line of the rear wheels. The chassis was designed by Gianpaolo Dallara, with wishbone and coil spring independent suspension all round. Slightly modified for practical use, it was bodied by Bertone, and the complete car created as great a sensation as the original chassis when it was shown at Geneva in 1966 as the P400 Miura.

Later that year it was put into production and it sold well.

The V-12 was in the 4-litre form used in the 400GT and was initially rated at 350bhp (10bhp less than in the front-engined model), while perhaps just to stimulate speculation a 430bhp *corsa* version was mentioned. The engine was twice uprated during the life of the Miura, to 370bhp in the P400S of 1969 and to 385bhp in the P400SV of 1971.

This shapely coupe was unquestionably a success in itself, for around 1200 were built before production ceased in 1972, the year after Lamborghini sold the company he had created. It was practical as a grand touring two-seater, it confounded critics by proving reliable, it had roadholding and handling near to racing standards, and – with an unladen weight of just under 1300kg – it was **fast**: 275kph (170mph)-plus even with the early version of the 4-litre engine.

Beyond that, it set a yardstick for the supercar manufacturers of the coming decade.

Specification
Engine: 60-degree V-12; 82 × 62mm, 3929cc; twin ohc per bank; six twin-choke Weber carburettors; 350bhp at 7000rpm, rising to 385bhp at 7850rpm.
Gearbox: five-speed manual.
Chassis: pressed steel; independent suspension front and rear by wishbones, coil springs, dampers and anti-roll bars; four-wheel disc brakes.
Dimensions: wheelbase 250cm/98½in; **track** 142cm/56in.

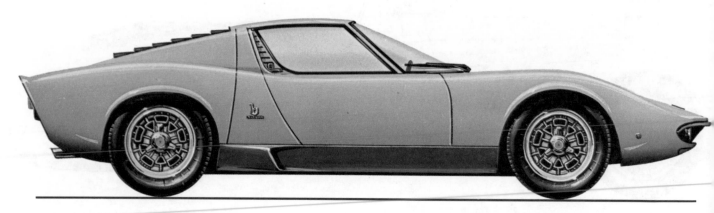

Lamborghini Countach

This extraordinary machine fulfilled all the 'supercar' high-performance functions, although a sports-car purist could well find it lacking in some respects. It was first seen as a show car at Geneva in 1971, and while other styling exercises in that category have reached production form – the Lancia Stratos was a near-contemporary example – the Countach hardly seemed likely to reach the roads. However, towards the end of 1973 it reappeared in production form and as Lamborghini's successor to the Miura.

In this form it had a tubular space frame in place of the prototype's semi-monocoque, with wishbone and coil spring independent suspension all round; it was clothed in the most eye-catching body of the decade, reality requiring that Bertone's original ultra-smooth lines be sacrificed only in the detail of air intakes. Doors hinged at the front, but opened upwards, giving access to a cockpit that was functional and little adorned, with good visibility – at least to the front and sides. The main luggage space was in the extremity of the tail. Unusually, the Countach did not put on weight in the development stage – dry weight was 1300kg.

The original concept had envisaged a 5-litre V-12, which could well have made the Countach a 320kph (200mph) car, but in the event the 4-litre V-12 was used, installed fore-and-aft. In the interests of a near-even weight distribution, the gearbox was mounted ahead of the engine, with a shaft running back to the final drive housed in an extension of the sump. This overall balance meant that the Lamborghini reputation for excellent handling and adhesion was maintained. The claimed maximum speed for this definitive Countach was over 300kph (190mph), although independent tests suggested that 280kph (175mph) was a more realistic figure.

The Countach was a costly car to develop, and when it appeared the general economic conditions favoured more modest cars, such as Lamborghini's smaller Urraco (a 3-litre V-8 260kph/160mph model). Nevertheless, this extravaganza did reach production, and a slightly modified S version appeared in 1977. By then, Lamborghini was heading towards receivership, although Countachs continued to trickle out of the Sant'Agata factory through to the end of the 1970s and beyond.

Specification

Engine: 60-degree V-12; 82 × 62mm, 3929cc; twin ohc per bank; six twin-choke Weber carburettors; 375bhp at 8000rpm.
Gearbox: five-speed manual.
Chassis: multi-tubular; suspension independent front and rear by wishbones, coil springs, dampers and anti-roll bars; four-wheel disc brakes.
Dimensions: wheelbase 252cm/99in; **front track** 150cm/59in; **rear track** 152cm/60in.

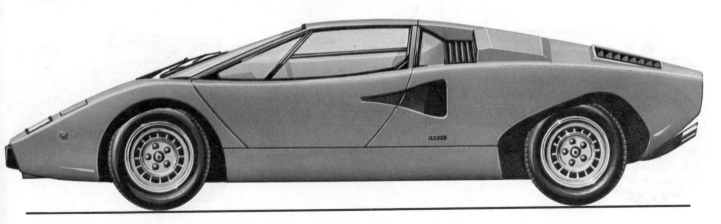

Lancia Lambda

Although its all round performance and roadholding were distinctly sporting, the Lancia Lambda was regarded in its own country more as a fast thoroughbred touring car. Some 13 000 were produced between late 1922 and 1931, engine size rising from 2·1 to 2·4 litres in 1926, then to 2·6 litres in 1928 for the last two of the nine series manufactured.

Recognised as Vincenzo Lancia's masterpiece, the Lambda differed radically in almost all major features from the average car of its time. Instead of a separate chassis, it had the world's first really successful unitary chassis/body construction, steel stampings making up the body sides, scuttle bulkhead and seat traverses, with the whole stressed structure covered by an aluminium skin.

The Lambda also had effective ifs by enclosed vertical coil springs on sliding pillars, which also served as kingpins, rigidly cross-braced by tubes. This system was pioneered on the British Morgan three-wheeler, but Lancia also incorporated telescopic hydraulic dampers – in 1922!

Unorthodoxy also reigned in the engine; a short, compact V-4 with staggered cylinders at approximately 13 degrees to each other, in an aluminium block with inserted steel liners, the vertical ohv being operated by a single ohc. The two exhaust pipes were at the back of the block, forming a hot spot for the inlet manifold in between. The gearbox, with three speeds until 1925, and four thereafter, had a remote control central-change lever.

Effective four-wheel brakes were fitted, the independent front end imparted quite exceptional roadholding and cornering qualities, and although the Lambda was never very fast, its outstanding suspension gave it a cruising speed close to its maximum, which ranged from 114kph (71mph) for the first, to 125kph (78mph) for the final models.

The car's advanced engineering was somewhat offset by its angular, gawky appearance, with long, flat-sided four-seater body, curious tail and high windscreen. Regrettably, Lancia's genius in dispensing with the separate chassis posed an important problem: in order to retain adequate beam strength, the door apertures were made both shallow and narrow, making normal saloon bodywork with full-size doors impracticable. From 1927 to 1931, therefore, a separate platform-type-chassis Lambda became available, while Lancia's next model, the larger Dilambda V-8 of 1929, dispensed with unitary construction altogether to give coachbuilders full rein.

1929 8th series Torpedo

Specification

Engine: *from 1st Series* – 13-degree V-4; 75 × 120mm, 2120cc; single ohc; single carburettor; 49bhp at 3250rpm.

7th Series – as above, but 79·4 × 120mm, 2370cc; 59·5bhp at 3250rpm.

from 8th Series – as 1st Series, but 82·5 × 120mm, 2570cc; 69bhp at 3500rpm.

Gearbox: three-speed manual, but four-speed from 1925.

Chassis: pressed steel integral with body (see text); front suspension independent by enclosed vertical coil springs on sliding pillars and hydraulic dampers; rear suspension by underslung semi-elliptic springs; friction dampers; four-wheel drum brakes.

Dimensions: wheelbase 310cm/122in, but 342cm/134½in from 1925; track 134cm/52½in, but 141cm/55½in from 1925.

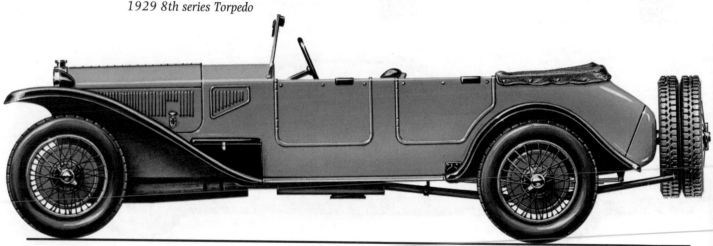

Lancia D20 to D25

Gianni Lancia committed his company to a competitions programme in the early 1950s, initially with the B20 Aurelia GT saloon, which gained excellent category results in 1951-52, and then with a more ambitious sports car challenge. Overall design supervision of this project was entrusted to Vittorio Jano, whose principal lieutenants were Ettore Mina (engines) and Francesco Falco (chassis).

The first sports-racer, the D20 coupe, made its debut in the 1953 Mille Miglia, when four started and the team gained third and eighth places. A major early success came in the spring, when Maglioli gained a Targa Florio victory for the still-new team. The D20 had a spaceframe of small-diameter tubes, all-round independent suspension with a trailing arm and transverse leaf spring at the front (in place of the traditional Lancia sliding pillar) and a similar system at the rear, while drum brakes were inboard front and rear. The engine was a dry-sump 2962cc V-6 rated at a useful 217bhp, but for Le Mans later in the year a Roots-type supercharger was combined with an engine of slightly reduced capacity (2683cc), which boosted output to 240bhp; these cars were not competitive, and in any case all four retired.

Later that year an open version designated D23 appeared, Felice Bonetto winning the Lisbon GP in one, while in the summer the D24 made its debut and was raced alongside the D23 for the rest of the season. The D24 was a shorter, *spyder* derivative, with the transverse-leaf rear suspension abandoned in favour of a de Dion layout; its normal engine was a 3·3-litre version of the V-6. Early failures were followed by first and second in a hill climb (these events still attracted major entrants in Italy at the time), then came a triumph in the Carrera Panamericana which led to these D cars being named 'Carrera'. In Mexico, D24s were first and second (Fangio, Taruffi) while Castellotti's D23 was third; victory was soured by Bonetto's death at the wheel of a D24. The next year opened with a second place at Sebring (and three retirements), followed by three worthy victories, Taruffi's in the Giro di Sicilia and the Targa Florio, and Ascari's win in the Mille Miglia.

Late in 1954 the D25 made its only race appearance, in the TT at Ards in Ulster. This was a substantially revised design, with 3·8-litre engine, five-speed gearbox and outboard front brakes. One placed third, behind a D24 and that proved to be the last major sports car race for Lancia, before the company turned to GP racing, and bankruptcy. While the sports-racers did not wholly fulfil their promise, they did win eight races and ten Italian hill climbs.

Specification

Engine: *D20* – 60-degree V-6; 86 × 85mm, 2962cc; twin ohc per bank; three Weber carburettors; 217bhp at 6500rpm (see text).

D24 – as above, but 88 × 90mm, 3284cc; 265bhp at 6500rpm.

D25 – as D20, but 93 × 92mm, 3750cc; 295bhp at 6200rpm.

Gearbox: four-speed manual, but five-speed on D25.

Chassis: space frame; on D20-D23, suspension independent front and rear by trailing arms, transverse leaf springs and dampers; on D24/25, front suspension as above, but rear suspension by de Dion axle, semi-elliptic springs and dampers; four-wheel drum brakes.

Dimensions: wheelbase *(D20)* 260cm/102½in, *(D24)* 240cm/94½in, *(D25)* 245cm/96½in; **front track** 129cm/51in; **rear track** 125cm/49in.

1953 D24 Carrera

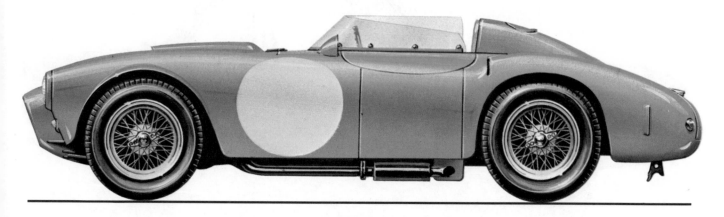

Lancia Fulvia

Remote from the traditional sports car in conception, the Fulvia coupe derived from a saloon, but in its HF sporting versions built up a formidable competitions record, as one of the last effective front-wheel drive cars in rallying. The attractive little 2+2 coupe first appeared early in 1965, the first lightweight HF car coming less than a year later, to be entered in rallies at a time when the Mini Cooper was all-conquering.

It used Lancia's narrow-angle V-4, mounted ahead of the front wheels, initially in 1212cc form and producing 80bhp (90bhp at 6000rpm in the HF, which was also substantially lighter by virtue of its alloy body panels and other components). The gearbox, four-speed in early models, five from 1969, was behind the front axle line. Dunlop disc brakes were fitted all round.

The early cars just had a 160kph (100mph) capability, but this speed was comfortably achieved by the 1298cc version which appeared in 1967, giving a 7bhp increase in the Rallye and Sport models, and – with a revised cylinder head and higher compression ratio – 14bhp more in the HF. At the same time, a bulbous Zagato coupe was built in small numbers, lacking the timeless simplicity of line of the normal production coupe, which remained the rally car for the works team and for many private entrants.

This car reached its peak with the Lancia V-4 in its final form, taken out to 1584cc to give 114bhp at 6000rpm in the 'civilized' 1·6 HF Lusso. The out-and-out competition version of this car – which was actually not far removed from the normal model – built up an excellent record, in events as varied as the RAC Rally (which Harry Kallstrom won in 1969 and 1970) and the Monte Carlo Rally (which Sandro Munari won in 1972). By then its early reputation for fragility was behind it, the engine was 'safe' to 8000rpm (and effective to 7500rpm, with 130bhp plus) in the works cars; handling in competition and production versions was taut and precise, bordering on nervous, the brakes powerful and sure.

The Fulvia was also raced, without conspicuous success, in the European Touring Car Championship and 'hotter' versions, including a *spyder*, were used in some international sports car events.

The Fulvia was displaced in rallying by the Stratos, but the little coupe remained in production until 1976, although by then only the 1298cc S3 was on offer as a 90bhp, 170kph (105mph) sporting coupe; the larger-engined models, together with the Fulvia saloons, had succumbed much earlier, as soon as the Beta appeared.

1969 1·6 HF factory rally car

Specification (*1971 1·6 HF Lusso road car*)
Engine: 13-degree V-4; 82 × 75mm, 1584cc; single ohc; twin Solex carburettors; 114bhp at 6000rpm.
Gearbox: five-speed manual.
Chassis: unitary, with steel body; front suspension independent by wishbones, transverse leaf spring, dampers and anti-roll bar; rear suspension by dead axle, semi-elliptic leaf springs, dampers, Panhard rod and anti-roll bar; four-wheel disc brakes.
Dimensions: wheelbase 233cm/91½in; **front track** 130cm/51in; **rear track** 128cm/50½in.

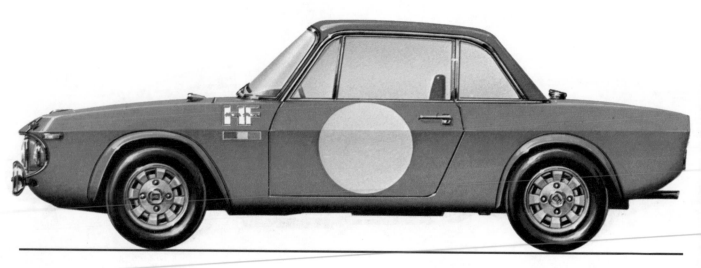

Lancia Stratos

The origins of the most effective and spectacular rally car of the 1970s were in a tiny, frail-looking Bertone styling exercise at the 1970 Turin Show. Outward appearance apart, however, the Stratos which was announced a year later, and which made its competition debut in the Tour de Corse just over 12 months after that, was a very different car. The Ferrari Dino V-6 took the place of the Fulvia V-4 of the Bertone show car, still mounted ahead of the rear wheels in a machine which followed the mainstream of competition car design, having a very strong chassis/body with a central monocoque and tubular subframes front and rear.

The car went through a lengthy development programme, being run in Italian national events (and the 1973 Tour de France, which it won) until it was homologated in autumn 1974. Sandro Munari then drove it to victory in its first two world championship rallies, the San Remo and the Rideau Lakes, and took third place in the RAC Rally (as if to dispel lingering doubts abouts its robustness), while Jean-Claude Andruet won in Corsica. More than the 400 necessary for homologation were produced; some were used as road cars, and a few were raced, with little success apart from the second place achieved by Munari and Andruet in the 1973 Targa Florio; the emphasis was on rallies.

The normal production V-6 was rated at 190bhp, while for competition versions up to 270bhp at 8000rpm was claimed for the two-valve engine (240bhp at 7800rpm was more normal), and a possibly-optimistic 285bhp for the four-valve derivative. The latter unit became ineligible after 1977, but the Group 5 Stratos which Pianta drove to win the 1978 Giro d'Italia had a 335bhp 24-valve engine, and 400bhp-plus was the target for a turbocharged racing programme, dropped after the death of development engineer Mike Parkes.

In rallies the Stratos did not have a great power advantage over its rivals, nor much of a weight advantage, but its balance and – above all – its traction, made the package almost unbeatable. It dominated the world and European rally championships until 1977, when changes in Fiat policy meant 'semi-retirement' for the works cars, but independent teams, notably that run by the French Lancia importers Chardonnet, continued to use the car into the 1980s. By the time its homologation had expired, the Stratos had a long list of outstanding achievements to its name, including four Monte Carlo Rally victories, second place on the Safari, three European Rally Championships and even the European Rallycross Championship.

Specification (*road car*)
Engine: 65-degree V-6; 92·5 × 60mm, 2418cc; twin ohc per bank; three Weber carburettors; 190bhp at 7000rpm (see text for competition units).
Gearbox: five-speed manual.
Chassis: monocoque, with tubular subframes front and rear; suspension independent front and rear by wishbones, coil springs, dampers and anti-roll bars; four-wheel disc brakes.
Dimensions: wheelbase 218cm/86in; **front track** 143cm/56½; **rear track** 146cm/57½in.

1975 factory rally car

Lancia Beta Montecarlo Turbo

To Lancia purists, the 1970s was a decade when the marque's individuality disappeared as it became Fiat's top-of-the-range brand name. But it was also the decade when Lancia gained many rally victories at the highest international level, and the 1980s opened with an international racing championship clearly falling to a Lancia works team. True, the sports car championship had become sadly debased by 1980, but it was won with fitting *élan* and with a car that was fittingly 'special' . . .

The Beta Montecarlo Turbo was a 'silhouette' car, related to the production Beta Montecarlo in little more than name, doors and roof-line in accordance with the regulations. It was a mid-engined sports-racer, with a low-drag (0·32) coupe body whose aerodynamic qualities had been proved in a wind tunnel before being demonstrated beyond question on the circuits. Square-tube subframes at each end of the centre section carried the suspension, the water radiator was in the nose, with oil coolers and the turbocharger intercooler in the left and right rear wings, each with prominent intakes.

The engine was a straight-four, mounted transversely ahead of the rear axle line and angled at 30 degrees. Like Beta production units, it was based on the Fiat twin-cam four, and because of its KKK K27 turbocharger was in linered short-stroke form to give a normal capacity of 1425cc, which put it into the 2-litre division of the championship, as a × 1·4 factor applied to turbocharged engines. In 1979, the engine was rated at 390bhp, for the opening race of 1980 at 400bhp, for the rest of that season at 410-415bhp. This conservative policy of restricting output well within known potential was proved sound in endurance races, where engine reliability was impressive. A Colotti five-speed gearbox and differential was standard.

The model's debut race at Silverstone was a fiasco, but matters improved through the rest of 1979 to the extent that Lancia won the 2-litre division of the championship. In 1980 Lancia fielded the only works team, with fast, reliable cars and strong driver pairings. They won three races outright (at Brands Hatch, Mugello and Watkins Glen), and almost invariably won their class (even when the works cars did not, as at Daytona, an independent Lancia succeeded). Team manager Cesare Fiorio took advantage of favourable conditions at Mugello and Vallelunga to run a car in the over-2-litre class; it beat the Porsches, thus foiling their class clean sweep, which meant that with an unbroken run of victories in their class Lancia took both the overall and Division 2 championships.

The development potential of the car was demonstrated in the German Group 5 Championship, where the short races and liberal regulations enabled Lancia to extract over 450bhp from the same basic engine; Hans Heyer duly won the 1980 series.

Lancia also contested the prestigious Giro d'Italia in 1979 and 1980, using a Montecarlo fitted with a 1995cc supercharged (not turbocharged) Abarth engine; this produced a mere 300bhp at 8000rpm, but offered a wide power band and no throttle lag. For circuit use in 1981 single- and twin-turbo 1775cc versions of the engine were developed, conservatively rated at 480bhp.

Specification *(mid-1980)*
Engine: straight-four; 82 × 67·5mm, 1425cc; twin ohc; Bosch indirect fuel injection with KKK turbocharger; 410bhp at 8800rpm.
Gearbox: five-speed manual.
Chassis: sheet steel centre section, with tubular subframes front and rear; suspension independent front and rear by wishbones, coil springs, dampers and anti-roll bars; four-wheel ventilated disc brakes.
Dimensions: wheelbase 230cm/90½in; front track 172cm/67½in; rear track 192cm/75½in.

1980 factory racer

Lister

Brian Lister's sports-racing cars bridged a gap in the late 1950s, between the fading of the Jaguars and the new breed of lightweight rear-engined cars. They were a sideline for a light engineering company, for whom enthusiasm and publicity were not sufficient to justify the continuation of the marque into a new age, with its predictable sophistication and high costs.

The first Lister appeared in 1954, with a large-diameter tube chassis and de Dion rear end, and with an MG engine. This gave way to a Bristol engine in the following year, and Lister-Bristols began to make a mark in the 2-litre class. A Maserati engine was successfully used for a season, then in 1957 Lister built his first car with a 3·4-litre Jaguar D-type straight-six.

The following year this went into 'production' (fewer than 40 were built) as the definitive Lister. The basic chassis was retained, consisting of 8cm diameter main members cross-braced by tubes and the floor pan, with box sections to carry the front suspension and a de Dion rear end. Although international races were then run under a 3-litre limit, and cars intended for championship events were fitted with Jaguar units at that capacity, most Listers appeared with 3·4-or 3·8-litre Jaguar engines, or the small-block Chevrolet V-8 in sizes up to 5·7 litres. The latter were fitted by Lister's US agent, Carroll Shelby (with GM gearboxes instead of the Jaguar unit), rated as high as 400bhp – considerably more than the Jaguar engine and, save perhaps in the most extreme state of tune, with greater reliability. Whatever the engine, it was mounted well back, and combined with tanks at the rear, this gave a weight distribution of 50/50.

In appearance, these Listers were extraordinarily belligerent, with prominent wheel arches and a bulge over the engine, which in cars run under international regulations rather cleverly offset part of the effect of the mandatory 25cm-deep windscreen, as on these Listers the base line for this measurement was well below the top line of the bonnet (in the USA, especially, smaller screens tended to be used). Down the years many cars were modified, and together with the introduction of the smoother, marginally longer and wider, Costin-designed body in 1959, this was to lead to some discussion about the eligibility of some Listers for historic races ...

In international events the fragility of the 3-litre versions of the Jaguar engine told against the Listers, but with the larger power units used in lesser British and American races they were highly successful. A spaceframe design was essayed for 1960, but only one car was built and the Lister line ended.

1958 Lister-Jaguar

Specification *(Lister-Jaguar)*
Engine: Jaguar straight-six; 76·5 × 83mm, 2986cc; twin ohc; Weber carburettors; 254bhp at 6300rpm (see text).
Gearbox: four-speed manual.
Chassis: tubular; front suspension independent by equal-length wishbones, coil springs, dampers and anti-roll bar; rear suspension by de Dion tube, radius arms, coil springs and dampers; four-wheel disc brakes.
Dimensions: wheelbase 230cm/90½in; **front track** 136cm/53½in; **rear track** 140cm/55in.

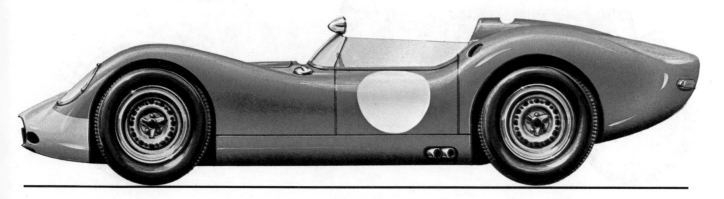

Lea-Francis Hyper

The peak of a remarkably chequered car manufacturing career spanning 56 years was attained by Lea-Francis of Coventry in 1928 when they won the classic Ulster TT, a gruelling 410-mile (660km) road race for production sports cars. The successful car, which defeated a front-drive Alvis by a mere 13 seconds, was the 1½-litre four-cylinder supercharged S-type Hyper, a rakish sports two-seater produced in the face of the financial strictures which afflicted so many smaller concerns in the late 1920s.

The production Hyper had a Type 4ED Meadows engine with a Cozette No.8 vane-type supercharger installed at the front and compressing the mixture at 7psi. Drive passed through a four-speed gearbox and open propellor shaft to a spiral bevel rear axle. Suspension was by semi-elliptic springs which employed phosphor-bronze sliding trunnions instead of shackles, while vacuum servo four-wheel brakes were fitted.

A low, wide-track chassis gave good stability, and the Meadows unit in standard form put out 61bhp at 4100rpm, making the production Hyper a tractable 145kph (90mph) road car. The competition model which won the TT and gained excellent placings and class wins elsewhere, differed internally, having special needle-roller engine bearings, tubular connecting rods and an oil radiator between the front dumbirons; the Cozette supercharger was a No.9 blowing at 15psi and giving 79bhp at 4500rpm. This meant a vivid performance throughout the rev range to a maximum of over 150kph (95mph), offset by fuel consumption of around 20mpg.

Fabric bodywork was used in 1928, but aluminium panels were adopted thereafter, while a distinctive sloping radiator enhanced the lines. For dependable road performance the Hyper required conscientious maintenance, with special attention to the lubrication of the engine and supercharger. Nearly 200 examples of the model, carrying either four-seater touring, coupe or TT two-seater bodywork, were sold, but the world economic depression ended the Hyper's chances and early in 1931 precipitated Lea-Francis into the second of three major financial crises that blighted its history.

Specification
Engine: *production model* – Meadows straight-four; 69 × 100mm, 1496cc; pushrod ohv; single Cozette carburettor and Cozette supercharger; 61bhp at 4100rpm.
  competition – as above, but 79bhp at 4500rpm.
Gearbox: four-speed manual.
Chassis: pressed steel side members; semi-elliptic springs and friction dampers front and rear; four-wheel servo-assisted drum brakes.
Dimensions: wheelbase 282cm/111in; **track** 127cm/50in.

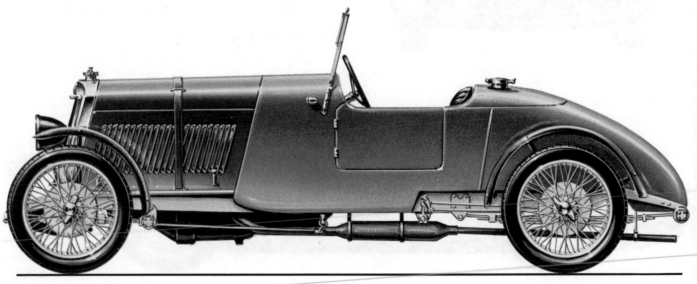

Lorraine-Dietrich Le Mans

Defeat was ever a strong spur, and when the Lorraine-Dietrich team from Lunéville in Eastern France finished eighth and 19th in the first Le Mans 24-hour race in 1923, and second and third in 1924, they returned in 1925 thirsting for the victory they had so narrowly missed – and those defeats produced cars greatly improved over their predecessors, once again demonstrating the great advantages of motor racing as a forcing house for design.

Designed by Marius Barbarou, formerly with the Benz company, the Lorraines which ran at Le Mans in 1923 were production-based 15CV tourers, tuned only as far as the then-rigid rules allowed. The engine was a very strong and flexible 3445cc ohv six with notably slender pushrods and Delco coil ignition, and the cars had left-hand drive and Sankey artillery wheels with two-wheel brakes.

Following 1923 experience the 1924 cars were distinctly more sporting, with twin Zenith carburettors, enlarged valves, raised compression, dual ignition, and slightly shorter, lighter and lower chassis with Rudge-Whitworth wire wheels. The 75 × 130mm engine had a four-bearing crankshaft and put out a lusty 70bhp at 3600rpm, while the sturdy chassis, with long cantilever rear springing and most efficient servo-assisted four-wheel brakes, with-

stood the stress and strain of the rough Le Mans circuit.

In 1925, its motor now giving 75bhp, a 3½-litre Lorraine won the race outright, with another car third, while at Spa one finished second in the Belgian 24-hours race.

In 1926, their golden year, the big blue French cars scored a triumphant one-two-three at Le Mans, averaging a record 106·34kph (66·08mph) and defeating strong Bentley, Peugeot and OM opposition. Naturally Lorraine-Dietrich marketed a replica of their Le Mans winner, and if it lacked the keen edge of the actual race cars, the Type Le Mans B36-S was a fine sporting model of the Vintage era. The engine produced a notably flexible 70bhp and a three-speed gearbox sufficed until 1928, when the weight of option-al cabriolet and coupe bodywork made four speeds desirable.

The Le Mans open four-seater, some examples of which survive in France today, had fine lines with a raffish tail and distinctive vee-formed mudguards, while the quality of manufacture and finish was on a par with that of Lorraine's great rival, the Bentley. Despite a road weight of over 1470kg, maximum speed was around the 145kph (90mph) mark. The B36-S was built in limited numbers until 1930.

Specification *(B-36S)*
Engine: straight-six; 75 × 130mm, 3445cc; pushrod ohv; twin Zenith carburettors; 70bhp at 3000rpm.
Gearbox: three-speed manual; optional four-speed from 1928.
Chassis: pressed steel side members; semi-elliptic front springs; cantilever rear springs; friction dampers; four-wheel servo-assisted drum brakes.
Dimensions: wheelbase 289cm/114in; track 140cm/55in.

1926 Le Mans

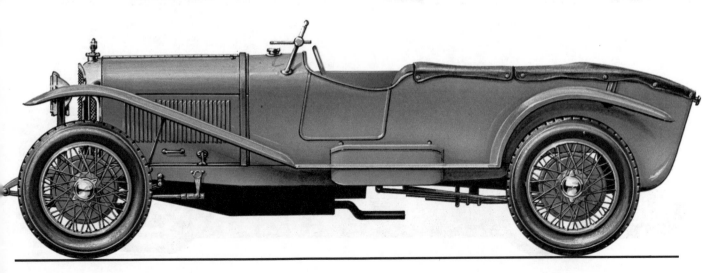

Lola T70

Eric Broadley's first big-engined Lola was his Ford V-8-engined GT car of 1963, which was effectively shelved when he committed himself for more than a year to the Ford GT40 project. In 1965, however, he returned to his Lola independence, with single-seaters and then the T70, which was destined to become one of the most widely used of all big competition sports cars.

It was introduced as an open sports-racer, primarily for the USA although 'two-seater racing car' competition did enjoy a brief European flowering, mainly in Britain, during its life. The T70 chassis was built around a very stiff centre section, a monocoque with a sheet steel floor, side pontoons in steel and alloy housing the fuel tanks, and steel box structures front and rear, the former carrying suspension, the latter with twin extensions for engine mountings and rear suspension. The body was in glass fibre, simple in its lines and effective. Suspension was conventional, with rear brakes inboard of the hub carriers.

The T70 was essentially a 'customer' car, and was from the outset designed to accept virtually any American V-8 (the Chevrolet 5·4-litre unit came to be regarded as 'standard'), while the gearbox could be either a Hewland LG500 four-speed or a ZF five-speed. Fifteen of these first T70s were built, and John Surtees' 1966 CanAm championship stimulated demand for an improved version.

The Mk2, appeared in 1966; its main improvement was in weight saved by using aluminium in place of steel in some areas. International regulations then led to the best-remembered T70, the Mk3 GT, in 1967. This had a sleek coupe top added to the body (which was extended at the rear to allow for the obligatory spare wheel and luggage space above the transmission). The suspension was beefed up, and was not interchangeable with that of the earlier cars, but it remained a weak point. The normal power units were Chevrolet V-8s, but the Mk3 first appeared with a 5-litre (98 × 83mm) twin-ohc Aston Martin V-8 which looked the part – compact and robust – but proved heavy, unreliable and none too powerful, so that the project was short-lived.

A Mk3B (or T76), lighter and generally tidied up, came in 1969. That year saw the best results for the coupes, with a first and second in the Daytona 24 hours its outstanding international result. Generally, however, the T70 needed the steady development it would have received if a proper works team had been run: it lacked stamina for endurance races, although in shorter secondary events T70 entrants gained many good results. Over 100 Mk3s were built (total T70 production reached 150); odd ones were converted for road use, and nine years after production ceased, Lola built three more to meet orders, using parts they held in stock ...

1967 Mk 3 GT

Specification

Engine: *(representative – see text)* – Chevrolet 90-degree V-8; 81·9 × 102·7mm, 5463cc; pushrod ohv; four twin-choke Weber carburettors; 460bhp at 6300rpm.
Gearbox: four-speed Hewland manual or five-speed ZF manual.
Chassis: monocoque; front suspension independent by upper wishbones, lower links, coil springs, dampers and anti-roll bar; rear suspension independent by radius arms, lower wishbones, upper links, coil springs and dampers; four-wheel disc brakes.
Dimensions: wheelbase 241cm/95in; **track** 137cm/54in.

Lotus Seven

Here was an uncompromising car, in which performance in all respects had absolute priority over other considerations such as mere comfort. They were road cars, but even without change they made effective club racing cars, especially in their early Seven and Super Seven forms.

The Seven replaced the Six, Colin Chapman's first production car, in 1957. It was marketed as a kit car, purchasers thereby avoiding payment of some taxes, although an inspection service was available. As the financial advantage of kit purchase dwindled, it became available complete, was slowly evolved, and survived into the 1980s. Almost a decade earlier it had become an anachronism in the Lotus range, and would have been discontinued had not Caterham Car Sales acquired the rights to it in 1973.

The efficiency of any Seven was strictly limited to its primary functions. Cockpit comfort rated low priority, especially for drivers of above-average height or girth, while even large feet could be an embarassment; but a driver could feel at one with a Seven as with few other road machines except two-wheelers. Even a heater was an optional extra in 1980 . . .

Basis of the Seven was a light tubular frame, with Lotus ifs, rear suspension incorporating a BMC (later Ford) rigid axle, and initially such engine alternatives as the Ford 100E or BMC A-series units, in each case offset to the left. Few early cars conformed rigidly to a specification, but matters became tidier when the first Super Seven appeared in 1962.

Relatively, this was almost refined – no more comfortable, but with better weather protection, flared full-size wings to deflect the road spray that swirled past the earlier cycle wings, and a Ford all-synchro gearbox. Engine was the Ford 118E, from subdued 65bhp at 5200rpm form to a Cosworth-modified version producing 95bhp at 6000rpm, usually coupled with such extras as close-ratio gears and an oil cooler. In this form, the car had extraordinary acceleration – 0-80kph (50mph) in 5·7 sec – although this began to fall off towards its 166kph (103mph) maximum – when aerodynamics overcame the power to weight ratio.

Caterham Cars correctly sensed that a demand for the Seven would continue, and usually had a waiting list as component supply problems restricted production to no more than 150 a year (sold in 'kit' form in the UK, fully-built for overseas markets). Caterham discarded the 'softer' Series 4, introduced by Lotus in 1970 with more complex and bulkier glass fibre body, and concentrated on the Mk3. This was offered with the 1·6-litre Lotus Twin Cam, its 126bhp cutting that 0-50 time to 4·4 sec, and raising top speed to almost 180kph (110mph), or the 1·6-litre Ford production engine. The Seven became one of those very rare cars to remain in production beyond the 21st anniversary of its introduction.

1958 S3

Specification

Engine: *Super Seven (1962)* – Ford-Cosworth straight-four; 80·63 × 72·75mm, 1498cc; pushrod ohv; two twin-choke Weber carburettors; 95bhp at 6000rpm.

S3 – Ford straight-four; 80·97 × 77·62mm, 1598cc; pushrod ohv; one Weber carburettor; 84bhp at 6000rpm.

S3 Twin Cam – Lotus-Ford straight-four; 82·55 × 72·75mm, 1558cc; twin ohc; two twin-choke Dellorto carburettors; 126bhp at 6500rpm.

Gearbox: Ford four-speed manual.

Chassis: tubular; front suspension independent by wishbones, coil springs and dampers; rear suspension by live axle, radius arms, coil springs and dampers; disc front/drum rear brakes.

Dimensions: wheelbase 218cm/86in; **track** 124cm/49in.

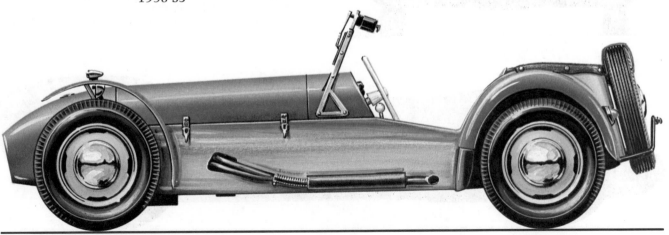

Lotus sports-racing cars

Small-capacity sports car racing was enlivened and changed beyond recognition in the second half of the 1950s by a brilliant succession of cars, with Lotus and Lola setting a development pace which others such as Elva could seldom match. Colin Chapman and Eric Broadley achieved staggering all-round performance advances with very modest resources and using relatively modest engines – sophistication in the areas of suspension, spaceframes, weight-saving and aerodynamics were their keys to success.

The first aerodynamic Lotus sports-racer was the 8 of 1954. It had a rigid lightweight spaceframe, coil-spring divided swing axle front suspension and de Dion rear with inboard drum brakes. The body was Frank Costin's first automotive design, all-enveloping from a low penetrating nose to pronounced tail fins (Costin was worried about the stability of such a light car, especially in cross winds). There was a full-length undertray, and the passenger seat could be covered. The body was partly stressed on the first car; this increased rigidity but complicated repair work, and panels were detachable on subsequent 8s.

Normal engine was a Laystall-headed MG unit, but Climax and Connaught engines were also used, and modifying the design to house a Bristol engine (and disc brakes) produced the 10.

In 1954 racing, the 8 proved fast and fragile, the prototype often being driven by Chapman himself. The 9 was lighter and shorter, with less pronounced tail fins, and was offered in Club and Le Mans forms, the latter intended for internationals and named after Lotus' first outing in the 24-hour race (in 1955, when the 9 was disqualified after Chapman had reversed it out of a sandbank). The Le Mans had a Climax 1100cc engine, MG gearbox and de Dion rear, while the Club was simpler, with a Ford back axle. The model was successful on both sides of the Atlantic.

The 11 (illustrated) appeared in 1956, sleeker with only slight fins, usually with a faired head rest, sometimes with full-width screens where regulations or road use required. The Le Mans models (75 and 85) had FWA or FWB Climax engines, de Dion rears and disc brakes (outboard front, inboard rear), while the Club and Ford 100E-engined Sports were simpler. Graham Hill started racing in an 11, Chapman and Mike Hawthorn duelled in them, Stirling Moss broke class records in one at Monza, and many others won races with 11s; perhaps above all, an 1100cc team car was an astonishing seventh overall at Le Mans.

A Le Mans 150 with FPF engine and wishbone front suspension was added to the Series 2 range in 1957, when the race success story of the 11 continued at Le Mans (an 1100 was ninth, while a 750cc version won its class and the prized Index of Performance).

Specifications

Lotus 11 (1957 Le Mans 85)
Engine: Coventry-Climax straight-four; 72·4 × 66·6mm, 1098cc; single ohc; twin SU carburettors; 84bhp at 6800rpm.
Gearbox: four-speed manual.
Chassis: spaceframe; front suspension independent by wishbones, coil springs, anti-roll bar and dampers; rear suspension by de Dion axle, coil springs and dampers; four-wheel disc brakes.
Dimensions: wheelbase 224cm/88in; **front track** 115cm/45½in; **rear track** 119cm/47in.

Lotus 23
Engine: *23* – Cosworth-Ford straight-four; 85 × 48·4mm, 1097cc; pushrod ohv; twin Weber carburettors; 100bhp at 7500rpm (see text).

23B – Lotus-Ford straight-four; 82·55 × 72·75mm, 1558cc; twin ohc; twin Weber carburettors; 143bhp at 8000rpm.
Gearbox: *23* – Renault four-speed manual (see text).

23B – Hewland five-speed manual.
Chassis: spaceframe; front suspension independent by wishbones, coil springs, dampers and anti-roll bar; rear suspension independent by wishbones, radius arms, coil springs, dampers and anti-roll bar; four-wheel disc brakes.
Dimensions: wheelbase 229cm/90in; **front track** 131cm/51½in; **rear track** 127cm/50in.

Lotus 11

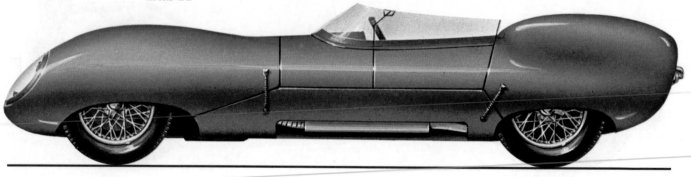

A Lotus 23 in Ian Walker's colours, at Aintree in 1962

The 15 had Chapman strut rear suspension and the FPF engine in 2·0- and 2·2-litre capacities, canted in the chassis at 60 degrees, while the 17 of 1959 was intended for smaller capacity FWM or FWE engines. Although Lotus' Le Mans fortunes deserted them, these were still successful cars elsewhere, until sports derivatives of the rear-engined 18 out-dated them.

Chapman had to embrace the rear-engined faith for his competition cars as the 1960s opened, and his first essay on these lines, the 18, soon led to the 19 sports-racing derivative. This could be seen as a response to the Cooper Monaco, and was rather cheekily named Monte Carlo. It used the main components of the F1 18, including the 240bhp Coventry Climax 2½-litre engine, with a tubular frame wide enough for two seats (the door sill on the left actually contained the fuel tank) and a full-width body which retained a 'family resemblance' to the 17, and of course full electrical equipment. The 19 (and the 19B one-off variant with a Ford V-8) was a successful sports-racer, but it was overshadowed by the 23 which came in 1962.

This elegant little car derived from the 20/22 FJ cars, using the 22 suspension and other mechanical components, with a two-seat width spaceframe in which the two main longitudinal tubes carried oil and water (separately!) between engine and nose radiators. The simple, clean glass fibre body had a somewhat confined cockpit with the markedly reclined driving position then coming into vogue. Standard specification – as far as that term could be applied to this type of car – included a 1097cc Cosworth-Ford and a Renault four-

speed gearbox. Sometimes allied with Hewland five-speed gearboxes, other engines were to be used: 997cc, 1096cc and 1498cc Fords modified by Cosworth, or – most notably – the first engine to carry the name Lotus, the 1558cc Ford unit with twin-ohc cylinder head devised for Lotus by Harry Mundy.

The Twin Cam was first raced in the 23 with which Jim Clark sensationally led the first 11 laps of the 1962 Nurburgring 1000km, and it became standard in the 23B of 1963. This was generally beefed up to cope with the engine's 143bhp (compared with the 100bhp of the first engine used in the 23). The 23/23B gained many class and outright race victories. Around 30 cars had been ordered when the 23 was announced, and 23/23B production eventually reached 131. But it was the last successful Lotus sports-racing car.

Much was expected of the bigger 30 which appeared in 1964, designed to take the 350bhp Ford 4727cc V-8. It had a deep central backbone frame, with a box-section front transverse member, and opening out at the back to two arms linked by a box bridge member behind the engine; 5·5- and 7-inch wide wheels, and their fat tyres, led to large protrusions at each corner which spoiled the car's otherwise low sleek lines. One of the few things to admire about a 30 on the circuits was Clark's efforts to master it. The car was a failure, and the revised version (designated 40) that came in 1965 was certainly no improvement. By that time Chapman's racing thoughts were focussed on single-seaters, and his Lotus sports-racing line just faded away . . .

133

Lotus Elite

Colin Chapman's 14 marked a new step for his still-infant Lotus company, for it was a GT car, widely admired for its conception, its lines and its staggering performance with a small engine, often unloved because of its fragility and unreliability. In perspective, its positive qualities outweighed the problems, both those encountered by owners, and the wider construction and marketing problems which it brought to Lotus' Cheshunt works.

The Elite was a road car with racing car suspension, giving excellent controllability; people were surprised to find that it also provided a comfortable ride, however, as firmness was coupled with a low overall weight (just over 680 kg). But the real innovation was its three-piece chassisless hull of glass fibre, the principal mouldings being a 'floor' (up to the wheel arches), a sandwich layer – an inner layer which through the transmission tunnel, etc., contributed structural rigidity – and the upper part. Metal was used in a hoop running up from the jacking points through the front of the door spaces and over the windscreen (thereby avoiding bulky pillars), and in the nose. The mechanical parts and running gear were mounted directly to the hull, which varied in thickness according to loadings; its quality was therefore critical, and eventual manufacture was entrusted to the Bristol Aeroplane Co. The sleek lines of the car were the work of Kirwan-Taylor, Frayling and Costin and its

drag coefficient of 0·29 confirmed visual impressions of aerodynamic efficiency.

Engine was a 1216cc sohc Coventry Climax FWE, in single-carburettor (75bhp) or twin-carb (80bhp) forms, the former giving a 180kph (110-plus mph) top speed, and the latter almost 195kph (120mph). Noise, much of it body resonance, was a drawback, while the hull almost seemed to amplify vibration from engine and transmission and kit builders in particular had to work very carefully if this was to be kept down.

The Elite first shown at Earls Court in 1957 was one of those show non-runners, and the few cars built in 1958 were mainly used on circuits. There the Elite excelled, for example taking eighth place overall when it first appeared at Le Mans in 1959, also winning its class then and in succeeding years (as it did in many many other events); as if to prove a point it also twice took the efficiency award in the 24-hour classic.

Series 2 and Special Equipment models came in 1960, with improved rear suspension and ZF gearbox in place of the BMC unit, but still with the anachronism of wire wheels. In sophistication, the Lotus 14 was years ahead of contemporary sports cars. Commercially, however, Chapman's struggle to get it into production never paid off, and production ended in 1963 after 998 had been built.

Specification *(1960)*
Engine: Coventry-Climax straight-four; 76·2 × 66·6mm, 1216cc; single ohc; SU carburettor; 75bhp at 6100rpm.
    SE model (1962) – as above, but twin SU carburettors; 85bhp at 6300rpm.
Gearbox: BMC four-speed manual (ZF on SE model).
Chassis: glass-fibre-reinforced plastics three-piece monocoque; front suspension independent by wishbones, coil springs, dampers and anti-roll bar; rear suspension independent by radius arms, coil springs and dampers; four-wheel disc brakes (inboard at rear).
Dimensions: wheelbase 224cm/88in; **front track** 119cm/47in; **rear track** 123cm/48½in.

Lotus Elan

This was by no means the first road-going Lotus, but it was the first to have a five-figure production run and become widely known. Introduced at the 1962 London Motor Show, the Type 26 Elan was a particularly well balanced design, with several novel features. Foremost among these was Colin Chapman's backbone chassis, fabricated in steel and forked front and rear to the suspension mountings, with engine and gearbox between the 'prongs' of the front fork and the transmission running along the boxed backbone. This neatly avoided the need for a conventional tubular chassis, which otherwise would have been necessary to support the un-stressed glass fibre body (the glass fibre chassis/body of the Elite would have been impractical for an open car, and in any case had proved unexpectedly costly). The Elan body had very neat lines, with a clean nose achieved through use of an integral bumper and then-novel retractable headlights; it had a comfortable and sensibly laid out cockpit, and even adequate luggage space in the cut-off tail. Suspension followed that of the Elite.

The earliest Elans had the 1498cc Lotus twin-ohc conversion of the Ford 116E engine (100bhp at 5700rpm) but in 1963 this was superseded by the 1558cc version, which gave a 180kph (110mph) maximum speed and acceleration appropriate to a larger-engined car (although the Metalastik 'doughnut' driveshaft couplings mitigated against slick changes).

The S2 with minor refinements came in 1964, and a coupe (designated Type 36) was introduced in 1965. This had even more attractive lines, carried through to the S3 (Type 45) of 1966, which also had suspension revisions and engine uprated by 10bhp to 115bhp. This was perhaps the most popular version of the Elan, and the most widely used in racing. It gave way to the S4 in 1968 with detail styling and safety equipment changes.

Two final versions appeared in 1967: the Plus 2 was wider and 60cm longer, to accommodate two occasional rear seats; it was inevitably heavier but had its engine uprated to 118bhp in com-pensation. The other model was the Sprint, in which power was increased to 126bhp; the engine remained flexible and had good torque characteristics (and drove through a five-speed gearbox) so that acceleration was preserved, coupled with a 190kph (120mph) top speed.

Through its years in production, the Elan was transformed from a sports car into a true GT car, thus accurately foreshadowing Lotus road car trends in the 1970s. When production ceased in 1973, total Elan production had reached 12 224.

Specification (*1964*)
Engine: Lotus-Ford straight-four; $82 \cdot 55 \times 72 \cdot 75$mm, 1558cc; twin ohc; twin Weber carburettors; 105bhp at 5500rpm.
  Sprint – as above, but twin Dellorto carburettors; 126bhp at 6500rpm.
Gearbox: Ford four-speed manual.
Chassis: steel backbone with unstressed glass fibre body; front suspension independent by wishbones, coil springs and dampers (anti-roll bar on later models); rear suspension independent by wishbones, coil springs and dampers; four-wheel disc brakes.
Dimensions: wheelbase 214cm/84in; **front track** 117cm/46in; **rear track** 122cm/48in.

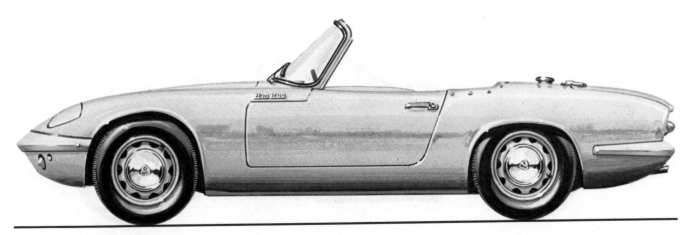

Lotus 46 and 47

The Lotus Type 46 Europa was the first production mid-engined coupe to be listed by a British manufacturer, its name summing up marketing intentions to sell it in Europe, in association with Renault. To this end, the Renault R16 engine/transmission was used, adapted for rear mounting; the 1470cc engine was tuned (with increased compression ratio, high-lift cams and carburettor changes) to give 78bhp at 6000rpm when the Europa was announced at the end of 1966. The 47 was outwardly similar, but intended for competition, with 1·6 litres of fuel-injected Ford-Cosworth to give an adequate 160bhp, transmitted through a Hewland five-speed gearbox.

Both cars echoed the Elan in having steel backbone chassis and similar ifs; the 46 had a rear suspension of radius arms and lower links along Elan lines, while in the 47 conventional radius rods were substituted for the long fabricated components, and other changes were made to facilitate quick circuit adjustments (and disc brakes were fitted all round).

The glass fibre body had sleek nose lines, but a high deck above the engine enforced a slit of a rear window, while fins alongside the hinged lid over the engine and luggage compartment further cut rearward visibility. Access was difficult, and although well equipped, the cockpit of early cars was cramped (this was improved by a revised chassis, with a lower floor pan).

In one respect – aerodynamic efficiency – the body was beyond criticism, and allied with light weight this contributed to the Europa's maximum speed of 185kph (115mph), achieved with modest power. Its performance was inevitably compared with that of the front-engined Elan, however, and seldom to the Europa's credit – the precise, impeccable, handling was, for example, offset by a cumbersome gear linkage.

Many Europa shortcomings were overcome in the Twin Cam, with the 1558cc, 105bhp Lotus twin-ohc version of a Ford engine, which appeared in 1971 (the 1565cc Renault 16TS engine was available for some markets). The rear fins were also cut down. The car was further improved in its Europa Special guise, with the Lotus 'Big Valve' engine, from 1972. A fifth speed was added to the gearbox, which meant that effective use could be made of the engine's 126bhp, moving the Europa into a performance area more fitting to its handling, with a claimed maximum speed of 200kph (125mph). It continued in this form until 1975, when production was ended to make way for the Esprit.

The 47 became familiar, and successful, in the colours of Lotus Components (illustrated), Gold Leaf and private owners; a T62 derivative, with a substantially different body, was raced by Gold Leaf Team Lotus, but was generally less widely seen as Lotus' racing was concentrated on Formula 1.

1967 Type 47

Specification (*Europa Special*)
Engine: Lotus-Ford straight-four; 82·55 × 72·75mm, 1558cc; twin ohc; twin Dellorto carburettors; 126bhp at 6500rpm.
Gearbox: modified Renault five-speed manual.
Chassis: steel backbone with unstressed glass fibre body; front suspension independent by wishbones, coil springs, dampers and anti-roll bar; rear suspension independent by transverse links, radius arms, coil springs and dampers; disc front/drum rear brakes.
Dimensions: wheelbase 231cm/91in; **track** 135cm/53in.

Lotus Elite and Eclat

The Lotus road-car range from the mid-1970s comprised a rear-engined model – the Esprit – and a pair of related front-engined cars, the Elite and the Eclat, which in many respects were more realistic in everyday terms. All three used the Lotus Type 907 slant-four twin-cam engine, against the trend for expensive high-performance cars, but appearing more sensible with each successive fuel crisis and price increase!

The basic differences between the front-engined cars were in styling, the Elite being a genuine four-seater sporting car with distinct wedge lines carried back to give near-estate car proportions, while the Eclat was a cheaper 2 + 2 fastback. Each had numerical designations indicating the ex-factory equipment state, Elites running from 501 to 504, Eclats from 520 to 524, the highest numbers in each case referring to the most expensive versions, with power steering and automatic transmission (the Elite was the first Lotus type with an automatic option).

Lotus continued the backbone chassis theme in these models, coupling it with glass fibre bodywork finished to high standards, and which was aerodynamically efficient. This was built around a 'steel safety frame' and in 1976 – to Lotus' obvious delight – the Elite became the first GRP-bodied car to be awarded the Don Safety Award.

The engine was rated at 160bhp when the Elite was introduced in 1974, and this power output was held when it was modified to meet 1977 European emission requirements (the enforced camshaft change in fact gave the positive benefit of increased torque). In 1980 a 2174cc 'high-torque' version of the 16-valve light-alloy engine was fitted in the Series 2·2 range of models, giving improved intermediate acceleration times.

Manual versions were initially fitted with a five-speed gearbox using Austin Maxi internals, giving light and positive changes (only four speeds were offered in the 'economy' Eclat), but this gave way to a Getrag box in the Series 2·2.

The Eclat was fractionally lighter than the Elite, its aerodynamics perhaps fractionally better, and it thus more convincingly reached the 200kph (125mph) maximum speed initially claimed for both models. In handling and road-holding terms, both were well above average and – like most Lotus road cars – almost above criticism.

This could not be said of some more tangible aspects during the first year, but matters improved when stricter quality control was applied in 1975, from the lavish interiors to mechanical parts, and the specifications were improved in detail. These models played a significant role in Lotus' shift up-market, and in helping the company's recovery from a lean period.

Specification

Engine: Lotus straight-four; 95·25 × 69·2mm, 1973cc; twin ohc; twin Dellorto carburettors; 160bhp at 6500rpm.

Series 2·2 – as above, but 95·25 × 76·2mm, 2174cc.

Gearbox: five-speed manual (see text) or optional three-speed automatic.

Chassis: steel backbone with unstressed glass fibre body; front suspension independent by upper wishbones, lower links, coil springs, dampers and anti-roll bar; rear suspension independent by trailing arms, transverse links, coil springs and dampers; disc front/inboard drum rear brakes.

Dimensions: wheelbase 248cm/98in; **front track** 149cm/58½in; **rear track** 150cm/59in.

1978 Elite

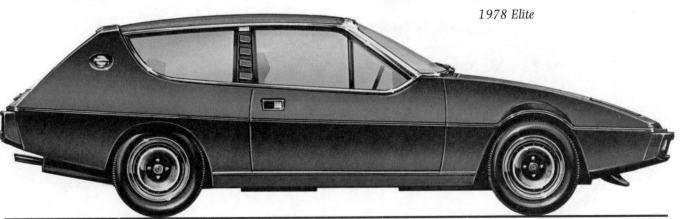

Lotus Esprit

The introduction of the Esprit late in 1975 marked the fulfilment of a policy intended to move the complete Lotus range 'up-market'; this model took the place of the Europa – albeit at a considerably higher price, and one that was to almost double by 1979 – while the Elite and Eclat effectively replaced the Elan. Most Lotus cars have been characterized by sophisticated mechanical design, and these cars carried that philosophy through to creature comforts – they were prestige cars with outstanding sports car attributes.

Unlike the Elite/Eclat, the Esprit was mid-engined, with the mass of the Lotus 907 16-valve dohc power unit ahead of the rear axle and canted at 45 degrees to the left, following racing car practice for optimum weight distribution. The engine was efficient in itself, producing 81bhp/litre. Drive was through a five-speed gearbox, with none of the linkage problems sometimes associated with rear- (or mid-) engined cars. Suspension was independent all round, giving high standards of adhesion, traction and ride. Following common Lotus practice, bought-in components such as the Citroen SM gearbox were used.

Lotus' backbone-cum-space frame chassis was clothed in elegant glass-fibre-reinforced plastics bodywork designed by Giugiaro, following the lines of a 1972 show car. There was no 'occasional' seats pretence – the Esprit was strictly a two-seater. Accommodation was comfortable, although not generous, and the cockpit equipment – rather pompously referred to as 'command and information services' – was sensibly arranged. The visibility problem common to this type of car was further from solution in the Esprit than in some of its contemporaries, and was not improved in the S2 version of 1978.

In the manner of its going, the Esprit set high standards, with a 210kph (130mph-plus) maximum speed from two litres comparing remarkably well with the potential of rival models with considerably larger engines. Performance was complemented by striking good looks and excellent manners. Although there was obvious competition potential in the Esprit, Lotus' racing was confined to Formula One and it was left to independents to develop sports-racing versions, though they were raced without success in 1979 and 1980.

Early in 1980 the Esprit Turbo was introduced, using the 907-based 910 engine with Garrett AiResearch T3 turbocharger and with a substantially revised chassis and suspension. Claimed maximum speed was 245kph (152mph). Later in 1980 a Series 2·2 version of the normally-aspirated model was also announced, in line with the rest of the Lotus range. The chassis and suspension of the Turbo were adopted for the S3 Esprit which came in 1981, and which was outwardly identified by air scoops behind the side windows and wrap-round bumpers.

Specification

Engine: Lotus straight-four; 95·25 × 69·2, 1973cc; twin ohc; twin Dellorto carburettors; 160bhp at 6200rpm.

   Series 2·2 – as above, but 95·25 × 76·2mm, 2174cc.

   Turbo – as standard, but with Garrett AiResearch turbocharger; 210bhp at 6500rpm.

Gearbox: Citroen five-speed manual.

Chassis: steel backbone/spaceframe with unstressed glass fibre body; front suspension independent by unequal-length wishbones, coil spring/damper units and torsion bar stabiliser; rear suspension independent by trailing arms, lateral link, driveshafts and coil spring/damper units; four-wheel disc brakes (inboard at rear).

Dimensions: wheelbase 244cm/96in; track 151cm/59½in.

1978 Series 2

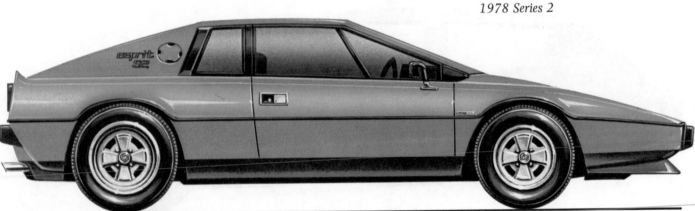

Marcos

British specialist car constructors were hardly conservative as the 1960s opened, but few departed so radically from established practices as Marcos with its 'wooden car'. Although the first model dated from 1960, Marcos Cars as such was formed in 1962 by Jem March and Frank Costin; Marsh was to run the company until it ceased operations, and had an immediate background in the Speedex company, supplying components and body shells to special builders, so he knew the market; Costin had Lister, Lotus and Vanwall body designs to his credit, and it was his idea that efficient car structures could be formed in modern marine plywoods. So the first Marcos was a wooden car, at least in its chassis structure of three primary longerons with stressed floor, and except for some glass fibre detail in its bodywork. Production running gear from Standard-Triumph was used, with the much-favoured Ford 105E engine. It was by no means a handsome device, but it proved Costin's principles; with a fully-tuned Ford engine it was capable of 190kph (120mph), handled well and found popularity with club racers (early Marcos drivers at this level included Jackie Stewart).

A much sleeker Volvo-engined model came in 1964, with a body design by Dennis Adams which was to last out the life of Marcos. The cockpit was cramped, with its semi-reclining seats fixed in place, the pedal assembly being adjustable. At a fairly high price, it gained a reputation for first-class roadholding, and had a 187kph (116mph) maximum speed. Variants with four-cylinder Ford engines followed, and there was a side step to the odd-looking Mini Marcos, which survived until 1970 (one was 15th at Le Mans in 1966).

In 1969 Marcos modified its main model to accept the 3-litre Ford V-6. Its additional weight brought a bonus in better road-holding, as the tendency for the nose to lift was reduced, and it gave the car a 200kph (125mph) top speed, although as a GT car it still had inadequate luggage space and that difficult of access cockpit.

A coil sprung live axle took the place of the telescopic de Dion linkage at the rear in 1969, while the following year the wooden chassis gave way to conventional square steel tubes. Ford 2-litre V-4 and 3-litre V-6 engines were optional, and for overseas markets the Volvo B30 straight-six was introduced. This 145bhp 3-litre unit gave the car virtually the same top speed as the Ford V-6, with fractionally better acceleration, but its main attraction was its full exhaust emission control, which it was felt would make the Marcos acceptable in the USA. The lure of market expansion was the company's undoing, for Marsh' sexpectations were not fulfilled, the new factory was never justified and the company collapsed. In spring 1981, however, Marsh set up a new and much smaller company trading under his own name, offering 'kit car' versions of the same design.

Specification *(1969)*

Engine: Ford 60-degree V-6; 93·67 × 72·42mm, 2994cc; pushrod ohv; Weber carburettor; 136bhp at 4750rpm.
Gearbox: four-speed manual with overdrive.
Chassis: wooden, with steel frames; front suspension independent by wishbones, coil springs, dampers and anti-roll bar; rear suspension by live axle, upper and lower links, Panhard rod, coil springs and dampers; disc front/drum rear brakes.
Dimensions: wheelbase 227cm/89½in; **front track** 123cm/48½in; **rear track** 130cm/51in.

1969 (Ford-engined version)

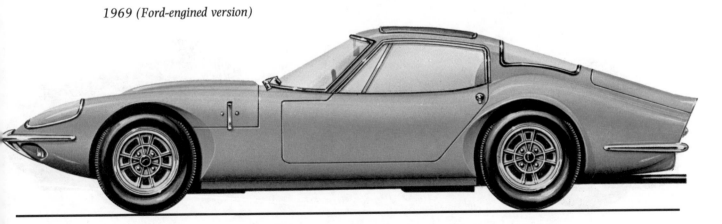

Maserati A6GCS

The Maserati brothers sold their company to the Orsi family in 1937, but retained day-to-day control under contract for the next ten years. When they finally left, one of their legacies to the Modena company was a sports car design, until then a rarity in the Maserati repertoire, but a harbinger of things to come ...

When the first car was completed in 1947 it adhered closely to a concept of a sports-racing car that was soon to be swept away as Cisitalias, Jaguars and others set the new pattern with full-width bodywork. During its spasmodic production life, therefore, the A6GCS was transformed from a spartan cycle-winged *spyder* to an elegant little two-seater with bodywork the equal of its mid-1950s contemporaries.

The A6 engine, owing something to a pre-war racing straight-six, was initially in 1488cc, 65bhp form, but in 1947 it appeared in its definitive 1978cc capacity, giving up to 130bhp. A single-ohc cast iron unit, it was superseded in 1952 by a twin-cam light alloy six, which was developed by Massimino and eventually rated at 165bhp, or 170bhp with higher compression ratio and higher revs.

The rest of the car was simple, comprising a tubular ladder frame with conventional ifs and live rear axle arrangement. A minimal body, with dual half-moon screens, almost seemed to proclaim its designers' racing car preferences – indeed, the cycle wings and single headlight in the traditional Maserati grille could simply be removed, together with all passenger facilities, to transform it into

a racing car. Production of this first A6CGS was only 15 cars, spread over four years.

A notable early success came in the 1947 Circuit of Modena, where the then-new Maseratis finished first and second, Ascari in his first winning drive heading Villoresi. During the next few seasons, there were a few successes in secondary Italian events.

Revised – almost reconceived – under Colombo's direction for 1952, the car still carried the A6GCS designation. Apart from the new engine (mentioned above) it had revised rear suspension and, in standard form, a purposeful full-width body, with small cockpit and tiny cutaway doors – a car obviously intended for sporting rather than touring use. However, Pinin Farina produced a handful of elegant little fastback coupes on A6GCS chassis, and designed the subsequent A6G/2000, made by other coachbuilders in open and coupe forms until 1956.

The later A6GCS was more widely raced, frequently with full works backing and sometimes by the works (hence such luminaries as Fangio and Musso drove them). There were class victories in major events such as the Mille Miglia and Targa Florio in 1953-55, and some outright wins in lesser races. It was superseded by the 200S in 1956, although independents still raced them for a little longer. Either version of A6GCS was a typical Italian sports-racer of its period, tough and built for real road courses rather than the airfield circuits where sports-racers of the future were being evolved.

Specification

Engine: *1947* – straight-six; $72 \cdot 5 \times 81$mm, 1978cc; single ohc; triple Weber carburettors; 130bhp at 6000rpm.

1953 – as above, but $76 \cdot 5 \times 72$mm, 1988cc; twin ohc 170bhp at 7500rpm (see text).

Gearbox: four-speed manual.

Chassis: tubular ladder-frame; front suspension independent by wishbones, coil springs, dampers and anti-roll bar; rear suspension by rigid axle, radius arms, semi-elliptic springs (quarter-elliptics from 1953) and dampers; four-wheel drum brakes.

Dimensions: wheelbase 231cm/91in; **front track** 122cm/48in from 1947, 130cm/51in from 1953; **rear track** 116cm/45½in from 1947, 122cm/48in from 1953.

1947 model

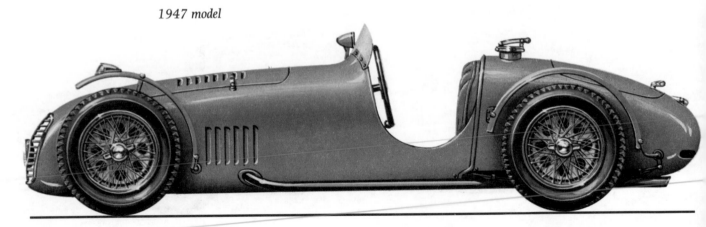

Maserati 300S and 450S

The lax and often crass regulations devised by the FIA to govern sports car racing during the 1950s encouraged some manufacturers to modify single-seater Grand Prix designs into so-called 'sports cars'. These did little to further the development of fast road cars, but they certainly provided some exciting racing. In 1954 Maserati was so tempted, developing a team of 3-litre sports-racing cars based on the Type 250F 2½-litre six-cylinder twin-ohc Grand Prix single-seater, to contest the World Sports Car Championship introduced the previous year.

The conversion was relatively simple: a wider multi-tubular frame to support an enveloping body wide enough to take two seats and carry lighting equipment, and an engine increased from 84 × 75mm to 84 × 90mm (2991cc), when it gave a brake reading of 260bhp at 6500rpm. The five-speed gearbox, set transversely in unit with the final drive, the de Dion rear axle with transverse-leaf spring, and the coil-spring front suspension all followed Maserati GP pattern.

With so many proven components the Type 300S (for Sport) should have been fully raceworthy in its first event, but Maserati's own limitations as a racing organisation, with mechanics hard-pressed to look after teams of GP and sports cars, cost the 300S victories which better preparation could well have secured. In its first full season, 1955, the car failed to win a single championship race, although it did win events at Bari, Monza, Oporto and

Venezuela. A batch of cars was also built for sale to private owners in Europe and the USA and these added several regional victories to the list.

In 1956, the 300S scored Maserati's first championship race victories in 1000km races in Argentina and at the Nurburgring. These successes could not prevent the rival Ferraris winning the title, but works or private 300S cars scored more non-championship wins at Bari, Nassau, in Venezuela and Montlhéry, Australia and in the USA.

For 1957, Maserati went all out for the championship, developing a fierce new 4½-litre four-ohc V-8 engine which was fitted into an elaborate multi-tube spaceframe. Suspension was much as on the 300S, and 370bhp on petrol or 420bhp on alcohol earned the V-8 the nickname 'Bazooka'; its all-out speed was reckoned at over 295kph (185mph). The 'Bazooka' won the Sebring and Swedish rounds of the 1957 contest, but with the title in the balance at the final race, the GP of Venezuela, Maserati met dire disaster: of the three V-8s competing, two crashed and were wrecked, while the third was destroyed by fire after crashing into one of the works 3-litre Maserati sixes also running!

A 1958 change in the race rules, limiting engine size to 3 litres, sealed the fate of these magnificent monsters, and Officine Maserati, by then in serious financial trouble, withdrew from all racing at the close of 1957.

1957 450S

Specification

Engine: *300S* – straight-six; 84 × 90mm, 2991cc; twin ohc; three Weber twin-choke carburettors; 260bhp at 6500rpm.

450S – 90-degree V-8; 93·8 × 81mm, 4477cc; twin ohc per bank; four Weber twin-choke carburettors; 370bhp at 7000rpm.

Gearbox: five-speed manual, transversely-mounted in unit with final drive.

Chassis: *300S* – multi-tube frame; front suspension independent by wishbones, coil springs and dampers; rear suspension by de Dion axle, transverse leaf spring and dampers; four-wheel drum brakes.

450S – as above, but tubular spaceframe.

Dimensions: wheelbase 235cm/92½in; **front track** 132cm/52in; **rear track** 127cm/50in.

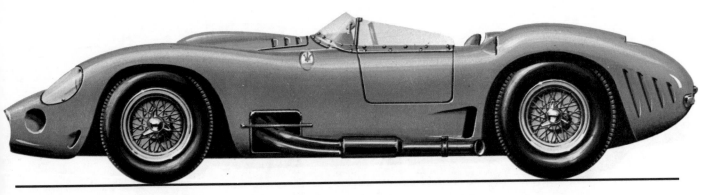

Maserati T60/61

Motor racing being second nature to Maserati, it was inevitable that as soon as some financial stability had been achieved, this proud Italian marque would find its way back to the world's circuits. Count Orsi's main stipulations were that all racing cars had to be built for paying customers, and that as many production parts as possible should be incorporated into their designs. Clearly Grand Prix racing was out of the question, but there was a healthy market for sports-racing cars, particularly in the USA; moreover, Maserati already had a suitable engine.

The Tipo 200S, a four-cylinder twin-ohc 2-litre unit built in 1956 for European racing, hillclimbing and speedboating, formed the basis. Its lubrication system was modified to dry sump to permit 'angling' of the engine at 45 degrees in the chassis to secure a low profile, and it gave a consistent test-bed reading of 195bhp at 7800rpm with satisfying reliability.

This unit was installed at the front of a novel chassis, formed from innumerable lengths of small-diameter steel tubing (between 1 and 1·5mm), allegedly chosen because it was surplus stock at Modena. Welded into a series of stressed triangulations, these made a remarkably strong but light spaceframe, with extra bracing from the lower body and floor panels welded into the structure. The multiplicity of tubes earned the car the nicknames of 'Spaghetti special' and the 'Birdcage', the latter enduring although the official designation was Tipo 60.

Suspension followed Tipo 250F Grand Prix pattern, while the engine drove back through a long propellor shaft to a transverse five-speed gearbox whose magnesium housing was in unit with the final drive. The open bodywork of 'two-seater' width was short, stubby and lacked grace, but with a wheelbase of only 223cm and a weight of 560kg, this new Maserati had a highly effective power-to-weight ratio.

It won its very first race at Rouen in July 1959, and its first hillclimb in August, subsequently scoring many more class wins in Europe and America.

Officine Maserati then enlarged the bore to 100mm, producing the 2·9-litre T61, a formidable 240bhp contender for the 3-litre class. Over a dozen were ordered in the USA before the first was completed, and the 'Birdcage' won the 1959 Nassau GP, the 1960 and 1961 Nurburgring 1000km races, and American races at Riverside, Laguna Seca, Palm Springs, Elkhart Lake and also elsewhere.

With proper team preparation and organisation, the T61 would undoubtedly have won more classic races. It led every round of the 1960 World Sports Car Championship – at Buenos Aires, Sebring, the Targa Florio, Nurburgring and Le Mans – but won only one event and broke down in the rest. Yet it remained an impressive example of improvisation, and earned the company some much-needed money.

1959 Tipo 61

Specification

Engine: *Tipo 60* – straight-four; 92 × 75mm, 1993cc; two twin-choke carburettors; 195bhp at 6800rpm.

Tipo 61 – as above, but 100 × 92mm, 2890cc; 240bhp.
Gearbox: five-speed manual, transversely-mounted in unit with final drive.
Chassis: welded multi-tube spaceframe; front suspension independent by wishbones, coil springs, dampers and anti-roll bar; rear suspension by de Dion axle, transverse leaf spring and dampers; four-wheel disc brakes.
Dimensions: wheelbase 224cm/88in; **front track** 127cm/50in; **rear track** 122cm/48in.

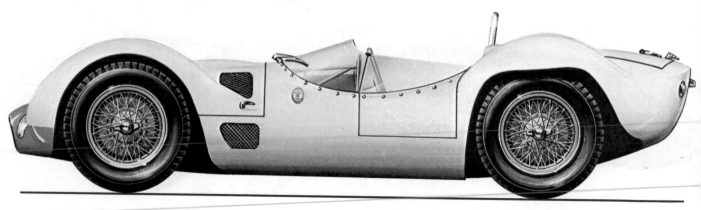

Maserati 3500GT

After the catastrophic end to Maserati's 1957 motor racing season, the orders of the proprietor, Count Adolfo Orsi, were to retrench, recoup and rationalise, with the Modena factory concentrating on the production of saleable cars able to turn a profit. In 1956 a 3½-litre version of the Type 300S sports car engine had already been tried in racing, and for 1957 this 86 × 100mm, 3485cc twin-ohc unit, fitted with two twin-choke carburettors, wet sump lubrication, and roadgoing electrical and other equipment, was inserted in a welded steel tubular frame of 300S derivation, but with longer wheelbase and wider track, designed to carry distinctive Grand Touring and sporting coachwork.

The 3500GT was intended to appeal to European and American connoisseurs and this new Maserati made its debut at the 1957 Geneva Show, wearing a handsome coupe body built by Carrozzeria Touring on their well-known *Superleggera* system. The specification was straightforward: instead of the 300S's costly five-speed gearbox in unit with the de Dion-type rear axle, the GT car had a German ZF four-speed all-synchromesh box in unit with the engine, a British-made GKN-Salisbury rigid rear axle with semi-elliptic leaf springs, and Girling disc brakes.

Even in detuned GT form Maserati's lovely twin-cam six gave 236bhp at 5500rpm, and could idle along at 30kph (20mph) in top or blast the car up to 225kph (140mph) or more with little apparent effort. The 3500GT went into production at 20 cars per month in 1958, and besides coupe bodywork by Touring and Vignale, a convertible by Frua and a *spyder* by Vignale also became available. A more sporting engine gave 270bhp and over 250kph (155mph), a five-speed gearbox was optional, and in 1963 the standard 3½-litre model was supplemented by one of 3·7 litres, equipped with Lucas fuel injection and named the Mistrale.

An even larger six-cylinder unit of 4136cc went into the Quattroporte, a fast and luxurious four-door sporting saloon of handsome appearance, while Maserati also produced limited numbers of a V-8 model, the 5000GT, with a 4935cc four-ohc engine derived from the ill-favoured sports-racing V-8 of 1957. The chassis used many components of the 3500GT but was slightly longer in wheelbase. With a maximum speed of 270kph (165mph) this was one of the fastest of all road cars in the 1950s, and was the forebear of several later Maseratis of note, including the Ghibli, the Indy and the mid-engined Bora.

Specification

Engine: *GT* – straight-six; 86 × 100mm, 3485cc; twin ohc; two twin-choke carburettors; 236bhp at 5500rpm.

GTI – as above, but with Lucas fuel injection optional from 1963; 270bhp.

Gearbox: four-speed manual; optional five-speed manual.

Chassis: tubular frame; front suspension independent by wishbones, coil springs and dampers; rear suspension by rigid axle, radius arms, semi-elliptic leaf springs and dampers; four-wheel disc brakes.

Dimensions: **wheelbase** 260cm/102½in; **track** 139cm/55in.

1963 GTI coupe

Maserati Merak

The Merak was not one of the out-and-out supercars of its decade but an honest attempt to market a realistic mid-engined car with all the desirable sporting attributes, 'executive' comfort, and an engine sensible in size, mechanical make-up and fuel demands. Design was by Giugiaro.

Introduced in the autumn of 1972, the Merak used the suspension, platform and many body parts from the Bora – in silhouette the pair appeared almost identical – but whereas the fastback of the Bora was fully glazed, the Merak simply had skeletal members above a flat engine deck to complete the line from cockpit roof to tail (the engine cover lifted between these, and in the first cars for the USA was humped to accommodate a full spare wheel, whereas others had a 'spacesaver' spare). Suspension was fully independent, giving a ride generally rated 'harsh' on the early cars, but improved in the Merak SS which came in 1975.

The engine was a version of the V-6 used in the Citroen SM, with enlarged bore and giving 190bhp in the first Meraks, 220bhp in the SS, but only 208bhp in its 1980 specification. Other Citroen components derived from that brief Italo-French marriage: the gearbox came from the SM, and the Citroen hydraulic system was used for brakes and pop-up headlights, and in neither employment (or under-employment when the complex plumbing is considered) was it found completely satisfactory. It was therefore discarded in the SS, which also had a ZF gearbox.

The 2+2 cockpit was comfortable, although not generously provided with stowage space or room for passengers in the occasional rear seats. All-round visibility was better than in most rear/mid-engined contemporaries. The 190bhp engine gave the Merak a top speed of 225kph (140mph), little improved in the SS.

The Merak was one of a family of small-series cars, others such as the Ghibli, Indy and Bora having race-bred V-8s, which carried this famous old name through the 1970s, and – with the aid of de Tomaso – through the vicissitudes of the Citroen alliance and into the 1980s.

Specification *(1974)*
Engine: 90-degree V-6; 91·6 × 75mm, 2965cc; twin ohc per bank; three twin-choke Weber carburettors; 190bhp at 6000rpm.
Gearbox: five-speed manual.
Chassis: integral; suspension independent front and rear by wishbones, coil springs, anti-roll bars and dampers; four-wheel disc brakes (inboard ventilated at rear).
Dimensions: wheelbase 260cm/102½in; **front track** 147cm/58in; **rear track** 145cm/57in.

1972 Merak SS

Matra M530

The Matra aerospace company entered the motoring world when it took over the financially weak Bonnet company in 1964, and with it Rene Bonnet's existing Renault-engined Djet, which was continued in production while Matra Sports designed a successor (and built the first of the F3 and F2 single-seaters which were to initiate the French racing resurgence).

Matra's first road car, the M530A, was announced at the 1967 Geneva Motor Show. While its lines appeared a little odd from some aspects, this was a sophisticated 2 + 2, which like the later Fiat X1/9 demonstrated that a mid-engined layout need not restrict accommodation or visibility. The basis was a steel hull, with bolted-on glass fibre body panels; roof panels were detachable, and could be stowed in a shallow front boot, leaving a longitudinal brace running forward from the built-in roll bar at the back of the cockpit (there was adequate luggage space behind the engine).

Effective independent suspension, a dry weight of 820kg, and a 47/53 weight distribution made for good handling and ride qualities, the former more than adequate for the available power.

This came from the Ford Taunus 17M V-4, a compact unit ideal for a car of this configuration, which drove through a Ford 15M transmission, with a rod-and-lever linkage which proved trouble-free. The engine was used in standard form, its 73bhp being good for a claimed maximum speed of 170kph (106mph) – but a genuine top speed of under 160kph (100mph) – with acceleration a little below par for a 1·7-litre sports car, although economy was excellent.

The measurable performance of the M530A was lower than that of its outwardly sleeker Djet predecessor, but that shortcoming did not result from Matra aerodynamics, rather from the tuned Renault engines, giving up to 103bhp, that had been used in the Djet. Despite its 'performance image' of the time, Matra was intent on a road-going sports car in the M530A, rather than a competitions-orientated pseudo-road car, and in this the design staff were successful. In general marketing terms, however, the car made only a modest impact, and although it continued into the 1970s, Matra's affiliation with Simca only two years after its introduction effectively limited its life.

Specification

Engine: Ford Taunus 60-degree V-4; 90 × 66·8mm, 1699cc; pushrod ohv; single Solex carburettor; 73bhp at 4800rpm.
Gearbox: Ford four-speed manual.
Chassis: steel platform; front suspension independent by wishbones, coil springs, dampers and anti-roll bar; rear suspension independent by trailing arms, coil springs, dampers and anti-roll bar; four-wheel disc brakes.
Dimensions: wheelbase 255cm/100½in;
front track 144cm/56½in; **rear track** 141cm/55½in.

Matra sports-racing cars

Matra entered a single 'all-French' car in the 1968 Le Mans 24-hour race as a symbol of intent; in 1974 they completed a hat-trick of Le Mans wins and dominated the world sports car championship, to fulfil that 1968 promise to French enthusiasts.

Effectively, the programme began with the MS630 using BRM and Ford engines in 1966-67, and in the following year when MS630/03 was entered at Spa and Le Mans with Matra's own 3-litre V-12. Also intended as a Formula One engine, this was designed by Georges Martin and the Moteur Moderne consultancy group, and with its primary F1 purpose in mind was a narrow-angle V-12. It was a straightforward twin-ohc four-valve unit, recalling Ferrari and BRM practice.

In its first form, the 630 was an ungainly coupe. It retired very early in the Belgian 1000km race, but surprised even the Matra team at Le Mans, where it ran second for part of the race and lasted for 21 hours. The endurance qualities of the engine having been demonstrated, Matra initiated design work on two possible chassis for it. Robert Choulet designed MS640, which was abandoned after an accident when it flipped at modest speed during trials at Le Mans (on a public road closed for the occasion, such is the importance of a prestige project in France). Bernard Boyer headed the parallel team which developed MS630 and MS650, the first open 650 being a rebodied semi-monocoque 630. Two 630/650s were in the team with a 630 and a 650 at Le Mans in 1969, where the 650 was fourth and a 630 fifth.

For 1979 Matra was hyphenated with Simca on the 650 *spyders*, but the season was a disaster, with the consolation of 'best 3-litre car' coming only in the Monza 1000km. There was a Tour de France victory, and this was repeated in 1971, when, apart from the Paris 1000km, Matra's sports-racing effort was confined to a solo MS660 at Le Mans, where it retired.

This car was developed as the MS670 for 1972, still along sound orthodox lines around a monocoque centre section with tubular sub-frames front and rear and the V-12 detuned for this purpose to 440bhp. Preparation was meticulous. The team was dominant at Le Mans, taking the first two places, and that was encouragement enough to challenge Ferrari in the 1973 series.

Slightly modified, 670s won eight of the nine races contested in 1973, while Le Mans fell to a 670B, which differed only in detail. Up to 480 bhp was available in the 1974 V-12, with impressive reliability, while on the 670C the rear brakes were moved inboard and details such as the rear aerofoil were tidied. Nine victories could be set against one defeat, with a first and third at Le Mans and a second world championship. At the end of the season Simca withdrew their support and, although there would have been Gitanes backing to carry through from 1974, finances were marginal; moreover, harsh fuel consumption regulations were announced for Le Mans. These factors persuaded Matra to abandon sports car racing, and as a finale their two winning 670Cs in the Kyalami Six Hours crossed the line side by side.

1972 MS670 (Le Mans winner)

Specification *(1974 MS670B)*
Engine: 60-degree V-12; 79·7 × 50mm, 2993cc; twin ohc per bank; Lucas fuel injection; 480bhp at 11 200rpm.
Gearbox: five-speed manual.
Chassis: monocoque centre section, with tubular subframes; front suspension independent by wishbones, upper arms, coil springs, dampers and anti-roll bar; rear suspension independent by upper arms, lower links, coil springs, dampers and anti-roll bar; four-wheel disc brakes.
Dimensions: wheelbase 256cm/100in; track 152cm/60in.

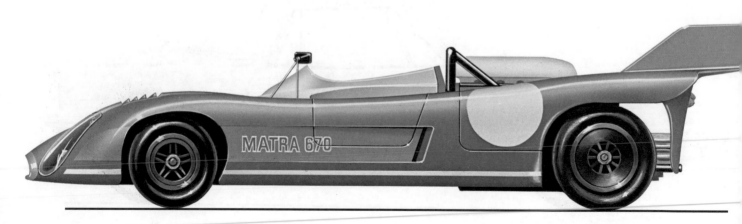

Matra-Simca Bagheera

Once the Matra-Chrysler link was forged in 1969, a replacement for the Matra M530 was obviously called for – that car had hardly been a great success, and although it was in the commercial hands of Simca it was powered by a Ford engine. Its successor came in the spring of 1973, and offered a novel solution to the problem of seating more than two people in a mid-engined coupe. Like other modest-production high-performance cars it incorporated mass-produced components, and it was successful – it might not have had enormous competition potential, but it lived through the decade to become a sporting Talbot, as Chrysler sold their European interests.

The instant captivating feature of this Bagheera was its three-abreast seating, with the driver slightly isolated from his passengers (who had to travel in intimate proximity, as overall width was only 173cm, but they at least had adequate leg room as the floor was flat). The plastics body, with two main bonded assemblies, was Matra-designed; it was therefore aerodynamically efficient, and stiff and strong as it was carried on a substantial chassis of tubular and boxed members, with a built-in roll-over structure.

Simca 1100 suspension was adopted, but after trials with prototypes designated M550, Matra redesigned the rear trailing arm/torsion bar layout. The engine came from the same fwd source, in its 1294cc TI version, installed transversely at the rear and driving through an 1100 gearbox. The power unit was ahead of the rear axle line, but also ahead of a quite generous boot, so that access to it was cramped. A maximum speed of 185kph (approaching 115mph) was claimed for the Bagheera; acceleration was not out-standingly brisk, and the gearchange came in for criticism, while at well below 160kph (100mph) the car became uncomfortably noisy.

Although there were some styling oddities in the cockpit, the Bagheera showed more than a touch of well-directed overall flair, with none of the idiosyncracies which characterized slightly earlier French essays in the class, and sales amply justified the initial planned production of 10 000 a year. A larger-engined version was stillborn, but in itself the Bagheera was an original, and worthwhile, addition to the Simca, Chrysler and later Talbot ranges.

In 1981, it was superseded by the restyled Murena, still with three-abreast seating, but powered by a choice of 1·6- or 2·2-litre Talbot engines.

Specification
Engine: Simca straight-four; 76·7 × 70mm, 1294cc; pushrod ohv; twin Weber carburettors; 84bhp at 6000rpm.
Gearbox: Simca four-speed manual.
Chassis: tubular; front suspension independent by wishbones, torsion bars and dampers; rear suspension independent by trailing arms, torsion bars and dampers; four-wheel disc brakes.
Dimensions: wheelbase 237cm/93½in; front track 138cm/54½in; rear track 143cm/56½in.

Mazda RX-7

The Togo Kogyo company kept faith with the rotary engine while others put it to one side – the millionth Mazda with this form of power unit was produced in 1979 – and introduced its first large-scale production rotary-engined sports car, the RX-7, early in 1978 (the less-than-inspiring Cosmo Sports having been built in small numbers from 1967-70).

The RX-7 was a shapely coupe, in appearance more than a match for its class contemporaries such as the Porsche 924 and Triumph TR7. Like them, it was front-engined, the compactness of the rotary unit meaning that it could be set well back from the nose, thereby providing a 51/49 weight distribution and facilitating good aerodynamics (drag coefficient with headlights retracted was only 0·34 in the 1981 RX-7SE). Suspension followed the well-tried McPherson strut ifs and live rear axle combination which worked well enough, even if back end behaviour was not entirely faultless in hard driving.

The engine was a refined version of the twin-rotor unit used in the RX-3 saloon, appropriate for a sports car because of its narrower power band and its above-average fuel consumption (when driven hard), both aspects being more acceptable in this employment. An exhaust thermal reactor largely kept the emission problem in check,

and save for minor details the engine was standard for all markets. Equivalent capacity was 2292cc ($2 \times 2 \times 573$cc) and it was rated at 105bhp, which proved good for a 188kph (117mph) maximum speed and acceleration only marginally below par for the class. Up to 165bhp was developed in 'production' racing versions, while in 1980 the BAE Turbosystems turbo version was approved; this raised maximum bhp to 171 at 5500rpm, and the claimed maximum speed to 217kph (135mph).

The RX-7 was nominally a 2+2 in European markets, but was more realistically listed as a two-seater in the USA, with a flat luggage platform behind the seats; the cockpit was well fitted-out, and visibility was reasonable.

Mazda produced competition accessories, such as spoilers and suspension components, early in the car's life, and from 1979 the RX-7 was actively raced in various guises, especially in the USA, where good placings fell to RX-7s in IMSA events and two cars placed fifth and sixth in the 1979 Daytona 24-hours, while another broke world class records at Bonneville. It was also seen in British production saloon racing, where its appearance (let alone its first outright victory!) led to some acrimony; in 1980, the RX-7 won this Group 1 championship.

Specification (*road cars*)
Engine: Wankel rotary with twin rotors in line; 2292cc; side inlet/circumferential exhaust valves; Nippon carburettor; 105bhp at 6000rpm.
Gearbox: five-speed manual.
Chassis: unitary; front suspension independent by McPherson struts, coil springs and anti-roll bar; rear suspension by live axle, upper and lower trailing arms, coil spring/damper units and anti-roll bar; disc front/drum rear brakes.
Dimensions: wheelbase 242cm/95½in; **front track** 142cm/56in; **rear track** 140cm/55in.

McLaren M8

McLarens built out-and-out sports racers, straightforward no-nonsense machines which dominated the CanAm series for four years. The M8 directly derived from the M6, which had an equally impressive season in 1967, was put into limited production by Trojan, and was the basis of the road-going M6GT prototype (abandoned after Bruce McLaren's death).

McLaren had been responsible for the broad concept of the M6, which was designed by Robin Herd, and the M8, which was the work of Gordon Coppuck and Jo Marquart. The M8 was built around an aluminium monocoque and the alloy-block dry-sump Chevrolet ZL-1 7-litre V-8, developed by McLarens to give an initial 620bhp, thus investing the M8 with a formidable power-to-weight ratio. It was a stressed member, mounted to the rear bulkhead which also carried the suspension radius arms and two subframes for the gearbox and the other rear suspension elements. The forward bulkhead mounted the front suspension. Transmission was through a Hewland LG500 gearbox. The bodywork added considerable bulk to the bare car, but was well-proportioned and aerodynamically efficient.

From 1968 onwards, the M8s were developed simply and logically (some team cars being rebuilt in revised form for the new season), while near-replicas without all the current refinements were built by Trojan for independent teams. The M8B of 1969 featured a high, suspension-mounted rear aerofoil; when these were banned the M8D of 1970 had its rear wing neatly mounted between longitudinal 'fences' running back from mid-wheelbase above each flank. The M8F was a smoother development, again with slightly extended track. The Trojan 'production' version was the M8FP.

Engines in the orange works cars were constantly increased in size and power outputs, to 7·6-litres and 625bhp in the M8B, to 670bhp in the M8D, and to 8·1-litres and 740bhp in the M8F, while even larger units were tried, although not regularly raced.

Power of this order, coupled with a very sound basic car, an efficient team, and driver strength centred on Denny Hulme, with Bruce McLaren himself, Peter Revson, Peter Gethin and Dan Gurney in turn as team mates, gained 32 victories for the works team in 37 CanAm races between 1968 and 1971, while independents gained many good placings in McLarens. Similar cars were also successful in the 1971 Interseries, but even a turbocharged version with up to 820bhp was outclassed by the Porsche 917/10s in 1972, as was the M20 successor to the M8F in CanAm racing.

Sadly, Bruce McLaren was killed in a test accident driving the first M8D at Goodwood early in 1970.

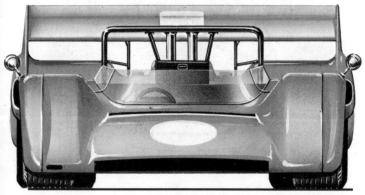

1970 M8D

Specification

Engine: *M8A* – Chevrolet 90-degree V-8; 108 × 95mm, 6990cc; pushrod ohv; Lucas fuel injection; 620bhp at 7000rpm.

M8F – as above, but in 7·6, 7·8 or 8·1 litre forms in works cars; 740bhp at 6400rpm (varying capacities affecting torque rather than gross power)

Gearbox: Hewland four-speed manual.

Chassis: monocoque; front suspension independent by wishbones, coil springs, dampers and anti-roll bar; rear suspension independent by upper links, lower wishbones, radius arms, coil springs, dampers and anti-roll bar; four-wheel ventilated disc brakes.

Dimensions: *M8A* – wheelbase 239cm/94in;
front track 146cm/57½in; **rear track** 137cm/54in.

M8F – wheelbase 249cm/98in;
front track 152cm/60in; **rear track** 147cm/58in.

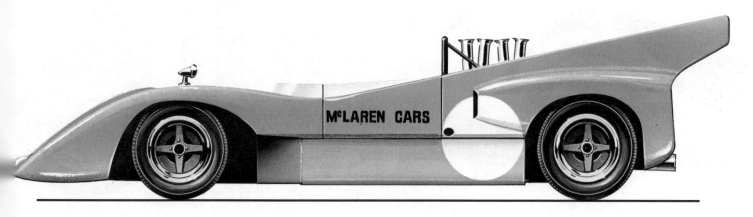

Mercedes-Benz S models

The big six-cylinder Mercedes-Benz sports cars designed by Dr Ferdinand Porsche rank high among the truly legendary Vintage machines. For size, noise, performance and sheer aura they were awesome indeed.

Like W O Bentley, Dr Porsche knew that the best way to high performance with reliability at that stage of development was a big, efficient, unhurried engine; the striking race successes of the big white German cars proved how right he was. There were four stages in their evolution – S, SS, SSK and SSKL – and their common antecedent was an under-braked and over-weight touring car, the 6·2-litre Model K which was equipped with a vertical Roots-type supercharger to give its performance a much-needed boost.

From the K, Dr Porsche first evolved the S (meaning Sport), with 6·8-litre engine, aluminium head and long four-seater body, which won the 1927 German sports-car GP and other races. Next came the SS (Super Sport) with a bigger bore, 7·1-litre engine in a lowered frame, and this car won the 1928 German GP and the 1929 Ulster TT. Porsche then advanced to the SSK (the K denoting *Kurz* or short) with lighter, shorter wheelbase chassis and 225bhp beneath its massive bonnet. This powerful but agile beast was good for 200kph (125mph) in the right places, and won numerous European hillclimbs, the 1930 Irish GP and the 1931 Belgian 24-hour race.

Finally the much rarer SSKL (L for *Leicht* or Light) was a further lightened SSK with drilled chassis and larger 'elephant' blower giving 265bhp. 'Light' was relative, for it still weighed 1700kg, but this fabulous monster won the 1931 Mille Miglia as a sports car, and the 1931 Avus, Eifel and German GPs stripped down to racing trim.

On all these cars the Roots supercharger blew through twin carburettors rather than inhaling through them as was normal practice. Nor was it permanently engaged, but was brought into action through a clutch when the driver fully depressed the accelerator. When in action it emitted a blood-curdling scream which added to the Merc's devilish image, besides giving ample warning to rival drivers that they were about to be overtaken. The best days of such vast, exciting machines ended after 1931, when science – in the shape of smaller, higher-revving engines in smaller, better-suspended cars – took over.

Specification

Engine: *S* – straight-six; 98 × 150mm, 6789cc; single ohc; twin carburettors and Roots-type supercharger; 180bhp at 3000rpm.
  SS – as above, but 100 × 150mm, 7069cc; 200bhp at 3000rpm.
  SSK – as SS, but 225bhp at 3300rpm.
  SSKL – as SS, but 265bhp at 3300rpm.
Gearbox: four-speed manual.
Chassis: pressed steel side members; semi-elliptic springs front and rear; hydraulic/friction dampers; four-wheel drum brakes with servo assistance.
Dimensions: wheelbase *S and SS* – 337cm/132½in, *SSK and SSKL* – 295cm/116in; **track** 141cm/55½in.

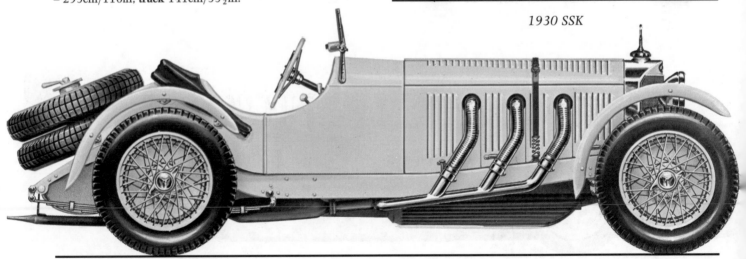

1930 SSK

Mercedes-Benz 300 SL

The 'Gullwing' was one of the sensational cars of the 1950s, as were the W194 sports-racer of 1952 and the W198 production version which followed in 1954. It was the car which marked one of Mercedes' occasional returns to main-line motor sport, with the success which seemed almost customary, for although the team gained 'only' second and fourth places in their first outing they convincingly won all the other events contested in 1952. And in its production form, the car had a rarely equalled glamour ...

Mercedes was at that time by no means over-endowed with money, and when the decision to go ahead with a new sports car was taken in 1951, economy dictated that a modified version of the straight-six from the 300S saloon was used, together with that model's transmission, ifs and swing-axle rear suspension. The novelty in the Sport Leicht was its multi-tube spaceframe and, consequent upon the need to maintain its integrity as far as possible, doors that were hinged on the roof, actually comprising windows and part of the roof. Aerodynamic – and aesthetic – qualities were improved by the low bonnet, achieved by canting the 171bhp dry-sump engine. The differential was bolted to the chassis, with half shafts hinged on trunnions and no conventional longitudinal location. The body was sleek, and virtually unadorned. The first race for the 300SL was the Mille Miglia, where the performance of the car (and a one-two-three in the Prix de Berne) alarmed Mercedes'

potential Le Mans opponents, a factor which contributed towards the first and second placings for the 300SLs in the 24-hour race. A similar result in the Carrera Panamericana was perhaps a greater triumph, after which the works put away the W194 (ten had been made).

However, Mercedes' US agent guaranteed a 1000-car order for a civilized derivative, so the W198 was launched in New York early in 1954. This was refined in appearance, with some chrome trim, bumpers, bonnet-side vents, and some spaceframe purity sacrificed to admit larger doors. Bosch direct fuel injection boosted engine power to 240bhp. The theoretical maximum speed was 260kph (162mph); in practice, this seems to have been around 225kph (140mph).

Although the production 'Gullwing' is best recalled for its rally career – events such as the Liege-Rome-Liege falling to it along with the 1956 European Championship – it was also raced, one notable achievement being Fitch's fifth overall in the 1955 Mille Miglia in one of the 29 alloy-bodied cars (steel-panel bodies were standard).

Production of the 'Gullwing' ceased in 1956 after 1400 had been built, and in 1957 it was succeeded by the 300SL Roadster, with 250bhp engine, low-pivot swing axles to give more predictable handling, and disc brakes on the final cars. 1858 Roadsters were made before production ended in 1962.

1957 'Gullwing'

Specification *(road cars)*
Engine: straight-six; 85 × 88mm, 2996cc; single ohc; Bosch fuel injection; 240bhp at 6100rpm.
Gearbox: four-speed manual.
Chassis: spaceframe; front suspension independent by wishbones, coil springs, dampers and anti-roll bar; rear suspension by swing axles, coil springs and dampers; four-wheel drum brakes.
Dimensions: wheelbase 240cm/94½in; **front track** 140cm/55in; **rear track** 145cm/57in.

Mercedes-Benz 300 SLR

This was an out-and-out sports-racer, deriving from the W196 Grand Prix car (as its W196S factory designation clearly indicated) rather than from the 300SL, although the association with the latter was a more useful marketing aid. Nine cars were completed, and raced for just one season in only six events, yet they contributed mightily to Mercedes' reputation for racing near-invincibility.

The cornerstone of Mercedes' mid-1950s competitions programme was the W196 F1 car, and the demands of Grand Prix racing meant that the sports car to follow up the 300SL successes could not be ready for racing until 1955 (first tests were run in the autumn of 1954). The square engine followed the straight-eight desmodromic GP unit closely, although the two blocks of four cylinders were cast in silumin instead of fabricated in steel and there were numerous detail variations, as well as those essential sports car additions, generator and starter. Power output varied according to fuel and anticipated race demands, up to 302bhp at 7500rpm on normal fuel, up to 340bhp on alcohol fuels.

The engine was canted in the space frame, and the transmission with ZF gearbox in unit with the final drive came from the W196, as did the suspension and massive inboard drum brakes. This was one area where Mercedes were less confident than the known opposition, especially the disc-braked Jaguars, and it led to the air brake used in two races (this was hydraulically operated, and followed experiments on a 300SL coupe). Body styles varied slightly, for example with twin headrests when a two-man crew was used, and coupe bodies were built for two cars, one of which was used as a road car by Rudolf Uhlenhaut – and was timed at 290kph (180mph) on a closed autobahn.

Stirling Moss and co-driver Denis Jenkinson scored a spectacular debut victory for the 300SLR in the 1955 Mille Miglia, averaging 157·63kph (97·95mph) over the 1596km (992 miles) and finishing well ahead of team mate Fangio. A one-two-three in the Eifelrennen followed, and 300SLRs were running first and second at Le Mans when they were withdrawn after a tragic accident involving the third car in the team. Two more victories, in the Swedish GP and the accident-marred TT, meant that Mercedes had to contest and win the Targa Florio to take the sports car championship.

The race was intensely dramatic, Moss and Peter Collins winning in a 300SLR despite an off-road excursion (by Moss) and an assault on a Sicilian wall (by Collins). Thus Mercedes gained a third title, to add to the GT championship gained by 300SLs and their overwhelming Grand Prix honours.

Specification

Engine: straight-eight; 78 × 78mm, 2979cc; twin ohc; Bosch fuel injection; 302bhp (see text) at 7500rpm.
Gearbox: five-speed manual.
Chassis: spaceframe; front suspension independent by wishbones, torsion bars and dampers; rear suspension by swing axles, torsion bars and dampers; four-wheel drum brakes.
Dimensions: wheelbase 238cm/93½in; **front track** 128cm/50½in; **rear track** 138cm/54½in.

Mercedes-Benz 450 SLC/500 SLC

The 450SLC seemed another model in the excellent range of road-sters and coupes produced through the two decades in which Mercedes broadly turned away from main-line motor sport (although they occasionally rallied with saloons). The 450SLC had been a big four-seat car which seemed to have less sporting potential than others in the range, but it was nevertheless chosen to spearhead the company's first sustained competition effort since the great racing teams of the mid-1950s.

In the late 1970s, however, the emphasis had shifted to rallies; by the end of the decade it was obvious that a full Mercedes works team, in all but name, was operating again, and right at the end of 1979 that team gained its first victory: the 450SLCs crushingly won the Bandama Rally, taking the first four places to team orders . . .

The 450 range had been introduced in 1973, gaining the Car of the Year award for qualities that (apart from thirst, in a time of fuel crises) were outstanding. The common engine to the series was a 4520cc iron-block, alloy-head V-8, effectively the 3·5-litre engine with increased stroke, gaining in torque rather than power (initially eight per cent up at 217 bhp). A 5-litre light-alloy V-8 was also developed, initially for the German market. The Mercedes-Benz three-speed automatic transmission was standard. Suspension was independent all round, with anti-dive geometry at the front, anti-squat linkage at the rear. The whole car was sophisticated and elegant, with a maximum speed of just over 210kph (130mph), but on the face of it hardly a competitions sports car . . .

This impression was not really contradicted by private efforts, such as Tony Fowkes' comfortable drive to a class win in the 1976 Tour of Britain, but after Andrew Cowan and Fowkes placed 280Es first and second in the 1977 London-Sydney Rally, Mercedes' thoughts increasingly turned towards rallying, and four quasi-works 280Es were run in the 1978 Safari Rally.

When a team returned to that event in 1979, it included 450SLCs (Hannu Mikkola placed one second) and thereafter the team majored on this model. Although, of necessity, it was a team on the grand scale, it was run out of the experimental department rather than by a competitions department, and manager Eric Waxenberger stressed that it was competing with virtually standard production cars rather than competition specials, albeit using 5-litre 310bhp light-alloy V-8s and suspension modified in the light of rough-terrain experience.

After the Bandama triumph, selected 1980 European events were contested, but the size and weight of the 450SLC told against it on these tighter rallies. In Portugal, cars placed fourth and fifth, while on the Acropolis the only car to finish was a lowly 14th. A very strong team, with cars now in Group 2 guise designated 500SLC, was run in the Argentine Codasar rally, where one finished in a less-than-impressive second place. After taking first and fifth in the Cote d'Ivoire Rally (with a private entrant second), the team was abruptly wound up, its achievements having far from matched expectations for this 'flagship' undertaking.

Specification

Engine: *road cars* – 90-degree V-8; 92 × 85mm, 4520cc; ohv; Bosch electronic fuel injection.
    rally cars – as above, but 96·5 × 85mm, 4973cc; approx. 320bhp.
Gearbox: three- or four-speed automatic.
Chassis: integral; front suspension independent by double wishbones, coil springs, dampers and anti-roll bar; rear suspension independent by semi-trailing arms, coil springs, auxiliary rubber springs, dampers and anti-roll bar; four-wheel disc brakes.
Dimensions: **wheelbase** 280cm/110in; **front track** 145cm/57in; **rear track** 144cm/56½in.

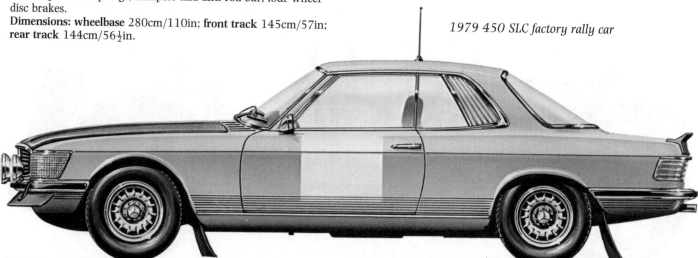

1979 450 SLC factory rally car

Mercer Type 35

Before 'Type 35' meant anything to Bugatti admirers, the designation was applied to a highly revered American sporting car, the Mercer Raceabout. Standing out from the dull ruck of average American designs, the Mercer enterprise was master-minded by W A Roebling, who belonged to the engineering family which built the Brooklyn Bridge, but who died on the Titanic in 1912. The Raceabout used a conventional but vigorous 4·9-litre four-cylinder T-head engine in a short chassis accommodating two people in bucket seats, a bolster tank and a pair of spare wheels.

Produced from 1911 to 1914, the car was intended for wealthy amateur motorists, being virtually hand-built from top quality materials, and while its exposed body, devoid of hood or other protection, probably restricted sales to the drier American states, there was always a waiting list for the car during the four years it was produced.

The basic design was conservative, with the four cylinders cast in pairs, dimensions being 111×127mm giving a total displacement of 4916cc. A meticulously balanced, pressure-lubricated three-bearing crankshaft was employed, the two camshafts in the crankcase being gear-driven and connecting with the 57mm diameter valves via rocking arms and 'lifters'. There were two plugs per cylinder, sparked by magneto, and a single carburettor; a brake reading of 58bhp at 1700rpm on Mercer's own dynamometer was obligatory. The engine was mounted in a subframe, and a separate three-speed gearbox was employed, although a heavier five-seater touring edition had four speeds.

Suspension was by the usual semi-elliptics, the springs being made of vanadium alloy steel, and Hartford friction dampers were fitted. The 110kph (70mph) Raceabout with its open scuttle, steeply-raked steering column, huge brass lamps, 'monocle' windscreen for the driver only, exhaust cut-out and popular canary yellow paintwork set a fashion in US sporting machinery also taken up by Stutz, National, Marmon and others. About a score of Mercer's evocative T-head Raceabouts still exist, fondly cherished.

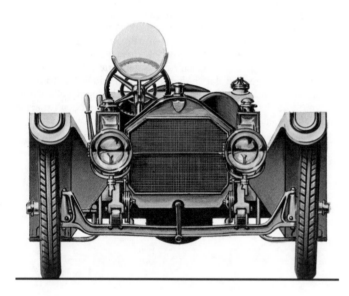

Specification
Engine: straight-four; 111×127mm, 4916cc; side valves in T-head; single carburettor; 58bhp at 1700rpm.
Gearbox: separate three-speed manual.
Chassis: pressed steel side members with engine and gearbox in subframe; semi-elliptic springs and friction dampers front and rear; rear-wheel drum brakes and transmission brake.
Dimensions: wheelbase 274cm/108in; **track** 145cm/57in.

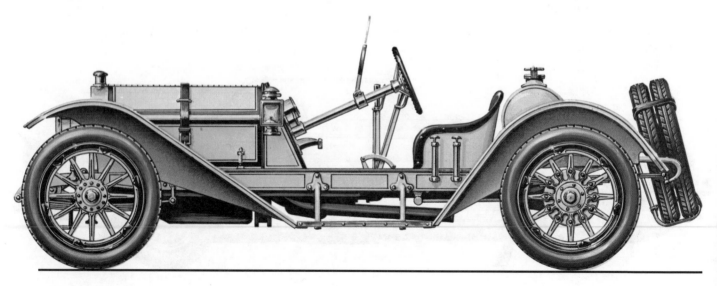

MG 18/80

It is often completely forgotten that there was once a 'big' MG of considerable promise, destined to die prematurely in the face of opposition from its own kin. As is well-known, the first MG sports cars were based on Morris products, but by 1928 the marque had achieved a separate identity, although still in close association with Morris, and was established in its own factory at Cowley. Cecil Kimber, the company 'kingpin', now sought a more powerful engine than the old 1802cc side-valve Morris Oxford used since 1926; he found the answer in another Morris unit.

For an unsuccessful 1927 model (the Light Six) Morris Motors had produced a 69 × 110mm, 2468cc six which, surprisingly for that somewhat pedestrian make, had its valves operated by a chain-driven overhead camshaft. MG improved the engine with a new cylinder head and twin SU carburettors, adapted Morris's three-speed gearbox, and designed a new chassis with wheelbase and track identical to the abortive Light Six but with a sturdier bulkhead, Rudge knock-off wire wheels, and a very smart new radiator with a central tiebar.

This was the first MG Sports Six, the rather high-built model making its debut in chassis and coupe forms at the 1928 Olympia Show. When production got under way it became the 18/80 (Mark I) for obscure reasons, its actual output being 58bhp at 3200rpm. It was a pleasant car, the 2½-litre six-cylinder ohc engine being notably flexible right up to its 125kph (78mph) maximum, the roadholding good, and the instrumentation and internal treatment excellent.

Twelve months later Kimber added to the MG range with an improved 18/80 Mark II, with four speeds, a new, sturdier frame, larger brakes and a 10·2cm wider track. Unfortunately these improvements also added weight, and for 1930 a special 130kph (80mph) Speed Model on the Mark I chassis was introduced, rather eclipsing the more luxurious and expensive Mark II. Almost simultaneously a Mark III Tigress competition model appeared, with a very special 83bhp engine featuring dry-sump lubrication, cross-flow head and 12 plugs, and AIACR regulation bodywork.

However, the profusion (and confusion) of MG models was simplified during the next two years owing to the resounding success of the smaller, cheaper MG Midget. Only five Mark IIIs were built, while the last Mark I came off the line in July 1931; the Mark II continued while stocks of parts were used up, and production of MG's first 'big six' finally ended in the winter of 1932-33.

Specification

Engine: *MksI and II* – straight-six; 69 × 110mm, 2468cc; single ohc; twin SU carburettors; 58bhp at 3200rpm.

  MkIII – as above (but see text); 83bhp at 4300rpm.
Gearbox: *MkI* – three-speed manual; *MksII and III* – four-speed manual.
Chassis: pressed steel side members; semi-elliptic springs and friction dampers front and rear; four-wheel drum brakes.
Dimensions: wheelbase 290cm/114in; **track** *MkI* – 122cm/48in, *MksII and III* – 132cm/52in.

MG Midget M-type

On the same stand as the new six-cylinder MG 18/80 at the 1928 Olympia Show was another newcomer, the MG Midget, of unforeseen but immense significance to the future of the still young company. With economic depression imminent, the motor industry was 'thinking small', and this, plus the challenge of the successful Austin Seven, had brought a new 'baby', the 847cc Morris Minor, to that same 1928 Motor Show.

This car's pleasing little four-cylinder engine had an overhead camshaft and a short, sturdy two-bearing crankshaft, producing about 18bhp to propel a minimal two-door saloon on a 198cm wheelbase. The engine was designed and built by Wolseley, which had been taken over by Morris in 1927, and Cecil Kimber of MG procured an early prototype Minor with a particularly lively engine. Intrigued by its potential, he replaced the saloon body with a sparse open two-seater, tested it and saw the makings of a best seller.

Thus was born the M-type Midget, a pretty little boat-tailed two-seater with neat fixed cycle wings, vee screen and fabric covered body. It used the Minor chassis and suspension (somewhat lowered), the engine (in 20bhp form), three-speed gearbox, transmission, axles and wheels; it weighed only 500kg, was good for 105kph (65mph) and inevitably sold like hot cakes. The first year's production of Midgets exceeded the entire MG production up to then, and the company, outgrowing its Cowley works, moved to Abingdon early in 1930.

The Midget was then launched into racing, with devastating effect. The little ohc engine was constantly improved, and what began with class wins by privateers in 1930 became outright victories in 1931, preceded by a shattering feat at Montlhéry where a supercharged, much-modified linered-down M-type in an underslung chassis became the first 750cc car ever to exceed 100mph (160kph).

With typical speed, MG introduced a competition sports car, the 750cc Montlhéry, with or without supercharger, based on the record car; in an overwhelming 1931 season, such C types won the Brooklands Double-12, Irish GP and Ulster TT sports car races. Handicapping helped, of course, but so did the altogether unprecedented performance of these little 'bombs'. These racers owed little to the original M-type, but in the light of their brilliant achievements these worthy little cars sold splendidly in open and coupe forms until mid-1932, a total of 3235 being produced before they were replaced by an updated Midget.

Specification

Engine: straight-four; 57 × 83mm, 847cc; single ohc; single SU carburettor; 20bhp at 4000rpm, rising to 27bhp from 1930.
Gearbox: three-speed manual, with optional four-speed manual from 1930.
Chassis: pressed steel side members; semi-elliptic springs and friction dampers front and rear; four-wheel drum brakes.
Dimensions: wheelbase 198cm/78in; **track** 107cm/42in.

MG Midget J2

The racing experience gained by MG with the Midgets in 1930 and 1931 was applied to the design of a new production model to succeed the M-type. The J2, which appeared in August 1932, was a clever, well-proportioned and attractive replacement, with fixed cycle-type wings, a neat two-seater body with windscoops and cutaway door sides, and a slab rear tank mounting the spare wheel.

If all this smacked of 'pseudo-Le Mans', it could be strongly argued that MG needed no fake racing image; they had raced over most of Europe, Le Mans included, and the J2 was the pleasingly functional result, setting a style which was so widely copied. Its wheelbase, at 218cm, was 20cm longer than the M-type's, but the track remained the same. The semi-elliptic springs slid in trunnions rather than on shackles, and the chassis, more rigid than the M, was underslung at the rear like that of the competition C-type.

The engine, too, owed much to the C-type. While retaining the old bore and stroke of 57 × 83mm (847cc) and the two-bearing crankshaft, it now had a cross-flow head with twin SU semi-downdraught carburettors, and 36bhp was realised at a busy-sounding 5500rpm,

almost twice the output of the Minor-based M-type. Again as on the M, the vertical drive to the ohc still served as the armature spindle for the vertical dynamo, where oil would eventually permeate the windings with disturbing effect.

Rudge centre-lock wire wheels were fitted, the 8-inch diameter brakes looking rather skimpy, while a four-speed gearbox was an improvement with a neat central remote-control lever. Its ratios were rather wide, but overall the J2 provided most enjoyable sports car motoring for two, while an aesthetically less-pleasing four-seater, the J1, was also offered.

Racing J3 and J4 derivatives with supercharged 750cc engines were also available for competition work, but clearly Abingdon's 'bread and butter' was chiefly earned by the J2, which attracted over 2000 satisfied customers in under two years' production. The last few hundred built were fitted with long, swept front wings in place of the open cycle-type; the new style certainly gave greater protection from the wet, and foreshadowed their use on the P-type which succeeded the J2.

Specification

Engine: straight-four; 57 × 83mm, 847cc; single ohc; twin SU carburettors; 36bhp at 5500rpm.
Gearbox: four-speed manual.
Chassis: pressed steel side members, underslung at rear; semi-elliptic springs and friction dampers front and rear; four-wheel drum brakes.
Dimensions: wheelbase 218cm/86in; **track** 107cm/42in.

MG Magnette K3

One of the most inspiring and exclusive of MGs, the K3 was essentially a competition model, available in sports or racing form in 1933-34. The Magnette derived from the 1931-32 Magna, which was the first small six produced by MG, and had a bore and stroke of 57 × 83mm – identical to that of the M-type Midget, but with two more cylinders, giving a capacity of 1271cc.

This engine was virtually that of a Wolseley Hornet, giving an inadequate 37·2bhp at 4100rpm. Also inadequate was the Magna chassis, with the same 8-inch brakes and 107cm track as the Midget, but a 41cm longer wheelbase. For the 1932 Motor Show, therefore, Cecil Kimber laid down an improved, higher performance MG six of under 1100cc, its stroke shortened to 71mm, and having three SU carburettors, a cross-flow head and magneto ignition. This was called the Magnette, and was marketed in KA and KB forms, with underslung chassis, 15cm wider track, and open four-seater or pillarless four-door saloon bodywork.

An innovation on the KA was a Wilson four-speed preselector gearbox, with selector lever on the gearbox, but the KB retained a normal 'crash' box, and there were some bewildering permutations of engines, gearboxes and chassis including the rare K2 with the Magna 1271cc power unit in a Magnette chassis. The definitive '1100' competition K3 emerged early in 1933 when, following a typically brief prototype period, a team of three achieved the boldest British racing coup since Bentley first won Le Mans.

These MGs, their 1087cc engines fitted with Powerplus superchargers, challenged the Maseratis and Fiats in the 1100cc class of the Mille Miglia, Italy's classic 1000-mile road race, and they won the first two places and the team prize. Five months later a similar K3 scored MG's second Ulster TT victory, while many class wins at home and abroad also fell to this brilliant car in 1933-34. Further development was halted by Lord Nuffield's 1935 edict that MG withdraw completely from motor racing.

In 1934, however, the company introduced a new road model Magnette, the N-type, with 1271cc engine and manual gearbox, and some very chic sporting bodywork in which the classic slab tank was replaced by an elegant outswept tail. A racing variant, the NE, won the 1934 Ulster TT, and N-types, the last of the pre-war 'real' Magnettes, endured until late 1936 with detail changes.

Specification

Engine: straight-six; 57 × 71mm, 1087cc; single ohc; single SU carburettor, with Powerplus supercharger (1933) or Marshall supercharger (1934); approx. 125bhp at 6500rpm.
Gearbox: Wilson four-speed preselector.
Chassis: pressed steel side members; semi-elliptic springs and friction dampers front and rear; four-wheel drum brakes.
Dimensions: wheelbase 239cm/94in; **track** 122cm/48in.

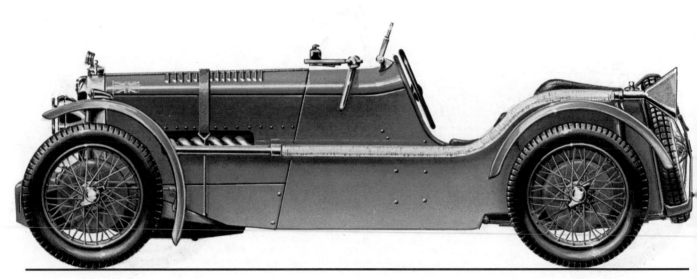

MG T-series Midgets

The T series of sports MG Midgets began in 1936, a few months after MG withdrew from motor racing by edict of Morris Motors, the company's new proprietors. At the same time, a programme of rationalisation began, and instead of the sporting ohc engine and 'crash' gearbox of former Midgets, the new TA had a long-stroke 1292cc pushrod ohv four-cylinder power unit (with twin carburettors) and four-speed gearbox, basically as used in the Morris Ten and Wolseley 10/40 saloons. The first Midget to have hydraulic brakes, it was roomier and less stiffly sprung, with some precious extra centimetres added to wheelbase, track and body, while the pushrod engine proved both zestful and reliable.

The TA became the TB in 1939, when the shorter stroke Morris 12 engine of 1250cc was adopted, along with a closer-ratio gearbox, but the Second World War stopped production almost before it had started.

Six years later, the war over, MG returned to car manufacture under vastly changed conditions. For Britain it was 'export or die' to a car-hungry world, so it was common sense to revive a proven pre-war design. With only slight suspension and body changes, therefore, production of the TB two-seater as the TC was soon under way, although severe problems of component and material supply retarded the initial output. For three years MG could not build

enough TC Midgets, many of them going to the USA and kindling a new American interest in sports cars and road racing.

By 1949, MG felt that the time had come for some modernisation, and the Midget was given a sturdier box-section frame with coil spring ifs, rack and pinion steering, larger brakes, with two leading shoes at the front, five-stud pressed-steel wheels of smaller diameter than the quick-release wire type, and bumpers front and rear.

This TD horrified MG's more reactionary diehards until it proved its virtues of pleasant ride, good roadholding and general 'Abingdon zest', demonstrated successfully at sundry motor race meetings at circuits such as Silverstone, Dundrod, and numerous American venues. A TD MkII 'competition' model with larger carburettors had 3-4bhp extra and more flexibility, and between late 1949 and late 1953 an impressive 29 664 MG TD Midgets were built.

The next change was merely cosmetic, BMC only sanctioning a face-lift for the TD, which emerged as the TF at the 1953 London Show. It had the 1¼-litre MkII engine, a curved radiator grille and more sweeping wings with faired-in headlights, separate bucket seats and optional wire wheels, but public reception was lukewarm. A full 1½-litre, 63bhp engine brought a decided improvement in performance, the TF 1500 Midget being produced until superseded by the MGA in mid-1955.

Specification

Engine: *TA* – straight-four; 63·5 × 102mm, 1292cc; pushrod ohv; twin SU carburettors; 52·4bhp at 5000rpm.

TB, TC and TD – as above, but 66·5 × 90mm, 1250cc; 54·4bhp at 5200rpm.

TD MkII and TF – as TB, but 57bhp at 5500rpm.

TF 1500 – as TA, but 72 × 90mm, 1466cc; 63bhp at 5000rpm.

Gearbox: four-speed manual.

Chassis: *TA, TB and TC* – pressed steel side members; front and rear suspension by semi-elliptic leaf springs and hydraulic dampers; four-wheel drum brakes.

TD and TF – as above, but box-section side members; front suspension independent by wishbones and coil springs.

Dimensions: *TA, TB and TC* – **wheelbase** 239cm/94in; **track** 114cm/45in.

TD and TF – **wheelbase** 239cm/94in; **front track** 120cm/47in; **rear track** 127cm/50in.

1950 TD

MG MGA

The MGA was the first post-war MG sports car to have 'contemporary' lines, with full-width bodywork to complement its flawless ancestry. Its outward shape recalled the one-off TD raced at Le Mans in 1951, and more directly the three EX182 team cars run in the 1955 24-hour race: these heralded the September 1955 introduction of the A, and like them the pre-production cars had some light-alloy body panels, while the chassis came via the EX179 record car. The engine was the 1489cc BMC B-type, used in the badge-engineered BMC ZA/ZB Magnette saloon which ran from 1953; it produced 68bhp when the A was launched and was uprated to 72bhp after the car had been in production for a year.

There was nothing novel in the suspension, but the whole car was well-balanced, with virtually 50/50 weight distribution. Maximum speed was just short of 160kph (100mph), while in less tangible qualities the A was a worthy sports car for even the most reactionary marque enthusiasts (perhaps it was for them that a wire wheel option was offered!).

Initially the works competition effort inclined towards racing, but major accidents in 1955 saw it re-directed into rallies, although the MGA was still widely raced in club events and it did return to Le Mans in coupe form in 1959-61, winning the 2-litre class in 1960, but retiring in 1959 and 1961.

The Twin Cam appeared in 1958 with disc brakes all round and 108bhp, but a 180kph (113mph) top speed was small compensation for an embarrasssingly troublesome engine and this model was dropped early in 1960. Meanwhile, the MGA engine was uprated in 1959, to 1588cc and 75bhp, with improved torque, while disc brakes took the place of the front two-leading-shoe drums. The MkII came in 1960, with the engine further bored out to 1622cc, and sufficient power to make it a genuine 160kph (100mph) car, certainly in hard-top form, for this version always had better aerodynamics.

Production passed 100 000 early in 1962, but sales were falling in the face of competition and the MGA was discontinued that year.

Specification (1959)

Engine: straight-four; 75·39 × 88·9mm, 1588cc; pushrod ohv; twin SU carburettors; 75bhp at 5300rpm.
Gearbox: four-speed manual.
Chassis: unitary with steel body; front suspension independent by wishbones, coil springs and dampers; rear suspension by live axle, semi-elliptic leaf springs and dampers; disc front/drum rear brakes.
Dimensions: wheelbase 239cm/94in; **front track** 121cm/47$\frac{1}{2}$in; **rear track** 123cm/48$\frac{1}{2}$in.

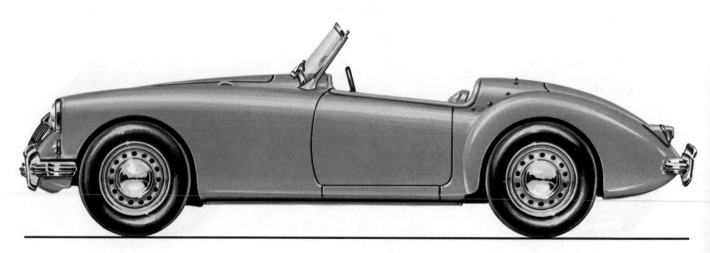

MG MGB

Until the parent conglomerate more or less streamlined MG out of existence at the end of the 1970s, the MGB was one of the great survivors. It was launched in 1962 but the origins of some major parts went back much further (engine to 1947, front suspension via the YA to before the Second World War); it was 'old-fashioned' for much of its life, but its traditional virtues proved to have lasting appeal.

It took the place of the MGA, then fading in the face of TRs and similar rivals. Running gear was similar to that of the A, but the B series engine was bored out, to give 95bhp and substantially improved torque. Coil-and-wishbone front suspension and a live rear axle made for responsive handling and ride qualities acceptable in a sports car. Top speed nudged 175kph (110mph), but was later to be lower in all but two variants.

These were the C of 1967, an unhappy model using the BMC six-cylinder 2·9-litre engine, which propelled it at almost 193kph (120mph) but which also, by its weight, totally upset the balance of the car; and the MGB GT V-8 coupe introduced in 1973.

This had the Rover-developed light-alloy 3·5-litre V-8, the handling was comparable with that of the basic B and it boasted a 200kph (125mph) top speed. It could not be sold in the USA, MG's principal market, and was discontinued at the end of 1976.

Meanwhile, the B gained a five-bearing version of its engine in 1964, the GT version appeared in 1965, all-synchromesh gears in 1967 (with an automatic transmission option), and a styling facelift in 1969. There were minor improvements until 1974, when – to the dismay of marque purists – the car had to be 'Federalised', with a greatly increased ride height to locate correctly US-specification bumpers; with this came a drop in engine power. A year later, suspension revisions offset the extra roll that had been an unfortunate consequence of the 1974 changes.

Although further minor improvements came in 1977, the B was showing its age, and was by then barely a 160kph (100mph) car. It nevertheless remained popular with a minority, and stayed in production, even after its profitability disappeared, until the MG factory at Abingdon was finally closed late in 1980.

1963 model

Specification

Engine: straight-four; 80·3 × 89mm, 1798cc; pushrod ohv; twin SU carburettors; 95bhp at 5400rpm in 1962, falling to 84bhp at 5500rpm in 1977.
Gearbox: four-speed manual, with optional automatic from 1967.
Chassis: integral with steel body; front suspension independent by wishbones, coil springs and dampers; rear suspension by live axle, semi-elliptic leaf springs and dampers (anti-roll bars from 1965); disc front/drum rear brakes.
Dimensions: wheelbase 200cm/78½in; **track** 125cm/49in.

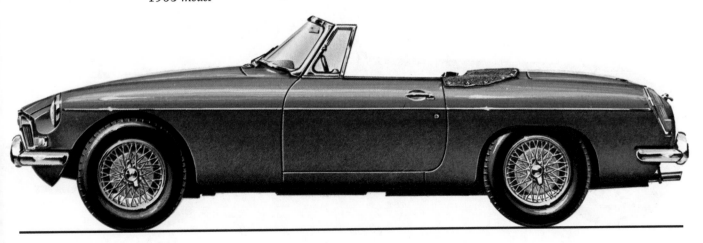

Morgan

That unique English marque, Morgan of Malvern Link, earned international fame with its spritely three-wheelers for a quarter century, before turning to four wheels in 1936. The first such car, the 4/4 (four wheels/four cylinders), used the same ifs system (coil springs on vertical sliding pillars) that featured on the very first Morgan in 1909 – and which still featured on Morgans in the 1980s!

The 4/4 was given a low, rigid ladder-type chassis with unusual Z-section side members, underslung at the rear, where a live axle was suspended on semi-elliptics. The engine was a 1122cc, 34bhp four-cylinder Coventry Climax with overhead inlet and side exhaust valves, driving through a separate four-speed gearbox. An open two-seater body with sweeping valanced wings, running boards and a neat sloping tail was hand-built by Morgan and this pretty little newcomer cost £194 when the MG TA Midget cost £222. An open four-seater and a two-seater coupe soon augmented the range, followed by a rarer 'Le Mans Replica' with fixed cycle-type front wings, justified by a second in class at Le Mans in 1938.

Almost all subsequent design changes concerned the engines, the chassis remaining basically unchanged into modern times, apart from periodic strengthening to accept more power. The first change of unit came in 1938, when the Climax gave way to an ohv Standard 10 unit. After weathering the Second World War the Morgan remained unchanged until 1950, when Standard's rugged 2·1-litre Vanguard engine was fitted. In this form it became the Plus Four, with 5cm wider track and 8cm wider body, although still a compact two-seater with exhilarating performance and leech-like roadholding, which also earned it competition successes of all kinds.

Triumph TR2, TR3 and TR4 twin-carburettor engines served after the Vanguard – making the Plus Four a 160kph (100mph) car – while even a BMC 1500 ohv engine was briefly used in an export model. The 4/4 was revived in 1955 in Series 2 form, powered by the side-valve 1172cc Ford 10 engine, with a three-speed gearbox; the 997cc ohv Anglia 105E engine with four speeds was introduced in 1960, and was succeeded by the 1340cc Classic 109E in 1961.

Apart from a lapse in the somewhat globular glass fibre Plus-Four-Plus aerodynamic GT coupe, of which only 49 were made, Morgan's styling remained 'pre-war', although a curved radiator and more sloping tail did improve the bodywork after 1955. Quick-release wire wheels were an attractive extra option, while braking was updated as performance rose, disc front brakes being adopted in 1960,

There were also Super Sports variants of the Plus Four with twin double-choke Weber carburettors, alloy bodywork and a range of other performance extras, and in 1962 one example, with a TR3 engine, won the 2-litre class at Le Mans, its performance surprising rivals with 'modern' specifications and aerodynamics. Production of the Plus Four ended early in 1969, but the Ford 1600cc Cortina ohv engine was fitted to the 4/4, giving it a speed of over 150kph (almost 95mph).

The most exciting Morgan of all made its debut at the 1968 Earls Court Show. Called the Plus Eight, it employed the 3½-litre Rover aluminium V-8 engine (of Buick origin), the torque from this 155bhp unit permitting an effortless 200kph (125mph) and a 0 to 100kph (60mph) figure of under 7 sec. To contain such performance, a stiffened frame with 5cm more wheelbase, 8cm wider track, larger tyres on broad-rim alloy wheels, a limited-slip differential and larger servo brakes were fitted. Initially a four-speed manual gearbox was used, until Rover's five-speed unit became available as an option.

Frankly old-fashioned apart from its engine, basic rather than refined, hard in suspension and only just weatherproof, the Plus Eight is glorious to drive on roads with corners of any kind, with its confidence-inducing understeer and inbuilt stability. Morgan's 'traditional' bodywork with separate wings and running boards tapering into the bodysides was deliberately retained, contributing to the unique vintage character of a marque built by vintage methods in a vintage factory; in 1981 it still enjoyed a healthy and envied waiting list of orders from home and abroad.

1956 4/4 series II

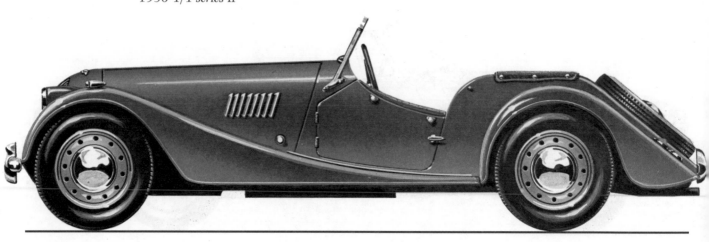

Specification

Engine: *4/4 (1936-38)* – Coventry Climax straight-four; 63 × 90mm, 1122cc; overhead inlet/side exhaust valves; single carburettor; 36bhp at 4500rpm.

4/4 (1939-49) – Standard straight-four; 63·5 × 100mm, 1267cc; pushrod ohv; single carburettor; 40bhp at 4300rpm.

4/4 (1955-60) – Ford straight-four; 63·5 × 92·5mm, 1172cc; side valves; single carburettor; 30bhp at 4000rpm.

4/4 (1960-61) – as above, but 81 × 48·4mm, 997cc; pushrod ohv; 41bhp at 5000rpm.

4/4 (1961-65) – as above, but 81 × 65mm, 1340cc; 56bhp at 4900rpm.

4/4 (1966-68) – as above, but 81 × 72·75mm, 1498cc; 83bhp at 4600rpm.

4/4 (from 1968) – as above, but 81 × 77·6mm, 1598cc; 93bhp at 4750rpm.

Plus Four (1950-54) – Standard Vanguard straight four; 85 × 92mm, 2088cc; pushrod ohv; single carburettor; 68bhp at 4000rpm.

Plus Four (1954-58) – Triumph TR2 straight-four; 83 × 92mm, 1991cc; pushrod ohv; twin carburettors; 90bhp at 4800rpm.

Plus Four (1958-62) – as above, but TR3 engine; 100bhp at 5000rpm.

Plus Four (1962-69) – as above, but TR4 engine; 86 × 92mm, 2138cc; 105bhp at 4750rpm.

Plus Eight – Rover 90-degree V-8; 89 × 71mm, 3528cc; pushrod ohv; twin carburettors; 155bhp at 5200rpm.

Gearbox: *4/4 (1936-50)* – separate four-speed manual.

4/4 (1955-59) – separate three-speed manual.

4/4 (from 1960) – separate four-speed manual.

Plus Four – separate four-speed manual.

Plus Eight (from 1968) – separate four-speed manual.

Plus Eight (from 1973) – four-speed manual (in unit with engine); optional five-speed manual.

Chassis: Z-section side members; front suspension independent by vertical sliding pillars, coil springs and dampers; rear suspension by rigid axle, semi-elliptic leaf springs and dampers; four-wheel drum brakes, but from 1959 disc front/drum rear brakes.

Dimensions: *4/4 and Plus Four* – **wheelbase** 244cm/96in; **track** 114cm/45in.

Plus Eight – **wheelbase** 249cm/98in; **track** 127cm/50in.

1969 Plus Eight

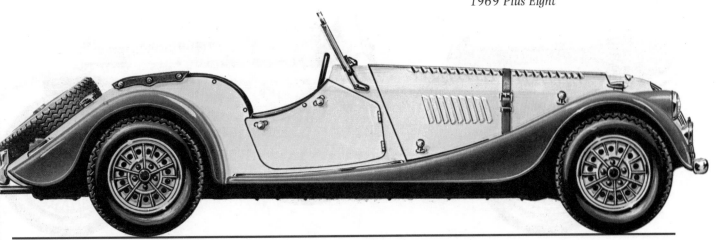

OM T665

At a time when overhead valves, frequently operated by overhead camshafts, were widely regarded as essentials in any sports car worthy of the name, the Italian OM defied fashion by having side valves. Quite why the Officine Meccaniche of Brescia did this is open to question, but the OM was nevertheless a remarkably lively performer which surprised its rivals by winning several motor races. Possibly, simplicity and reliability were the motives.

The first 2-litre six appeared in touring form in 1925 as the Type 665 Superba, its monobloc engine having a detachable head in which the combustion chambers embodied Ricardo patents. Dimensions were 65 × 100mm (1991cc) and a fully machined and dynamically-balanced crankshaft ran in four plain bearings, the centre pair being cooled by water jacketing. With a single Zenith carburettor and coil ignition, only 45bhp was achieved, but like most Latin marques, OM found the call to go racing irresistible, even with side valves.

By the use of twin carburettors, raised compression and razor tuning, the 665's output was boosted to about 60bhp at 4000rpm; the engine was installed in a shortened chassis possessing the virtues of strength, good weight distribution and roadholding, and excellent four-wheel braking, using the Perrot system at the front. All these features were demonstrated at Le Mans in the famous 24-hour race, when 665s finished fourth and fifth in both 1925 and 1926, winning the Rudge Whitworth 'handicap' Cup in the latter year.

The works OMs also won the 2-litre class in the Monza 24-hour and Spanish 12-hour races of 1926, while their achievements peaked in 1927 with a sweeping one-two-three triumph in the first 1000-mile Mille Miglia race over Italian public roads. Later that year, the 665 Sport MM was introduced with twin carburettors, underslung axles and larger brakes.

British racing driver/engineer R F Oats developed a special pushrod-ohv 12-plug head for the 2-litre, scoring several home successes with it, but the manufacturers chose Roots supercharging to boost output of their side-valve engine to 80bhp at 4000rpm. That secured them several more good placings in sports car races, but the twin-cam supercharged Alfa Romeos were now eclipsing the cars from Brescia. Capacity was raised to 2·2 litres, then to 2·35 litres in 1930, but production ceased in 1931, after which OM concentrated on commercial vehicles.

Specification

Engine: *Superba* – straight-six; 65 × 100mm, 1991cc; side valves; single Zenith carburettor; 45bhp at 3500rpm.

    Sport – as above, but 60bhp at 4000rpm.

    Sport MM – as above, but twin Zenith carburettors; 65bhp.

Gearbox: four-speed manual.

Chassis: pressed steel side members; semi-elliptic springs and friction dampers front and rear; four-wheel drum brakes.

Dimensions: wheelbase 310cm/122in (but 279cm/110in on Sport); **track** 132cm/52in.

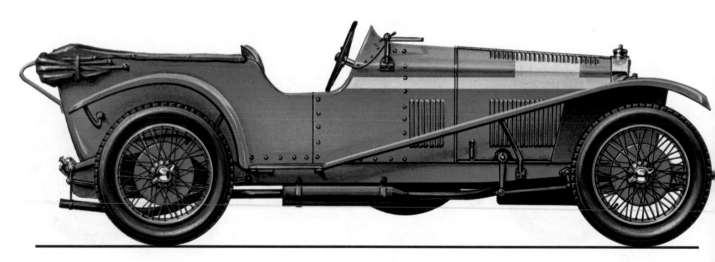

Panther Lima

With the Lima, Panther moved down-market from its grandiose recreations of previous years, to a car intended to recapture the spirit of the sports car of three or four decades earlier – at any rate visually and without any deliberate 'replicar' intent – but with modern standards of ride and performance. It was also the first Panther to be produced in quantity, although with output still modest, it was inevitable that use should be made of mass-produced components, in this case largely from Vauxhall (which association also brought marketing and service advantages). Unlike the cars which inspired its design, no competition role was envisaged for the Lima (although one did present an anachronistic sight in some major rallies and others ran in British club racing categories).

The design was based on the Vauxhall Magnum 2300 floorpan, used that car's suspension, steering, brakes, engine and transmission. The floorpan was modified to facilitate installation of the engine behind the front-wheel centre line, thus favouring weight distribution to the benefit of acceleration, and the gearbox also had to be shifted rearwards in the two-seater cockpit. The floor pan was reinforced, with substantial longitudinal tubes running under the door sills. MG doors made for an all-metal cockpit; the rest of the body was of moulded glass fibre.

In standard form the engine was rated at 108bhp, but Dealer Team Vauxhall conversions to various states of tune were available (as were DTV suspension parts), while a turbocharged version was announced in the autumn of 1978.

The Lima was a practical car as well as a fun car, although for touring the luggage space behind the rear seats was hardly adequate. It was fast – 190kph (almost 120mph) – predictable and stable, this last virtue being in part due to a front spoiler which largely obviated the aerodynamic shortcomings of the large flowing wings, so much a part of the originals which inspired it.

By the end of 1979, however, an attempt to broaden its market was being held at least partly responsible for Panther Westwinds' dire financial crisis, during which one of the first acts forced on it was to cut back Lima production. The company continued a curious on/off existence during 1980, and at the end of that year was acquired by the South Korea-based Jindo Industries, with Panther's founder Bob Jankel returning. Lima production restarted early in 1981, and in the spring a sparsely-equipped 1756cc version, the 1800ES, was introduced.

Specification (*standard car*)
Engine: Vauxhall straight-four; 76·2 × 97·5mm, 2279cc; single Stromberg carburettor; 108bhp at 5000rpm.
Gearbox: four-speed manual, with optional automatic or five-speed manual.
Chassis: pressed steel; front suspension independent by wishbones, coil spring/damper units and anti-roll bar; rear suspension by live axle and coil spring/damper units.
Dimensions: wheelbase 246cm/97in; **front track** 133cm/52½in; **rear track** 132cm/52in.

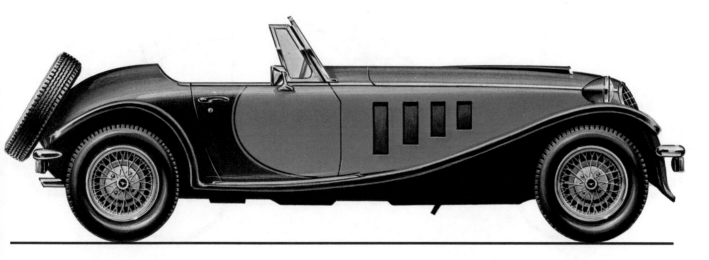

Pegaso

The first Pegaso was exhibited at the 1951 Paris Show and set the automotive world buzzing, for its specification was advanced, its appearance striking and its background extraordinary – an improbable mix of a yearning for prestige, frustrated personal ambition, and a finishing school for technical craftsmen. It lacked the one essential ingredient of commercial sense; thus the marque Pegaso flowered only briefly . . .

A Spanish national commercial vehicle company, ENASA, was set up in the one-time Hispano Suiza factory in Barcelona in 1946, and Wilfredo P Ricart was appointed to run it. He had a wide background, and a particular reputation as an engine designer. He got ENASA on the rails, then lavishly equipped a department where sophisticated engineering could be practised. Its energies were directed to an advanced GT car to be almost entirely built in-house.

The basis was a dry-sump twin-ohc alloy V-8, initially of 2474cc but enlarged to 2·8 or 3·2 litres in the definitive Z102, with a supercharging option (even a two-stage supercharger, although it seems unlikely that this attracted any customers). Claimed power outputs ranged from 165bhp for the first unit, to 225bhp for the blown 3·2s. Use of a transaxle, with gearbox behind the rear axle driving forward to a ZF-type limited-slip differential, made for a spacious cockpit. Torsion bars were used in the suspension, with a de Dion axle at the rear. Disc brakes would have been a benefit to these heavy cars, but were not then available to Pegaso; 14-inch ventilated drums were therefore used, inboard at the rear.

A variety of bodies was mounted on the Z102's strong platform-type chassis, the largest number by Saoutchik, and the most attractive coupes and *spyders* by Touring, but Pegaso's own coupe lacked overall balance with its deep flanks and heavy nose treatment. Top speed of a 3·2 coupe, the most common type, approached 190kph (120mph).

Pegaso's competition efforts were largely confined to minor Spanish events – certainly its successes were. A twin-hull device, the Bi-torpedo with 2·5-litre supercharged engine, was used in record attempts, but two coupes entered for Le Mans in 1953 failed to start. A 3·2-litre *spyder* showed well in the 1954 Carrera Panamericana before crashing.

A Z103 was launched in 1955, but the end of Pegaso cars was less than two years away, by which time total production was estimated at around 110 cars.

Largely hand-built, complex, costly and temperamental, there was really no place for these Pegasos in the 1950s.

Specification

Engine: 90-degree V-8; 85 × 70mm, 3178cc; twin ohc per bank; Weber carburettor; 195bhp at 6000rpm.
Gearbox: five-speed manual.
Chassis: platform; front suspension independent by double wishbones, torsion bars and dampers; rear suspension by de Dion tube, radius arms, torsion bars and dampers; four-wheel drum brakes.
Dimensions: wheelbase 234cm/92in; **front track** 132cm/52in; **rear track** 129cm/51in.

Pontiac Firebird TransAm

This was the last survivor of the 'pony-car' era of the late 1960s and early 1970s, when the major US manufacturers had their final fling with high-performance cars before emission controls and fuel crises bit hard. It was perhaps far from the traditional idea of a sports car, yet this most muscular of Firebirds was capable of matching many revered types in performance, and it did fulfil a sports or GT motoring role. It survived because the demand for the sort of performance it offered did not dry up as image-conscious manufacturers turned away from performance as a virtue, *per se*. Regulations and social attitudes took their toll, however and late 1970s versions were enfeebled, although still capable of over 170kph (110mph), a rarity among US production cars.

The Trans Am came from the same GM stock as the Camaro, to fulfil the ambition of Pontiac divisional manager John DeLorean to match Chevrolet in the SCCA Trans American series. The undistinguished base Firebird dated from 1967, and the first Trans Am appeared in 1969 (ironically, DeLorean moved to Chevrolet in the same year) with 6·5-litre 345bhp V-8, uprated suspension and bolt-on goodies such as a boot-lid spoiler. Only a few hundred were made before the line was restyled for 1970, with the 6·5-litre Formula 400 and Trans Am at the top of the new range. It was a big brash 2 + 2, but the overall lines were well balanced, and the nostril nose with merging chin spoiler made it distinctive. It ran for more than a decade without fundamental body changes.

The running gear was straightforward, but the heavy-duty springs and dampers combined with anti-roll bars front and rear stiffened it to advantage, while the progressive-rate power steering allowed some feel through to the driver.

Power plants varied, and although the Trans American Championship regulations had a capacity limit of 305cu in (5-litres), the 400cu in (6·5-litre) V-8 was used in street Trans Ams, until in 1973 Pontiac released cars with the Super Duty 455, then rated at 310bhp; this was down to 290bhp by 1974, when it was dropped, and when brought back in 1976, its 7458cc produced all of 200bhp (tighter Californian regulations meant that cars were sold there with the 6604cc L80, producing an even more modest 185bhp).

Nevertheless, by 1976 most of the other 'pony cars' had gone, and half the Firebird sales in that year were Trans Ams. Pontiac kept it on, and brought in the Firebird Turbo Trans Am at the end of the decade, its 4·9-litre V-8 fitted with that panacea for emission and performance problems, a turbocharger (an AiResearch unit) which at least meant that 200bhp was still available.

In the hard-fought Trans American races of the late 1960s and early 1970s, Pontiac never came out on top, in part perhaps because its race programme had been built round Jerry Titus, who was killed before it really got under way. But the Trans Am was an honest sporty car, with a devoted following, the last of the American supercars with race breeding.

Specification *(road cars)*
Engine (representative – see text): *1973* – 90-degree V-8; 105·4 × 106·9mm, 7458cc; Rochester carburettor; up to 310bhp at 4500rpm, falling to 200bhp at 3600rpm from 1976.
  1979 – as above, but 101·6 × 76·2mm, 4940cc; Garrett AiResearch turbocharger; 205bhp at 4000rpm.
Gearbox: four-speed manual, but three-speed automatic from 1979.
Chassis: unitary; front suspension independent by wishbones, lower trailing links, coil springs, dampers and anti-roll bar; rear suspension by rigid axle, semi-elliptic leaf springs, dampers and anti-roll bar; disc front/drum rear brakes (but four-wheel ventilated discs from 1979).
Dimensions: wheelbase 274cm/108in; **front track** 155cm/61in; **rear track** 152cm/60in.

Porsche 356

This was the first car sold with the marque name Porsche, although it was the 356th project to come from the Porsche Buro since 1930. It was also the only Porsche in which Ferdinand Porsche could be said to have had even an indirect hand – the tubular-framed prototype was not far removed from the VW-based sports car he had designed before the Second World War – although he did no more than approve his son Ferry's plans to build Porsche cars.

That first car, completed early in 1948, used VW running gear, VW torsion bar suspension all round and a modified VW 1131cc engine positioned ahead of the rear wheels in a tubular frame. For very practical reasons, an alternative design was preferred, and the first 356s (a coupe and an open car) built at Gmund in the summer of 1948 had pressed-steel chassis frames with aluminium bodywork, and engines behind the rear axle line. The quoted power of the air-cooled flat-four was 40bhp at 4000rpm, and it propelled this light (almost 800kg) and aerodynamically efficient car up to a maximum speed of 140kph (85mph).

The 356 designation was retained until 1965, and in some respects the cars changed surprisingly little as 78 000 were built. That figure must have seemed beyond imagination while Porsche struggled to get established, moving to Germany after the first 50 cars had been built at Gmund (in Austria).

In 1951, 1·3- and 1·5-litre engines were introduced (the 1100 was continued until 1954), and a one-piece windscreen and synchromesh gearbox came in 1952. The 356A (1955) was of unitary construction with five ohv engine options, in varying states of tune from 1·3 to 1·6-litres: coupe and open bodies were offered, including the short-lived Speedster, which was effectively superseded by the first Carrera as the top model (with 115bhp engines in 1958). These Carreras were also the first production Porsches to use disc brakes. Through the 1959-63 life of the 356B the body was revised and a Roadster came into the range, while the top Carrera engine grew to 1966cc (130bhp) in 1961. Some of these 356Bs became more familiar under other designations – e.g.: 60, 75, Super 90 and 90 – which related to engine bhp.

Finally, 356 production started to tail off with the C of 1963-65,

Specification

Engine: *365A/1100* – flat-four; 73·5 × 64mm, 1131cc; pushrod ohv; single carburettor; 40bhp at 4000rpm.

365A/1500 – as above, but 80 × 74mm, 1488cc; twin Solex carburettors; 70bhp at 5000rpm.

356B/1600 – as 365A/1100, but 82·5 × 74mm, 1585cc; 60bhp at 4500rpm.

365B/S90 – as above, but 90bhp at 5500rpm.

365C/1600C – as 365A/1100, but 82·5 × 74mm, 1582cc; 75bhp at 5200rpm.

365C/1600SC – as above, but 95bhp at 5800rpm.

Gearbox: four-speed manual.

Chassis: punt-type steel; front suspension independent by trailing arms, transverse torsion bars, dampers and anti-roll bar; rear suspension by swinging axles, radius arms, torsion bars and dampers; four-wheel drum brakes on A and most B models, but discs on some B and all C models.

Dimensions: wheelbase 210cm/82½in; **front track** 129cm/51in on A models, 130cm/51¼in on B/C models; **rear track** 125cm/49in on A models, 127cm/50in on B/C models.

1954 356A/1500S

The first Porsche, a 356 spyder

as the 911 programme gathered momentum. The 356C differed only in detail from the B, but the range was reduced to two 1600s, C and SC.

Variations through the 356 series were numerous and bewildering, and competition use was extraordinarily widespread. The earliest cars were valued for their light weight and were adapted for competitions use, at least until the Carreras appeared. Three aluminium coupes with 48bhp engines were prepared by the works for the 1951 Le Mans 24-hour race; one started, and won its class, so marking the start of Porsche's long and honourable career in racing and rallying (cars used in competitions earlier had been privately prepared and entered). Also in 1951, a 1·5-litre 60bhp coupe finished third in the Liege-Rome-Liege.

S versions led to the Carreras, the first in 1955 with a 1·5-litre engine giving 100bhp. This 'series within the 356 series' reached its peak with the Carrera GTL of 1960; a number of these were built by Abarth with lightweight and aerodynamically-refined bodies, and a 1·6-litre engine which in its highest state of tune produced 135bhp at 7400rpm. One of these won its class at Le Mans in 1960. Later 356B Carreras had 2-litre engines (1961-63), but these did not match the light Abarth-Carreras in outright performance terms.

Meanwhile, the Porsche marque had become widely known through the 356 series, on the roads of the western world and more especially in races and rallies, where the cars were formidable contenders for production class honours.

The first 356 coupe nearing completion at Gmund later in 1948

169

Porsche 550 and RS

The 550 was Porsche's first sports-racing car, which became universally known as the Spyder despite the fact that some had coupe tops. They could be road-equipped, and some were rallied, but their real place was in racing. They echoed the first Porsche, in that the engine was ahead of the rear wheels and a tubular ladder-frame was used, but they also marked a significant step forward by the burgeoning company.

The inspiration for the first Spyders is generally credited to the Glöckler-Porsche specials built by Walter Glöckler in 1949-50, using Porsche mechanical components in light tubular frames. The 550, or 1500RS, was formally introduced at the 1953 Paris Motor Show, although prototypes had already been raced.

One of these prototypes had the twin-cam engine destined for the 550; it was normally seen as a 1·5-litre unit, although in search of class honours 550s sometimes ran with smaller versions. Designed by Fuhrmann, this Type 547 was a light-alloy dry-sump flat-four, with shaft-driven overhead camshafts. It was initially rated at 110bhp at 7000rpm, and output on non-exotic fuel was raised to 135bhp at 7200rpm in the 550A of 1957.

Transmission was through a four-speed gearbox (five on the 550A) and ZF limited-slip differential. Normal Porsche suspension was used, as were 356 brakes. Production cars had a ladder frame, although a spaceframe was to be evolved for the works 550A. External shape was improved along the way, from stubby to relatively sleek, and the hump over the engine compartment which was a characteristic of early production cars was soon abandoned. The light-alloy bodywork was flimsy – the whole car weighed less than 640kg – the rag top was ludicrous, the bolt-on coupe top was effective but far from handsome, and most cockpit fittings were standard Porsche parts.

The 550A was listed in 1957-58, and the Spyder name was carried over to the RS/RSK derivatives. More than 125 1500RSs were built, the largest number finding their way to the USA.

Debut race for a 550 as such was the 1954 Mille Miglia, when Herrmann took sixth place overall, and then came a Le Mans class win. This was repeated in 1955 (and in the 1100cc class), and there were others at Rheims, the Nurburgring, and many in lesser events.

The outstanding achievement of 1956 was Porsche's first Targa Florio victory, Umberto Maglioli winning by a generous margin in the sole works entry. This car was in effect the forerunner of the RSK, which appeared in the summer of 1957 and was to be built in 1958-59 in small numbers, with 1·5- and 1·6-litre engines rated at 148/150bhp. It had the tubular spaceframe essayed earlier and modified suspension, while the dumpy body was not enhanced by the twin rear fins sometimes used.

The RSK gained more sports car honours for Porsche, the 1958 season including a second overall in the Targa and third places in the Buenos Aires 1000km and Sebring 12 hours, as well as at Le Mans (backed up by fourth and fifth, and a class one-two-three) – results which meant that Porsche were runners-up to Ferrari in the World Championship of Makes. In 1959, the Targa was again Porsche's high point, RSKs finishing first and second, while none of the Le Mans entries finished.

The series continued in all but designation with the RS60 (1960-61) and RS61 (1961), built in small numbers with engines in 1·5 and 1·6-litre forms, producing 150bhp (RS60) and 160bhp (RS61). Rear suspension was revised, with a wishbone arrangement, while the bodies became distinctly sleeker. Several styles were essayed, including coupes and a near-coupe for Le Mans, in efforts to gain speed through streamlining.

More power was the real key to this, however, and the flat-four was taken out to almost 2 litres (one of these was used in the car placed fifth at Le Mans). A 2-litre 210bhp eight-cylinder engine belatedly became available in 1962, and was first raced in Sicily, where one car placed third in spite of problems with its new disc brakes. The following year an eight-cylinder Spyder won the Targa outright, driven by Bonnier and Abate. Then, while this model was to be prominent in hill climbs for another year, Porsche competition attention turned increasingly to the 904.

1954 550

170

*The first two 550s at Le Mans in 1953,
before the type was formally announced*

Specifications
1500RS/550

Engine: *550* – flat-four; 85 × 66mm, 1498cc; twin ohc per bank;
twin Solex carburettors; 110bhp at 7200rpm.

    550A – as above, but twin Weber carburettors; 135bhp.

Gearbox: four-speed manual, with five-speed manual on later
cars.

Chassis: ladder-frame; front suspension independent by trailing
arms, torsion bars and dampers; rear suspension by swing axles,
trailing arms, torsion bars and dampers; four-wheel drum brakes.

Dimensions: wheelbase 210cm/82½in;
front track 129cm/51in; **rear track** 125cm/49in.

RS61/1600

Engine: flat-four; 87·5 × 66mm, 1588cc; twin ohc per bank; twin
Weber carburettors; 160bhp at 7800rpm.

Gearbox: five-speed manual.

Chassis: spaceframe; front suspension independent by trailing
arms, torsion bars, dampers and anti-roll bar; rear suspension
independent by double wishbones, coil springs and dampers;
four-wheel drum brakes.

Dimensions: wheelbase 220cm/86½in;
front track 129cm/51in; **rear track** 125cm/49in.

1958 RSK

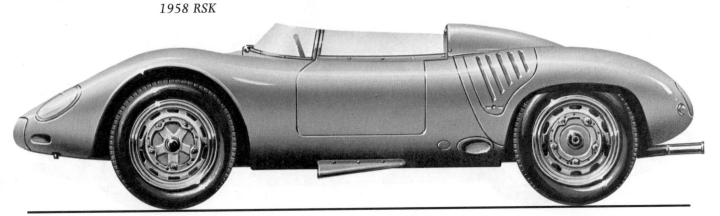

Porsche 904

Often known as the Carrera GTS, the 904 was the first of the 900 series intended specifically for competition use, although its equipment and manners were such that it could be used as a road car. It marked a major Porsche departure from its VW origins, and was planned specifically for the 2-litre GT class, which promised to be hotly contested in the early 1960s. The regulations called for a minimum production of 100 cars, and while some constructors adopted time-honoured but dubious means of achieving homologation, Porsche opted for the straightforward approach of laying down 100 cars and setting a 'list price' so low that private entrants were inevitably attracted ...

The 904 was in any case an attractive racing proposition in its own right, not quite as aerodynamically efficient as its low coupe lines suggested, perhaps, but tough and versatile, and highly competitive on road circuits. For the first time Porsche used a composite construction, with glass fibre bodies (made by Heinkel) bonded to a ladder-type frame of substantial pressed steel longitudinal and cross members to form a stiff structure. The wishbone and coil spring suspension derived from the 550 RSK series, and sometimes proved fragile on customer cars.

Although the original intention had been to use a six-cylinder engine and works cars did appear with sixes and eights, in standard form the 904 was the last 'production' competition Porsche to use the old four-cylinder engine, in 2-litre form and reworked to give 180bhp at 7200rpm in 1965, slightly more in 1966; that power came with open exhausts, and in detuned and 'street-legal' form 155bhp was claimed. The engine was installed ahead of the rear axle line, driving through a new five-speed gearbox behind the axle and a ZF limited-slip differential.

First race for the 904 was the 1964 Sebring 12 hours, where it won the 2-litre class outright; 904s then took the first two places overall in the Targa Florio and class victories in other major events. The next year opened with Eugen Böhringer taking second place in the Monte Carlo Rally with a works-entered 904 – an outstanding achievement in an event by no means suitable for a 'racer', and consequently more notable than the third, fourth, fifth and sixth placings by 904 crews in the 1964 Tour de France. At Le Mans that year, a 904 fitted with a 211bhp 911 engine won the 2-litre prototype class and the Index of Performance; a 'normal' works car won the 2-litre GT class almost as a matter of course, in a year when this class was dominated by the 904.

Works-run 904s with eight-cylinder engines achieved little, but an experimental *spyder* with this unit was second in the Targa Florio, immediately ahead of a normal coupe 904 with a 911 six and another with one of the eights derived from the F1 engine. More than 100 of the 120 production 904s were sold, and were still campaigned independently while the works team moved on to its successor surprisingly rapidly.

1964 Carrera GTS

Specification

Engine: flat-four; 92 × 74mm, 1966cc; twin ohc per bank; twin Weber or Solex carburettors; 180bhp at 7200rpm.
Gearbox: five-speed manual.
Chassis: ladder-frame; front suspension independent by wishbones, coil springs, dampers and anti-roll bar; rear suspension independent by twin radius rods, wishbones, coil springs, dampers and anti-roll bar; four-wheel disc brakes.
Dimensions: wheelbase 230cm/90½in;
front track 132cm/52in; **rear track** 131cm/51½in.

Porsche 906

The Carrera 6 carried on from the 904 – indeed, the earliest 906s were 904s with six-cylinder engines – yet the definitive car was by no means a 904 six, rather the first of a new generation of sports-racing Porsches. Effectively, it was the first model from a distinct competition department and for which there were no road-going intentions; 52 were to be built (50 being called for to qualify it as a Group 4 sports car under the 1968 regulations), and the specification was to be modified in detail as they were completed.

The engine/transmission had been developed in the 1965 904/6 prototype, and the basic 904 suspension was used, with mountings revised to obviate handling shortcomings (which were thought to have derived from rubber in the joints) and the then-novel Bilstein inert-gas dampers. In this car, Porsche returned to the spaceframe, which proved too flexible in its first form and had to be stiffened, for example with a cross tube over the engine bay.

The glass fibre body did not contribute to structural strength – its upper parts were distinctly flimsy – nor was it aesthetically pleasing from some angles (the nose, for example, was very low between prominent wheel arches). The cockpit was as narrow as the regulations permitted, and its roof line was continued neatly through a translucent louvred engine-bay cover to a neat spoiler above the Kamm tail. The pronounced 'inset' of the cockpit from the flanks meant that gull-wing doors were used; just behind them on either side were prominent air intakes for brakes and gearbox cooling. The compulsory luggage space was in the extremity of the tail, behind the gearbox. A long-tailed body was developed for fast circuits such as Le Mans and Daytona. The complete car was only marginally lighter than the 904, as a sprint race role was not envisaged for it.

Basically, the engine followed the 911 six, lightened by the use of magnesium in place of aluminium in the crankcase and other details, such as a magnesium carrier for the cooling fan. Initial power output was 210bhp, soon raised to 220bhp and slightly more when the Bosch fuel injection, developed for the engine during 1966, was adopted. The works team occasionally ran 906s with 2·2-litre, 250bhp eight-cylinder engines.

Race debut was in the 1966 Daytona 24 hours, when Herrmann and Linge placed the works 906 sixth overall, first in the 2-litre class. With only one interruption, this category belonged to the 906 through the year, and the 906 scored a sixth outright Targa Florio victory for Porsche. As with its predecessors, the 906 had a useful career with private owners long after the works team turned to the sleeker 910 in 1967.

1966 Carrera

Specification

Engine: flat-six; 80 × 66mm, 1991cc; single ohc per bank; twin Weber carburettors; 220bhp (see text) at 8000rpm.
Gearbox: five-speed manual.
Chassis: tubular spaceframe; front suspension independent by wishbones, coil springs, dampers and anti-roll bar; rear suspension independent by twin radius rods, wishbones, coil springs, dampers and anti-roll bar; four-wheel disc brakes.
Dimensions: wheelbase 230cm/90½in; **front track** 134cm/52½in; **rear track** 140cm/55in.

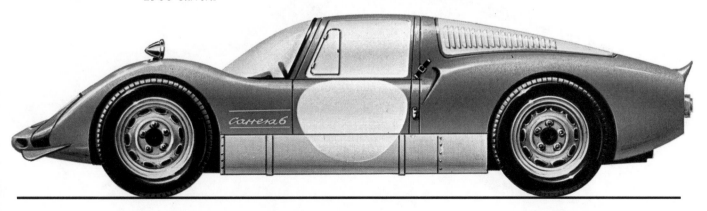

Porsche 911

The forerunner of the 911, the 901, was exhibited in 1963 as a future successor to the then-current road models; 20 years later its derivatives were still mainstream cars in the Porsche range, and for marketing purposes the number was applied to one of the outstanding 'supercars' of the 1970s. Meanwhile, there had been a wide range of variants and 911s had achieved no mean list of competition successes.

Production did not get under way until autumn 1964, when because of Peugeot objections the 901 model number was changed to 911. The engine was still air-cooled, still overhung at the back, but it was a new single-ohc six rated at 130bhp and it drove through a new five-speed gearbox (a pushrod 1·6-litre four was used in the 'economy' 912 which had the same body as the 911, and was in production 1965-68).

Despite a relatively short wheelbase, the external lines were both elegant and efficient, while two-seater room was adequate, even if the 'occasional' seats were distinctly constricting. The first version had a 210kph (130mph) top speed, although the noise level did not encourage driving at over 160kph (100mph), while handling called for familiarity, or skill . . .

First significant variant was the Targa in 1965, a convertible with a distinctive roll-over bar which stiffened the body as well as overcoming many traditional soft-top shortcomings. The 911S, with revised suspension and Bosch fuel-injected engine giving up to 170bhp and 220kph (135mph), followed in 1966; the E had the

Specification (*representative road cars*)
Engine: *911 (1964)* – flat-six; 80 × 66mm, 1991cc; single ohc per bank; six Solex carburettors; 130bhp at 6100rpm.

911S (1969) – as above, but 84 × 66mm, 2195cc; two Zenith carburettors; 190bhp at 6500rpm.

911S (1971) – as above, but 84 × 70·4mm, 2341cc; two Zenith carburettors or Bosch mechanical fuel injection; 190bhp at 6500rpm.

911S (1973) – as above, but 90 × 70·4mm, 2687cc; Bosch K-Jetronic fuel injection; 210bhp at 6300rpm.

Carrera (1977) – as above, but 95 × 70·4mm, 2994cc; 200bhp at 6000rpm.

Turbo (1978) – as above, but 97 × 74·4mm, 3299cc; Bosch fuel injection and turbocharger; 300bhp at 5500rpm.

911SC (1980) – as Carrera, but 188bhp at 5500rpm.
Gearbox: five-speed manual, with optional four-speed manual or Sportomatic semi-automatic (but four-speed manual only on Turbo).
Chassis: integral steel; front suspension independent by McPherson struts, transverse wishbones, torsion bars and anti-roll bar; rear suspension independent by trailing arms, transverse torsion bars, dampers and anti-roll bar; four-wheel disc brakes with drum handbrake.
Dimensions: *from 1964* – wheelbase 221cm/87in; **front track** 134cm/53in; **rear track** 132cm/52in.

from 1969 – wheelbase 227cm/89½in; **front track** 136cm/56½in; **rear track** 134cm/52½in.

from 1973 – wheelbase 227cm/89½in; **front track** 137cm/54in; **rear track** 135cm/53in.

1965 911

911 in the 1967 Swedish Rally

four-speed Sportomatic semi-automatic transmission as an alternative to the slick four-speed manual box; the base model was the 911T.

A 2·2-litre engine came in 1969, its principal benefit being improved torque rather than outright power, and in 1971 the enlargement was to 2·4 litres (actually 2341cc) with power outputs ranging from 130bhp in the 911T to 190bhp in the 911S. This 1971 change was complemented by a new gearbox (a four-speed, with the five-speed version an option).

Two years later a 2·7-litre engine with Bosch K-Jetronic continuous fuel injection was introduced on the 911 and 911S, which (with Carrera and Turbo variants) were to be the only designations applied to the model until 1976, when the 911 Lux and 911N were listed. In 1978 the 911SC appeared, sharing with the SC Sport the choice of coupe or Targa bodies and a 2994cc engine rated at 188bhp.

The Carrera of the 1970s used a slightly modified 911 body with a prominent rear aerofoil, a 2687cc engine from 1974, and a 2994cc unit from 1977.

An outstanding new member of the 911 family was unveiled at the 1974 Paris Motor Show: the Turbo. This carried the works internal designation Type 930, and that does seem to relate it more closely and realistically to the turbocharged competitions models of the decade, but for all external purposes Porsche referred to it as the 911 Turbo.

With its wide wheels, front air dam and substantial rear spoiler, the Turbo fitted naturally into the sporting 'supercar' category. Handling was rated exemplary for a rear-engined car, the very wide tyres giving high cornering power; braking could not be faulted, throttle lag was minimal, acceleration startling and top speed with the first 260bhp 3-litre engine was 250kph (155mph); the 300bhp 3·3-litre version that followed in 1978 gave 260kph (160mph).

Outwardly, there were many detail changes to 'normal' 911s – different wheels, modified nose spoilers, mandatory US bumpers, and so on – while through the second half of the 1970s rumours of its imminent decease were regularly proved premature as demand for it held up remarkably.

Porsche had introduced the 911 as a touring car rather than a sports car, but competition use was inevitable. Beyond the obvious sports and GT categories, the company contemplated entering it as a Group 2 Touring Car around 1970, to compete with cars generally regarded as saloons; that, however, would have strayed beyond the spirit of the rules ...

Nevertheless, the all-round sporting qualities of the 911 were thoroughly demonstrated during a distinguished competition career in which its circuit performances were transcended by its rallying achievements. These began in 1965 with fifth place on the Monte Carlo Rally and during the following year Porsche won the sports car (Group 3) section of the European Rally Championship. The first major victory came in 1967, when Vic Elford won the Lyon-Charbonnieres Rally, going on to win the Tulip and Geneva rallies to clinch another Group 3 title.

In 1968, Elford won the Monte Carlo Rally (with another Porsche second) while various drivers, including Bjorn Waldegaard and Pauli Toivonen, won major events in both 911T and 911S models, Toivonen eventually securing the European Championship in the face of strong opposition from Lancia, Saab, Alpine-Renault, Alfa Romeo and the new Ford Escort Twin Cam.

Waldegaard won the Monte Carlo for Porsche in 1969 and completed a hat-trick of wins on the Swedish Rally; in 1970 he again won the Monte, this victory helping Porsche win the manufacturer's section of that year's European Championship.

After this, the factory team concentrated on the prestigious Safari Rally in east Africa, an event which on the face of it was ill-suited to the car. Nevertheless, a 911 was placed fifth at its first attempt in 1971, and both 1972 and 1974 produced second places; despite massive efforts, however, subsequent forays failed to produce the elusive victory.

Privateers continued to campaign the 911 and its derivatives throughout Europe and in 1978 a most famous victory fell to a 3-litre Carrera prepared by the Almeras brothers, when Jean-Pierre Nicolas won the Monte Carlo Rally against factory opposition.

In racing, the 911 and its lighter offshoot, the Carrera RSR were prominent, with European GT classes falling to cars run by such teams as those of Kremer and Loos, and success in North America in the TransAm and IMSA championships.

Porsche 908

After an uncharacteristically faltering start, this Porsche became one of the most versatile and successful of all sports-racing cars. It won Porsche its first Manufacturers' Championship, came dramatically close to becoming its first outright Le Mans winner, and – until the *spyder* 917 – was the only car powered by a non-American engine to win a CanAm race. Even a dozen years after the 908 had first appeared, a privately-owned 908/03 ran with the leaders in international endurance races, although that said more for the lamentable state of sports-car racing in 1980 than for the 908 *spyder* . . .

When the 908 appeared in 1968, however, sports-car racing was healthy, and the new 3-litre limit for Prototypes suited Porsche admirably: for the first time, it intended to compete on level terms as far as engine capacity was concerned. For an engine, Porsche turned to the 1991cc twin-ohc six used in the 910 of 1967 and enlarged it by adding two cylinders and taking the bore out to 85mm, while the stroke remained at 66mm. Conception to test bed thus took only four months, and it immediately produced 320bhp, rising to 335bhp by the time it was first raced, and ultimately to 370bhp.

Porsche felt that the existing transaxle would not be able to cope with the power and torque of the flat-eight, so a dry-sump six-speed gearbox (designed for the 909 hill-climb special) was adopted. This was not satisfactory, however, and a new conventional wet-sump gearbox was developed for 1969.

The first chassis was almost identical with that of the 907 (the 3-litre engine first ran in public – at the 1968 Le Mans test weekend – in two long-tailed 907s as well as the first 908 coupe). The body was substantially wider than the 907, however, as wider tyres had to be accommodated, and the wheel arches were higher to allow for 15-inch wheels (instead of 13-inch) so that larger brakes could be used, and so that these sports cars could take direct advantage of Formula One tyre development.

The 908 was a problem child in 1968, with transmission faults and – in its long-tail version – with handling deficiencies. The first victory, the only one in a 1968 championship race, was gained by Jo Siffert and Vic Elford in a short-tail coupe in the Nurburgring 1000km. Later that year the long-tail cars were run with adjustable rear spoilers, the flaps working in conjunction with suspension movement, but this was not carried over to subsequent 908s.

The Prototype regulations for 1969 did not require luggage space or a spare wheel, or stipulate a minimum weight, all of which made

Specification

Engine: flat-eight; 85 × 66mm, 2997cc; twin ohc per bank; Bosch fuel injection; 335bhp at 8000rpm rising to 350bhp at 8450rpm.
Gearbox: six-speed manual, later reduced to five-speed manual.
Chassis: tubular spaceframe; front suspension independent by wishbones, coil springs, dampers and anti-roll bar; rear suspension independent by radius arms, upper and lower links, coil springs and dampers; four-wheel disc brakes.
Dimensions: wheelbase 230cm/90½in; front track 148cm/58½in (but 154cm/60½in on 908/03); rear track 145cm/57in (but 151cm/59½in on 908/03).

1969 works 908/02

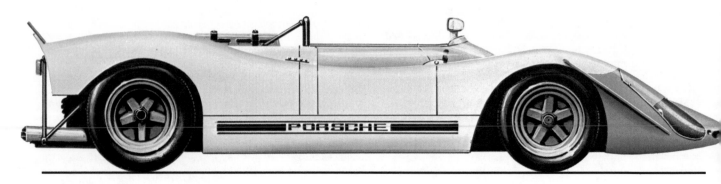

'908/04' at Brands Hatch in 1979

a *spyder* version of the 908 attractive. The 908/02 *spyder* had a slight power disadvantage compared with the Ferrari which was expected to be its principal rival, but it was considerably lighter, helped by the use of light alloy in place of steel in the spaceframe and suspension. Its debut came at Sebring, where it was hoped that the new car would offset the retirement of all five 908/01s at Daytona, but the best *spyder* was third.

Then the tide turned, with a one-two-three at Brands Hatch and a one-two-three-four in the Targa Florio with 908/02s and wins at Monza and Spa for the long-tail 908/01 coupes. Extra speed was then found for the 908/02, with a smoother body, in which form it won at Watkins Glen. Meanwhile, a 908/02 with the early *spyder* body won the Nurburgring 1000km, and a coupe was only narrowly defeated at Le Mans. The 908/02 continued in the hands of private entrants – an outstanding victory falling to Tony Dean in the 1970 Road Atlanta CanAm race – while a new variant was developed to complement the big 917s, which were not suitable for such races as the Targa Florio.

The engine remained unchanged in this 908/03, with power output up to 350bhp and more. The rest of the car echoed the original 909 special: compact and light, with its cockpit so far forward that it was almost between the front wheels. An aluminium alloy spaceframe and reinforced-plastics-sandwich bodywork made for light weight, while weight distribution was improved by moving the gearbox ahead of the rear axle line. The 908/03 won both the

Targa Florio and Nurburgring 1000km in 1970, but suffered a rare defeat in Sicily in 1971, although 908/03s took the first three places at the Nurburgring. The factory then sold the cars; ten years later, Siegfried Brunn's 908/03, in more or less original form, was by no means outrun in European 1000km races ...

In the mid-1970s, private entrants had seized on the idea of uprating the 908 by replacing the eight with the KKK-turbocharged, six-cylinder 2142cc engine used in the Carrera RSR Turbo. In long-distance race trim, this engine was rated at 445bhp in 1974, but with increased boost up to 500bhp was available and for Interseries events, engines up to 2·7-litres were used. Some works assistance was obtained, notably by Reinhold Joest. Outwardly, the cars were changed considerably, with large rear aerofoils and noses modified to achieve balance.

These 908/04s, as they were dubbed, did as well as could be expected of non-works entries in 1975, when – largely through the efforts of Joest and Casoni – Porsche was second in the World Championship of Makes. In 1976, Joest won the opening round, on the Nurburgring Nordschleife, thus contributing to Porsche's championship that year.

Finally, at Le Mans in 1980 there appeared a hybrid device with the designation 908/80. Built by Joest with Martini backing, it was outwardly a 936; under the skin it was a mixture of 908 and 936, with a twin-turbo producing some 500bhp. It led the 24-hour race until delayed by gearbox trouble, and ultimately finished second.

Porsche 917

This was the most powerful road-racing car ever built, the outcome of quite legitimate exploitation of a regulation naively intended to outlaw highly-specialized sports-racing cars. The regulation stipulated a minimum production of 25, a number which in no way deterred Porsche, and work started on the 917 project in the summer of 1968; in April 1969 25 examples were lined up for CSI inspection, and eventually 43 were built.

In its first season, the 917 gained a reputation for difficult handling and instability, but then it dominated the World Championship for two seasons, and later – in open form with turbocharged engines – the CanAm championship. Through these years, it brought to sports-car racing an element of spectacle which has since been sadly missed.

The engine was a flat-12, air-cooled in the Porsche tradition, initially of 4·5 litres and producing 580bhp. It was not a particularly complex unit and as its features had been proved in a flat-eight, its gestation period was short – basically, the Porsche Research and Development division added four cylinders to the 3-litre flat-eight to produce a 'boxer' 12. Air cooling meant that it was bulky (86cm long), with a large shrouded fan driven from the camshaft gear train above it adding to that impression (some engine heat was also

1970 917K Le Mans car

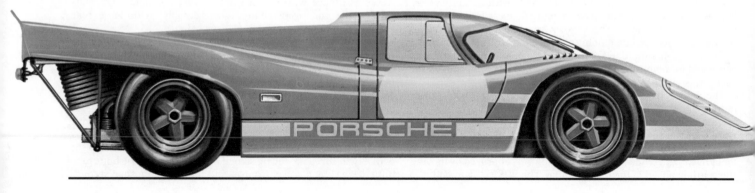

dissipated through a large oil radiator). That camshaft train was driven from the centre of the crankshaft.

The engine was progressively enlarged, first to 4·9 litres and then to the 'definitive' 5 litres (and 630bhp) in 1971; it rose to 5·4 litres for the 917-10 Group 7 car in 1972. The quoted power for the 1972 CanAm 5-litre turbocharged flat-12 was 950bhp at 8000rpm, but it had a 1000-plus potential bhp, while the very special 5·4-litre unit developed for the 917-30 produced 1100bhp.

The engine was mid-mounted in a very light aluminium spaceframe (a few special cars had magnesium frames). While the CanAm and Interseries cars were *spyders*, the sports car championship 917s had a variety of coupe bodies, basically short- or long-tailed, with several variations of each in pursuit of aerodynamic advantage. All these 917s were very close to the 800kg minimum weight limit, and thus had a formidable power/weight ratio.

The Porsche factory raced the 917 only while it was developed to raceworthiness, after which leading independent teams such as JW-Gulf and Porsche-Salzburg campaigned the cars in World Championship of Makes races. Here, the 917s scored 15 victories in 1969-71, the most notable being Porsche's first outright Le Mans victory, scored by Hans Herrmann and Richard Attwood in a

Porsche-Salzburg car in 1970 (heading a one-two that was repeated in 1971).

The first *spyder* appeared in 1969, in the form of the 4·5-litre 917PA, which was to all intents and purposes a cut-down coupe. It was followed by the 5-litre 917-10 in 1971. This was used in the CanAm series – where it ended the years of McLaren domination – and from 1972 in the European Interseries, for which some coupes had already been converted to *spyder* form as they became ineligible for world championship races (their presence, and the high costs of running them, virtually killed off any real international importance the Inter series might have had).

Porsche's CanAm interests were in the hands of Roger Penske, for whom the ultimate sports-racing car, the 917-30, was developed for 1973; the invincibility of this machine in the hands of Mark Donohue had much the same effect on this series ...

The 917 was timed at over 385kph (240mph) at Le Mans, and a 917-10 could accelerate from standstill to 160kph (100mph) in 3·9 sec. To show that figures of this order had real meaning in lap times, albeit on a track, Donohue was to lap Talladega at 355·84kph (221·11mph) before these extraordinary cars became museum exhibits.

The 1981 regulations admitting 5-litre cars encouraged the Kremer team to build a new 917 for Le Mans, largely to original specification and with the alternatives of a 4·5-litre engine or a 4·9-litre flat-12 rated at 600bhp.

Specification

Engine (representative): *917 coupe (1971)* – flat-12; 86·8 × 70·4mm, 4998cc; twin ohc per bank; Bosch fuel injection; 630bhp at 8300rpm.

917-30 CanAm – as above, but 90 × 70·4mm, 5374cc; twin turbochargers; 1100bhp at 7800rpm.

Gearbox: four- or five-speed manual.

Chassis: tubular spaceframe; front suspension independent by wishbones, radius rods, coil springs, dampers and anti-roll bar; rear suspension independent by lower wishbones, radius arms, coil springs, dampers and anti-roll bar; four-wheel ventilated disc brakes.

Dimensions: *917 coupe (1971)* – **wheelbase** 230cm/90½in; **front track** between 152cm/60in (on 305mm/12in wheels) and 156cm/61½in (on 381mm/15in wheels); **rear track** between 153cm/60in (on 381mm/15in wheels) and 158cm/62in (on 432mm/17in wheels).

917-30 – **wheelbase** 250cm/98½in; **front track** 167cm/65½in; **rear track** 156cm/61½in.

917-30 CanAm (Roger Penske team)

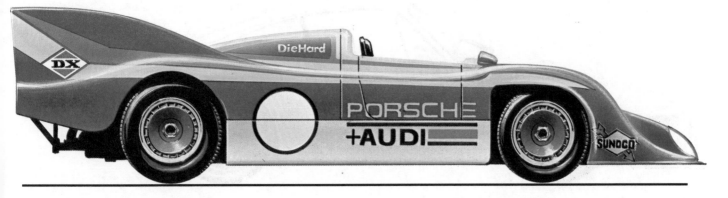

Porsche 934 and 935

In the year that the road Turbo was introduced (1974), Porsche gained racing experience with the look-alike Carrera RSR Turbo; this led to the 934, which can effectively be regarded as a production competition car partner to the 911-based Turbo.

In the 934, the standard suspension was modified as far as possible under the regulations – it was supplemented by coil springs and adjustable anti-roll bars – while mandatory safety equipment was built in, additional brake cooling was arranged; plastic wheel-arch extensions made for an aggressive appearance, while confusingly 934s running in Group 5 often wore 935 rear wings and had even wider wheels.

The fuel-injected engine combined water-cooled intercoolers with a KKK turbocharger; it was officially rated at 485bhp, but within two seasons private teams were extracting as much as 580bhp, using higher boost pressures through waste-gate modifications.

The 934 dominated GT categories in the second half of the 1970s, but for outright victories in the World Championship of Makes the 935 became the car to run, and private entrants always backed up the works team, or won in the name of Porsche when there was no works team.

The 935 had an ultra-light 'silhouette' body which was modified throughout its career, with coil springs in place of torsion bars in the suspension, 917 ventilated disc brakes, and a considerably developed version of the Turbo flat-six with a capacity of 2857cc (applying the regulation × 1·4 factor, this was equivalent to a 4-litre unblown unit). In 1976 this engine was rated at 590bhp, but the twin-turbocharged version in the 935/77 gave 630bhp (there was also a briefly-seen variant run in the 2-litre class to counter BMW and Ford, with a 1425cc engine producing 370bhp).

The 3211cc engine which appeared in the 1978 works cars was raced only three times; this had water-cooled heads along 936 lines, and developed a staggering 750bhp. This won at Silverstone, finished eighth at Le Mans with an oil leak, and retired at Vallelunga.

In overall terms, however, the record of the 935 was superb, the World Championship of Makes falling to it in 1976, 1977, 1978 and 1979. The outstanding single achievement in those four years was undoubtedly the 1979 Le Mans victory gained by a 935/K3, a version developed by the Kremer team, largely in aerodynamic respects, which demonstrated beyond question that in the 935 Porsche had produced a magnificent machine for professional teams.

Specifications

934

Engine: flat-six; 95 × 70·4mm, 2993cc; single ohc per bank; Bosch fuel injection and KKK turbocharger; 485bhp at 7000rpm (1976).
Gearbox: four-speed manual.
Chassis: integral; front suspension independent by McPherson struts, wishbones, torsion bars, auxiliary coil springs and anti-roll bar; rear suspension independent by trailing arms, torsion bars, auxiliary coil springs, dampers and anti-roll bar; four-wheel disc brakes.
Dimensions: wheelbase 226cm/89in; **front track** 148cm/58in; **rear track** 149cm/58½in.

935

Engine: flat-six; 92 × 70·4mm, 2857cc; single ohc per bank; Bosch fuel injection and KKK turbocharger (twin turbos on 935/77); 590bhp at 7900rpm rising to 630bhp at 8000rpm by 1977.
Gearbox: four-speed manual.
Chassis: integral; front suspension independent by McPherson struts, coil springs, wishbones and anti-roll bar; rear suspension independent by trailing arms, coil springs, dampers and anti-roll bar; four-wheel disc brakes.
Dimensions: wheelbase 227cm/89½in; **front track** 150cm/59in; **rear track** 156cm/61½in.

1976 works 935

Porsche 936

The uncertain state of sports car racing in the mid-1970s led Porsche to build another sports-racing *spyder*, although as its general policy had swung to competing with cars which broadly looked like production models the effort put into this 936 was relatively modest. That, in fact, precisely reflected the state of the World Championship for Sports Cars – Group 6 racing – for the FIA had introduced a 'rival' Group 5 championship at a time when the sports car world was hardly able to sustain even one championship. Only the Le Mans organizers were strong enough in 1976 to bring Groups 5 and 6 together (and to add Groups 2 and 4, IMSA, NASCAR and a couple of their own categories), so giving the manufacturers something real to aim for ...

Porsche turned to proven components for its weapon: the 936 used the production-based 2142cc air-cooled flat-six, with a single KKK turbocharger; this had been used in some 908/03s and in the 1974 RSR Carrera Turbo and developed 520bhp (slightly more than the Alpine-Renault V-6 of the obvious rival). The engine was positioned well ahead of the rear axle in the interests of weight distribution, while transmission stamina was ensured by use of the 917's transaxle.

The spaceframe chassis also derived from the 917, as did some suspension components. The first glass fibre body was so low that it dictated modifications to the engine induction system. After its first outing, however, the engine deck was raised and surmounted by a prominent air intake. Very large rear fins, with a full-width aerofoil between them, also characterized the car.

First time out, the 936 failed, a stretched throttle cable slowing it to finish fifth at the Nurburgring (although Joest saved the day for Porsche by winning in his 908/03). After that, the 936 won everything it was run in – Monza, Imola, Pergusa, Dijon and Salzburgring – to secure the championship. Le Mans justified a doubled entry – a wise precaution, as one car retired, leaving Jacky Ickx and Gijs van Lennep to win by more than ten laps, despite 20 minutes lost while an exhaust failure was repaired.

For 1977 the car was modified to reduce frontal area, while twin turbochargers raised engine power to 540bhp; Porsche interest was confined to Le Mans, however, where one car duly won while the second retired again.

One of the cars run at Le Mans in 1978 was in 1977 trim, while the engines of the other two had water-cooled cylinder heads and developed 580bhp, but the two cars which finished were placed second and third. Power was raised to 600bhp in 1979, and Essex colours replaced those of Martini, but neither of the Le Mans entries lasted the 24 hours.

The 1981 works 936 entry for Le Mans was powered by a 2·65-litre flat-six, conservatively rated well below its potential at 600bhp, to give the car a theoretical maximum speed in excess of 220mph.

Specification

Engine: flat-six; 83 × 66mm, 2142cc; twin ohc per bank; Bosch fuel injection and KKK turbocharger (twin turbos from 1977); 520bhp at 8000rpm rising to 600bhp in 1979.
Gearbox: five-speed manual.
Chassis: aluminium spaceframe; front suspension independent by wishbones, coil springs and dampers; rear suspension independent by radius arms, wishbones, coil springs and dampers; four-wheel ventilated disc brakes.
Dimensions: wheelbase 241cm/95in (but 240cm/94½in in 1978); front track 153cm/60in (but 148cm/58½in in 1978); rear track 148cm/58½in (but 145cm/57in in 1978).

1977 Le mans winner

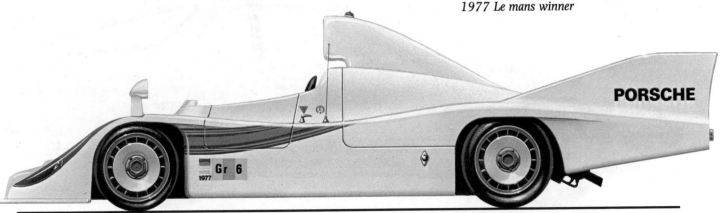

Porsche 924

This was the first front-engined, rear-drive model to carry the Porsche badge (it might have been launched as an up-market VW to succeed the unhappy VW-Porsche 914, but it appeared as the down-market model of the Porsche range). The last 914 was built late in 1975, just before the 924 became available, to be proclaimed by Porsche as "our idea of a good sports car".

It departed from the company's previous idea of a good sports car in more than its basic configuration: in its use of stock VW components in the running gear, for example, and in its water-cooled engine, of Audi parentage. A single-ohc 125bhp four, this was inclined to the right at 40 degrees, with Bosch K-Jetronic continuous injection system fitted as standard, and – unusually for a Porsche – requiring premium fuel (although the US version, with lower compression ratio, smaller valves and emission equipment, was rated at 100bhp and would run on low-grade fuel).

Also unusual was a drive train which married a front engine to a rear transaxle. This was connected to the front-mounted clutch by a shaft housed in a rigid tube, which enforced a high 'transmission tunnel' in the cockpit. Initially an Audi four-speed gearbox was standard, but a Porsche five-speed unit became optional in 1978 and standard in 1979 (with a three-speed automatic optional throughout). This layout made the weight distribution close to 50/50 regardless of load, which gave excellent cornering to complement a firm but comfortable ride.

The 2+2 body may not have pleased Porsche purists, although it was one of the better examples of front-engined cars in this class, and had a better drag coefficient than the seemingly more aerodynamic 911, giving correspondingly good fuel consumption; maximum speed was acceptable for a 2-litre car at 200kph (125mph). This Porsche never gave the impression of being built down to a price, and found ready acceptance in the sports car market, sales passing the 100 000 mark early in 1981.

The basic engine was substantially modified for the 924 Turbo, which was announced in the autumn of 1979, having an entirely new light-alloy cylinder head, maximum power of 170bhp at 5500rpm and a top speed of 225kph (140mph).

A competition variant of the Turbo was shown when the road car was announced, and this was the first front-engined car run by the works. For this role it was lighter, had stiffer suspension, extended wheel arches and spoilers, and an engine rated at 320bhp for Le Mans in 1980, where the best placing for the team was sixth.

Just before that race, the 924 Carrera GT was announced, with a 210bhp turbocharged engine, as a production 'supercar' with competition potential. This was realised early in 1981, with the GTR (racing) variant having an engine rated at 375bhp and the GTS (rally) project with 280bhp. The production run was limited to 400, sufficient to qualify for Group 4 homologation, and – following its policy of not competing with its customers – Porsche turned out a 400bhp version for the works team to run in the GT Prototype category at Le Mans.

1977 model

Specification *(road cars)*
Engine: straight-four; 86·5 × 84·4mm, 1984cc; single ohc; Bosch fuel injection; 125bhp at 5800rpm.
Turbo – as above, but with single KKK turbocharger; 170bhp at 5500rpm.
Carrera GT – as Turbo, but 210bhp at 6000rpm.
Gearbox: five-speed manual transaxle, with optional four-speed manual or three-speed automatic.
Chassis: monocoque steel; front suspension independent by McPherson struts, coil springs, wishbones, dampers and anti-roll bar; rear suspension independent by semi-trailing arms, torsion bars, dampers and anti-roll bar; disc front/drum rear brakes, but four-wheel discs on Carrera GT.
Dimensions: wheelbase 240cm/94½in; **front track** 142cm/56in; **rear track** 137cm/54in.

Porsche 928

With the 928, Porsche entered another sector of the market, producing a model with the accent as much on luxury as on high performance; and it was another front-engined model at that. In marketing terms the decision – taken during the 1973-4 fuel crisis – was sound, being confirmed by the 1978 Car of the Year Award and subsequent full order books; in design terms the layout was determined by constraints as diverse as the need to provide accommodation for four (not wholly achieved, the car being a 2+2 rather than a full four-seater) and the various safety regulations in main markets.

Some 928 features appeared on the 924, which was in production before the 928, although conceived later. Although Porsche followers may have been conditioned to the new era by the 924, the 928 was not wholly satisfying in appearance – it lacked the crispness of the 924 in its overall lines, with curvaceous side panels, a very sleek nose (in which the retractable headlights sensibly did not have covers) but a curiously rounded tail, and unattractive details such as the alloy wheels, in either its first form (illustrated) or the later 928S.

However, the beauty and efficiency under the skin were appreciated when the 928 was announced in 1977. The first version of the light-alloy single-ohc V-8 had a capacity of 4·5 litres, producing 240bhp quietly and smoothly, with abundant torque, and on low-grade fuel. It was bored out to 4·7 litres for the 928S (announced in 1979), to produce 300bhp at 5900rpm. In 1979, incidentally, Porsche experimented with V-8s in which half the cylinders were cut out in light-load conditions, showing up to 23 per cent improvement in fuel consumption.

In the transmission a transaxle was used again, with the gearbox positioned immediately ahead of the final drive unit; the possibility of gear change linkage vagaries was obviated by carrying this along the rigid tube housing the propeller shaft. The Porsche-Weissach rear suspension incorporated links to counter toe-in variations, and thus cut out oversteer in normal driving conditions (when the 928 was reassuringly stable).

The 928 found ready acceptance for what it was, a luxury sports 2+2 with a high degree of equipment in its rather oddly upholstered cockpit and a lightly-stressed engine giving more than adequate performance – maximum speeds of the 928 and 928S were 225kph (140mph) and a claimed 250kph (155mph).

Specification

Engine: *928* – 90-degree V-8; 95 × 78·9mm, 4474cc; single ohc per bank; Bosch K-Jetronic fuel injection; 240bhp at 5850rpm.
    928S – as above, but 97 × 78·9mm, 4664cc; 300bhp at 5900rpm.
Gearbox: five-speed manual; optional three-speed automatic.
Chassis: steel monocoque, with some alloy panels; front suspension independent by double wishbones, coil springs, dampers and anti-roll bar; rear suspension independent by lower wishbones, upper transverse links, coil springs, dampers and anti-roll bar; four-wheel ventilated disc brakes.
Dimensions: wheelbase 250cm/98½in; **front track** 155cm/61in; **rear track** 153cm/60in.

Railton

Although the snobbish sports car enthusiast may dismiss the Railton as 'an Anglo-American bastard', the formula of a big, low-stressed engine in a light chassis made good sense for both performance and price. The Cobham-built Railton was the unlikely descendant of the Eric Campbell, the Silver Hawk and the Invicta, all of which were launched by Captain Noel Macklin, but whereas the first three makes all failed, the Railton's career was only terminated when the Second World War broke out.

Founded in mid-1933, the marque took its name from Reid A Railton, famous designer for Thomson & Taylor of Brooklands. Taking as a basis the 4-litre straight-eight Hudson Terraplane, he lowered and modified the chassis and suspension, fitted friction dampers supplemented by André Telecontrols, added higher-geared steering, and tuned the big side-valve engine with its splash-lubricated big ends, raising the compression ratio and gaining an extra 19 horsepower over the basic unit's 94bhp.

The standard Hudson three-speed gearbox was adopted, and the mechanicals were elegantly clothed in lightweight British bodywork with a distinctive straight-sided radiator and incisive bonnet lines. With the engine's remarkable low speed torque and a road weight of around 1100kg, the power-to-weight ratio was

formidable, and the acceleration of any Railton in any gear was outstanding: 0 to 80kph (50mph) in 9 sec, and 0 to 100kph (60mph) in just over 12 sec were normal figures for a closed model, with a maximum of over 145kph (90mph).

In 1935 a special 990kg 'Light Sports' tourer with doorless light alloy open body and fixed cycle wings was introduced; its performance was electrifying, with a 0–100kph (60mph) figure of under 9 sec and a maximum of over 170kph (110mph). One of the three built set a new sports car record at Shelsley Walsh in 1938.

For the lazy driver the gearbox was scarcely necessary, the torquey Hudson engine starting the car off at 500rpm in top gear and running up to 145kph (90mph) in smoothness and silence on a par with the contemporary Rolls-type Bentley – but costing almost one third the price. The Railton's pace was, of course, qualified by suspension, steering and braking limitations which even Reid Railton could not wholly eradicate, but on a point-to-point journey over pre-war British roads, a well-driven Railton was hard to beat.

Hudson hydraulic brakes were adopted in 1936, and in 1937 a longer wheelbase chassis became available, the cars carrying more luxurious coachwork and growing heavier and less agile, although no straight-eight Railton was ever a sluggard.

Specification

Engine: *1933-34* – Hudson straight-eight; 75 × 114mm, 4010cc; side valves; single carburettor; 113bhp at 3800rpm.

From 1935 – as above, but 76 × 114mm, 4168cc; 124bhp.

Gearbox: Hudson three-speed manual.

Chassis: pressed steel side members; front suspension by radius arms, semi-elliptic leaf springs and friction/hydraulic dampers; rear suspension by semi-elliptic leaf springs and friction/hydraulic dampers; four-wheel drum brakes, mechanically-operated from 1933, hydraulic from 1936.

Dimensions: wheelbase 287cm/113in, but 295cm/116in from 1935 and optional 323cm/127in from 1937; **track** 142cm/56in.

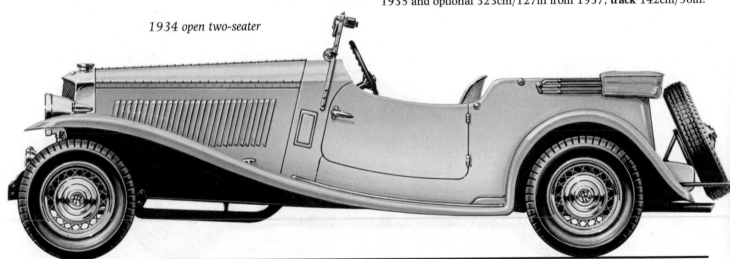

1934 open two-seater

Renault sports-racing cars

Renault's sports-racing programme with turbocharged cars lasted four years, with the clear-cut objective of victory at Le Mans. That was eventually achieved, at considerable cost in effort and time – the A442 won its first race, at Mugello in 1975, but did not win another until the all-important 24-hour race in 1978.

Alpine started on the quest for outright Le Mans victory with the 3-litre A220 coupes in 1968-69, but these were under-powered and were never competitive.

With a much greater emphasis on Renault, therefore, a new sports car programme was built around the CH V-6 designed by François Castaing at Renault's Viry-Chatillon engine development facility during 1972. In 2-litre form, this produced 270bhp for an exploratory 1973 season in the A440 (this car was designed by André de Cortanze, and like all Renault-Alpines until 1977 was built at the Alpine plant at Dieppe). For 1974 the power output of the 24-valve iron-block V-6 was modestly increased to around 285bhp, and it was used as a semi-stressed member in the A441. With the A440 and A441, the works team dominated the European 2-litre Championship, winning all seven races it contested.

Le Mans became a realistic objective when the CHS turbocharged version of the engine was built for 1975. With a Garrett turbo, output was increased dramatically to around 500bhp, while engine speed (and hence internal stresses) rose only fractionally. This was used in the A442, a straightforward semi-monocoque car which was intensively developed – there were, for example some 140 changes for the 1976 season – although at times it was handi-capped by the patriotic decision to run on Michelin steel-braced radial-ply tyres.

Driven by Gérard Larrousse and Jean-Pierre Jabouille, the A442 scored its debut victory in a championship race at Mugello, but for the rest of the season, while showing speed in practice sessions, the car too often suffered turbocharger teething problems or punctures in actual races, so that a couple of second placings were its next-best results.

With development, and against apparently negligible opposition, 1976 should have been better. But in terms of results, there were only three second places in championship races to show for a major programme; a sensational Le Mans pole position time – 6½sec faster than the next car – was a mitigating factor.

Renault then concentrated on Le Mans, and four cars were entered for the 1977 race (where a pair of Mirages also had the CHS V-6). At half distance Renaults were first and second, but all the team cars retired and there was only a second place for one of the Mirages to salvage pride. In 1978 the team ran two modified 1977 cars (A442A), an A442B which had substantial bodywork modifications and an A443, with a 520bhp 2140cc engine, 15cm longer wheelbase, long-tailed body and semi-enclosed cockpit. This time Renaults led throughout, with either the A443 or the A442B in which Jean-Pierre Jaussaud and Didier Pironi eventually won; one of the 1977 cars was fourth. It was perhaps as much with relief as with jubilation that Renault then turned away from sports car racing.

Specification *(A442)*

Engine: 90-degree V-6; 86 × 57·3mm, 1997cc; twin ohc per bank; Kugelfischer fuel injection and Garrett AiResearch turbocharger; 500bhp (approx) at 9900rpm.
Gearbox: five-speed manual.
Chassis: semi-monocoque; front suspension independent by wishbones, coil springs, dampers and anti-roll bar; rear suspension independent by radius arms, wishbones, coil springs, dampers and anti-roll bar; four-wheel disc brakes.
Dimensions: wheelbase 231cm/91in; **front track** 142cm/56in; **rear track** 143cm/56½in.

1978 A442B

Riley Nine Brooklands

Among the truly significant cars of the 1920s, the Riley Nine Monaco of 1926-27 is well remembered for a coachbuilding 'first' – the stepped closed body with integral boot. But that car's engine, designed by Percy Riley, was perhaps even more notable: departing from the customary side valves of its time, the 60·3 × 95·2mm 1087cc four cylinder engine had inclined overhead valves in hemispherical combustion chambers, like costly racing units.

Riley achieved it on a low-priced car by employing twin 'high' camshafts, one each side in the crankcase, operating 90-degree valves through short, light pushrods and rockers. The potential of this design was realised by that great Brooklands driver and engineer, J G Parry Thomas, who set out to produce a high-speed version. By fitting twin Solex carburettors, special camshafts and other modifications, he extracted some 50bhp at 5000rpm from the engine, despite its two-bearing crankshaft.

Thomas also shortened and lowered the frame, sweeping in the tail end, and producing a car only 91cm high at the scuttle. Unfortunately Thomas was killed in a record attempt early in 1927, but work on the Riley was continued by his partner Reid Railton, who not only completed the car but won a race with it at Brooklands in autumn 1927, with a fastest lap at a truly staggering 158·7kph (98·62mph).

Riley then took over manufacture, marketing the low-slung Nine as the Brooklands Speed Model. The specification included a dropped frame, underslung at the rear, and with a fold-flat screen and rudimentary hood the production road model was good for 130kph (80mph) – and much more with special tuning,

By 1928 the Brooklands was a forceful contender in the 1100cc class formerly dominated by French Salmsons and Amilcars. It broke numerous speed records, scored four consecutive class wins in the Ulster TT between 1928 and 1931, and won both this race and the Brooklands 1000 Miles race outright in 1932. The car was too stark and hard-riding for extensive road use, although it performed well in the milder kind of trial despite its low ground clearance. From Percy Riley's clever ohv four a larger six-cylinder unit was evolved, and from this sprang the supercharged 1½-litre ERA engine which would power those highly-successful English single-seaters to so many victories.

Specification
Engine: straight-four; 60·3 × 95·2mm, 1089cc; pushrod ohv; twin carburettors; 50bhp at 5000rpm.
Gearbox: four-speed manual.
Chassis: pressed steel side members, underslung at rear; front and rear suspension by semi-elliptic leaf springs and friction dampers; four-wheel drum brakes.
Dimensions: wheelbase 244cm/96in; **track** 121cm/47½in.

Riley Imp and MPH

A Riley bearing the name 'Imp' first appeared at the 1933 Olympia Motor Show, having a shortened Nine chassis onto which was crammed a two/four-seater body with the rear seats well behind the rear axle. The following summer the Riley design staff, despite the profusion of models characteristic in those days, got round to revising the Imp.

They produced an extremely pretty two-seater body with flared wings, a fold-flat screen and a nicely rounded tail supporting the spare wheel. With a wheelbase of only 230cm and large-diameter wire wheels the proportions were admirable, but the Imp must have disappointed buyers who expected a fast car as well as 'fast looks'.

The chassis, underslung at the rear, was a sturdy affair with 15cm-deep boxed side members and generous cross bracing, while the engine – a special series version of the well-known 1087cc Nine unit, had twin SU carburettors, a Scintilla vertical magneto, and an output of 41bhp at 5000rpm.

With the car scaling 860kg with the normal four-speed 'silent third' gearbox (slightly more with a Wilson preselector) this meant a maximum speed of no more than 115kph (70mph) – a lot less than the less civilised Brooklands model which the Imp succeeded. More important, the admittedly smaller and more spartan MG Midget J2 managed the same speed on 847cc and cost £199–10s to the Riley's £298.

An optional extra was Riley 'Preselectagear' transmission, which meant a Wilson four-speed preselector gearbox with Newton automatic centrifugal clutch.

The Imp proved popular for rally work, scoring several successes in British events, but it lacked the power for racing; a works team of specially prepared 'Ulster Imps' ran unsuccessfully in the 1934 TT, while 'B Bira', the famous Siamese prince, began his racing career at Brooklands with a private Imp in 1935.

The slightly longer Riley MPH with similar bodywork, 1·5-, 1·6- or 1·76-litre six-cylinder engine, larger brakes and a 140kph (85mph) maximum seemed more promising but cost far more, and overall both these strikingly good looking models disappointed, production ending in 1935.

1935 Imp

Specification (*Imp*)
Engine: straight-four; 60·3 × 95·2mm, 1089cc; pushrod ohv; twin SU carburettors; 41bhp at 5000rpm.
Gearbox: four-speed manual; optional four-speed Preselectagear (see text).
Chassis: box-section side members, underslung at rear; front and rear suspension by semi-elliptic leaf springs and friction dampers; four-wheel drum brakes.
Dimensions: wheelbase 230cm/90½in; track 121cm/47½in.

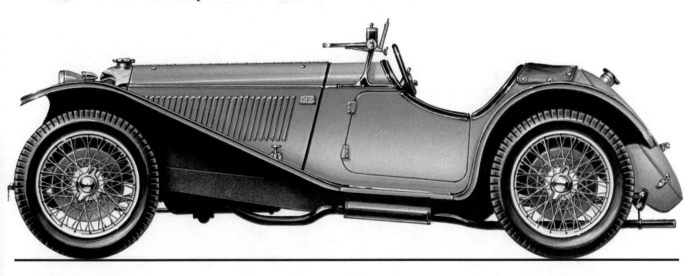

Riley Sprite

In 1934 Riley introduced an enlarged edition of its famous four-cylinder Nine engine, increasing the bore and stroke from 60·3 × 95·2mm to 69 × 100mm (1496cc). All the excellent characteristics of the classic Riley design with its 'high' camshafts and angled valves in hemispherical heads remained, but a new and very rigid three-bearing balanced crankshaft was employed, and this engine in single-carburettor form driving through a Wilson preselector gearbox, went into the new Riley Falcon saloon released at the 1935 Motor Show.

This same engine, in twin-carburettor boosted form, giving 61bhp at 5000rpm, made an admirable replacement for the heavy six in a revised version of the MPH called the Sprite. As on the MPH, there was a choice of a four-speed manual gearbox or a wide-ratio Wilson epicyclic box (as fitted to the Falcon saloon). The open two-seater bodywork was considerably restyled, however, with sweeping valanced wings harmonising with the shapely MPH-style tail; the radiator was shrouded in an unusual 'fencer's mask' cowling, curving forward over the dumbirons to merge with the front wings, giving an attractive long-bonnet effect.

The chassis remained of basic MPH type, apart from the adoption of Girling rod-operated brakes with ribbed drums, electron back-plates and airscoops. A long undershield was also fitted, enclosing the transmission and brakework, and improving both the aerodynamics and the draught-proofing. Maximum speed was 140kph (85mph), but the engine's ready response to tuning encouraged its use in 1½-litre sports car racing.

The 1935 Ulster TT saw a quartet of specially prepared Sprite-based Rileys, with long-tailed bodies and cycle wings, one winning outright and others placing sixth and ninth. The same cars placed one-two-three-four in the 2-litre class of the 1936 French GP and in the 1936 TT, the 1935 victory was repeated.

During that year the Sprite engine became optional in the Riley Kestrel saloon and the Lynx tourer, making them into desirable 130kph (80mph) cars.

1937 brought more Sprite race victories at Montlhéry in France, at Crystal Palace and elsewhere, but financial troubles then struck Riley and in 1938 the company was taken over by the Nuffield Group.

Specification

Engine: straight-four; 69 × 100mm, 1496cc; pushrod ohv; twin carburettors; 61bhp at 5000rpm.
Gearbox: four-speed manual; optional Wilson four-speed preselector.
Chassis: box-section pressed steel side members, underslung at rear; front and rear suspension by semi-elliptic leaf springs and friction dampers; four-wheel Girling drum brakes.
Dimensions: wheelbase 248cm/97½in; track 122cm/48in.

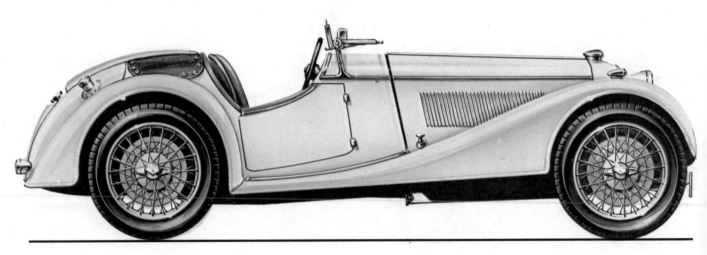

Saab Sonett

Saab saloons have gained splendid sporting reputations, but the company's attitude to its only sports car seemed reticent, and little attempt was made to exploit its potential, marketing being largely confined to the USA. The diminutive open Sonett I, based on Saab 93 components and shown in 1956, was shelved and it was not until 1965 that the Sonett II coupe was announced. It was put into limited production late that year.

A design by Bjorn Karlstrom was preferred to a Targa-top exercise by Sason; both were inevitably inhibited by the need to use available components, so that the Sonett II looked dumpy, sitting on wheels from the contemporary 96, which were just too large for it. However, they tied in with the saloon's suspension, engine (in its 841cc 60bhp Monte Carlo form) and transmission, naturally with front-wheel drive. The glass fibre body was mounted on a shortened 96 chassis pan, and soon grew a bulge over the bonnet as it was modified to accept the 1·5-litre German Ford V-4 in 1968. This change to a four-stroke was largely at the insistence of US distributors, and its extra 10bhp made virtually no difference to

performance because of its greater weight, both versions of the II having maximum speeds approaching 160kph (100mph).

There were still too many shortcomings, and Sonett III was evolved for 1972. Sergio Coggiola was commissioned to design a new body, and he came up with a longer, sleeker three-door hatchback, and tidied up the interior. The largest of the Ford V-4s was used, a 1·7-litre unit rated at only 65bhp, as its compression ratio was lowered to suit unleaded fuel. Maximum speed was still almost 160kph (100mph), good aerodynamic characteristics helping to offset the near-910kg unladen weight of this solid little car. Although the V4 was mounted ahead of the front wheels, the Sonnet was not a nose-heavy car, having light and neutral steering suited to twisty roads.

The first year of the Sonett III was the model's best in sales terms, with over 2000 built. Saab people were fond of jokes about the 'toy' in their range, but the total production of 8351 Sonett IIIs justified its existence, even if further development was not possible and production of this 97 ceased after 1973.

Specification *(Sonett III)*
Engine: Ford 60-degree V-4; 90 × 66·8mm, 1699cc; pushrod ohv; single Solex carburettor; 65bhp at 4700rpm.
Gearbox: four-speed manual.
Chassis: steel platform; front suspension independent by wishbones, coil springs and dampers; rear suspension by beam axle, coil springs and dampers; disc front/drum rear brakes.
Dimensions: wheelbase 215cm/84½in; track 123cm/48½in.

Sonett III

Salmson 1100

Apart from a few short-lived deviations, the French sports Salmson adhered consistently to the 1100cc class through the 1920s. During that period the Billancourt concern built air-cooled vee-twins (under GN licence), water-cooled fours and even a straight-eight, but the Salmson that gave so much inexpensive motoring pleasure to so many enthusiasts had four cylinders, either with pushrod ohv or twin ohc. At first they were spidery creations called 'cyclecars', denoting a specially cheap taxation category devised by the French, but when the concession ended in 1925 they became *voiturettes* or light cars.

The first Salmson fours had two-bearing crankshafts and hemispherical heads with eight inclined overhead valves operated by four pushrods only, a mechanical 'miracle' achieved by each pushrod actuating both the inlet and exhaust valves of each cylinder through a system of T-bars and springs. Such economy in moving parts from a lesser maker might have been derided, but Salmson had several years' experience of making aircraft engines, and the four-pushrod engine worked well, remaining in production from 1921 to 1927, when it was succeeded briefly by an eight-pushrod touring model.

Light weight being obligatory to qualify for the French cut-price tax, the 1921 Salmson chassis was a simple 'bedstead' with quarter-elliptic springs projecting fore and aft. A three-speed gearbox in unit with the engine, shaft drive and a differential-less rear axle also featured, while a gossamer open two-seater body was normal wear, with fittings such as a spare wheel, electric lighting, instruments etc. rating as optional extras above the 350kg weight limit.

While the four-pushrod engines went into production, new and sophisticated twin-ohc heads and three-bearing bottom ends were quickly developed for a team of special 1100cc eight-plug racers which won first time out in the 1921 Cyclecar GP at Le Mans, and swept the 1100 board clean for the next four years. Production twin-cam models – the first by any marque in the world – were announced in 1922, and marketed in touring, sports and racing forms up to 1930.

With exotic model names such as Grand Prix, Grand Sport and San Sebastian, these were the much-loved 'Sammies' that sold briskly and figured successfully in all branches of motor sport, from trials and rallies to sprints and road and track racing, all with impressive reliability.

1926 Sports two-seater

Specification

Engine: *'four-pushrod' models (see text)* – straight-four; 62 × 90mm, 1087cc; pushrod ohv; single carburettor; 22bhp (approx) at 3000rpm.
   twin ohc models – as above, but twin ohc; 33bhp (approx) at 3800rpm.
Gearbox: three-speed manual, but four-speed manual on twin-ohc Grand Sport model.
Chassis: pressed steel side members; front suspension by reversed quarter-elliptic leaf springs and friction dampers (but semi-elliptic springs from 1922); rear suspension by quarter-elliptic leaf springs and friction dampers; rear-wheel drum brakes from 1921, four-wheel drum brakes on twin-ohc models and on all models from 1925.
Dimensions: *'four-pushrod' model* – **wheelbase** 259cm/102in; **track** 107cm/42in.
   twin ohc model – **wheelbase** 254cm/100in; **track** 114cm/45in.

Singer Le Mans 9

Derided by purists as a 'phoney' sports-racer with its ostentatious 'slab' rear tank, windscoops, cutaway doors and superfluity of stone-guards, the 972cc Singer Le Mans nevertheless offered brisk performance at modest price, achieved some notable competition successes, and gave its owners ample enjoyment.

Its best feature was probably the four-cylinder ohc engine. Singer of Coventry was an early user of ohc in small cars, beginning in 1926 with the Junior, which grew into the more sporting Porlock by 1929 and the 105kph (65mph) Nine sport four-seater by 1932. This had a sturdy two-bearing 60 × 96mm engine with chain-driven single ohc and twin carburettors, producing around 45bhp and able to turn at over 5500rpm.

Fitted into a lowered, shortened chassis, wearing fixed cycle wings, Rudge knock-off wire wheels, and with a remote control four-speed synchromesh gearbox and hydraulic brakes, the Nine sold at a price which ensured its popularity and confronted MG with a serious rival on the cheap sports car market.

First time out, the Nine won a Glacier Cup in the gruelling Alpine Trial of 1932, and Singers boldly entered one for the Le Mans 24-hour race in 1933. The rear seats were replaced by a 'slab' petrol tank and lighter wings were fitted, the car making a trouble-free run to place 13th overall, being the third under-1000cc car to finish.

The resulting 972cc Le Mans Singer of 1934 was a lively if rather brash little car with 40bhp twin-carburettor engine, shapely swept wings minus running boards, twin spare wheels mounted behind the slab tank, all the Le Mans trimmings – and a rorty exhaust note. It could attain 120kph (75mph) and scored numerous successes in British trials, rallies and driving tests, thanks to low gearing which in other circumstances was less of an advantage.

At Le Mans it this time became the first under-1000cc finisher, taking 15th place overall. In 1935 Singers produced a special long-tailed 'Replica' Nine based on the Le Mans, a team of these winning the Brooklands Relay Race, and a 'Replica' also won the 1-litre class at Le Mans yet again. At the Ulster TT, however, Singer suffered collective calamity, when three of the four team cars crashed at the same point through steering drop-arm breakages. This did considerable harm to Singer's sports car reputation, and a change of company policy after 1936 ended the Le Mans line.

Specification(*Nine Le Mans*)
Engine: straight-four; 60 × 86mm, 972cc; single ohc; twin carburettors; 40bhp at 4700rpm.
Gearbox: four-speed manual.
Chassis: pressed steel side members; semi-elliptic leaf springs front and rear; four-wheel Lockheed hydraulic drum brakes.
Dimensions: wheelbase 231cm/91in; **track** 114cm/45in.

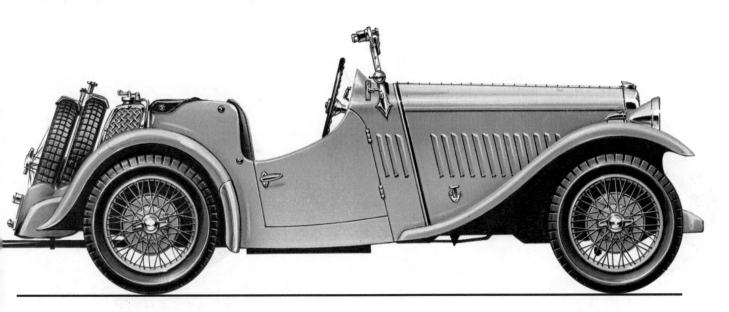

Squire

The story of the Squire car is a sad one. Adrian Squire was a talented young engineer with very decided ideas about sports cars. After serving an apprenticeship with Bentley he joined MG as a draughtsman, leaving two years later to found Squire Motors at Remenham Hill, near Henley-on-Thames, in 1931. The company earned its bread-and-butter by garage work and petrol sales, while plans for building a Squire sports car went forward; a separate company was formed in 1934, with racing driver Manby-Colegrave as a director.

A proprietary engine, the all-alloy 69 × 100mm (1496cc) twin-ohc Anzani, was adopted, fitted with a Roots-type supercharger which raised output from around 70bhp to 105bhp at 5000rpm. A separate ENV-Wilson preselector four-speed gearbox was used, while the remainder of the specification was typical of pre-Second World War British cars: channel section frame with semi-elliptic springing, beam axles and wire wheels.

Squire's design, however, possessed outstanding merits in appearance, roadholding and braking. It looked glorious with its impressively low build, massive hydraulic brakes, a beautiful and expensive-looking inclined radiator and lovely body lines ending in a neat tail. The chassis was very rigid with cruciform bracing, two wheelbases were offered, and a variety of two- and four-seater bodywork was available.

Every car was guaranteed to have exceeded 160kph (100mph), but the big snag was the price: £1220 for the cheapest model (a short chassis open two-seater) at a time when a 1½-litre Aston Martin cost £610, an Alvis £495, a supercharged MG Magnette £795, and even a blown 1750cc Alfa Romeo from Italy could be had for only £850.

In an effort to prove the car's effectiveness one was prepared for racing at Brooklands in 1935, without success apart from third place in a short handicap.

A 'cheap' two-seater was built to sell at £995, but with only seven cars made and five sold in two years an idealist's ideal had manifestly failed and the company had to be wound up in July 1936. The following year, however, one of their few customers, Val Zethrin, took over the remaining Squire parts, improved the design in detail, and built three more cars before war intervened. Efforts to resume manufacture when peace returned were to no avail. As for poor Adrian Squire, he joined WO Bentley at Lagonda in 1936, then Bristol Aircraft factory, only to be killed in an air raid in 1940.

Specification

Engine: Anzani straight-four; 69 × 120mm, 1496cc; twin ohc; SU carburettor and Roots supercharger; 105bhp at 5000rpm.
Gearbox: separate Wilson four-speed preselector.
Chassis: pressed steel side members with cruciform bracing; front and rear suspension by semi-elliptic leaf springs and hydraulic dampers; four-wheel drum brakes.
Dimensions: wheelbase 259cm/102in or 312cm/123in; track 137cm/54in.

Stutz Black Hawk and Bearcat

Twin-cam straight-eights in the USA, land of iron side-valve engines in the 1920s, were a rarity indeed, and it took a near-victory in the world's most famous sports car race to produce such a novelty. The Stutz company of Indianapolis was the instigator, producing a new, low-line model, the DV16 or 'Vertical 8 Safety Car' in 1926, with a 4·7-litre 80bhp ohc straight-eight. The DV16 had a double-drop frame and underslung worm rear drive, and despite carrying heavy sedan coachwork could reach almost to 130kph (80mph) with dynamo smoothness due in part to a fully balanced nine-bearing crankshaft. It also had early Timken-type hydraulic brakes, using water and alcohol.

Its performance was so promising that Stutz made a rather long open four-seater 'boat tail' version for 1927, raising engine size to 4·9 litres and output to 95bhp. This was called the Black Hawk Speedster, and won all but one AAA stock car races that year. For 1928 power was stretched to 115bhp, and the boosted engine was inserted in a shorter 'boat tail' which (in stripped form) clocked a record 171·44kph (106·53mph) at Daytona.

That precipitated the Black Hawk into racing; one ran at Le Mans in 1928, finishing a brilliant second amid solid Bentley opposition. In 1929 Stutz tried with three cars, now with 5·3 litres and four speeds, while one was run experimentally with a Roots super-charger engaged at will by the driver. This car caught fire, and a modest fifth with another car was the only 1929 reward.

Trying for a third time, the cars were given a new chain-driven twin-ohc head with four valves per cylinder, showing over 150bhp on the brake. Such enterprise was ill-rewarded with the destruction of one car by fire, and total retirement.

The company then developed the 5·3-litre 32-valve four-speeder into a high performance road car, called the DV32 or Bearcat, an open model guaranteed to exceed 160kph (100mph). A Super Bear-cat with shorter wheelbase was introduced in 1931, but buyers were few in such an economically-bleak year, so Stutz cheapened it in 1932 by fitting a three-speed synchromesh gearbox – few drivers had used the four-speed box anyway, with so much torque – but the inevitable happened and Stutz had ceased production of its superbly-engineered cars by 1934 and was out of the automobile business a year later.

Specification

Engine: *Black Hawk (1927-29)* – straight-eight; 82·5 × 114·3mm, 4888cc; single ohc; twin carburettors; 95bhp at 3200rpm rising to 115bhp at 3600rpm by 1928.
   Black Hawk (1930-34) – as above, but 85·7 × 114·3mm, 5350cc; 113bhp at 3300rpm.
   Bearcat and Super Bearcat – as above, but twin ohc; 156bhp at 3900rpm.
Gearbox: three-speed manual from 1927; four-speed manual from 1929; three-speed manual from 1932.
Chassis: pressed steel side members; semi-elliptic leaf springs front and rear; friction dampers in 1927, but hydraulic dampers thereafter; four-wheel drum brakes, Timken hydrostatic in 1927, Lockheed hydraulic thereafter, with vacuum servo assistance.
Dimensions: wheelbase 333cm/131in (but 295cm/116in on Super Bearcat); **front track** 144cm/56½in; **rear track** 149cm/58½in.

Sunbeam Alpine and Tiger

Introduced in 1959, this Sunbeam Alpine (the Rootes Group had used the name on a short-lived model six years earlier) was by no means a full-blooded sports car, but a handsome, responsive and comfortable open tourer with sporting characteristics. It was a happy amalgam of Rootes components, the 1494cc engine and transmission coming from the Rapier and the floorpan from the Husky, while the suspension was the stolid mix of coil spring and wishbone ifs and semi-ellipitic live rear axle. It was to all intents and purposes a 160kph (100mph) car, with a weight of 1000kg telling against its acceleration figures.

The Series II of 1960 had its engine bored out to 1592cc, to produce 85·5bhp, but performance fell off again in the Series III of 1963 with power down to 80·5bhp, falling further – to 77bhp – in the new hardtop GT model. That lasted only a year, replaced by the Series IV, which had slightly modified lines (most noticeably, the tail fins were cut down), 82bhp and optional three-speed automatic transmission, which few found attractive. In the Series V, which came in 1965, the 92·5bhp of the Rootes 1725cc engine did not quite restore the magic 100mph (160kph) top speed, and the pretence of two occasional seats was abandoned.

There were modest attempts to use the Alpine in competition, but the impetus to make it a genuine high-performance car came from the west coast of the USA, spurred by the success of the AC Cobra. Shelby inserted a 141bhp, 4·2-litre Ford V-8 into a Series IV Alpine; this prototype was tested by Rootes, further modified, and in 1965 was put into production as the Tiger.

Tigers performed creditably in secondary races throughout the mid-1960s, although a works attempt at Le Mans in 1964, using cars which had been partly-developed by Lister, was a failure.

The Tiger's fate was sealed in 1967 when industrial troubles at Rootes precipitated the company's takeover by Chrysler; the new owners were naturally less than enthusiastic about using a Ford engine and production was discontinued after just over 7000 had been made (including a few Tiger IIs with a more potent 4727cc Ford V-8). Finally, in 1968, Chrysler terminated production of the Alpine.

1960 Alpine Series II

Specification

Engine: *Alpine Series I* – straight-four; 79 × 76·2mm, 1494cc; pushrod ohv; Zenith carburettors; 83·5bhp at 5300rpm.

Alpine Series II – as above, but 81·5 × 76·2mm, 1592cc; 85·5bhp.

Tiger I – Ford 90-degree V-8; 96·5 × 73mm, 4262cc; pushrod ohv; Ford carburettor; 164bhp at 4400rpm.
Gearbox: four-speed manual; optional Borg Warner three-speed automatic on Series IV and V.
Chassis: unitary; front suspension independent by wishbones, coil springs, dampers and anti-roll bar; rear suspension by live axle, semi-elliptic leaf springs and dampers; disc front/drum rear brakes.
Dimensions: *Alpine* – **wheelbase** 218cm/86in; **front track** 130cm/51in; **rear track** 124cm/48½in.
Tiger – **wheelbase** 218cm/86in; **front track** 132cm/52in; **rear track** 123cm/48½in.

Talbot 90 and 105

The so-called 'Roesch' Talbots built at Barlby Road, North Kensington, between 1926 and 1936 were decidedly 'wolf-in-sheep's-clothing' motor cars of medium size, medium price, high quality and surprising performance. They were lofty in build and staid looking, especially under the bonnet where a clean and simple pushrod-ohv single-carburettor engine sat with ample space around it.

Certainly Swiss designer Georges Roesch's 14/45 of 1926 had no sporting pretensions, but was a brilliant passenger-carrying car by one who disliked complication, noise, friction and wasteful litres. Its engine was a straightforward 1·6-litre six with vertical ohv operated by needle-thin pushrods and rockers on friction-saving knife-edge fulcrums, and a four-bearing crankshaft required to turn at 4500rpm. The rigid chassis had semi-elliptic front springs and quarter-elliptics at the rear, the brakes were excellent, and the 14/45 was lively, reliable and pleasant to drive. That such a car could form the basis of a Le Mans, TT or Brooklands racing car seemed very remote, but that was exactly what happened.

Roesch first evolved the Talbot 75, with engine enlarged to 2276cc and given a fully-balanced seven-bearing crankshaft. This performed so well that the Fox & Nicholl racing stable persuaded Roesch to produce a competition version for the 3-litre sports car class. Raising the compression to 10:1, he extracted 93bhp at 4500rpm from the 2·2-litre engine, which held this figure on the brake for 24 hours. Tests established the car's maximum speed as near enough 90mph (145kph), so the new competition Talbot became the 90.

Performing in swift, unfussed silence, the lofty white-painted Talbots won their class in four consecutive major races in 1930, at Le Mans, Phoenix Park, Ulster and Brooklands. When, inevitably, Fox & Nicholl asked for more, Roesch raised the engine size for 1931 to 2969cc, giving 100bhp and 105mph (169kph) – and a new type number for the next competition Talbot. In 1931 the 105 placed third at Le Mans, while at Brooklands it scored one-two-three in class in both the 1931 Double 12 and the 1932 1000 Miles race, when Talbots also placed second and took the team prize.

Such was Talbot versatility that a team of 105s in a very different element, the gruelling Alpine Trial, finished without loss of marks in 1931, 1932 and 1934, also taking the team prize in the two latter years. The 90 and 105 were both marketed as superbly tractable, long-lasting road cars with a wide choice of bodywork, some of the most beautiful by Talbot itself. While still a healthy profit-maker, Talbot was sold to Rootes, who killed the proud Roesch pedigree and crossed it with Humber and Hillman designs.

Specification

Engine: *90* – straight-six; 69·5 × 100mm, 2276cc; pushrod ohv; single carburettor; 70bhp at 4500rpm (but 93bhp on competition cars).

105 – as above, but 75 × 112mm, 2960cc; 100bhp at 4000rpm (138bhp at 4800rpm on competition cars).

Gearbox: four-speed manual; optional Wilson four-speed preselector from 1932.

Chassis: pressed steel side members; semi-elliptic front springs; quarter-elliptic rear springs; friction dampers, but hydraulic dampers from 1930; four-wheel drum brakes.

Dimensions: *90* – **wheelbase** 282cm/111in, but 290cm/114in from 1930; **front track** 141cm/51½in; **rear track** 141cm/55½in.

105 – **wheelbase** 290cm/114in; **track** 141cm/55½in.

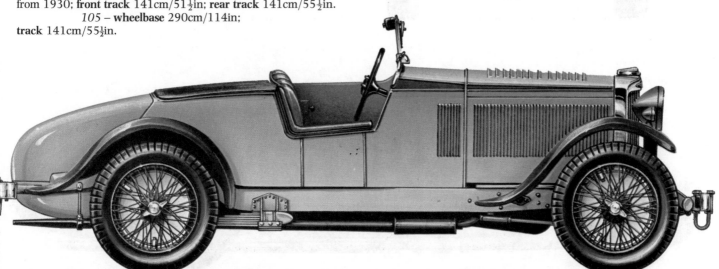

Talbot-Lago

Antonio, Antoine, Anthony or Tony Lago was Venetian-born, but spent much of his working life in England and France. In 1933 he joined Sunbeam-Talbot-Darracq in the twilight years of that combine, going to Paris to reorganise the old Talbot-Darracq works at Suresnes, where French Talbot cars were being built in desultory fashion. Other than belonging to the same group, these had nothing to do with Georges Roesch's London-built Talbots; the best of the French range was a 3-litre ohv six with four-bearing crankshaft and a chassis with ifs by transverse leaf spring.

Lago saw potential in it, and in 1934 he and designer Becchia drew up a new hemispherical head with inclined valves to fit the old block, utilising the single camshaft in the crankcase with angled pushrods to actuate the inlet and exhaust valves through rockers. In 1935 S-T-D collapsed, Lago enlisted fresh financial support, and Automobiles Talbot was refloated as an independent concern.

Then came the French sports-car racing rennaissance, and Talbot laid down a team of competition 4-litre machines for 1936. Developed from the 3-litre, the new engine had a seven-bearing crankshaft and triple Solex carburettors, and its 170bhp was transmitted through a Wilson self-change gearbox. Teething troubles dogged its first season, but by 1937 the Talbot had found its form,

winning several major sports-car races including the British TT and the French Grand Prix.

Concurrently, a prestige high-performance road car, the Lago Sport-Spéciale or SS, was launched with the same engine in milder 140bhp form. With its low, short chassis and large wheels this was a magnet to French coachbuilders, who produced a variety of curvaceous close-coupled coupés, some gloriously shaped, others an excess of wild radii and curlecues. Underneath them all, that solid six-cylinder engine was able to waft the car along at an easy 185kph (115mph) without stress or strain.

After the Second World War, the sports Talbots were enlarged to 4½ litres, and the cross-pushrod head was reworked, acquiring twin 'high' camshafts operating inclined ohv (in Riley fashion) through short pushrods. That and hydraulic brakes apart, the cars were little changed from pre-war, though now called Grand Sport and with 190bhp beneath their shapely bonnets, plus the extra prestige of a 1950 Le Mans victory and several wins from the same engine in single-seater Grand Prix Talbots. France's implacable tax system (which heavily penalised owners of high-priced cars) killed off such splendid automobiles, and in 1959 Talbot-Lago was absorbed by Simca.

Specification

Engine: *Lago Sport Spéciale (1936-39)* – straight-six; 90 × 104·5mm, 3994cc; pushrod ohv; twin or triple carburettors; 125bhp at 4100rpm, rising to 140bhp (and 165bhp on competition models).

    Lago Grand Sport (from 1946) – as above, but 93 × 110mm, 4482cc; twin 'high' camshafts operating pushrod ohv; 165bhp at 4200rpm, rising to 190bhp (and 240bhp at 4700rpm on competition models).

Gearbox: four-speed Wilson preselector.

Chassis: box-section side members; front suspension independent by transverse leaf spring; rear suspension by semi-elliptic leaf springs; friction dampers from 1936, hydraulic/friction dampers from 1945; four-wheel drum brakes, Bendix mechanical from 1936, Lockheed hydraulic from 1945.

Dimensions: wheelbase 264cm/104in or 295cm/116in; front track 142cm/56in; rear track 149cm/58½in.

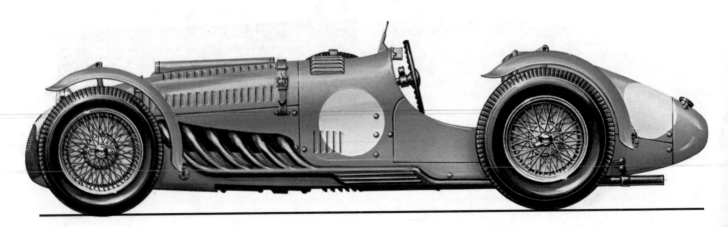

Triumph Dolomite

This was one of the great might-have-beens of motoring history, for it promised to be a British sports car to match contemporary pace-setting models. There were two main problems: Triumph could not adequately finance such a project in a difficult economic period; and when the first Dolomite was shown at the 1934 Motor Show, Alfa Romeo objected to the undeniable fact that it bore a remarkably close resemblance to its own classic supercharged straight-eight models.

Donald Healey, then Triumph's development engineer, had ambitions to produce a car to match the Alfa Monza, and to this end a second-hand example was closely examined; Alfa may have had strenuous objections to the Dolomite, although not to the extent of a law suit (as was rumoured at the time).

The Dolomite brochure promised that "each car is built and tested under the supervision of Mr Donald Healey", and would be delivered with a guarantee that it had covered a flying mile at a speed in excess of 160kph (100mph), with full touring equipment. It was a handsome car, not so svelte as its Italian inspiration, perhaps, but thoroughly purposeful.

Resemblance to Alfa Romeos was most obvious under the bonnet, in a straight-eight with its cylinders in two RR-Hiduminium light-alloy blocks of four with the twin ohc gear-driven from the centre of the ten-bearing crankshaft. The gear-driven Roots supercharger, on the right, had a pressure of approximately 10psi. Preselector control for the Armstrong Siddeley Wilson-type gearbox was mounted on the steering column, and transmission was by open propellor shaft. Semi-elliptic suspension front and rear, with the chassis stiffer at the front, gave a board-hard ride in the sports-car tradition. Enormous Lockheed brakes, in 16-inch Elektron drums, gave adequate stopping power.

Initially, parts for six cars were gathered, but all were not assembled. *The Autocar* experienced one at Brooklands, where it achieved 164·91kph (102·47mph), while another was written off when Donald Healey had his famous accident with a Danish train during the 1935 Monte Carlo Rally.

Triumph abandoned the model, and the surviving cars and parts were acquired by High Speed Motors, re-appearing as the HSM-Dolomite. With an engine bored out to 2·4 litres (and higher supercharger pressure) one was run by APR Rolt in speed trials and circuit events. Triumph later revived the name 'Dolomite' for a roadster and for saloons, decades apart and with nothing like the exciting potential of the first Dolomite.

Specification

Engine: straight-eight; 60 × 88mm, 1990cc; twin ohc; twin Zenith carburettors and Roots-type supercharger; 140bhp at 5500rpm.

Gearbox: four-speed Wilson preselector.

Chassis: deep-section main members, upswept over rear suspension, plus crossmembers; front and rear suspension by live axle, semi-elliptic leaf springs and dampers; four-wheel drum brakes.

Dimensions: wheelbase 356cm/140in; **track** 137cm/54in.

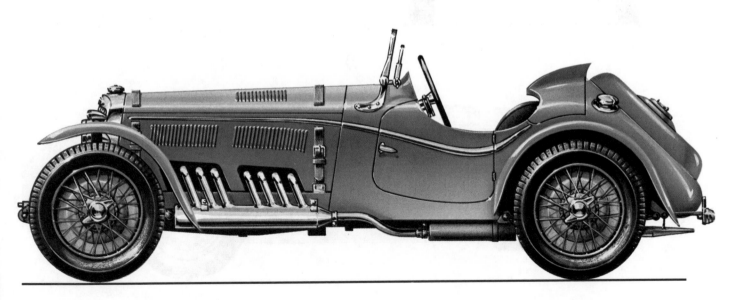

Triumph TR2 to TR6

The essence of the early TRs was simplicity, reflected in low construction costs and competitive prices, and a robust rather than elegant appearance. The first Triumph sports car project after the company's acquisition by Standard in 1945 was the complex TRX, which was never put into production, but a new low-budget programme resulted in the TR2. This was introduced late in 1952, although not marketed until the following summer.

Components from existing models were used where possible: the Standard Vanguard engine (linered down to below 2 litres), gearbox and back axle, and Triumph Mayflower front suspension. The simple body comprised mainly single-curvature pressings. The TR2 had a maximum speed of just over 160kph (100mph), was economical and reliable, and had acceptable handling resulting from development work by Ken Richardson. Production was a mere 8628, before it was succeeded in 1955 by the slightly more 'civilized' TR3.

This was distinguished by its grille, and by an initial increase in power from 90bhp to 95bhp (cylinder head modifications early in 1956 raised that to 100bhp). Late in 1956 it became the first British production car fitted with front disc brakes. The TR3A followed in 1958, with an optional hardtop (and outside door handles!) and a 175kph (110mph) capability. TR3 production reached 83 500 before it gave way to the TR4 in 1965.

The early TRs became familiar in competitions, from club to international level: in 1954, TR2s took team prizes in events as diverse as the Tourist Trophy and the Alpine Rally, while the latter event in 1956 saw TR3 crews take no fewer than five Coupe des Alpes for finishing without loss of marks.

A first attempt at Le Mans, with a TR2 in 1954, was moderately successful (15th of 18 finishers), but in 1956 all three works cars finished, the highest placing being 14th. TRS derivatives with the twin-ohc 'Sabrina' engine were run at Le Mans 1959-61: all three retired in 1959, but all finished in 1960 and in 1961 they placed ninth, eleventh and fifteenth to take the team award. The works then turned away from racing, although they did support efforts in SCCA categories, and the TR4 was briefly used by the resurrected rally team in 1962.

A square-cut Michelotti body was fitted to a widened version of the TR3 chassis to produce the TR4, which was powered by a 105bhp four-cylinder 2183cc engine. The coil spring ifs and semi-elliptic rear suspension were retained until the TR4A appeared early in 1965 with the coil spring irs from the Triumph 2000. Engine power was marginally increased (to 104bhp), but in top speed terms this did not offset the greater weight; 68 800 TR4s were produced.

Effectively, the body and running gear were carried over to the TR5 PI, along with a fuel-injection six-cylinder engine producing 150bhp to give a real improvement in performance, to speed rising to 190kph (120mph); a carburettor version was also available for some export markets. The TR5 had a relatively short production life, 11 694 being built before the TR6 was announced in 1969.

This was another logical update, with Karmann Ghia body superimposed on similar mechanical parts and inner structure, with detail improvements such as wider wheels (to complement its 'masculine' lines) and a front anti-roll bar. During its production years, the power of the Lucas-injected engine was twice reduced, from 150bhp in 1970 to 125bhp in the CR series in response to 1976 European emission regulations; engines of TR6s destined for the USA always had Stromberg carburettors to satisfy Federal regulations, and a consequent 126bhp.

This was a 190kph-plus (120mph) car in its prime, with a very taut ride verging on the harsh, which made for stability. It was the last TR to have that 'traditional British sports car' feel and by the end of production 88 000 had been made.

1953 TR2

TR6 of the Group 44 team

Specifications (representative)
TR2 and TR3
Engine: *TR2* – straight-four; 83 × 92mm, 1991cc; pushrod ohv; SU carburettors; 90bhp at 5000rpm.

TR3 – as above, but 100bhp.

Gearbox: four-speed manual; optional overdrive.

Chassis: steel, with separate body; front suspension independent by coil springs, wishbones and dampers; rear suspension by live axle, leaf springs and dampers; four-wheel drum brakes on TR2, disc front/drum rear brakes on TR3.

Dimensions: wheelbase 224cm/88in; **front track** 114cm/45in; **rear track** 116cm/45½in on TR2, 117cm/46in on TR3.

TR6 PI
Engine: straight-six; 74·7 × 95mm, 2498cc; pushrod ohv; Lucas fuel injection; 150bhp at 5500rpm.

Gearbox: four speed manual with overdrive.

Chassis: steel, with separate body; front suspension independent by wishbones, coil springs, dampers and anti-roll bar; rear suspension independent by semi-trailing arms, coil springs and dampers; disc front/drum rear brakes.

Dimensions: wheelbase 223cm/88in; **track** 128cm/50½in.

1962 TR4

Triumph Spitfire

When it appeared in the autumn of 1962, the Spitfire was greeted as a traditional British sports car with an unusual dash of sophistication – it had, for example, irs instead of the time-honoured live axle. It derived from a more staid model, the Herald, with an engine that went back to Standard days – a hand-down approach that also had a smack of tradition about it, dictated by the development budget and the anticipated sales. Like others before it, the Spitfire outlived its 'parent', continuing into 1980 by which time the Herald was long gone.

The Herald contributed chassis, gearbox and final drive ratios, ifs and that transverse spring irs, which was fine for all but hard cornering, when the swing axle jacked up and the wheels tucked under (more disconcerting perhaps to an observer than to an alert driver, and largely overcome in the works team cars). The 1147cc engine was rated at 63bhp, enough to push the Spitfire to over 145kph (90mph), for its body was efficient as well as attractive. Wind-up windows cramped the cockpit, and a tall driver was at a disadvantage with the soft top erected, or under the hard top which was offered from 1963. The complete nose section was hinged at the front, giving splendid engine accessibility.

The Mk2 came in 1965, with another 4bhp. By that time the Spitfire was well established in competitions, notably in fastback form, and used in rallies and races. The works had already blessed

tuned engines giving up to 90bhp, and in its team cars used extensively-revamped units giving around 100bhp. A primary aim was class honours at Le Mans; the 1964 achievement was a disappointing 21st, but in 1965 two of the cars placed 13th and 14th and took the class from Alpine. There were other class victories in lesser events. The works also ran Spitfires in rallies, sometimes with fastback bodies and in 1965 with 117bhp 1296cc engines. Notable results included a class win in the 1964 Tour de France and second overall in the 1965 Geneva Rally. Changed regulations ruled them out of international competition after 1965.

A production fastback body was introduced for the Spitfire-based GT6 of 1966, which had a 1998cc six-cylinder engine. The Spitfire Mk3 followed in 1967 with a 1296cc engine initially developing 70bhp but uprated to 75bhp before the Mk4 was introduced in 1970 (when an all-synchro gearbox was at last standardized). However, US-specification engines were by this time being emission-controlled, the single-Zenith 1296cc unit for that important market producing only 58bhp.

A 1500 engine was introduced for 1974, giving cars sold outside the USA a top speed nudging 160kph (100mph). Although there were some external changes, some such as bumpers being obligatory, the Spitfire which saw out the decade was still remarkably similar to the little sports car introduced in 1962.

Specification (representative)

Engine: *Mk1* – straight-four; $69 \cdot 3 \times 76$mm, 1147cc; pushrod ohv; twin SU carburettors; 63bhp at 5750rpm.

   1500 – as above, but $73 \cdot 7 \times 87 \cdot 5$mm, 1493cc; 71bhp at 5500rpm.

Gearbox: four-speed manual.

Chassis: backbone frame; front suspension independent by double wishbones, coil springs, dampers and anti-roll bar; rear suspension by swing axles, transverse leaf spring, radius rods and dampers; disc front/drum rear brakes.

Dimensions: wheelbase 211cm/83in; **front track** 125cm/49in; **rear track** 122cm/48in.

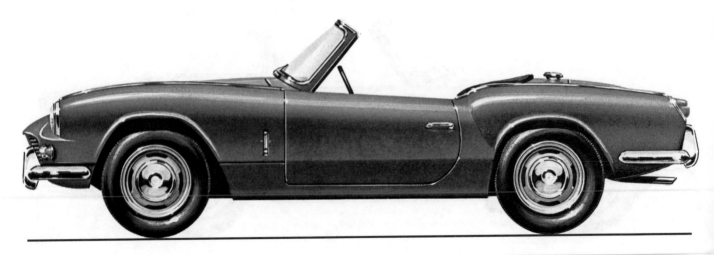

Triumph TR7

The TR7 was the BL model selected for development funding in the 1970s, owing little to the earlier TR models but a great deal to American requirements, for the USA was the most important market for sports cars. After investigations in the USA in 1970, the design was finalized in coupe form, for it was then felt that open cars might be forbidden on safety grounds; this anticipated regulation never materialized, but an open version of the TR7 did not appear until 1979.

Although a mid-engined layout was rejected, the TR7 had fashionable wedge body lines. These gave it a good drag factor, but their aesthetic effectiveness depended very much on paint schemes, and problems were caused by US bumper height regulations and the ground-to-headlight-centre stipulation (leading, incidentally, to the use of pop-up headlights). The sharply-raked windscreen resulted in some visibility problems.

The engine was derived from the Triumph Dolomite saloon's 16-valve slant-four. When the TR7 was introduced early in 1975, US versions were fitted with a low-compression engine delivering 90bhp; when a catalytic convertor was added in response to emission regulations in 1977 this dropped to 86bhp, the performance loss being partly offset by a five-speed gearbox. Cars for

markets free of the US restrictions had 105bhp engines, with improved acceleration and a 169kph (105mph) top speed.

McPherson strut ifs was used, while at the rear a live axle was adopted in place of the TR6 irs, a retrograde step made less noticeable by adequate wheel travel and damping.

While successful racing versions of the TR7 were developed for SCCA production events, the works competition emphasis was on rallying. John Buffum was very successful in North American rallies, but the more intensely-competitive European events saw weight and relatively modest power tell against the TR7, and on rough or unseen roads the short wheelbase/wide track relationship caused problems. Even with up to 300bhp of the Rover-developed V-8 in the car, major successes eluded the team, although in 1978 and 1980 Tony Pond gained good secondary event victories with it; but the works programme was wound up after the 1980 RAC Rally.

A roadgoing TR8 using the Rover-developed V-8 was introduced for the US in 1980, and in its drophead form was well received. Acclaim, however, was not matched by commercial returns and for this reason TR production was terminated in 1981.

Specification

Engine: *European specification (1976)* – straight-four; $90·3 \times 78$mm, 1998cc; single ohc; SU carburettors; 105bhp at 5500rpm.

Gp4 rally car – 90-degree V-8; $88·9 \times 70·35$mm, 3495cc; pushrod ohv; 280bhp at 7500rpm on four twin-choke Weber carburettors, rising to over 300bhp at 7500rpm on Pierburg fuel injection.
Gearbox: four-speed manual on early models; five-speed manual or optional Borg Warner three-speed automatic on later models and all TR8s.
Chassis: Steel unitary monocoque; front suspension independent by McPherson struts, coil springs, lower lateral links and anti-roll bar; rear suspension by live axle, lower trailing arms, upper arms, coil springs, dampers and anti-roll bar; disc front/drum rear brakes (but four-wheel discs on rally cars).
Dimensions: wheelbase 216cm/85in; **front track** 141cm/55½in; **rear track** 140cm/55in.

Turner

John Turner introduced his limited-production sports car series in 1955 and built them at Wolverhampton for eight years. During this period they gained a good reputation among club racing drivers, although some of their circuit virtues meant that Turners had road-use shortcomings. In common with several similar, but usually less pretty, models from other British specialists, the Turners were marketed in 'kit' form, although complete cars were exported.

Austin A30 and A35 components were extensively used, with a conventional chassis frame of two main tubular side members and cross members, with a sheet steel subframe and glass fibre body shell, mounted on Austin ifs and rear axle. These Turners were strictly two seaters, with tidy, well-instrumented cockpits but with seats whose adjustment called for spanner work and with the oddity of the filler cap for the small fuel tank being inside the modest boot. Detachable side screens were normal, but sliding side windows became optional when a hard top was introduced in 1961.

For 1960 the Coventry Climax FWA 1098cc was offered as an alternative to the 948cc BMC A-series unit; with the FWA, front disc brakes became standard. Outwardly, a wide grille distinguished these cars, earlier 803cc and 948cc versions having a narrower half-moon grille.

With the FWA, the Turner just reached 160kph (100mph), while if the revs were used freely its acceleration matched that of the MGA. The engine proved surprisingly docile and tractable for everyday use, albeit noisy. As tuned by Alexander, the A-series engine gave closely similar performance, while the Ford 105E became a third engine option in 1961. Turner road-holding was above average for the class.

With a good competition record behind them these cars were more than a match in all but price for rival models such as the Sprite, and they brought the Turner company to its high point in the early 1960s. In 1962 a more sophisticated GT was added to the range, but by that time the company's fortunes were declining in the face of rival models from major manufacturers and production ceased in 1966. A few of the functional little two seaters lingered on in club racing for years afterwards.

Specification (*Turner-Climax*)
Engine: Coventry Climax straight-four; 72·4 × 66·6mm, 1098cc; single ohc; twin SU carburettors; 75bhp at 6000rpm.
Gearbox: four-speed manual.
Chassis: tubular; front suspension independent by wishbones, coil springs, dampers and anti-roll bar; rear suspension by live axle, longitudinal torsion bars, radius arms and dampers; disc front/ drum rear brakes.
Dimensions: wheelbase 204cm/80½in; **front track** 116cm/45½in; **rear track** 114cm/45in.

TVR M-series

By the mid-1970s TVR was one of the few survivors of the once-prolific British specialist car industry, most of the other little companies having succumbed to a simple lack of business acumen, to reputations for poor reliability and meagre back-up services, or even to the introduction of VAT (which removed much of the justification for kit cars). By that time, TVR's uncertain years – with company crises, cash-draining ventures into racing, and impressive but impractical prototypes – were over. From the introduction of the M-series models in 1972, managing director Martin Lilley committed the company to a policy of model evolution rather than innovation, and that saw TVR safely through the decade.

Forerunner of the M-series was the Triumph-engined 2500 of 1971, which followed the Vixen and Tuscan but with the body adapted to a new chassis. While following the same backbone lines, with outriggers to carry the body, this was a stronger structure in round- and square-section tubing and was easier to produce. It was retained in the M, where the most noticeable change was in the body – the 'dumpy' look which had characterized most production TVRs gave way to a longer body, with sleeker nose and tail sections (interiors, too, were simplified). Finish of this glass fibre body was better than on previous models, distinctly so after a fire closed the

Blackpool factory for months in 1975, perhaps providing a sabbatical for self-criticism! The established running gear was retained, with independent suspension all round.

Apart from the 2500M, which continued for the North American market until 1977, as the Triumph engine met emission requirements, Ford engines became the TVR norm. The 1600M used the Cortina engine, while the 3000M used the 3-litre V-6, rated at 142bhp in normal form. A departure from that came with the Turbo of 1976, which had a Broadspeed-prepared turbocharged V-6 producing 230bhp, and later 265bhp.

Body improvements came with the three-door hatchback Taimar and the Convertible, both available in Turbo form, the latter being a rare late-1970s open car with real high performance – TVR claimed a 230kph (145mph) top speed for it, some 30kph (20mph) faster than the normal 3-litre models.

In 1980 TVR announced the Tasmin, with a slightly larger and sleeker body by ex-Lotus designer Oliver Winterbottom, a revised tubular chassis retaining the backbone but with a perimeter frame added to the body-carrying outriggers, and the 2·8-litre fuel-injected German Ford V-6. The Tasmin retained the continuity of this small company's series of high-performance road cars.

1978 3000M

Specification (3000M)
Engine: Ford 60-degree V-6; 93·97 × 72·41mm, 2994cc; pushrod ohv; Weber carburettor; 142bhp at 5000rpm.
    Turbo – as above, but with Broadspeed turbocharger; 265bhp at 5500rpm.
Gearbox: four-speed manual.
Chassis: tubular backbone; front suspension independent by wishbones, coil springs, dampers and anti-roll bar; rear suspension independent by wishbones, coil springs and dampers; disc front/drum rear brakes.
Dimensions: wheelbase 229cm/90in; **track** 137cm/54in.

Vauxhall Prince Henry and 30/98

One of the better known ancestors of the sports car, the Vauxhall 'Prince Henry' earned wide renown before the First World War for its speed, flexibility and good roadholding. The Vauxhall concern in those days was all-British, with strong sporting inclinations, as emphasised by an impressive outright victory in the 1908 RAC 2000 Miles Trial held in Great Britain. Numerous racing and record-breaking successes at Brooklands track and in sprints, hillclimbs and reliability trials further enhanced the performance, stamina and reputation, and in 1910 the marque tackled the big German Prince Henry Trial, for which the premier award was donated by the Kaiser's brother, Prince Heinrich (Henry) of Prussia.

The regulations for this forerunner of the modern rally encouraged long-stroke, large-capacity engines, but Vauxhall's chief designer, L H Pomeroy, adapted his 1908 four-cylinder A-type for the contest. A team of three cars was prepared, their L-Head monobloc side-valve engine of only 3 litres capacity, with a five-bearing crankshaft which was fast-revving for the time at 2500rpm, assisted by raised compression, modified camshaft and special valves to give an effective 60bhp. A light open four-seater body was graced by a sharp vee-radiator embodying vestigial flutes, which then featured on all Vauxhall production models until the late 1970s.

The Vauxhall trio completed the very rugged 1900km (1205miles) course without trouble, although with their relatively small engines their performance was eclipsed by European cars with engines of over 7 litres. They returned with 'Prince Henry' plaquettes nevertheless, and in 1911 a production version of the Trial cars was marketed with 55bhp, 3-litre engine as the C-type Prince Henry, 43 examples being sold.

In 1912 Vauxhall introduced an improved version, the D-type, with an enlarged 4-litre engine giving 75bhp at 2500rpm. This proved an extremely brisk performer, with over 130kph (80mph) maximum speed and pleasing flexibility. It shone brightly in British hillclimbs and races, while many speed records also fell to a special single-seater Vauxhall using a D-type engine. Still more significantly, the 4-litre Prince Henry provided the basis of the 4½-litre 30/98.

The birth of the 30/98 was almost accidental. A prosperous textile engineer, Joseph Higginson, chose speed hillclimbing as one of his hobbies and aspired to break the Shelsley Walsh record. He asked LH Pomeroy, the Vauxhall designer, to build him a suitable car.

Pomeroy took one of the Vauxhall 4-litre Prince Henry engines, enlarged it by rather drastic methods to 4½ litres, and inserted the resultant 90bhp unit into one of Vauxhall's 1912 Coupe de l'Auto racing chassis. In 1913 Higginson got his record, over 8 sec faster than the old one, and Vauxhall got a hefty fee and the basis of a fine new sporting model.

With a new crankshaft and a stronger cylinder block, the new engine went into limited production in a short, whippy two-wheel-braked chassis carrying stark open four-seater bodywork. This car, the E-type 30/98, was announced late in 1913 and only 13 were built before the First World War.

In 1919, however, the E-type was revived, its design more Edwardian than Vintage yet with charms including superb flexibility, stirring acceleration and over 130kph (80mph) from the lusty, thumping 'big-four' engine, limited only by the inadequacies inherent with rear-wheel and transmission brakes only.

Early in 1923 a new 4·2-litre ohv edition, the OE, was introduced; 22 extra bhp meant even more vigour, making the 30/98 the fastest British sporting car of its time, while the same year also brought the sorely needed four-wheel brakes. Exponents reaped a rich harvest in sprints, hillclimbs and short races, although the car was never seriously raced in long-distance events as was its great rival, the Bentley.

Fewer than 600 30/98s were built, the last appearing in mid-1927 when the company had been taken over by General Motors. The last few months' cars had hydraulically-operated front brakes, several engine improvements, and a new gearbox, bringing considerable refinement, but the 30/98 epitomised the rugged spartan, and immensely lively early-Vintage sports car.

The 1919 30/98 E-type

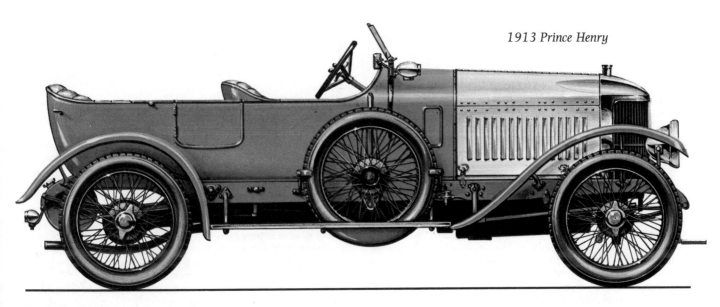

1913 Prince Henry

Specification

Engine: *C-type* – straight-four; 90 × 120mm, 3055cc; side valves; single carburettor; 52bhp at 2500rpm.

    D-type – as above, but 95 × 140mm, 3969cc; 75bhp.

    E-type – as above, but 98 × 150mm, 4525cc; 90bhp at 3000rpm.

    OE – as above, but 98 × 140mm, 4224cc; pushrod ohv; 112bhp at 3300rpm.

Gearbox: separate four-speed manual.

Chassis: pressed steel side members; front and rear suspension by semi-elliptic leaf springs and friction dampers; rear-wheel drum brakes plus transmission brake, but four-wheel drum brakes on OE.

Dimensions: *C-type* – **wheelbase** 290cm/114in; **track** 137cm/54in.

    D-type – **wheelbase** 312cm/123in or 323cm/127in; **track** 137cm/54in.

    E-type – **wheelbase** 295cm/116in; **track** 137cm/54in.

    OE – **wheelbase** 297cm/117in; **track** 137cm/54in, rising to 142cm/56in.

1924 30/98

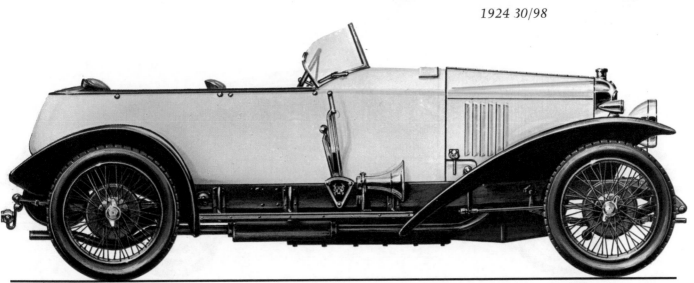

Volvo P1800

This GT coupe was the only sporting Volvo to become widely known – the open P1900 of the mid-1950s having been built in very limited numbers (167) – and it survived for more than a decade. This perhaps reflected its sturdy Swedish qualities, rather than scintillating performance or inspired styling, for it lagged behind its contemporaries in both respects.

The P1800 was introduced in 1960, with the 1778cc four-cylinder engine from the 120-series saloons, an ifs/live rear axle arrangement which proved quite adequate for its grand touring role, and a unitary body which was initially built by Jensen. Curiously high-waisted, and with a niggardly glass area, it seemed almost outmoded in the early 1960s, especially as it was embellished with prominent fins. These were retained in the eminently sensible 1800ES 'sports wagon', introduced in 1971, which gave rear-seat passengers a view of the outside world denied them in the earlier claustrophobic version – although they had no more room, and in both styles the space behind the front seats was more suited for extra luggage, adding to the GT virtues of this Volvo. The E and the ES were produced in parallel into 1972, so the ES extended the life of the model by only a year.

The other major changes during the car's life were in its engine: in 1963 an uprated version of the B18 unit was introduced, and the car was redesignated 1800S. That lasted until 1968, when in common with other Volvo models an increase in bore made for a 1986cc unit, rated at 118bhp. That was followed a year later by a fuel-injected version giving 130bhp in the 1800E, a 160kph (100mph) car. It drove through a gearbox inherited from the 164, with four speeds plus overdrive.

Apart from the ES body, little effort was made to update the 1800 beyond the introduction of alloy wheels and a slightly different grille on the E, although prototypes more appropriate to the 1970s were prepared. The 1800 remained a solid car, with virtues offsetting its increasingly dated specification, and when production ceased in 1973, 44 965 had been sold, over 8000 of them ES 'sports wagons'.

Specification (*1800E*)

Engine: straight-four; 88·9 × 80mm, 1986cc; pushrod ohv; Bosch fuel injection; 130bhp at 6000rpm.
Gearbox: four-speed manual with overdrive.
Chassis: unitary; front suspension independent by wishbones, coil springs, dampers and anti-roll bar; rear suspension by live axle, trailing arms, Panhard rod, coil springs and dampers; four-wheel disc brakes.
Dimensions: wheelbase 239cm/94in; track 133cm/52½in.

1963 1800S

206

Wolseley Hornet

Although derided by true sports car believers as an amalgam of inferior production car components masquerading as the real thing, the six-cylinder Wolseley Hornet gave pleasure to many young people during the bleak first half of the 1930s. Perhaps the most deplorable part of the Hornet story was its beginning: at that time manufacturers mindful of balance sheets rather than engineering principles and aesthetics were squeezing oversize engines into undersize chassis with little conscience, in quest of family markets.

In 1930 the two-door Morris Minor three-speed saloon was worked on by Wolseley, who lengthened the frame by 30cm and inserted a 1271cc six-cylinder version of the Minor engine. With boxey body and skinny, over-long bonnet, the new Hornet's appearance was ludicrous, but the single-ohc six gave a pleasing reserve of power, easy top gear driving and over 95kph (60mph), with hydraulic brakes as well.

Its potential for sporting use was not lost on the London distributors, Eustace Watkins, who swiftly commissioned an open two/four-seater version to be built by Abbey Coachwork. Soon other coachbuilders came in on the act, and rather showy 'sports' Hornets helped fill the Brooklands, Donington and Shelsley Walsh car parks.

Very conscious of this growing extra market, Wolseley in 1932 produced a sporting twin-carburettor 40bhp four-speed Hornet Special in chassis form only, with wider track, larger brakes and a weight of 600kg. Coachbuilders draped it with sports bodies decked out with Le Mans-style 'go-faster' gear such as slab rear petrol tanks, cycle wings, stoneguards, bonnet louvres, over-size 'racing instruments', scuttles with windscoops and folding screens. Hard put to top 110kph (70mph), the cars might seem foolish now but they were fun for the undiscerning and reliable if not over-driven.

The next step came in 1934 with a cross-flow cylinder head, raising output to 47bhp, some necessary chassis stiffening, and a rear-underslung frame; in 1935 a larger 1604cc engine from the Wolseley 14 was installed, bringing the ultimate in Hornet performance with 50bhp and 120kph (75mph). Production of sports Hornets ended in 1935.

Specification

Engine: *Hornet (1930-32)* – straight-six; 57 × 83mm, 1271cc; single ohc; single carburettor; 32bhp at 4300rpm.
Hornet Special (1932-35) – as above, but twin SU carburettors; 43bhp at 4500rpm, rising to 47bhp from 1934.
Hornet Special 14 (1935) – as above, but 61·5 × 90mm, 1604cc; 50bhp.
Gearbox: three-speed manual, but four-speed manual from 1932.
Chassis: pressed steel side members, underslung at rear from 1934; front and rear suspension by semi-elliptic springs and hydraulic dampers; four-wheel Lockheed hydraulic drum brakes.
Dimensions: wheelbase 230cm/90½in; **track** 107cm/42in, but 114cm/45in from 1932.